Prompt Engineering

Hands-on guide to prompt engineering for AI interactions

Eric C. Richardson

bpb

www.bpbonline.com

First Edition 2025

Copyright © BPB Publications, India

ISBN: 978-93-65892-963

To View Complete
BPB Publications Catalogue
Scan the QR Code:

Dedicated to

*To my mother, **Joanne**, who encouraged me to read
my wife, **Stacie**, who encouraged me to write
my daughters, **Katie** and **Maddie**, who encourage me to dream*

About the Author

Eric C. Richardson has 30 years of experience in technology. He was first exposed to an early home computer, the Altair 8800, when he was in primary school when his father built one. He never stopped working with computers and technology. He is currently focusing on artificial intelligence, security architecture, and technology governance, risk, and compliance. He spent 17 years at Microsoft Security in their digital supply chain in a variety of roles. He has been a CISO of startups and various senior leadership roles in other companies but has always focusing on integrity and security.

Eric has also been a volunteer teacher in high school for AP computer science and has taught college-level courses. He has published multiple books and articles on technology and the internet since the mid 1990's. He holds an undergraduate degree in Management Information Systems, a Master's in Computer Science with an emphasis on cybersecurity engineering, and a Master's degree in Business Administration with a focus on technology management. Eric is a passionate supporter of STEM education and Neurodiversity support in tech. He has been married for thirty years to his amazing wife, Stacie, and has two daughters: Katherine and Madelyn. He is an experienced technology consultant who enjoys the process of partnering with an organization to move towards a stronger future empowered by technology.

About the Reviewers

❖ **Maxim Salnikov** is a tech and cloud community leader based in Oslo. With over two decades of experience as a web developer, he shares his deep expertise in web platforms, cloud computing, and AI by speaking at and delivering training sessions at developer events worldwide.

By day, Maxim drives cloud and AI solution development across European companies as the go-to-market leader of Microsoft's application innovation and developer productivity businesses.

In his spare time, he organizes events for Norway's largest web and cloud development communities and advises startups on AI technology and strategy as a board member.

Maxim is passionate about exploring and experimenting with generative AI, including AI-assisted development and autonomous AI agents. To foster global discussions and connect with like-minded professionals, he founded and organized the Prompt Engineering Conference—the first of its kind on a global scale.

❖ **Dr. Michael Seller** is an AI strategist, prompt engineering expert, and business consultant specializing in AI-driven solutions. He holds a Doctorate in Business Administration and certifications in AI and data analytics. As the founder of AI Alchemy, he has developed over 200 tailored prompts across various domains, helping businesses and nonprofits optimize their operations. Dr. Seller has conducted AI training workshops for organizations such as the Humanity House Foundation, the Center of Public Safety for Women, and Ampac, equipping professionals with practical AI skills. His work spans academia, consulting, and technical reviewing for AI publications.

Acknowledgement

I would like to express my sincere gratitude to all those who contributed to the completion of this book.

First and foremost, I extend my heartfelt appreciation to my family and friends for their amazing support and encouragement throughout this journey which motivated me to learn, grow and share.

I would like to thank the great staff of BPB Publications, who were there every step of the way through the writing process and were a source of immense guidance that was always welcome and appreciated.

I would also like to take a moment to acknowledge the technical reviewers, and editors who provided valuable feedback and contributed to the refinement of this manuscript. Their insights and suggestions have significantly enhanced the quality of the book.

I would also like to thank the readers of this book for their support.

Thank you to everyone who has played a part in making this book a reality.

Preface

Forty years ago the world thought artificial intelligence was just around the corner. In the last several years, we are finally seeing AI begin to fit the potential we all thought it could. This book acts as a resource for individuals who wish to master complex methods that influence our engagement with AI systems. Developers, researchers, and enthusiasts alike will find that the insights presented here work to improve your knowledge and abilities in constructing effective AI prompts. The book opens with a fundamental introduction to machine learning (ML) and artificial intelligence (AI) while exploring their fundamental principles. Beginning with AI philosophical foundations pioneered by Alan Turing and progressing through machine learning paradigms like supervised and unsupervised learning, the book establishes essential knowledge to grasp complex interactive developments. Exploration of prompt engineering specifics reveals how transformer-based models act as transformative elements critical for contemporary AI applications. Exploring the functions of generative models such as GANs and transformers helps readers understand the advanced architecture that drives current AI systems. The subsequent chapters examine practical prompt engineering methods. This section teaches how to build and refine prompts that create improved interactions with AI systems. The discussion encompasses practical applications of AI, ethical challenges, and societal impacts to deliver a comprehensive analysis of prompt engineering consequences. Ultimately, this book aims to deliver educational value along with inspirational insights. This work provides guidance to help you face AI challenges and opportunities through innovative, ethical applications of your learning. This book serves as an indispensable guide for your prompt engineering skills development regardless of if you work on refining chatbots or creating sophisticated AI systems.

Chapter summaries:

Chapter 1: A Brief Overview of ML and AI - This chapter offers a succinct introduction to the domains of ML and AI. It starts by explaining basic definitions and foundational concepts, preparing the readers to comprehend the wider applications of these technological fields. This chapter details the development of machine learning throughout and divides machine learning into distinct categories based on the different methods used to process data for model training. The chapter examines emerging learning paradigms while showcasing their distinctive methods and impacts on the field. The chapter provides new ML and AI learners with a straightforward, structured introduction that highlights the field's diverse and dynamic transformative technologies.

Chapter 2: Evolution of Machine Learning - This chapter examines the evolution ML by exploring its beginnings with symbolic AI and following its development into today's statistical learning techniques. The discussion initiates by examining early machine learning methodologies. We also cover significant historical achievements in neural network research and the backpropagation algorithm's importance since its introduction in 1986. We explore how support vector machines (SVMs) gained prominence during the 1990s and their significant influence on machine learning. The chapter examines how big data, together with advanced computational abilities enabled by hardware innovations such as GPUs and TPUs played a transformative role. The rise of deep learning is also introduced.

Chapter 3: Development of Generative Models - This chapter examines how generative models evolved into an essential part of artificial intelligence. The chapter starts by explaining generative models and demonstrating how they differ from discriminative models through their capability to synthesize new data samples. We examine the development of generative models by understanding their historical evolution. Our exploration covers the functioning of GANs by examining generator and discriminator networks as well as demonstrating their wide-ranging uses in image synthesis and text generation beyond these areas. The concluding section of the chapter prepares readers for the emergence of transformers by suggesting their future transformative influence on generative AI.

Chapter 4: Rise of GPT and Transformer-Based Models - This chapter explores how GPT models and Transformer architectures emerged and shaped AI development. It provides an account of how transformer-based models developed and became crucial in AI through their application in prompt engineering. The chapter starts by tracing machine learning model development before introducing the revolutionary emergence of transformer-based architectures. We examine the self-attention mechanism and look into major models, including BERT and GPT. The chapter covers fundamental elements of Transformer architecture, including scaled dot-product attention and multi-head attention alongside position-wise feed-forward networks and positional encoding. We also cover the benefits of the self-attention mechanism and combine a comprehensive description of AI technology developments with discussions on how these models advance prompt engineering capabilities while serving as essential reading material for those seeking knowledge about emerging AI technologies.

Chapter 5: Transformer-based Models in Prompt Engineering - This chapter explores the essential function of transformer-based models as they apply to prompt engineering. The chapter presents successful case studies demonstrating real-world instances where transformer-based models have enhanced AI solutions through improved efficiency and effectiveness. We examine transformer models by contrasting them with classic prompt engineering models, including LSTM and GRU networks. The comparative analysis shows that transformer models excel at managing extended data sequences and demonstrate superior capabilities in tasks that involve understanding intricate textual dependencies. This chapter delivers a complete survey of transformer-based models' role in prompt engineering while highlighting their revolutionary impact on AI interaction enhancement and development.

Chapter 6: Transformer Architecture Concepts - This chapter delivers an in-depth analysis of transformer architecture progress while focusing on GPT from OpenAI. The chapter starts by explaining the original GPT model's basic architecture before examining the development of GPT-2 and GPT-3. We also look at various uses of these models, starting from natural language processing applications to creative fields, such as writing and art, before looking at practical industry applications like customer service automation. The narrative demonstrates how these models create transformative changes across multiple sectors while offering a detailed view of their potential and technological advancements.

Chapter 7: The Prompt Ecosystem - This chapter provides an insightful examination of prompt engineering which stands as a vital component when working with transformer-based models in AI and ML domains. The section begins with an explanation of prompt engineering and its goals while clarifying how creating effective prompts can improve AI system performance and accuracy. By analyzing practical examples, the chapter demonstrates that effective prompts enhance AI model performance while ineffective prompts result in ambiguous or inaccurate results. The text explores the different elements that form a prompt and explains prompt structures, dividing them into informative, interrogative, and directive categories. The chapter presents active learning to improve prompts through AI feedback and introduces methods for evaluating prompt performance. This chapter examines the entire prompt ecosystem and demonstrates its essential role in AI and ML while delving into the technical aspects and creative process of prompt engineering.

Chapter 8: Prompt Types In-Depth - The chapter thoroughly examines the different categories of prompts with special emphasis on their application in AI and ML domains and categorizes prompts into several types. We examine open-ended and close-ended prompts. The chapter examines multi-modal prompts that merge text with images and additional data formats to assess their flexible and intricate nature. The discussion includes contextual prompts that demonstrate their ability to produce appropriate responses by utilizing existing information. The chapter surveys additional prompt types that are less prevalent yet hold comparable significance while demonstrating how they can be applied across various sectors. The chapter presents essential insights into how various prompts can be effectively applied to improve AI system interactions and result quality.

Chapter 9: Understanding Tokens - This chapter explores the basic concept of tokens in AI by examining their definition and function along with their working mechanisms within AI models such as GPT-4. The section starts by defining tokens and explaining their crucial role in constructing inputs for machine learning systems to process and generate responses. We examine the tokenization process and demonstrate its complexity and flexibility through examples from different languages. The chapter investigates how token limitations work in AI models and how token limitations affect the structuring of prompts and the general performance of AI systems. This chapter delivers comprehensive insights into token operations and their limitations.

Chapter 10: Efficiency in Prompt Engineering - The chapter thoroughly examines why creating efficient prompts is essential for AI and ML applications. We start by demonstrating the essential role of efficiency in prompt engineering alongside significant advantages that well-designed prompts deliver through enhanced response precision and better system performance. We move forward to examine different methods for creating efficient prompts. The chapter outlines techniques for both evaluating prompt performance and making improvements to their efficiency. The content presents evaluation tools and metrics for prompt assessment and demonstrates the differences between optimized and non-optimized prompts through comparative examples. The chapter intends to provide readers with essential knowledge and tools through which they can improve their prompt engineering skills to boost AI application performance.

Chapter 11: Critical Role of Syntax - This chapter gives a detailed account of how syntax can affect the efficiency of prompts in AI systems. We look at typical syntactical errors while providing guidance on how to prevent making those mistakes. This chapter presents a conversational model along with language techniques that enable actors to maximize that model's effectiveness. The latter portion of the chapter examines advanced techniques in syntax construction.

Chapter 12: Techniques and Strategies for Prompt Engineering - This chapter delivers a comprehensive guide to developing effective AI system prompts. We begin by presenting best practices in prompt crafting. The chapter proceeds to examine advanced prompt engineering techniques and how few-shot learning and zero-shot learning techniques enable AI models to process prompts without needing extensive previous examples. We also cover prompt tuning and optimization methods to enhance prompt effectiveness for specific needs and explain how to manage multi-turn conversations, which are essential for developing more interactive AI exchanges. The chapter demonstrates practical applications by showing real-world examples of these techniques in operation. The content offers case studies and lessons learned from successful implementations.

Chapter 13: Challenges of Quality Prompts - This chapter examines the challenges faced when creating effective prompts to operate AI systems. The initial section identifies fundamental elements that define high-quality prompts, which consist of clear instructions, specific details, and relevant context, along with suitable tone and style. The chapter advances by examining typical obstacles that arise within the field of prompt engineering. We examine how ambiguous prompts produce unexpected or off-topic responses in AI systems and prompt design bias. We learn about the barriers to effective, prompt design while demonstrating the consequences of these challenges.

Chapter 14: Tools and Platforms for Prompt Engineering - This chapter is a critical resource for understanding the different tools essential for creating high-quality AI application prompts. We start by presenting an overview of widely-used platforms such as GPT-3 Playground, Hugging Face Transformers, and the OpenAI API and cover their technical capabilities, user interfaces and distinct features. Subsequently, the chapter provides a practical manual for the effective utilization of these tools and a step-by-step guide for setting up and configuring each platform, along with best practices for crafting and testing prompts as well as methods to analyze and interpret results. The final section of this chapter addresses the integration process of prompt engineering tools into current workflows.

Chapter 15: Ethics in Artificial Intelligence - The chapter examines significant ethical issues that arise throughout the development and application of AI and ML technologies. We start by examining bias and fairness and how AI systems risk reinforcing existing prejudices if not properly managed. The chapter stresses the need to detect and reduce biases to achieve equitable and inclusive results in AI systems. Next, the importance of safeguarding user data and stopping unauthorized access to AI systems becomes the focal point of privacy and security concerns. The text analyzes how technologies such as GPT and other advanced AI systems affect society through job displacement and economic changes, as well as their roles in spreading misinformation and generating deepfakes. The chapter analyzes the regulatory and governance structures to monitor AI development and usage and examines fundamental principles necessary for ethical AI development. We learn the obstacles and essential frameworks for ethical AI implementation and understand how AI technology can advance in a way that supports human rights while being beneficial to society.

Chapter 16: Finances of Prompts and Cost Management - This chapter examines the financial considerations involved in the design and application of prompts within AI systems. We start with an analysis of how various prompt designs affect their processing costs in AI. The discussion transitions to methods that help control and minimize these costs. The chapter explains how AI capabilities help automate repetitive tasks which result in reduced operational costs. The book includes case studies that demonstrate practical applications of cost-efficient prompt engineering in real-world scenarios.

Chapter 17: Future Directions and Challenges of AI and ML - The chapter delivers a forward-looking examination of AI and ML advancements and their ongoing evolution. We examine the recent progress in AI and ML, which concentrates on building new AI models and combining AI with emerging technologies like IoT and quantum computing. The discussion moves forward to explore some upcoming obstacles. The chapter outlines various technical challenges encountered while developing advanced AI technologies that require stronger algorithms and sophisticated management of complex data structures. We learn about the ethical and regulatory dilemmas associated with AI adoption and underscore the necessity for frameworks that promote responsible deployment by tackling privacy, bias, and transparency issues. The chapter investigates future AI applications while emphasizing hybrid models.

Chapter 18: Legal Framework for Artificial Intelligence - This chapter deeply examines legal aspects related to AI creation and distribution of AI-generated content. It starts by providing a comprehensive overview of current legal structures that manage artificial intelligence through national and international regulations. The chapter investigates intellectual property challenges related to AI technologies with a focus on patents and copyrights. We learn about the General Data Protection Regulation (GDPR) along with multiple data protection laws that influence data management practices in AI systems. The security issues organizations encounter while implementing AI technologies are also covered.

Chapter 19: Practical Examples of Chatbots and AI Systems - This chapter delivers an extensive examination of cutting-edge chatbots and AI systems that influence the current conversational AI field. The chapter starts with an examination of leading systems like ChatGPT and ChatGPT Plus while detailing their functions and technological foundations. The text discusses Google's Bard and Gemini by showing what unique features they offer for processing complex questions. We also learn about some practical, real-world examples of prompts that you can implement.

Coloured Images

Please follow the link to download the
Coloured Images of the book:

https://rebrand.ly/7sho73g

We have code bundles from our rich catalogue of books and videos available at **https://github.com/bpbpublications**. Check them out!

Errata

We take immense pride in our work at BPB Publications and follow best practices to ensure the accuracy of our content to provide with an indulging reading experience to our subscribers. Our readers are our mirrors, and we use their inputs to reflect and improve upon human errors, if any, that may have occurred during the publishing processes involved. To let us maintain the quality and help us reach out to any readers who might be having difficulties due to any unforeseen errors, please write to us at :

errata@bpbonline.com

Your support, suggestions and feedbacks are highly appreciated by the BPB Publications' Family.

Did you know that BPB offers eBook versions of every book published, with PDF and ePub files available? You can upgrade to the eBook version at www.bpbonline. com and as a print book customer, you are entitled to a discount on the eBook copy. Get in touch with us at :

business@bpbonline.com for more details.

At **www.bpbonline.com**, you can also read a collection of free technical articles, sign up for a range of free newsletters, and receive exclusive discounts and offers on BPB books and eBooks.

Piracy

If you come across any illegal copies of our works in any form on the internet, we would be grateful if you would provide us with the location address or website name. Please contact us at **business@bpbonline.com** with a link to the material.

If you are interested in becoming an author

If there is a topic that you have expertise in, and you are interested in either writing or contributing to a book, please visit **www.bpbonline.com**. We have worked with thousands of developers and tech professionals, just like you, to help them share their insights with the global tech community. You can make a general application, apply for a specific hot topic that we are recruiting an author for, or submit your own idea.

Reviews

Please leave a review. Once you have read and used this book, why not leave a review on the site that you purchased it from? Potential readers can then see and use your unbiased opinion to make purchase decisions. We at BPB can understand what you think about our products, and our authors can see your feedback on their book. Thank you!

For more information about BPB, please visit **www.bpbonline.com**.

Join our book's Discord space

Join the book's Discord Workspace for Latest updates, Offers, Tech happenings around the world, New Release and Sessions with the Authors:

https://discord.bpbonline.com

Table of Contents

1. A Brief Overview of ML and AI 1

    Introduction 1

    Structure 2

    Objectives 2

    Key milestones in early AI history 2

        Turing and the concept of a thinking machine 2

        The Turing test 4

        John McCarthy and the Dartmouth conference 4

    Fundamental concepts of machine learning and artificial intelligence 6

        Overview of machine learning and statistical analysis 6

        Overview of artificial intelligence 7

        Algorithms and models 7

        Types or components of artificial intelligence 8

        Data training and their importance in ML 10

    Historical context and evolution of AI and GPT 15

    Conclusion 17

2. Evolution of Machine Learning 19

    Introduction 19

    Structure 19

    Objectives 20

    Symbolic artificial intelligence to statistical learning 20

    Rule-based systems to data-driven models 23

        Limitations of rule-based systems 23

        Emergence of data-driven models 23

        Challenges and considerations 25

    Neural networks 26

        Development of neural networks 27

    Use of the backpropagation algorithm 28

Introduction of backpropagation 28

Support vectors.. 28

    Rise of support vector machines 29

Advancements in artificial intelligence.. 29

    Impact of big data and computational power 29

    Big data... 30

    Computational power 30

    Growth of large datasets and databases... 31

    Enhanced learning and performance.. 31

    Improved model robustness 32

    Accelerated development and innovation.. 32

    Scalability and infrastructure 32

Advances in graphics and tensor processor hardware........................... 33

    Speed and efficiency.. 33

    Wide adoption and support 33

    Tensor processing units 33

Emergence of deep learning 34

Conclusion.. 35

3. **Development of Generative Models**... **37**

Introduction... 37

Structure... 38

Objectives 38

Overview of generative models 38

    Early generative models 38

    Motivations behind developing generative models 39

    Early uses of generative models.. 40

    Generative models versus discriminative models...................................... 40

        Generative model 40

        Discriminative model 41

        Differences between discriminative and generative models 41

        Benefits of generative models.. 42

Benefits of a discriminative model 43

Different types of generative models 44

  Gaussian mixture models 44

  Naive Baynes models 45

  Markov chains 46

  Probabilistic graphical models 46

  Hidden Markov models 46

  Boltzmann machines 48

  Variational autoencoders 49

Generative adversarial networks 51

Conclusion 53

4. Rise of GPT and Transformer-Based Models **55**

Introduction 55

Structure 56

Objectives 56

Overview of Transformer-based models 56

  Importance and relevance of Transformer-based models 56

History of Transformer-based models 57

  Technical background for Transformer-based models 58

    Feed-forward neural networks 59

    Self-attention mechanism 59

    Input tokenization 60

    Vectors in tokenization 61

    Encoder and decoder layers 62

    Connected network 62

    Positional encoding 62

    Multi-head attention 63

    Training and optimization 63

    Scalability and efficiency 63

  Evolution of machine learning models 65

  Key breakthroughs and milestones 65

BERT and GPT...*66*

Looking back..*69*

Conclusion...69

5. Transformer-based Models in Prompt Engineering..............................**71**

Introduction...71

Structure...72

Objectives 72

Evolution of prompt engineering 72

Defining the scope and significance.......................................*73*

Transformers in contextual prompt design *73*

Advancements enabled by Transformers 74

Improved contextual understanding......................................*75*

Handling long-range dependencies..*76*

Scalability and parallelization..*76*

Sentiment analysis and text classification..................................78

Customizing Transformers for specific tasks 79

Fine-tuning techniques *79*

Transfer learning in NLP..*80*

Methodologies in prompt engineering 81

Crafting effective prompts...*81*

Measuring prompt efficacy..*82*

Comparison with other models used in prompt engineering *83*

Specific applications in prompt engineering...............................84

Generative tasks *84*

Conversational AI *85*

Language translation and summarization...............................*86*

Sentiment analysis and text classification *87*

Conclusion...88

6. Transformer Architecture Concepts..**89**

Introduction.. 89

Structure... 89

Objectives 90

Transformer models 90

   The advent of GPT by OpenAI 90

     Concept and architecture.. 90

     Contextual reference to detailed Transformer model exploration........ 91

     Start of GPT 91

     Scaling up and improved performance with GPT-2.................... 92

     Large scale and broad capabilities with GPT-3 93

     Popularity and scale improvements with GPT 4 94

     GPT-4o as the latest innovation 94

Technical details of GPT models 96

   Architecture and training 97

   Learning GPT's architecture... 97

   Training GPT and the need for computational power...................... 99

   Language modelling and transfer learning 100

   GPT models learning language patterns................................... 100

   Transfer learning and its benefits... 101

Comparison with other AI models 102

   Applications and impact of GPT models................................... 102

     Enhancing chatbots and virtual assistants 102

     Language translation and summarization 102

     Sentiment analysis and text classification 103

     Creative applications 103

     Marketing opportunities 103

     Educational content creation... 104

     The ultimate chatbot.. 104

Conclusion.. 105

7. The Prompt Ecosystem **107**

Introduction 107

Structure 107

Objectives 107

The prompt ecosystem 108

    Conceptual overview 108

        Prompt ecosystem's role in AI-driven models 109

        Differentiating from other artificial intelligence subsystems 109

        Shaping model outputs 109

    Importance of the prompt ecosystem 110

        Significance of prompts in artificial intelligence 110

        Implications on artificial intelligence applications 110

Components of the prompt ecosystem 111

    Structural elements 111

        Anatomy of a prompt 112

        Types of prompts 112

Dynamics of prompt creation 113

    Crafting effective prompts 113

        Prompt iteration and refinement 114

    Detailed elements of a prompt 115

        Setting clear objectives 115

        Contextualization and background information 116

        Providing context 116

        Managing prior knowledge 117

    Specificity and precision in instructions 118

        Instructional clarity 118

        Desired depth and scope 119

    Examples, analogies and constraints 120

        Using examples and analogies 120

        Defining constraints and limitations 121

    Tone, style and edge cases 122

        Specifying tone and style 122

Addressing edge cases... 122

Conclusion.. 123

8. Prompt Types In-Depth **125**

Introduction... 125

Structure.. 125

Objectives 126

Creative potential of open-ended prompts 126

Nature of open-ended prompts 126

Use cases for open-ended prompts... 127

Challenges and considerations 127

Precision and clarity with closed-ended prompts........................ 128

The nature of closed-ended prompts... 128

Use cases for closed-ended prompts.. 129

Challenges and considerations 129

Discovery with exploratory prompts 130

Nature of exploratory prompts 130

Use cases for exploratory prompts... 130

Challenges and considerations 131

Enhancing the effectiveness of exploratory prompts 131

Diverse data inputs with multi-modal prompts............................ 132

Nature of multi-modal prompts 132

Use cases for multi-modal prompts 133

Multi-source data synthesis 133

Challenges and considerations 134

Enhancing accurate responses with contextual prompts 135

The nature of contextual prompts 135

Use cases for contextual prompts... 136

Challenges and considerations 136

Sequenced prompting with procedural prompts 138

Nature of procedural prompts 138

Use cases for procedural prompts.. 138

Challenges and considerations 139

Dynamic interactions with adaptive prompts 140

Nature of adaptive prompts 140

Use cases for adaptive prompts 141

Challenges and considerations 142

Conclusion 143

9. Understanding Tokens **145**

Introduction 145

Structure 146

Objectives 146

Introduction to tokens 146

Definition and role of tokens in artificial intelligence 146

Overview of tokenization in artificial intelligence models 147

Tokens central to artificial intelligence communication 147

Using tokens in processing and generating responses 148

Importance of tokens for efficient computation 148

GPT-4 and token optimization case study 149

Tokenization process 149

Breaking down text into tokens 149

Detailed steps in the tokenization process 150

Role of vocabulary in tokenization 150

Examples of tokenization in various languages 151

Challenges in tokenizing morphologically rich languages 151

Tokenization of programming languages 151

Token limitations 152

Effect on memory and processing power 152

Designing effective prompts within token constraints 153

Example scenarios of prompt optimization 153

Implications for artificial intelligence system design 154

Tokenization and model architecture 154

Role of tokens in scaling artificial intelligence models 155

Custom tokenization for domain-specific tasks 155

Future of tokenization in artificial intelligence 157

Potential developments 158

Conclusion 160

10. Efficiency in Prompt Engineering 161

Introduction 161

Structure 161

Objectives 162

Introduction to prompt efficiency 162

Scope of efficiency in prompt engineering 162

Role of prompt engineering in AI performance 163

Efficiency impacts resource utilization 163

Examples of efficiency leading to better outcomes 163

Impact of efficiency on computational costs 164

Resource optimization to reducing API calls 165

Lowering operational expenses 165

Improving response times and user experience 166

AI in customer support 166

Real-time AI applications 166

Enhancing model performance with well-designed prompts 167

Benefits of efficient prompts 168

Reducing cognitive overload 168

Scaling AI systems efficiency to managing workloads 169

Enhancing accessibility and inclusivity 170

Strategies for efficient prompt design 171

Balancing detail and brevity 171

Measuring and optimizing efficiency 172

Examples of optimized versus non-optimized prompts 173

Future considerations for efficient prompt engineering 174

Future evolution of prompts in generative AI 174

Automation and efficiency 175

Adapting prompt efficiency strategies 175

Conclusion... 177

11. Critical Role of Syntax **179**

Introduction... 179

Structure... 180

Objectives 180

Importance of syntax in prompts.. 180

Effect of syntax on artificial intelligence 180

Meta prompting.. 181

Examples of syntactical variations and their impacts.............. 181

Structural prompts in question-answering systems 182

Syntax and ambiguity in language.. 182

Best practices for syntactical precision.. 183

Using clear and unambiguous language.................................. 183

Structuring prompts for maximum clarity.............................. 184

Avoiding common syntactical pitfalls...................................... 185

Influence of human syntax on artificial intelligence responses.............. 185

Advanced syntactical techniques... 188

Using specific keywords and phrases for desired outcomes.............. 188

Employing syntactical structures to guide AI responses............... 188

Leveraging complex syntax for sophisticated outputs 189

Balancing simplicity and complexity.. 190

Implications for efficiency in prompt engineering......................... 191

Efficiency-accuracy tradeoff in syntax 191

Speeding AI task execution with optimized syntax 191

Prompt iteration for improved results....................................... 192

Future trends in syntax-driven prompt engineering 193

Learning and adapting to human syntax.................................. 193

Role of multilingual syntax in AI development....................... 194

Human-AI collaboration towards more natural prompts 194

Conclusion.. 195

12. Techniques and Strategies for Prompt Engineering............................ 197

Introduction... 197

Structure... 198

Objectives 198

Major AI players 198

OpenAI ChatGPT 198

Meta LLaMA... 199

Google Gemini... 200

Claude... 201

Microsoft Copilot... 203

Midjourney... 204

Best practices for crafting prompts 205

Understanding the audience 206

Iterative testing and refinement 207

Leveraging feedback and metrics... 207

Real-world applications and outcomes.................................. 208

Lessons learned from successful implementation................. 209

Advanced prompt engineering techniques 209

Few-shot and zero-shot learning 210

Prompt tuning and optimization 210

Handling multi-turn conversations....................................... 212

Conclusion... 213

13. Challenges of Quality Prompts 215

Introduction... 215

Structure... 215

Objectives 216

Designing effective prompts.. 216

Clarity and specificity 216

Context and relevance 217

Tone and style considerations... 219

Common challenges in prompt engineering.................................. 222

Ambiguity 222

Bias 223

Best practices for ensuring neutral and fair prompts 223

Complexity 223

Advanced prompt optimization techniques 224

Iterative refinement 224

Prompt chaining 225

Prompt templates and automation 226

Creating reusable prompt templates for consistency 226

Automating prompt generation for efficiency 227

Metrics for quality assessment 227

Measuring relevance, accuracy, and completeness 227

Human versus machine evaluation of prompted outputs 228

Identifying and resolving failures 229

Troubleshooting misinterpretations and incorrect responses 229

Understanding the model's limitations 229

Evaluating prompt performance 230

Conclusion 230

14. Tools and Platforms for Prompt Engineering 231

Introduction 231

Structure 231

Objectives 232

Developer tools 232

The OpenAI Playground 232

Hugging Face Transformers 233

OpenAI API 235

Other tools and emerging platforms 235

Using the tool effectively 236

Setting up and configuring tools 236

GPT in OpenAI Playground 237

Writing and testing prompts via tools 238

Analyzing and interpreting results..238

Integrating prompt engineering into workflows.................................239

    Workflow automation..239

    Collaboration and version control..240

    Continuous improvement and scaling..240

Advanced use cases and real-world applications 241

    Building custom assistants and chatbots......................................241

    AI as the tool for generating code and documentation....................242

    AI in decision-making..243

Challenges and future trends in prompt engineering tools................244

    Limitations and bias mitigation..244

    Handling API limitations and failures..245

    Trends to watch..245

    Testing and evaluating prompts..246

    Example of creating a content generator....................................247

Conclusion...247

15. Ethics in Artificial Intelligence...**249**

Introduction...249

Structure..249

Objectives 250

AI and ML ethics 250

    Defining ethics in AI and machine learning................................251

    Reasons ethics matter in AI development 251

        Overview of ethical challenges 251

Bias and fairness in AI 253

    Types of bias in AI models..253

    Detecting and addressing bias in data 254

    Case studies on algorithmic bias 254

    Achieving equity and inclusivity through fairness........................255

Privacy and security concerns in AI 256

    Privacy risks in AI-powered applications 256

Data anonymization and privacy-preserving techniques 257

Securing AI models 257

Ethical considerations for data usage 258

Societal impact of GPT and advanced AI 259

Role of AI in misinformation and deepfakes 260

Implications for trust and public perception 260

Regulation and governance of advanced AI 261

Addressing bias and fairness in AI models 261

Identifying and mitigating biases in training data 262

Techniques and strategies for an inclusive AI design 262

Auditing and monitoring AI for fairness 263

Real-world examples of fair AI implementations 263

Best practices to follow for AI ethics 264

Privacy by design using privacy-centric AI 264

Data governance and ownership in AI systems 265

Ensuring robustness and resilience in AI models 265

Securing the AI development lifecycle 265

Conclusion 266

16. Finances of Prompts and Cost Management 267

Introduction 267

Structure 267

Objectives 268

Cost management in AI 268

Cost management importance in prompt engineering 268

Microsoft and Google AI platforms 269

Other AI GPT service platforms 270

Financial considerations in prompt engineering 271

Economics of AI 271

Pricing models of AI services 272

Knowing fixed versus variable costs 272

Usage-based pricing 273

Efficiency in writing prompts...274
    Understanding token consumption pricing.....................................274
        Optimizing prompt length for cost control...........................274
    Strategies to minimize prompt iterations......................................275
    Using low-resource models for simple tasks................................275
    Batch processing prompts...276
Cost management in running your AI service......................................277
    Allocating resources..277
    Model selection optimization on use case basis.............................278
    Scalability and cost scaling..278
    Managing API calls and minimizing latency................................279
    Cost implications of fine-tuning models.......................................279
Financial optimization techniques for AI services..............................280
    In-house models versus cloud-based costing.................................280
    Leveraging discounts and reserved instances...............................281
    Financial optimization techniques for AI services........................281
    Multi-cloud strategies for cost management.................................282
    Monitoring usage and setting budgets...282
Conclusion...283

17. Future Directions and Challenges of AI and ML.....................**285**
Introduction...285
Structure...285
Objectives...286
Advancements in artificial intelligence and machine learning...........286
    Next-generation artificial intelligence models.............................286
    Alignment of AI with other technologies.....................................287
Improving prompt engineering using cutting-edge AI........................288
    State-of-the-art prompt design...288
    Artificial intelligence and customizing user experience...............289
    Long-term projections for prompt engineering............................290
Future prospects for prompt engineering at scale...............................291

Technical hurdles 291

Future state ethical and regulatory challenges 292

Potential future applications 293

Hybrid models and integration of AI tools 294

Artificial intelligence for social good 295

AI in health care, from screening to therapy 295

AI in environmental protection 295

AI in schools for intelligent education 296

Future of AI-driven prompt engineering 296

Augmented and virtual reality compatibility 297

Conclusion 298

18. Legal Framework for Artificial Intelligence **299**

Introduction 299

Structure 299

Objectives 300

Existing legal frameworks 300

Current national and international AI laws 300

Other key jurisdictions 301

Important legal principles and guidelines 301

Intellectual property and artificial intelligence 303

Patents and copyrights in AI systems 303

Ownership issues in AI-generated content 304

Ownership of content in prompt engineering 305

Content moderation and liability responsibilities 305

Data privacy and security 306

Privacy laws on AI prompts 306

Security challenges in AI deployment 307

Ethical considerations in prompt engineering 309

Bias and fairness in prompt outcomes 309

Accountability in automated prompting systems 310

Compliance and enforcement mechanisms 311

Standards and best practices impacting AI prompts 311

Standards and guidelines for AI prompts 313

Conclusion.. 314

19. Practical Examples of Chatbots and AI Systems.. 315

Introduction.. 315

Structure.. 315

Objectives 316

Simple and helpful prompts... 316

Complex examples 317

Examples of prompts and responses 320

Chatbot planning.. 323

Create a context prompt 324

Simple Chatbot example 325

Setting up the prompt.. 325

Running the prompt... 326

Conclusion... 329

Index **331-340**

CHAPTER 1

A Brief Overview of ML and AI

Introduction

It is nearly impossible to read any news today that does not mention **artificial intelligence (AI)**, **machine learning (ML)**, or any related areas associated with it. The rapid advancements in AI and ML have created a demand for new skills and knowledge. Prompt engineering is a critical skill for anyone working with AI models, as it directly impacts the quality and reliability of the outputs generated.

Whether you are a seasoned AI practitioner or a newcomer to the field, understanding prompt engineering will enhance your ability to harness the full potential of AI models. By mastering this skill, you can improve the performance of AI systems, create more engaging user experiences, and contribute to the responsible development of AI technologies.

Before we learn about what prompts and, by extension, prompt engineering is, we will need to learn some background information. So, in this chapter, we will introduce some basic foundational elements such as learning AI, ML, and prompt engineering and will touch a bit on the history. By having a solid understanding of how we got here, you will best understand where prompt engineering is going and be ready to unlock the power of prompts, paving the way for a new era of human-AI collaboration.

Structure

This chapter will cover the following topics:

- Key milestones in AI history
- Fundamental concepts of machine learning and artificial intelligence
- Historical context and evolution of AI

Objectives

When you complete this chapter, you will understand the basics of the origin of ML and AI and the historical context in which they arose. You will have an overview of AI and ML from a big-picture perspective. You will understand the basics of the evolution of AI and begin to see the complexity of the area of study. Readers will also understand the various types of AI.

Key milestones in early AI history

Using machines to solve problems is something that defines civilization. The better our machines, the better we can use them. Computers are electronic versions of mechanical computing devices which have existed a very long time, the Middle Ages saw clocks track astronomical events, what they did with gears and rotors was actually create ways to mathematically predict the motion of celestial bodies. These were early mechanical computers effectively. Let us talk about how the descendants of those machines (computers) were used to create a new area of scientific study: AI.

Turing and the concept of a thinking machine

The notion of machines **solving** problems is not new, of course. The roots of what we know of AI today goes back to World War II. A secret group of code breakers was formed at the **Government Code and Cypher School (GC&CS)** on the grounds of the British country house *Bletchley Park* in *Buckinghamshire*. It was an amazing team, and one of the best-known among them was *Alan Turing*. Turing was a brilliant mathematician who was recruited as the leader of GC&CS to help use electromechanical devices to break the code of the German electromechanical enciphering device. The German machine is now known as the Enigma machine.

Figure 1.1: *A photograph of an actual Enigma machine from World War II:*
From the author's personal collection

To defeat Enigma the solution was, by our standards, a primitive computer, but quite capable for its time. It was called the **Colossus**, a group of computers used from 1943 to the end of the way. It was the world's first computer in terms of it being a digital programmable platform.

Figure 1.1 shows an actual WWII Enigma machine at the *Flying Heritage & Combat Armor Museum* in *Everett Washington, USA*. The Enigma machine was a device to encrypt and decrypt messages. Simply, it had a keyboard to type and used an electro-mechanical device to encipher the message. Every time you press a key, the machine would change what the next letter could be; if two machines were set up with the right key, one could decrypt another.

To decode a message, the recipient would need an Enigma machine set up like the sender's. They would type in the encoded message, and the machine would reverse the process to reveal the original text.

From a cybersecurity perspective, the Enigma machine represents an early example of a symmetric key encryption system. Both parties need to share a secret (in this case, the rotor settings) to communicate securely. It is also a great example of how mechanical and electrical engineering can be used to create complex cryptographic systems. As someone who has worked in cybersecurity for 25 years, it is quite similar to how cryptography is used today. For example, we would call the agreed-on rotor settings the public key. The rotor settings were changed every day; there was an agreed-on list of settings tied to the date published. Those were amongst the most secret of all documents.

Those secret rotor settings were made up of letters. Although a weakness in the plan was humans preferring a real word as opposed to scrambled letters. Hence, the GC&CS was able to narrow down the possible choice of words that fit the six-character rotor settings.

Using only known six-letter German words, the team using Colossus (then known as the **Bombe**) iterated through every single six-letter word in the day with a simulation of the inner workings of the Enigma machine. As they became successful in this iterative approach, known today as a **brute force attack**, they used this information to help war end faster. Not only was this the first significant example of computers doing calculations faster than humans, but it also eventually gave rise to AI. It was also the first instance of what one could call cyberwarfare since, primarily, cybersecurity today is focused on encryption in one way or another.

The Turing test

After World War II, *Alan Turing* wrote about *Computing Machinery and Intelligence* in an academic paper in 1950. In that paper, he proposed the concept of machine intelligence, which is now known as the Turing test. Rather than providing a direct definition of machine intelligence, Turing suggested an operational approach. He posited that a machine could be considered intelligent if it could engage in a conversation with a human without the human realizing that they were conversing with a machine. This idea is encapsulated in the imitation game, where a machine attempts to mimic human responses well enough to be indistinguishable from a human interlocutor. In some cases, programs that effectively focus chatbots have been able to deceive people into thinking they are conversing with an actual human.

Turing's concept of machine intelligence hinges on the ability of a machine to exhibit behavior indistinguishable from that of a human, particularly in the context of linguistic and conversational tasks. This focus on behavior and performance, rather than internal processes or consciousness, marks a foundational shift in thinking about AI. Turing is one of the individuals who can claim the title of **the father of computer science**, and to this day, the Turing test is taught to computer science students. The question of whether a system analysis can evaluate and then create a judgment and articulate it is at the heart of AI. Others took his efforts and built upon it. The next milestone happened a few years later.

John McCarthy and the Dartmouth conference

The Dartmouth conference, which occurred in 1956, marked the birth of AI and, broadly, computer science as a formal field of study. Early AI programs grew out of this to define the initial approaches to AI problem-solving.

That conference was held at *Dartmouth College* in *New Hampshire* and organized by *John McCarthy, Marvin Minsky, Nathaniel Rochester,* and *Claude Shannon*. It was considered a seminal event in the history of AI. This conference marked the formal birth of AI as a distinct academic discipline. *McCarthy* coined the term AI during this event, setting the stage for decades of research and development. The goal of this conference was to explore the idea that human intelligence could be replicated by machines, laying the groundwork for future AI research. The collaborative environment fostered by this conference brought together prominent researchers who would become pioneers in the field, establishing foundational concepts and stimulating widespread interest in AI. The Dartmouth conference catalyzed significant advancements in computer science, leading to the development of early AI programs and setting a vision that continues to drive the field today.

At that time, outside of science fiction, the notion of machines being able to emulate even rudimentary human intelligence was considered a farcical notion. At the conference, however, they acknowledged that the rapid advancements in computer science and the successful implementation of early computing machines created a fertile ground for such ambitious ideas. Researchers were increasingly interested in exploring the potential of these new machines beyond mere number-crunching. They wondered whether computers could be programmed to perform tasks that required human-like intelligence, such as reasoning, learning, and understanding language.

At that time, *McCarthy* was a young assistant professor who joined *Dartmouth College* a year before. He was particularly captivated by the idea of a computer being able to emulate human intelligence. He envisioned a future where machines could think and solve problems autonomously. To explore this vision, he proposed a summer research project to bring together leading minds in mathematics, engineering, and computer science to discuss and develop the concept of AI.

McCarthy, along with other researchers *Minsky, Rochester, and Shannon*, crafted a proposal that articulated their bold vision to take a few individuals to study the nature of AI for about a year in 1956. Their prominent goal stated that regarding human-equivalent intelligence, *".. a machine can be made to simulate it"* (*McCarthy, John; Minsky, Marvin; Rochester, Nathan; Shannon, Claude (1955)*).

This proposal was groundbreaking in daring to pose that a computer or machine could even resemble a human in terms of abilities. It suggested that human cognitive processes could be understood and replicated by machines, a hypothesis that would drive AI research for decades to come. The conference aimed to explore a variety of topics, including automatic computers, how a machine could be programmed to use a language, neuron nets, and self-improvement, all of which are foundational elements in AI research.

That conference gave us not only the term AI, as we stated, but also defined AI, starting an entirely new area of academic research. It is important to note that computer science degrees had only just begun to be given out a few years before 1953. So, the world had a new area of research created just as the first graduates of an entirely new related field were heading into the workforce.

It was not just computer scientists involved; from the beginning, AI had to be an interdisciplinary field of study. Professionals from mathematics, psychology, engineering, and computer science needed to come together. The notion of ML, **natural language processing (NLP)**, and symbolic reasoning were evolving together.

Possibly the most important thing that came out of that conference was that it inspired other institutions to begin their own research into AI. To this day this is considered the moment of AI's birth after about a decade of great minds considering what the future could be. This conference started the journey towards modern AI.

Fundamental concepts of machine learning and artificial intelligence

Understanding the fundamental concepts of ML and AI involves grasping key ideas crucial for any modern executive. At its core, AI is a broad field concerned with creating systems capable of performing tasks that typically require human intelligence. These tasks include problem-solving, understanding natural language, recognizing patterns, and making decisions. ML, a subset of AI, focuses specifically on the development of algorithms that enable computers to learn from and make predictions based on data.

Data is the lifeblood of these technologies; the quality and quantity of data available directly impact the performance and accuracy of the models. This is why data collection, cleaning, and preprocessing are critical steps in any AI project. By understanding these fundamental concepts, executives can better appreciate the potential and limitations of AI and ML. They can make more informed decisions about their implementation and guide their organizations toward strategic, ethical, and effective use of these powerful technologies.

Overview of machine learning and statistical analysis

Computers are excellent at doing calculations. Data is what they use, so it is logical that statistical analysis on very large data sets has been a crucial use for computing for years. Big Data or **business intelligence** (**BI**) are business/technical methods to draw insights from the signals in the data. Often, deep statistical analysis needs to be done on the data to draw useful insights, and just like humans can make mistakes, so can computers. The focus is, therefore, on having particularly good data and refined and tested calculations. This is where ML comes into play.

ML is a field of computer science that uses statistical techniques to allow computers to learn from data without being explicitly programmed for specific tasks. It is about designing and implementing algorithms that enable machines to utilize data for improvement and to make decisions with minimal human intervention. It involves a variety of methods, such as **supervised learning**, where the algorithm learns from labeled training data; unsupervised learning, where it identifies patterns in unlabeled data; and **reinforcement learning**, where an agent learns to make decisions by performing actions and observing the results.

At its core, ML relies on **optimization**—the process of adjusting the parameters of models to minimize a cost function. This is often done through gradient descent or other optimization algorithms that iteratively adjust parameters to improve the model's predictions. Just like any statistical model, it is best when adjusted and often as the sample size increases you can make better and better adjustments.

Overview of artificial intelligence

The goal is to develop models that can generalize from their training data and perform well on unseen data. This is measured by various performance metrics such as accuracy, precision, recall, and F1 score for classification tasks, or mean squared error and R-squared for regression tasks, which would be familiar to those who have experience with statistical analysis. Think of it as ML enabling AI systems to adapt to new scenarios and perform tasks by recognizing patterns and inferring rules from data. ML and AI are closely related. ML is effectively the behind-the-scenes, and AI is where the statistical analysis occurs and inferences are made. ML is the foundation that AI is built upon, and as we read further in the book, we will discuss AI as the foundation, chatbots/GPTs are built upon, so there is a clear foundational approach of one technology leveraging another.

In terms of AI, ML enables computers to build models from sample data to make predictions or decisions rather than following strictly static program instructions. This adaptive nature of ML is what breathes life into AI. For instance, NLP helps in understanding and generating human language, and in computer vision, it is used to recognize images and videos. These capabilities are not just theoretical; they are used in real-world applications like virtual assistants, self-driving cars, and personalized medicine, highlighting the transformative power of ML in AI. That is why ML is the backbone that allows AI to continuously evolve, enhancing its intelligence over time.

Algorithms and models

Training, validation, and testing are critical stages in the development of AI and ML models. Each of those serves a distinct purpose in ensuring the effectiveness and reliability of the model. During the training phase, the model is exposed to a large dataset from which it learns patterns and relationships. This phase is akin to schooling, where the model adjusts its parameters based on the input data to minimize errors in its predictions.

Following training, the validation phase comes into play. Here, the model is evaluated on a separate set of data, known as the **validation set**, which was not used during training. The goal of validation is to fine-tune the model's parameters and ensure that it is not merely memorizing the training data but is capable of generalizing to new unseen data. This step helps detect and mitigate overfitting, a scenario where the model performs well on the training data but poorly on new data.

The testing phase involves assessing the model's performance on another distinct dataset, called the test set. This stage provides an unbiased evaluation of the model's effectiveness and accuracy in real-world scenarios. The test set acts as a final exam, giving a clear indication of how well the model is likely to perform when deployed.

Types or components of artificial intelligence

AI can be broadly categorized into narrow (or weak) AI and general (or strong) AI.

AI encompasses a wide range of technologies and concepts, each with its own specific focus and applications. Narrow AI, also known as weak AI, is designed to perform specific tasks, such as facial recognition or recommendation systems, and is the most common form of AI today. In contrast, general AI, or strong AI, aims to replicate human intelligence in a more holistic way, capable of understanding, learning, and applying knowledge across a broad range of tasks—though this remains largely theoretical. Deep learning, a subset of ML, uses neural networks with many layers to analyze complex patterns in data, powering advancements in areas like image recognition and autonomous vehicles. NLP enables AI to understand and interact with human language, facilitating technologies like chatbots and translation services. Expert systems mimic human decision-making in specific domains by applying rules and logic to a predefined knowledge base. Cognitive computing focuses on simulating human thought processes, helping with tasks that require judgment and decision-making in complex scenarios. Finally, robotics integrates AI with physical machines, allowing them to perform tasks autonomously in environments ranging from factories to hospitals. Together, the following components illustrate the diverse and evolving landscape of AI technologies, each contributing to how machines can augment and interact with human capabilities:

- **Narrow AI:** It is designed to perform specific tasks within a limited domain. These systems excel at their designated functions but lack the ability to transfer knowledge or adapt to new situations outside their programming. Examples include chess engines, voice assistants, and recommendation systems. While highly effective in their niches, narrow AI systems do not possess true understanding or consciousness.

- **General AI:** Also known as strong AI or **artificial general intelligence (AGI)**, it refers to hypothetical AI systems that would match or exceed human-level intelligence across a wide range of cognitive tasks. Such systems would be capable of reasoning, problem-solving, learning, and adapting to new situations much like humans do. As of now, general AI remains a theoretical concept and a long-term goal in AI research.

- **Deep learning:** It is a subset of ML that uses artificial neural networks inspired by the human brain. These networks consist of multiple layers of interconnected nodes, allowing them to process and learn from vast amounts of data. Deep learning has led to significant breakthroughs in areas like image and speech recognition, NLP, and game-playing AI.

- **NLP:** It is a field of AI focused on enabling computers to understand, interpret, and generate human language. NLP combines linguistics, computer science, and AI to bridge the gap between human communication and computer understanding.

Applications of NLP include machine translation, sentiment analysis, chatbots, and voice assistants. Recent advancements in deep learning have greatly improved NLP capabilities, leading to more sophisticated language models and applications.

- **Expert systems**: They are a type of AI designed to mimic the decision-making abilities of a human expert in a specific domain. They are composed of two main components: a knowledge base and an inference engine. The knowledge base contains a collection of facts and rules about the domain, while the inference engine applies logical rules to the knowledge base to deduce new information or make decisions. Expert systems are used in various fields, such as medical diagnosis, financial forecasting, and technical support, where they help users make informed decisions by providing expertise and recommendations based on the data and rules programmed into the system. Despite their effectiveness in narrow domains, expert systems are typically limited by the quality of the knowledge they contain and the complexity of the rules they can process.

- **Cognitive computing**: It refers to advanced AI systems designed to simulate human thought processes in a computerized model. These systems use technologies such as, NLP, ML, and reasoning to understand, interpret, and respond to complex data in a way that mimics human cognition. Unlike traditional AI, which follows predefined rules, cognitive computing systems can learn and adapt over time, making them capable of handling unstructured data and performing tasks such as speech recognition, sentiment analysis, and decision-making. The goal of cognitive computing is to enhance human decision-making by providing insights and recommendations based on the system's ability to analyze vast amounts of data, recognize patterns, and understand context. These systems are often used in areas like healthcare, finance, and customer service, where they can assist in making more informed and timely decisions.

- **Robotics**: It is a branch of AI that involves the design, construction, and operation of robots—machines that can perform tasks autonomously or semi-autonomously. Robotics combines elements of computer science, engineering, and AI to create systems capable of interacting with the physical world. These robots are equipped with sensors to perceive their environment, processors to analyze data and make decisions, and actuators to carry out physical actions. Robotics is applied in various fields, from manufacturing and logistics, where robots handle repetitive tasks with precision, to healthcare, where they assist in surgeries or provide care to patients. The goal of robotics is to develop machines that can perform complex tasks safely and efficiently, often in environments that are challenging or hazardous for humans. As AI continues to advance, robotics is becoming increasingly sophisticated, enabling robots to learn from experience, adapt to new situations, and work alongside humans in a collaborative manner.

Data training and their importance in ML

Data is a cornerstone of ML and AI. For these technologies to function effectively, they require vast amounts of data to learn from and make accurate predictions. The importance of data cannot be overstated, as it serves as the foundation upon which ML models are built and trained. Quality data enables models to recognize patterns, make informed decisions, and ultimately deliver valuable insights and predictions. Bad data means bad results; it is that simple.

When considering ML and AI, data plays several critical roles. The first critical role data plays is training models, which help them understand the relationships between different variables. We will talk about training in more detail later, but it is how various types of AI learn what they know. High-quality and relevant data ensures that models can learn accurately and make reliable predictions. This data is used for validation and testing, ensuring that models generalize well to new, unseen scenarios and do not simply memorize the training data.

The quality and quantity of data directly impact the performance of AI and ML models. Clean, well-structured data free from biases and errors leads to more accurate and trustworthy models. As we touched on, poor-quality data can result in flawed models that produce unreliable predictions which can have significant negative consequences in real-world applications.

For people in the organization who may not be exceptionally technically skilled, understanding the importance of data in AI and ML is crucial for several reasons. It highlights the need for robust data collection and management practices, emphasizes the value of data governance and ethics, and underscores the necessity of investing in data infrastructure. By prioritizing data quality and availability, organizations can ensure that their AI and ML initiatives are built on a solid foundation, leading to more successful and impactful outcomes moving any business forward.

The AI system learns what it knows through distinct types of learnings or teachings. This is no different from how information (data) is loaded into the system in question.

Understanding the distinction between supervised and unsupervised learning is fundamental. Supervised learning is a type of ML where the model is trained on a labeled dataset. This means that each input data point is paired with the correct output. For instance, in a system designed to recognize images of cats and dogs, the training data includes images labeled as either cat or dog. The model learns to map inputs to the correct outputs, enabling it to make accurate predictions when presented with new, unlabeled data. This approach is highly effective for tasks like classification, where the goal is to assign input data to predefined categories, and regression, where the objective is to predict continuous values.

In ML and AI, it is critical to understand the distinction between supervised and unsupervised learning types. Let us go a bit deeper than we just discussed:

- Supervised learning is a type of ML where the model is trained on a labeled dataset. This means that each input data point is paired with the correct output. For instance, in a system designed to recognize images of cats and dogs, the training data includes images labeled as either cat or dog. The model learns to map inputs to the correct outputs, enabling it to make accurate predictions when presented with new and unlabeled data. This approach is highly effective for tasks like classification, where the goal is to assign input data to predefined categories, along with regression, where the objective is to predict continuous values.

- Unsupervised learning deals with unlabeled data, quite in opposition to supervised learning. Here, the model is tasked with identifying patterns, structures, or relationships within the data without prior knowledge of the correct output. This type of learning is akin to exploring a new city without a map and discovering landmarks and neighborhoods based on their natural groupings. Common applications of unsupervised learning include clustering, where the model groups similar data points together, and anomaly detection, where the model identifies data points that significantly differ from the norm.

These concepts are crucial for making informed decisions about which ML techniques to apply to different business problems. Supervised learning is typically used when there is a clear outcome to predict based on historical data, such as predicting customer churn or classifying email spam. Unsupervised learning is valuable for exploratory data analysis and for scenarios where discovering hidden patterns can provide strategic insights, such as segmenting customers into distinct groups based on purchasing behavior.

Knowing the two learning approaches allows executives to better leverage ML and AI technologies, aligning the right techniques with their business objectives and ensuring they harness the full potential of their data.

There is a variation on supervised learning called semi-supervised training. It is a bit of both supervised and non supervised, trying to come to a synthesis of the two for best results. In this methodology, the model is trained on a small amount of labeled data supplemented by large amounts of unlabeled data. This approach is particularly valuable when obtaining a fully labeled dataset is expensive, time-consuming, or impractical.

Semi-supervised learning offers the advantages of supervised learning—where the model benefits from the guidance of labeled examples—combined with the efficiency of unsupervised learning, which utilizes the vast amounts of available unlabeled data. For executives, understanding semi-supervised learning highlights a cost-effective and efficient strategy to harness AI and ML capabilities, enabling their organizations to make the most out of their data resources, even when labeling is a limiting factor. This approach can lead to improved model performance and broader applicability of AI solutions in various business contexts.

Additive to the choice of supervised versus unsupervised AI training is an advanced concept that deals with AI using ML to potentially make predictions. This is what we are seeing today with the many chatbots. These learning techniques are called few-shot learning and zero-shot learning:

- **Few-shot learning**: It refers to the ability of a model to learn and make accurate predictions after being exposed to only a few examples of each class. Traditional ML models typically require large amounts of labeled data to perform well. Few-shot learning leverages advanced techniques to generalize from a limited number of examples, making it highly valuable in applications where data is scarce or rapidly changing. In this scenario, an example would be learning data for personalized healthcare, where a model trained with few-shot learning can adapt to a new patient's unique medical profile using only a small number of past records. Medicine broadly is an area where statistical analysis is central to the successful treatment of patients.

- **Zero-shot learning**: It takes few-shot learning further by enabling models to make accurate predictions for classes they have never seen before. This is achieved through leveraging auxiliary information, such as descriptive attributes or relationships between classes. Here is an example: a zero-shot learning model trained to recognize animals might use descriptive attributes like **stripes** and **is large** enough to correctly identify a new, unseen animal, such as a Zebra, based on these characteristics.

Note: When someone uses an AI website, Chatbot, etc., the data is logged and could be turned into learning, if applicable. Sometimes, the individual interacting with the AI can impact its training. Read the terms and conditions of any AI service to be sure.

Here is a real-world example I tried. A random AI website was asked a question, which, as a preview for the rest of the book, is the prompt we will be spending a significant amount of time talking about. In this example, Microsoft co-pilot was used (https://copilot.microsoft.com/), which they branded an AI companion for this experiment. I started by uploading a photo of the inscription of the ring of power from the book series: Lord of the Rings, asking to translate it. I give it a hint by quoting a movie about them in *Figure 1.2*. It was not able to translate the information:

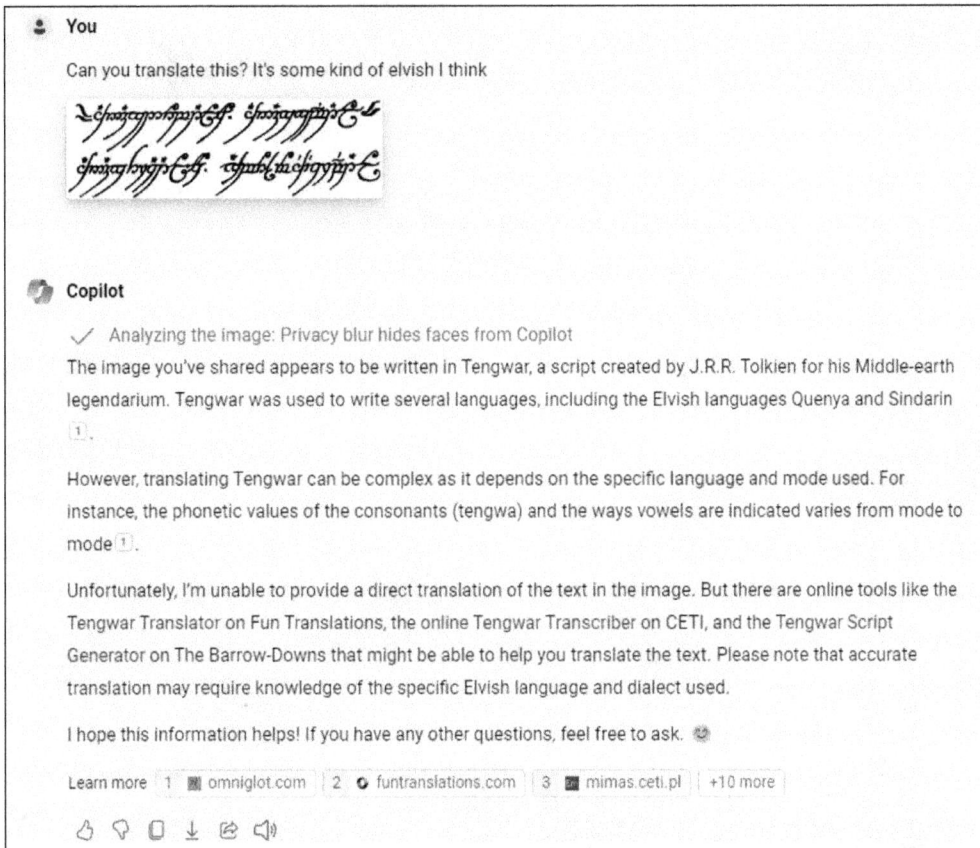

Figure 1.2: Asking Co-Pilot to translate an image from a fictional book

In *Figure 1.3*, you can see that a better hint was given, and it did respond properly. The attempt was effectively a zero-shot learning attempt, where interacting with it is the learning. In the second attempt, more data was provided so it could predict better what was asked for. This is a simple few-shot learning example:

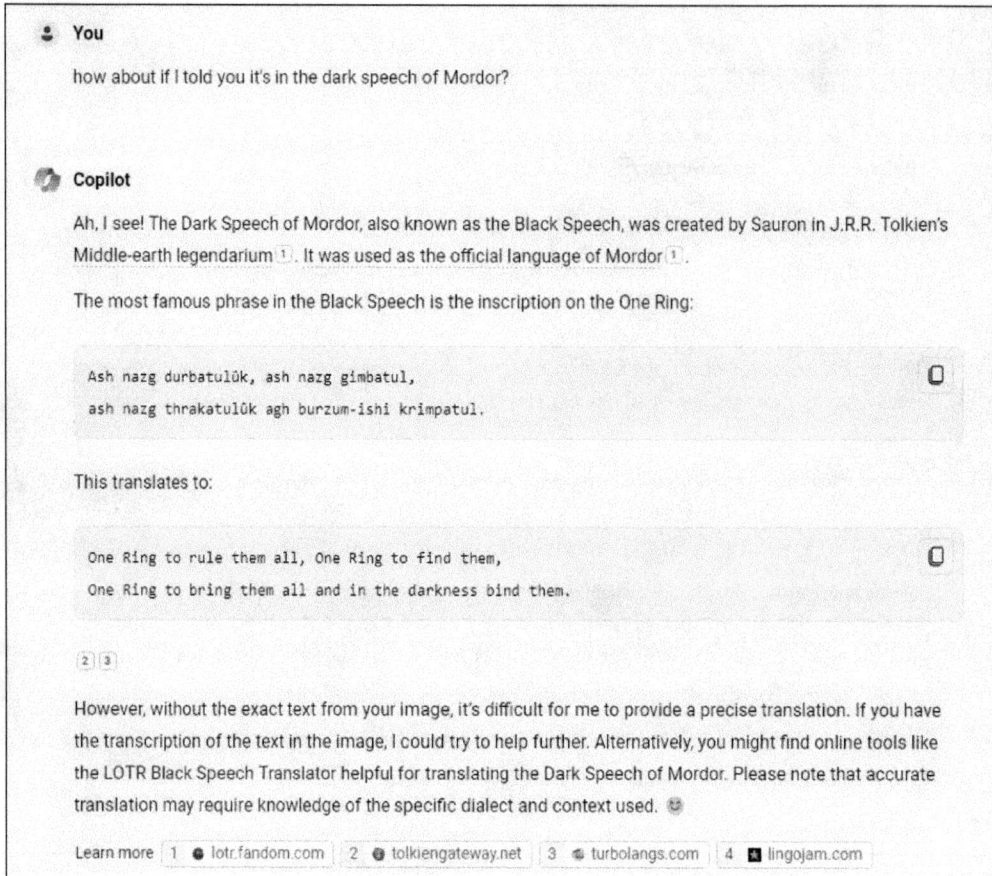

Figure 1.3: *Giving the system a bit more context*

In *Figure 1.4*, the first question was asked again, this time with no clue at all. From the learning just done, it gave a correct response:

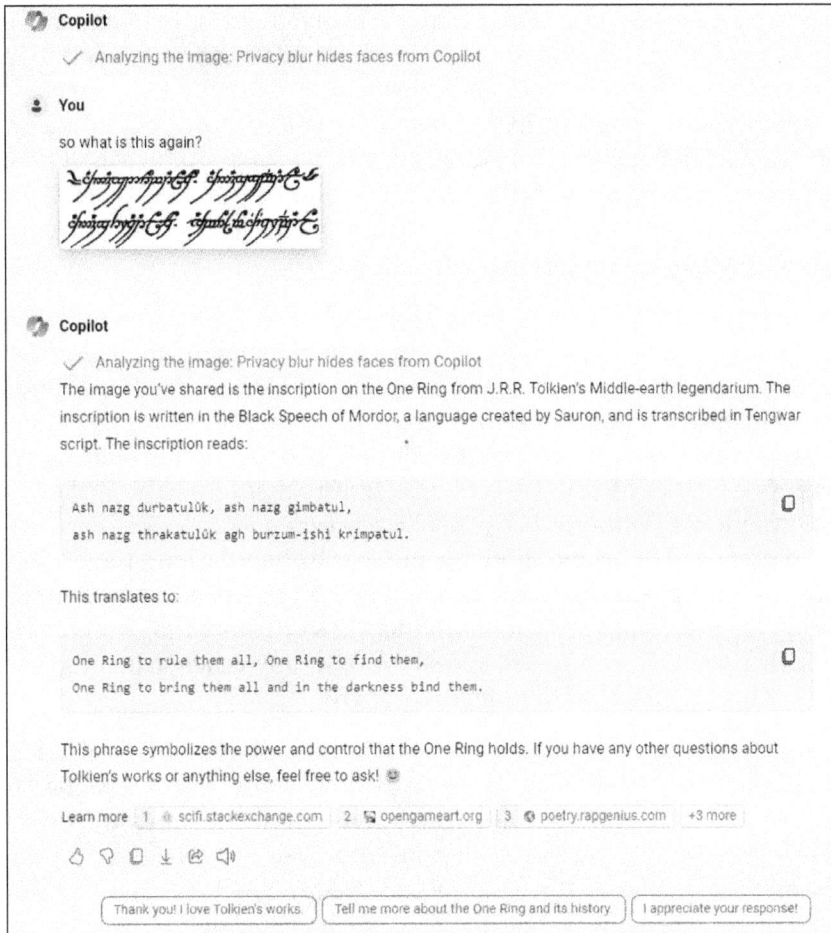

Figure 1.4: The correct answer based on the learning given

Historical context and evolution of AI and GPT

Modern AI broadly encompasses a wide range of technologies and methodologies aimed at creating systems capable of performing tasks that typically require human intelligence.

On the other hand, **general AI**, often called **strong AI,** is the concept of a machine with the ability to apply intelligence to any problem rather than just one specific problem, essentially mimicking the cognitive abilities of a human. This type of AI would have self-awareness, sentience, and consciousness. General AI can learn, understand, and apply knowledge in different domains, making it a more flexible and adaptable form of intelligence. Today, general AI remains a mostly theoretical concept and has not been achieved in practice, but it is worth mentioning.

The current wave of chat services like ChatGPT evolved out of the work being done on LLM systems. About a decade ago, an AI research foundation was formed to learn about AI and produce useful AI to be safe and beneficial. Eventually, they created ChatGPT, which was released in November 2022. ChatGPT changed how people interact with AI via what feels like a chatbot experience but is backed by deep AI and ML. It set off a storm as huge tech companies (Microsoft, Google, Meta, and of now, Apple, etc.) are working on their own versions of either ChatGPT or companies are hiring software engineers and computer scientists to help build their own.

One more concept to discuss now, a **large language model (LLM) is** an advanced type of AI designed to understand, generate, and manipulate human language. These models are typically built using deep learning techniques and are trained on vast amounts of text data to develop a broad understanding of language, including grammar, context, and various nuances. Examples of LLMs include OpenAI's GPT 4, and Google's BERT. Transformers are a type of neural network architecture that forms the backbone of LLMs. The transformer model, introduced by *Ashish Vaswani* and others from Google brain/ research, revolutionized NLP by allowing models to handle long-range dependencies and context more effectively than previous architectures like **recurrent neural networks (RNNs),** which are a type of artificial neural networks designed to recognize patterns in sequences of data, such as time series, speech, text, or any other sequential data. Pattern recognition is critical for an LLM to function properly.

What does this all have to do with the various GPT chat AI? The **GPT** in **Chat GPT** stands for generative pre-trained transformer. It is a type of AI model that is designed to generate text by predicting the next word in a sequence, given all the previous words within some text. This is achieved through a process known as pre-training, where the model is trained on a large dataset of text to learn the patterns and structures of language. Once pre-trained, GPT models can be fine-tuned on specific tasks such as translation, question-answering, and text completion.

Tip: Be aware that entering anything into any AI/Chatbot could become part of its learning. That is why companies often forbid employees from having AI do analysis of any internal information as it would make it potentially public. AI systems will frequently have an Opt In/Opt Out step so take care to read the terms and conditions.

GPT models are based on the transformer architecture, which uses mechanisms called attention and self-attention to weigh the influence of different words in a sentence. This allows GPT to generate coherent and contextually relevant text. OpenAI.com will have links and updates to the latest version of the model as it is evolving quickly.

Now, we can talk about what a prompt is and why it is so critical. Let us use a hypothetical situation that reflects a real-world scenario:

- **Question**: Why is hydro-power a good idea?
- **Answer**: It reduces electricity bills, decreases carbon footprint, and provides a renewable source of energy.

Simply put the preceding prompt as the question. It is all about the question. We talked about training models, specifically how they are trained through inputting prompt (question) and answer pairs. The more you enter over a wider range of expertise or depth, the better your LLM becomes. You do not need an LLM if you are only trying to calculate the optimal temperature setting of your thermostat. There are a few finite inputs, so you can only use ML, although anything complicated that relies on interpolation would need training. What is interesting here is that you do not just have to train an LLM on facts; there are trading methods where you do not give it an answer or give it bounds to work within. You can also train it on something made-up like **Prompt: tell me story about a space empress named Lyria**. If you use the right model, you will get a story. AI such as ChatGPT can do things like **Prompt: write python code to convert from Celsius to Fahrenheit**. Running this today against ChatGPT 4o will get the following two answers, a junior programmer answer and an experienced programmer answer:

- One that a junior programmer may create:

```
# Function to convert Celsius to Fahrenheit
def celsius_to_fahrenheit(celsius):
    fahrenheit = (celsius * 9/5) + 32
    return fahrenheit

# Example usage
celsius = 25
fahrenheit = celsius_to_fahrenheit(celsius)
print(f"{celsius} degrees Celsius is equal to {fahrenheit} degrees
Fahrenheit.")
```

- One that an experienced programmer may create as it explains how to pass a variable:

```
def celsius_to_fahrenheit(celsius):
return (celsius * 9/5) + 32
```

You can use this function by passing a temperature in Celsius as an argument, and it will return the equivalent temperature in Fahrenheit. You can respond with a more efficient approach; thus, improving it is learning. These learnings are often double-checked based on supervised learning.

Conclusion

In this chapter, we covered some important moments in AI history, and how systems work in general. We also discussed how those systems learn and how your interactions with them can affect their learnings.

In the next chapter, we will talk about the evolution of ML and its significance.

Join our book's Discord space

Join the book's Discord Workspace for Latest updates, Offers, Tech happenings around the world, New Release and Sessions with the Authors:

https://discord.bpbonline.com

CHAPTER 2

Evolution of Machine Learning

Introduction

This chapter looks into the historical progression of **machine learning** (**ML**), tracing its roots from symbolic AI to the modern era of statistical learning. It begins with an exploration of early ML approaches, highlighting the transition from rule-based systems to data-driven models. Key milestones in the field are discussed, including the definition and development of neural networks from the 1950s to the 1980s. The chapter emphasizes the significance of the backpropagation algorithm, introduced in 1986, which revolutionized the training of neural networks. Moving into the 1990s, the rise of **support vector machines** (**SVMs**) is examined, showcasing their impact on the field. The chapter also addresses the transformative role of big data and increased computational power, facilitated by advancements in hardware such as **graphic process units** (**GPUs**) and **tensor processing units** (**TPUs**) as well as **neural processing units** (**NPUs**). Finally, the emergence of deep learning is presented, marking a new era in ML driven by the growth of large datasets and sophisticated computational resources.

Structure

This chapter will cover the following topics:

- Symbolic artificial intelligence to statistical learning
- Rule-based systems to data-driven models

- Neural networks

- Use of the backpropagation algorithm

- Support vectors

- Advancements in artificial intelligence

- Advances in graphics and tensor processor hardware

- Emergence of deep learning

Objectives

When you complete this chapter, you will understand the background technologies that were needed to give rise to modern **artificial intelligence** (**AI**) and ML. You will learn the reliance of ML and modern AI on statistical analysis. You will also understand how the connection between biology and study of the brain to how neural networks function in AI.

Symbolic artificial intelligence to statistical learning

The origins of statistical analysis, which laid the groundwork for the field of ML, traces back to the early work in probability theory and statistics in the 18th and 19th centuries. One of the foundational figures in this area was *Thomas Bayes*, an English statistician and clergyman. The Bayes' theorem, introduced posthumously in 1763, provided a way to update the probability of a hypothesis as more evidence or information became available. This theorem forms the basis for Bayesian inference, a critical method in modern statistical analysis and ML. Evidently, using mathematics to solve problems is as old as humanity, this is just formalizing those steps.

A bit more recently, in the 19th century, the work of *Carl Friedrich Gauss* and *Pierre-Simon Laplace* further advanced the field. *Gauss* was a German mathematician who contributed significantly through his development of the Gaussian distribution (normal distribution), which describes how data points are distributed around a mean value. *Laplace* was a French mathematician who expanded on Bayes' work and introduced methods for estimating the parameters of statistical models. Their contributions were crucial in developing the mathematical tools needed for analyzing and interpreting data.

The early 20th century saw the formalization of many statistical methods, driven by the work of pioneers like *Ronald Fisher*, who is often generally regarded as the father of modern statistics. *Fisher's* introduction of maximum likelihood estimation and his development of the **Analysis of Variance** (**ANOVA**) provided powerful techniques for inferring relationships between variables. His work laid the foundation for many of the algorithms used in ML today. Today ANOVA analysis is part of many college-level statistical analysis courses, it is also a foundational concept used in quality systems such as Six Sigma, etc., as ANOVA analysis uses the data from a process to identify outliers or errors that would require re-work to fix. By understanding which step and sub-step in a process causes the error, an adjustment can be made to remediate it.

As computers became more powerful and accessible in the mid-20th century, the field of ML began to take shape. The advent of electronic computing allowed for the practical application of statistical methods on a large scale. In 1957 *Frank Rosenblatt* introduced the perceptron, which was an early type of artificial neural network inspired by the human brain's structure. This marked one of the first attempts to create machines that could learn from data, setting the stage for future developments in AI.

The 1960s and 1970s saw further advancements with the development of algorithms like **k-Nearest Neighbors (k-NN)**, decision trees, and SVMs. These algorithms were grounded in statistical principles and aimed at enabling machines to recognize patterns and make decisions based on data. The increasing availability of digital data and improvements in computational power fueled rapid progress in the field.

Symbolic AI which was also known as classical AI or **Good Old-Fashioned AI (GOFAI)**, played a significant role in the development of AI before the rise of statistical learning. Symbolic AI is based on the manipulation of symbols and the use of explicit, human-readable rules to represent knowledge and solve problems. This approach dominated AI research from the 1950s through the 1980s, effectively the first major leap in AI evolution.

Symbolic AI systems rely on logic and structured representations of knowledge, such as semantic networks, production rules, and frames. These systems were designed to perform tasks that required reasoning, planning, and problem-solving by following predefined rules and procedures. One of the early successes of symbolic AI was the **general problem solver (GPS)**, developed by *Allen Newell* and *Herbert A. Simon* in the late 1950s. GPS was a program capable of solving a wide range of problems by representing them as a series of logical steps.

Despite early successes, symbolic AI faced significant challenges. Those challenges were seen particularly in dealing with uncertainty and learning from data along with handling the complexity and variability of real-world environments. These limitations led researchers to explore alternative approaches, including statistical learning and connectionist models like neural networks.

The transition from symbolic AI to statistical learning marked a shift in focus from rule-based systems to data-driven approaches. Statistical learning, which includes methods like regression analysis, decision trees, and neural networks, emphasizes learning patterns and relationships from data rather than relying on explicitly programmed rules. This shift was driven by several key factors, which are as follows:

- **Data availability:** The increasing availability of digital data provided a rich resource for training ML models. Unlike symbolic AI, which required extensive manual encoding of knowledge, statistical learning methods could automatically learn from large datasets.

- **Computational power:** Advances in computing technology enabled the processing and analysis of large datasets, making it feasible to apply complex statistical methods to real-world problems.

- **Mathematical foundations:** The development of rigorous mathematical frameworks for statistical learning, such as probability theory, optimization, and information theory, provided a solid foundation for building effective ML algorithms.

- **Adaptability and scalability:** Statistical learning methods demonstrated greater adaptability and scalability in handling diverse and dynamic environments. These methods could generalize from data and improve performance with more training examples, addressing some of the limitations of symbolic AI.

A turning point in the transition was the resurgence of interest in neural networks; particularly with the advent of backpropagation in the 1980s. Backpropagation allowed for the efficient training of multi-layer neural networks, overcoming some of the computational challenges that had previously hindered their adoption. This led to the development of deep learning, a subfield of ML that leverages large-scale neural networks to model complex patterns and representations. We will speak about neural networks at length, later in this chapte, in the section *emergence of deep learning*.

The integration of statistical learning with symbolic AI approaches has also seen progress in recent years. Hybrid systems that combine the strengths of both paradigms aim to leverage the structured reasoning capabilities of symbolic AI with the flexibility and learning capacity of statistical methods. These efforts reflect an ongoing evolution in the field, seeking to create more robust and intelligent systems by drawing on the complementary strengths of different AI approaches.

The transition from symbolic AI to statistical learning represents a significant evolution in the field of AI. While symbolic AI laid the groundwork with its emphasis on logic and rule-based systems, the rise of statistical learning brought data-driven methods to the forefront, enabling more adaptive and scalable solutions to complex problems. This shift has been instrumental in advancing AI to its current state, where ML and deep learning are central to many applications and technologies.

When we look at the early history of statistical analysis, we see it is marked by the contributions of mathematicians and statisticians who developed the theories and methods that underpin modern ML. The transition from theoretical developments to practical applications was facilitated by advancements in computing technology. This is what led to the sophisticated ML algorithms we use today. This historical progression we have seen highlights the interdisciplinary nature of the field, drawing from mathematics, statistics, and computer science to create systems capable of learning and adapting from data.

Rule-based systems to data-driven models

Rule-based systems, which today, are known as expert systems, rely on explicitly programmed rules and logic to perform tasks. As the shift from rule-based systems to data-driven models occurred, several significant changes and developments emerged in the field of AI. This transition marked a fundamental shift in how AI systems were designed, developed, and implemented, leading to new capabilities and applications.

Limitations of rule-based systems

The rule-based system model did get the job done, but was not the final evolution of where they would end up. These systems were effective in structured and well-defined domains but encountered several limitations like:

- **Scalability**: Manually encoding knowledge and rules for complex systems was labor-intensive and impractical for large-scale applications.

- **Adaptability**: Rule-based systems struggled to adapt to new or unforeseen situations since they could only operate within the scope of predefined rules.

- **Handling uncertainty**: These systems found it difficult to manage uncertainty and variability inherent in real-world data and environments.

- **Knowledge acquisition bottleneck**: Extracting and formalizing expert knowledge into rules was a significant challenge, often leading to incomplete or outdated rule sets.

Emergence of data-driven models

The shift towards data-driven models was driven by the need to address these limitations and take advantage of the growing availability of digital data and increased computational power. Data-driven models, particularly ML algorithms, rely on learning patterns and relationships from data rather than being explicitly programmed with rules. Several major developments occurred while this shift was occurring, which are as follows:

- **Statistical foundations:** The application of statistical methods allowed for the modeling of complex relationships and patterns within data. Techniques such as linear regression, decision trees, and clustering provided the foundation for more sophisticated ML algorithms.

- **Neural networks and deep learning**: The resurgence of neural networks, particularly with the development of backpropagation in the 1980s (discussed later in this chapter in the section *use of the backpropagation algorithm*), enabled the training of multi-layer networks. This advancement led to deep learning, which uses large-scale neural networks to model intricate patterns and representations, significantly enhancing the capabilities of AI systems. We will specifically discuss deep learning later in this chapter, in the section *Wide Adoption and Support*.

- **Data availability:** The exponential growth of digital data from various sources, including the internet, sensors, and mobile devices, provided rich datasets for training ML models. This abundance of data was crucial for the development and success of data-driven models.

- **Computational advances**: Improvements in hardware, such as GPUs and cloud computing, enabled the efficient processing of large datasets and complex models. These advances made it feasible to implement and deploy data-driven AI systems at scale.

- **Algorithmic innovations**: The development of new algorithms and optimization techniques, such as SVMs, ensemble methods (that is, random forests and gradient boosting), and reinforcement learning, expanded the range of problems that AI systems could tackle.

- Symbolic AI and statistical learning are two great achievements in the history of AI, and both have their own approach to hard problems. Symbolic AI employs machine-readable rules and logic to play with symbols of ideas and relationships. It is great for formal logic and storage of knowledge but weak for uncertainty and variation. Statistical learning — which is gaining popularity thanks to the explosion of ML — works with large amounts of data and probabilistic frameworks to detect trends and make predictions. It is robust in highly variable and big data systems, but not typically interpretively or as accurate as symbolic AI. However, both methodologies have increasingly merged with one another to generate hybrid models that combine the power of symbolic reasoning and deep learning for stronger, more general AI.

Impact on AI applications-driven models has profoundly impacted AI applications by enabling more accurate, efficient, and scalable solutions across various domains. These models rely heavily on vast amounts of data to learn patterns and make predictions to improve performance over time. In fields such as healthcare, finance, and transportation, data-driven AI models can analyze complex datasets to uncover insights that humans might miss, leading to more informed decision-making and optimized processes. Remember at the end of the day it is a series of programs doing exceedingly rapid calculations. An example to consider would be in healthcare where AI models can predict patient outcomes, recommend personalized treatments, and even assist in diagnosing diseases with greater precision. In finance, those models drive real-time fraud detection, risk assessment, and automated trading strategies. Today we see AI at work in transportation as data-driven models power autonomous vehicles, optimizing routes and enhancing safety. The ability to process and learn from large datasets has also driven advancements in areas such as natural language processing, image recognition, and robotics, making AI applications more intelligent, adaptable, and capable of handling intricate tasks with minimal human intervention. The integration of data-driven models in AI has revolutionized how industries operate, driving innovation and efficiency to new heights. The shift to data-driven models led to significant advancements and expanded the scope of AI applications, some examples are:

- **Natural language processing**: ML models enabled breakthroughs in NLP tasks such as language translation, sentiment analysis, and speech recognition. Techniques like word embeddings and transformer architectures (we will discuss transformer architectures shortly) revolutionized the field. NLP has become a very important interface in recent years to allow for individuals to get a human-like response from a human asking a question. In the last two years, we have seen tremendous progress made in having a **conversation** with an AI of some sort. We will speak to this much more later on.

- **Computer vision**: Deep learning models, particularly **convolutional neural networks** (**CNNs**), achieved remarkable success in image and video recognition, object detection, and image generation, leading to applications in healthcare, autonomous vehicles, and surveillance.

- **Recommendation systems**: Data-driven approaches improved recommendation systems, providing personalized content and product suggestions on platforms like *Netflix*, *Amazon*, and *Spotify*.

- **Healthcare**: ML models are used for medical diagnosis, drug discovery, and personalized treatment plans, leveraging large datasets of medical records and genetic information.

Challenges and considerations

While data-driven models brought many advantages, they also introduced new challenges which constrained their growth and wider adoption. Let us look at some of them:

- **Data quality and bias**: The quality and representativeness of training data are crucial. Biases in data can lead to biased models, raising ethical and fairness concerns.

- **Interpretability**: Complex models, particularly deep learning networks, are often seen as **black boxes**, making it difficult to understand and explain their decisions. Efforts to improve model interpretability and transparency are ongoing.

- **Generalization**: Ensuring that models generalize well to new, unseen data is a critical challenge. Overfitting to training data can lead to poor performance in real-world applications.

- **Privacy and security**: The use of large datasets, particularly those containing personal information, raises privacy and security concerns. Techniques such as differential privacy and federated learning are being developed to address these issues. Ethics about what is done with potentially personal data of billions of individuals is something being hotly debated across the world today.

The shift from rule-based systems to data-driven models marked a transformative period in AI, enabling more powerful, adaptable, and scalable solutions. This transition was driven by advancements in statistical methods, computational power, and the availability of data, leading to significant progress in various AI applications. It has also introduced new challenges that continue to be the focus of ongoing research and development in the field.

Neural networks

A neural network is a computational model inspired by how biological neural networks in the human brain process information. Of course, human-created neural networks are much simpler and less capable than billions of years of evolution giving us the human brain. The basic principles of interconnected processing units and adaptive learning make them a powerful tool for solving complex problems in fields such as image recognition, speech processing, and decision-making.

In the human brain, neurons are specialized cells that transmit information through electrical and chemical signals. These neurons are interconnected, forming a vast and complex network that enables us to process information, learn, and make decisions. Similarly, in a neural network, artificial neurons (nodes) are connected by weighted links. Each artificial neuron receives input, processes it, and passes the output to the next layer of neurons. The neural network uses common biological terminology which one will come across often:

- **Neurons and nodes**: Just as biological neurons receive, process, and transmit signals. Artificial neurons in a neural network receive input, apply a mathematical function, and pass the result to the next layer.

- **Connections and weights**: In the brain, synapses are the connections between neurons, and they can strengthen or weaken over time thus influencing how signals are transmitted. In a neural network, connections between nodes have weights that are adjusted during training to improve the network's performance.

- **Learning and adaptation**: The brain learns and adapts through experience by adjusting synaptic strengths based on feedback. Neural networks learn through a process called training where the weights of the connections are adjusted based on the error of the network's predictions compared to the actual outcomes. This adjustment process often involves algorithms like backpropagation.

- **Layered structure**: The brain processes information through multiple layers of neurons. In a neural network data is processed through multiple layers of nodes, typically including an input layer with one or more hidden layers and an output layer. Each layer extracts different levels of features from the input data.

A neural network, therefore, consists of interconnected nodes (neurons) organized in layers, which are an input layer, one or more hidden layers, and an output layer, which we will speak about shortly. Each connection between nodes has an associated weight, which is adjusted during training to minimize the error in predictions. Neural networks are particularly powerful in recognizing patterns and making predictions based on complex data inputs. Let us discuss i neural networks in some depth.

Development of neural networks

The concept of neural networks dates to the 1950s when *Warren McCulloch* and *Walter Pitts* proposed a model of artificial neurons. In 1958, *Frank Rosenblatt* developed the perceptron, an early type of neural network capable of binary classification. Despite initial excitement, neural networks faced significant limitations, especially with multi-layer networks, due to the lack of efficient training algorithms. During the 1970s and 1980s, research interest waned as symbolic AI approaches gained prominence. However, foundational work continued, laying the groundwork for future breakthroughs. The basic structure of a neural network maps out those nodes and shows the connections. They are grouped in the three basic layers:

- Input layer is the initial layer of a neural network that receives the raw data. It serves as the entry point for the data into the network. Each node in the input layer corresponds to one feature or dimension of the input data. For example, in an image processing network, each node might represent the pixel values of the image. The input layer does not perform any computation; it simply passes the input data to the next layer (which is the first hidden layer).

- The hidden layers are the intermediate layers between the input and output layers. A neural network can have one or many hidden layers depending on its depth. Nodes in hidden layers perform computations on the data they receive from the previous layer. Each node in a hidden layer takes a weighted sum of the inputs, applies a bias, and then passes the result through an activation function to introduce non-linearity. This process allows the network to learn and model complex patterns and relationships in the data. As the data passes through successive hidden layers, the network extracts and transforms features at increasingly higher levels of abstraction.

- The output layer is the final layer of the neural network, producing the network's predictions or classifications. The nodes in the output layer correspond to the possible outcomes or classes in the task at hand. In a binary classification task, the output layer might have a single node representing the probability of one class, while in a multi-class classification task, it might have one node per class. The output layer processes the transformed data received from the last hidden layer, typically using an activation function suitable for the task. The result is the network's output which is then used for decision-making or further analysis.

Together, these layers enable a neural network to transform raw input data into meaningful output shown in *Figure 2.1,* this example shows two hidden layers:

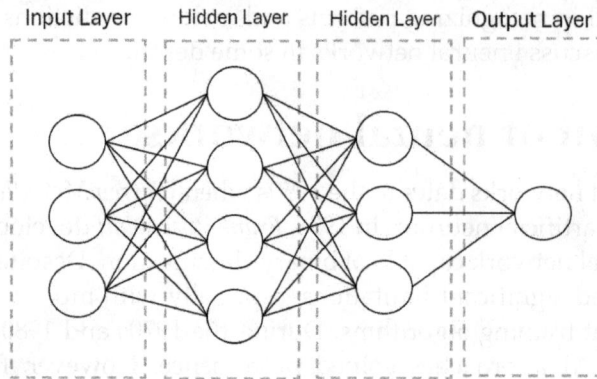

Figure 2.1: *A diagram of a neural network*

Use of the backpropagation algorithm

The backpropagation algorithm is a method used for training neural networks by minimizing the error between predicted and actual outputs. It works by propagating the error backward through the network, adjusting the weights of the connections based on the gradient of the error with respect to each weight. This process involves two main steps: forward propagation, where inputs pass through the network to generate predictions, and backward propagation, where the error is calculated and used to update the weights. Backpropagation enables the efficient training of multi-layer neural networks making it a cornerstone of modern neural network training.

Introduction of backpropagation

In 1986, *David Rumelhart, Geoffrey Hinton,* and *Ronald Williams* published a seminal paper that popularized the backpropagation algorithm. The primary purpose of backpropagation is to update the weights of the neural network to reduce the difference between the predicted output and the actual target values. This difference is measured by a loss function, which quantifies the error.

The work demonstrated that backpropagation could effectively train deep neural networks, overcoming many of the challenges that had previously hindered their development. This breakthrough revitalized interest in neural networks and laid the foundation for the deep learning revolution. The ability to train multi-layer networks using backpropagation unlocked new possibilities for AI applications, from image recognition to NLP.

Support vectors

Support vectors are data points that lie closest to the decision boundary in a classification problem. In the context of SVMs, these points are crucial because they define the position and orientation of the hyperplane that separates different classes. The goal of an SVM is to find the hyperplane that maximizes the margin between the support vectors of different classes, ensuring the most robust separation. Support vectors play a key role in determining the generalization ability of the SVM.

Rise of support vector machines

The 1990s saw the rise of SVMs as a powerful tool for classification and regression tasks. Introduced by *Vladimir Vapnik* and his colleagues, SVMs offered a novel approach to pattern recognition by focusing on maximizing the margin between different classes. This approach proved to be highly effective, especially in high-dimensional spaces, where traditional methods struggled. SVMs gained popularity due to their strong theoretical foundations and practical performance, becoming a standard tool in the ML toolkit. They were particularly successful in applications such as text categorization, image classification, and bioinformatics. The following key advances significantly shaped the field of ML:

- Neural networks provided a flexible and powerful framework for modeling complex patterns in data.

- The development of neural networks in the 1950s-1980s laid the groundwork for future breakthroughs, despite early challenges.

- The backpropagation algorithm enabled efficient training of deep neural networks, marking a major milestone.

- The introduction of backpropagation in 1986 by *Rumelhart*, *Hinton*, and *Williams* revitalized neural network research.

- Support vectors are critical elements in defining the decision boundary in classification tasks.

- The rise of SVMs in the 1990s introduced a robust and theoretically sound method for classification and regression, expanding the horizons of ML applications.

These developments collectively propelled the field of ML forward, enabling the sophisticated AI systems we see today. It took a relatively short amount of time to make such progress.

Advancements in artificial intelligence

AI advancement over time has significantly been driven by several key factors such as the explosion of big data as well as increased computational power and the growth of large datasets and databases, advances in hardware, and the emergence of deep learning.

Impact of big data and computational power

Big data refers to the enormous volumes of structured and unstructured data generated every day from various sources like social media, sensors, transactions, and more. This data is invaluable for AI because it provides the raw material that AI models need to learn and make accurate predictions. As the amount of available data has grown so has the ability of AI systems to analyze and extract meaningful insights from it. At the same time, computational power has increased dramatically, allowing these vast amounts of data to be processed more quickly and efficiently. This combination has enabled AI systems to become more sophisticated and capable of solving complex problems.

Big data

Computational power is central for training and running sophisticated ML models, as it directly influences the speed and efficiency of data processing and model inference. High-performance computing resources enable the execution of complex algorithms and large-scale computations, driving advancements in AI capabilities and real-time analytics:

- **Volume, variety, and velocity**: Big data is characterized by its large volume, variety, and velocity. The sheer amount of data generated from sources like social media, sensors, transactions, and **Internet of Things (IoT)** devices provides AI systems with rich and diverse datasets. This abundance of data is crucial for training AI models allowing them to learn from a wide range of examples and improve their accuracy and generalization capabilities.

- **Data-driven insights**: Big data enables AI to uncover patterns and insights that would be impossible to detect manually. In fields like healthcare, finance, and marketing, AI can analyze vast datasets to identify trends, predict outcomes, and make recommendations. An example could be in healthcare where AI can process patient records and medical imaging data to diagnose diseases more accurately and suggest personalized treatment plans.

- **Enhanced decision-making**: With access to big data, AI systems can make more informed and timely decisions. In real-time applications such as fraud detection, autonomous driving, and supply chain optimization, the ability to analyze large datasets quickly and accurately is critical. AI systems can detect anomalies, optimize routes, and adjust strategies on the fly, leading to more efficient and effective operations.

Computational power

Advances in computational power, particularly through the development of GPUs and TPUs, have been crucial for AI. GPUs, with their ability to perform parallel processing, significantly accelerated the training of deep learning models. TPUs, designed specifically for AI tasks, offer even greater efficiency and performance. This increased computational power allows for the training of larger, more complex models in a fraction of the time previously required:

- **Scalability:** Enhanced computational power enables the scaling of AI applications. Distributed computing frameworks and cloud-based solutions allow AI systems to leverage multiple processors and vast amounts of memory, making it feasible to handle massive datasets and perform complex computations. This scalability is essential for deploying AI solutions in real-world scenarios where data and computational demands can be immense.

- **Innovations in AI techniques**: The availability of powerful computational resources has spurred innovations in AI techniques. Researchers can now experiment with more sophisticated algorithms, deeper neural networks, and larger models. Techniques such as transfer learning, reinforcement learning, and **generative adversarial networks** (**GANs**) have benefited from increased computational capabilities, leading to breakthroughs in areas like NLP, image synthesis, and game playing.

The synergy between big data and computational power has been a driving force behind the rapid progress in AI. Big data provides the essential raw material for AI models to learn and improve, while advanced computational power enables the efficient processing and analysis of this data. Together they have expanded the boundaries of what AI can achieve, paving the way for innovative applications and solutions that enhance various aspects of our lives.

Growth of large datasets and databases

The availability of large datasets and advanced databases has been another crucial factor in AI's development. Large datasets provide diverse and rich examples that AI models need to learn effectively. We can see this in image recognition where large collections of labeled images allow AI systems to distinguish between different objects with high accuracy. Modern databases are designed to handle and manage these massive datasets efficiently thus ensuring that data is easily accessible and can be processed in real-time. This infrastructure supports the continuous training and improvement of AI models.

Enhanced learning and performance

Rich data for training large datasets provides AI models with a wealth of information to learn from. This diversity in data helps models generalize better and perform more accurately across various tasks. For example, in image recognition, a vast dataset with numerous images of different objects, scenes, and conditions allows the model to recognize and classify images with high accuracy.

When handling complex tasks, many AI applications such as NLP and speech recognition, require understanding and processing nuanced and complex data. Large datasets enable models to capture these complexities and subtleties, leading to more sophisticated and capable AI systems. An example of this would be training a language model on a massive text corpus which will help in understanding context, idioms, and various linguistic structures.

Improved model robustness

Mitigating overfitting is when a model performs well on training data but poorly on unseen data. Large datasets help mitigate this by providing a wide range of examples, which encourages the model to learn generalizable patterns rather than memorizing specific instances. This improves the model's robustness and reliability in real-world applications.

Real-world data is often noisy and variable. Large datasets that encompass this variability allow AI models to become more resilient to noise and better at handling different scenarios. This is particularly important in applications like autonomous driving, where the system must reliably interpret diverse and potentially noisy input data.

Accelerated development and innovation

Access to large datasets accelerates AI research and development. Researchers can experiment with new algorithms and techniques, leveraging the abundance of data to test and refine their models. Publicly available large datasets, such as ImageNet for image recognition or the Common Crawl dataset for NLP, have been instrumental in advancing AI research.

Large datasets are crucial for pre-training models that can be fine-tuned for specific tasks. Transfer learning leverages pre-trained models on large datasets and adapts them to new smaller datasets. This approach has been highly effective in improving performance while reducing the need for extensive labeled data in specialized applications.

Scalability and infrastructure

ML is a processor, storage, and compute-intensive. Scalability and infrastructure are crucial for meeting the growing demands of ML, as they enable efficient handling of large datasets and complex models across distributed systems. Robust infrastructure ensures that ML workflows can scale seamlessly, supporting increased computational requirements and faster deployment of AI solutions in diverse environments, which are as follows:

- **Advanced databases and storage solutions**: The growth of large datasets has driven the development of advanced databases and storage solutions. Modern databases are designed to handle vast amounts of data efficiently, ensuring that data is accessible and can be processed in real-time. Technologies like distributed databases, cloud storage, and data lakes support the scalable storage and retrieval of massive datasets.

- **Real-time processing and analysis**: With the rise of big data, the ability to process and analyze data in real-time has become critical. AI systems can now leverage real-time data streams to make immediate decisions and predictions. This capability is essential in applications such as fraud detection, personalized recommendations, and dynamic pricing.

The growth of large datasets and advanced databases has been a cornerstone in the evolution of AI. These datasets provide the foundation for training robust and accurate models, while advanced storage and processing solutions ensure scalability and efficiency. Together, they enable the development of innovative AI applications that can handle complex, real-world challenges with greater precision and reliability.

Advances in graphics and tensor processor hardware

Advances in hardware, particularly the development of GPUs and TPUs, have been game-changers for AI. GPUs were initially designed for rendering graphics in video games and graphical manipulation on screen. They are highly effective at performing the parallel computations required for training AI models. TPUs, which were developed by *Google*, are specialized for ML tasks and offer even greater efficiency. These hardware advancements have significantly reduced the time required to train complex AI models, making it feasible to experiment with larger and more sophisticated neural networks.

Speed and efficiency

The ability of GPUs to handle thousands of operations concurrently significantly speeds up the training process of neural networks. This efficiency is crucial for experimenting with large models and complex algorithms, as it reduces the time required for each training iteration. This faster training cycle allows researchers and developers to iterate quickly as well as refine models and achieve better results.

Wide adoption and support

GPUs have become the standard hardware for AI research and development. Major deep learning frameworks (popular examples you may run into are TensorFlow, PyTorch, and Caffe) are optimized to take full advantage of GPU acceleration. This widespread support has further solidified GPUs' role in advancing AI capabilities. GPUs have been used for non-graphic purposes for quite a few years, one of the first main non-graphical uses was in mining cryptocurrency. Now that same processing horsepower is desirable for AI. This drives GPU scarcity thus rising costs, which explains why high-end graphics cards are a challenge to obtain and why they are so expensive.

Tensor processing units

TPUs, unlike GPUs, are custom-designed to accelerate ML workloads. TPUs are specifically optimized for operations commonly used in neural networks such as matrix multiplications and convolutions. This specialization is why in many ways they are superior to GPUs. This specialization allows TPUs to perform these tasks more efficiently and with lower power consumption.

When looking to achieve performance gains, TPUs offer significant performance improvements over traditional CPUs and even GPUs for certain AI workloads. They can handle large-scale computations more quickly and efficiently, thus enabling the training of very large and complex models. This performance boost is particularly beneficial for applications that require real-time processing, such as natural language understanding, image recognition, and video analysis.

When there is a need to have a strong integration with cloud services, TPUs are integrated into cloud platforms like Microsoft Azure, making this powerful hardware accessible to a wide range of users without the need for significant upfront investment in physical infrastructure. This accessibility democratizes AI development and allowing businesses, researchers, and developers to leverage advanced hardware for their AI projects.

The overall impact on AI through enabling deep learning has helped drive the advances in GPUs and TPUs, which have been instrumental in the rise of deep learning itself. These hardware innovations have made it feasible to train deep neural networks on large datasets within reasonable time frames which is essential for achieving state-of-the-art performance in many AI tasks.

These new enhancements have been facilitating innovation with the enhanced computational capabilities provided by GPUs and TPUs. Researchers can explore more complex and novel AI architectures. This freedom to innovate has led to breakthroughs in various domains, including NLP (very much like the development of large language models), computer vision, and reinforcement learning.

Advanced adding hardware is what allows AI models to scale effectively to handle the ever growing usage occurring, as it has access to more compute power, storage, and greater network bandwidth. Organizations can deploy large-scale AI applications, such as recommendation systems, autonomous driving, and intelligent assistants which require processing vast amounts of data in real-time. The efficiency gains also translate to lower operational costs and energy consumption, making AI more sustainable.

Emergence of deep learning

Deep learning is a subset of ML that uses neural networks with many layers (hence **deep**) to model and understand complex patterns in data. The emergence of deep learning has been a major breakthrough in AI, enabling systems to achieve human-like performance in tasks such as image and speech recognition, language translation, and even playing strategic games. Deep learning models can automatically discover the features needed for a task directly from the raw data, reducing the need for manual feature engineering and allowing for more flexible and powerful AI solutions.

The development of algorithms like backpropagation, which adjusts weights in the network to minimize error, has been crucial for training deep neural networks. Additionally, innovations such as CNNs for image processing and **recurrent neural networks** (**RNNs**) for sequential data have enabled deep learning to tackle a wide range of tasks effectively.

In the field of computer vision, deep learning has set new standards for image and video analysis. CNNs have proven exceptionally effective for tasks like image classification, object detection, and facial recognition. Some applications we have touched on such as autonomous vehicles, which rely on real-time image processing to safely navigate, and medical imaging, where AI assists in diagnosing diseases from X-rays and MRI scans, also benefit.

The confluence of big data, enhanced computational power, with large datasets, databases, and advanced hardware. Not surprisingly, the rise of deep learning has propelled AI to new heights in the last few years. These factors have collectively enabled AI to tackle increasingly complex and diverse problems, transforming industries and enhancing our daily lives in unprecedented ways. Deep learning has been a transformative force in AI enabling machines to achieve unprecedented levels of understanding and performance across diverse applications. By automating feature extraction and learning from vast amounts of data, deep learning has expanded the horizons of what AI can accomplish, driving innovation and progress in both research and industry.

Conclusion

In this chapter, we covered the advances in statistical analysis, which ML is built upon. We covered the technology of what a neural network is and how it is based on human biology, as well as other areas of innovation affecting ML and AI, bringing them both faster into the future. We spent time on deep learning, an ingredient in the recipe of modern AI and chatbots. As ML continues to evolve, the development of generative models represents a significant leap forward, enabling machines to not only analyze and predict but also to create and innovate. These models have opened new frontiers in AI, allowing for the generation of realistic data, art, and even human-like text, pushing the boundaries of what machines can achieve.

In the next chapter, we will focus on the development of the generative models, which took the wealth of knowledge from ML to build the foundational algorithms for modern AI.

Join our book's Discord space

Join the book's Discord Workspace for Latest updates, Offers, Tech happenings around the world, New Release and Sessions with the Authors:

https://discord.bpbonline.com

CHAPTER 3
Development of Generative Models

Introduction

This chapter explores the fascinating evolution of generative models, a cornerstone of **artificial intelligence** (**AI**). We will begin by defining generative models and contrasting them with discriminative models, highlighting their unique ability to create new data samples. The chapter then traces the historical development of generative models, starting with early examples like *Naive Bayes* and *hidden Markov* models and progressing to more sophisticated approaches like *restricted Boltzmann machines* and *Autoencoders*. A pivotal moment in this journey is the introduction of **generative adversarial networks** (**GANs**), a revolutionary concept that pits two neural networks against each other in a creative duel. We will look into the mechanics of GANs, exploring the roles of generator and discriminator networks and showcasing their diverse applications in image synthesis, text generation, and beyond. We will speak about the advantages and disadvantages of each approach. The chapter concludes by setting the stage for the subsequent rise of transformers, hinting at the transformative impact they would have on the field of generative AI as they literally put the *G* in *Chat GPT*.

Structure

This chapter will cover the following topics:

- Overview of generative models
- Different types of generative models
- Generative adversarial networks

Objectives

This chapter will delve into the very foundations of AI and what a prompt is all about, the prompt interacts with a generative model in the system. Knowing how generative models work and their history helps to craft excellent prompts. We will talk about the history of generative models and move into discussing two of the major forms that models take: discriminative and generative. We will then walk through current models which you are likely to come in contact with, and touch on examples of how they functionally work.

Overview of generative models

When we talk about AI models, there are two main types we often refer to: generative models and discriminative models. Think of them as different tools in our AI toolbox, each with its own unique strengths and purposes.

Generative models are effectively a class of machine learning algorithms designed to generate new data points that resemble a given dataset. Unlike discriminative models, which focus on predicting label-given input data, generative models aim to understand the underlying distribution of the data and use this understanding to generate new, synthetic data. These models can learn the probability distribution of a dataset and can produce samples from this distribution, essentially creating new data that is statistically similar to the original data.

These models represent a significant advancement in the field of AI. Their ability to understand and replicate the underlying distribution of data opens up numerous possibilities across various domains, from enhancing data availability to creating entirely new forms of digital content. As the technology continues to evolve, the impact of generative models is expected to grow, driving innovation and transforming industries.

Early generative models

The development of generative models can be traced back to the early days of probability theory and statistical modeling. These models were initially developed to better understand and represent the underlying structure of data, allowing researchers to simulate, predict, and infer new data points based on observed patterns. The roots of generative models lie in the foundational work of probability theory by pioneers such as *Pierre-Simon Laplace* and *Carl Friedrich Gauss*. These early efforts focused on understanding how to model random events and distributions mathematically. The concept of the Gaussian (or normal) distribution, introduced by *Gauss*, is a cornerstone of many generative models. This distribution helped in understanding how to describe data that cluster around a mean value with a certain variance. This became a strong foundation for other mathematicians using stronger and stronger computers to build on.

Motivations behind developing generative models

Mathematicians have long recognized the need to develop generative models for AI to address the complexity and variability inherent in real-world data. Traditional deterministic models often fall short when dealing with the nuanced and unpredictable nature of such data, necessitating the use of probabilistic approaches that generative models offer. These models, grounded in mathematical theories and statistical principles, allow for the creation of new data instances that are representative of the underlying distribution of observed data. This capability is crucial for various AI applications, from natural language processing to image and speech recognition, where the goal is not just to analyze existing data but to generate new and plausible examples. By employing techniques that we will speak to, such as Bayesian inference, Markov chains, and neural networks, mathematicians have equipped AI systems with the ability to learn and generalize from limited datasets, improve robustness, and enhance the accuracy of predictions. The development of generative models represents a significant advancement in AI, enabling machines to mimic the creativity and adaptability of human intelligence more closely. Mathematicians and statisticians focused on the following five areas:

- **Understanding data**: Generative models were initially developed to better understand and represent the underlying distributions of data. By modeling how data is generated, researchers could gain insights into the structure and patterns within the data.

- **Simulation and prediction**: These models allow for the simulation of new data points, which is crucial in fields like meteorology, finance, and biology. Generative models can predict future events or generate synthetic data for various applications.

- **Unsupervised learning**: Generative models are pivotal in unsupervised learning, where the goal is to learn patterns and structures from unlabeled data. This capability is essential for tasks like clustering, density estimation, and anomaly detection.

- **Data augmentation**: In machine learning, generative models are used to create additional training data, enhancing the robustness and performance of supervised learning algorithms. This is particularly valuable when labeled data is scarce.

- **Creative applications**: Generative models have opened new frontiers in creative fields, enabling the generation of art, music, and literature. They allow for the exploration of new styles and the creation of novel content.

Early uses of generative models

Some of the earliest uses of generative models date back several decades. One of the initial applications was in speech synthesis, where models were developed to convert written text into spoken words, paving the way for modern text-to-speech systems. Simple image generation was also an early use, with computer graphics and procedural generation techniques in the 1960s and 1970s helping to create basic images and patterns. In the realm of statistical data modeling, generative models were crucial for simulating and understanding the statistical properties of various datasets across fields like economics and biology. Natural language processing, which we spoke about previously, saw the application of these models in the 1980s and 1990s for tasks such as predicting the next word in a sentence and generating coherent text based on statistical properties. Additionally, researchers experimented with music generation, using models to compose melodies and harmonies based on learned patterns from existing music. Another noteworthy application was handwriting synthesis, where generative models in the 1980s and 1990s enabled machines to generate handwritten text that closely mimicked human writing styles. These pioneering uses laid the groundwork for the sophisticated generative models we have today, such as GAN and **variational autoencoders** (**VAEs**), which can create highly realistic images, videos, and text. We will talk about GANs and VAEs in the section named GANs.

Generative models versus discriminative models

The two model types, generative and discriminative, that were developed are important to spend time on. These two serve different purposes in the field of AI, each with its own strengths and applications. The development of both types of models has been driven by their respective applications and specific needs for understanding data distributions and making precise predictions.

Generative model

To use an example of why you may use a specific model, let us take an example of assuming you have a team of chefs who have learned not just to follow recipes but to create new dishes that taste like the ones they have been taught to make. Generative models work in a similar way. They learn the patterns and details of existing data and can generate new, similar data. For instance, they can create new images, text, or even sounds that resemble the original data they have been trained on.

Generative models can help us create new products, designs, or even pieces of art by generating new ideas based on existing ones. They can create synthetic data to augment our datasets, which is especially useful when we have limited real data. By understanding what *normal* data looks like, they can spot anomalies or irregularities, which is valuable in fraud detection and quality control.

Generative models aim to model the joint probability distribution; think of a standard bell curve when plotted. By doing so, they can generate new data points that are similar to the observed data. These models learn the underlying distribution of the data and can generate new data instances. They are useful for tasks like data augmentation, anomaly detection, and simulation.

Discriminative model

One can think of discriminative models acting as skilled judges in a competition. They are trained to tell the difference between categories. For our example, let us say they can look at customer data and predict whether a customer will buy a product or not, or they can analyze images and determine if they contain a cat or a dog. They are using the ability to discriminate one thing from another in short.

These models are excellent at making precise predictions and classifications. This makes them ideal for tasks like identifying spam emails, predicting customer churn, or recognizing objects in images. They are generally quicker and simpler to train as compared to generative models, allowing us to deploy solutions faster.

Discriminative models focus on modeling the conditional probability distribution. Their primary goal is to discriminate between different classes in the data. These models aim to find the decision boundary between classes and are typically used for classification and regression tasks.

Differences between discriminative and generative models

In the case of generative models, they focus on creating new data that looks like the existing data. They can be more complex since they need to understand and replicate the entire data distribution. They are also useful in innovation, creating new content, and detecting anomalies.

In the case of discriminative models, they focus on distinguishing between different categories or making predictions based on data. They are best for making predictions, classifications, and efficiently handling large datasets.

From a more technical perspective, we can look at some of the major differences by differentiating via purpose, complexity, or the application of the model. Let us take a look at the following differences:

- **Purpose**:
  - **Generative models**: Focuses on creating new data that looks like the existing data.
  - **Discriminative models**: Focus on distinguishing between different categories or making predictions based on data.

- **Complexity**:
  - **Generative models**: More complex because they need to understand and replicate the entire data distribution.
  - **Discriminative models**: They are simpler, as they only need to find the boundary between different classes or outcomes.

- **Application**:
  - **Generative models**: Useful in innovation, creating new content, and detecting anomalies.
  - **Discriminative models**: Best for making predictions, classifications, and efficiently handling large datasets.

Both generative and discriminative models are crucial in the AI landscape, each serving distinct but complementary roles. Generative models excel in creating new data and identifying outliers, which can drive innovation and enhance our data capabilities. Discriminative models, on the other hand, are our go-to for making accurate predictions and classifications, helping us make informed decisions based on data. As an example, consider you are looking for bank fraud. The discriminative model would train on classifying the data as *Good* or *Bad* where the generative model would look more for patterns, showing fraudulent behavior versus legitimate behavior.

Do you have to choose one over the other? No, you do not, you can choose one or the other or combine then, we will touch on that. The choice between generative and discriminative models depends on the specific requirements of the task at hand. In many practical applications, combining the strengths of both types of models can lead to superior performance and more robust solutions. For example, using generative models to augment training data can enhance the performance of discriminative models, leveraging the best of both worlds.

Benefits of generative models

Generative models offer substantial benefits to AI, enhancing the scope and efficiency of AI systems across various domains. One of the primary advantages is their ability to generate new data, which can be especially valuable when working with limited datasets. For example, in image recognition, generative models can create additional images similar to the training set, thereby augmenting the dataset and improving the accuracy and robustness of the model. This capability extends to natural language processing, where generative models can produce diverse sentences or text to enrich training data, facilitating better performance in tasks such as translation and sentiment analysis. Ensuring the synthetic data is of high quality is important to get the best result.

Generative models excel in unsupervised learning, allowing AI systems to learn from unlabeled data, which is often more abundant and easier to obtain than labeled data. This ability is crucial for clustering and understanding data distributions without the need for extensive human annotation. It enables the discovery of patterns and structures within large datasets, revealing insights that might not be apparent through supervised learning techniques alone.

In the realm of creative applications, generative models are transformative. They enable the creation of novel content, such as images, music, and text, often with a high degree of originality and quality. Artists and designers leverage these models to produce unique artworks, musical compositions, and innovative designs. In the entertainment industry, particularly in video games and movies, generative models are used to create realistic environments, characters, and scenes, enhancing the immersive experience for users.

Generative models also play a crucial role in simulation and scenario testing. By simulating complex systems and generating realistic scenarios, they provide valuable tools for testing and analysis. For instance, in autonomous driving, generative models can create diverse driving scenarios to train and test vehicle behavior, ensuring safety and reliability in real-world conditions. Similarly, in finance, these models can simulate market conditions to test and optimize trading strategies, providing insights into potential market movements and investment outcomes.

Another major benefit of generative models is their ability to perform dimensionality reduction and feature learning. By learning a compact representation of data, they can reduce dimensionality while preserving important features, which is beneficial for data visualization, making high-dimensional data more interpretable. This capability also aids in efficient data storage and retrieval, as the reduced representations can be more easily managed and analyzed.

Generative models also are highly effective for anomaly detection. By learning the normal distribution of data, they can identify outliers or anomalies that deviate from the expected pattern. This is very useful in applications such as fraud detection, network security, and healthcare, where identifying unusual patterns can preemptively address potential issues.

Generative models significantly enhance the capabilities of AI systems by providing powerful tools for data generation, unsupervised learning, creative applications, simulation, dimensionality reduction, and anomaly detection. These advantages make generative models an essential component of modern AI, driving innovation and improving performance across a wide.

Benefits of a discriminative model

Discriminative models offer a robust framework for solving a wide array of supervised learning problems in AI. These models are designed to learn the boundaries that distinguish between different classes in a dataset rather than modeling the underlying data distribution. This focus on decision boundaries provides several distinct advantages that enhance the performance and applicability of AI systems.

Discriminative models are highly effective for classification tasks. They directly learn the mapping from input features to output labels, which allows them to optimize the decision boundaries between classes. This direct approach typically leads to higher accuracy in classification problems compared to generative models, which also need to model the distribution of each class. For example, in image recognition tasks, discriminative models like **convolutional neural networks (CNNs)** have shown superior performance in identifying objects and distinguishing between various categories with high precision.

Discriminative models are particularly adept at handling high-dimensional data, where the number of features can be very large compared to the number of samples. Techniques such as regularization are commonly used in discriminative models to manage overfitting and ensure robustness. Regularization methods are essential in fields like genomics and text classification where the datasets are inherently high-dimensional.

Many discriminative models are scalable to large datasets. For instance, linear classifiers and kernel methods can be extended to large-scale problems using stochastic gradient descent (we will get into that a bit later in the section *Boltzmann machines*) and other optimization techniques. This scalability is vital for applications in big data analytics, where processing vast amounts of data efficiently is a key requirement. Models that can scale effectively allow businesses and researchers to leverage large datasets to gain insights and make informed decisions.

Broadly discriminative models bring several key benefits to AI, including high accuracy in classification, simplicity and efficiency and robustness to high-dimensional data, scalability, interpretability, and flexibility with complex data. These advantages make discriminative models a critical tool in the AI toolkit, driving advancements in various fields and enabling the development of intelligent systems that can perform precise, efficient, and interpretable tasks. By leveraging these strengths, AI practitioners can build models that not only perform well but also provide valuable insights and solutions across diverse applications.

Different types of generative models

There are many models used today, and knowing them allows you to know which tool to use. You will not always be able to choose per se, but you can do research to see what model a specific AI system is using to effectively allow you to choose the method you want, at least sometimes. Let us talk about those models now!

Gaussian mixture models

These models assume that the data is generated from a mixture of several Gaussian distributions with unknown parameters. The **gaussian mixture model (GMM)** is a probabilistic model used to represent a distribution of data points in a multi-dimensional space. It is particularly useful when you believe that your data is generated from several different sources or processes. Each of these sources can be thought of as producing data that follows a Gaussian (or normal) distribution, which you might know as the classic bell curve. Instead of having data that fits a single Gaussian distribution, a mixture model assumes that your data comes from a mix of several Gaussian distributions. Each of these distributions represents a different subgroup within your data.

A use for GMM is, for example, when you have data about the heights of people, but you actually have measurements from different groups: children, teenagers, and adults. If you plot this data, it will not form a single bell curve but rather multiple overlapping bell curves. A GMM helps you model this scenario by allowing multiple Gaussian distributions to exist simultaneously and explaining the overall shape of your data.

Components are the individual Gaussian distributions within the mixture. Each component is defined by its own mean and variance. Each Gaussian component has a weight associated with it, which indicates the influence that particular component has in the overall mixture. The weights of all components add up to 1.

For the application of GMM, you can use it to group data points into clusters where each cluster corresponds to a different Gaussian component. By modeling the normal distribution of your data, GMMs can help identify outliers or anomalies that do not fit well within any of the Gaussian components. In image and speech processing, GMMs are used for tasks like segmenting images or recognizing spoken words.

A GMM is a powerful tool for understanding and modeling complex datasets that are generated by multiple sources. By combining multiple Gaussian distributions, GMMs provide a flexible approach to capturing the underlying structure in your data. Whether you are working in clustering, anomaly detection, or other fields, understanding GMMs can significantly enhance your ability to analyze and interpret data.

GMMs come with several downsides and risks, particularly concerning model complexity, selection, and computational demands. One of the main challenges is deciding the optimal number of mixture components; too many can cause overfitting, capturing noise as if it were meaningful data, while too few can result in underfitting, failing to adequately model the underlying distribution. Additionally, GMMs are sensitive to the initial parameter choices, which can influence the convergence of the solution and potentially lead to different outcomes based on these initial conditions. The scalability of GMMs can also be a concern, as they require extensive computation for probability densities, making them less suitable for large datasets. These factors necessitate careful consideration and testing to ensure that a GMM is appropriate for a given application and can perform effectively without undue computational expense.

Naive Baynes models

A Bayesian probabilistic machine learning model (where feature independence is assumed) that is used widely for classification purposes like spam detection, text classification and sentiment analysis because it is both fast and simple.

Markov chains

A Markov chain is a mathematical representation of a list of possible events, whose probabilities are derived from the state reached in the preceding event and it can be used to describe memoryless systems such as weather prediction, language understanding, or stock price prediction.

Probabilistic graphical models

A **probabilistic graphical model** (**PGM**) is a graph-based method to compute joint probabilities on large sets of variables (nodes denote random variables, edges conditional dependencies) which is useful in image processing, natural language processing and bioinformatics to simulate complex distributions over big sets of variables.

Hidden Markov models

A **hidden Markov model** (**HMM**)is a statistical model that represents systems that follow a Markov process with hidden states. In simpler terms, it is a way to model sequences of data where we believe that the system generating the data goes through a series of states, but we cannot directly observe these states. Instead, we observe some outputs (or emissions) that are generated from these hidden states. HMMs are widely used in temporal data and sequence modeling, such as speech and handwriting recognition.

HMMs rely on several specific concepts. Some of these are states, that is, the various conditions or modes the system can be in. In an HMM, these states are not directly visible (hidden), but they influence the visible outputs. Observations are the actual data points we can observe. Each observation is generated by a corresponding hidden state. Transition probabilities are the probabilities of moving from one state to another. They define the dynamics of how the system changes states over time. Emission probabilities are observing a particular output from a given state. They describe how each state produces observable data.

Applying these concepts, a way to think about an HMM is to imagine that you are trying to guess the weather (hidden states) based on whether people are carrying umbrellas (observations). You cannot see the weather directly (it is hidden), but you can see the umbrellas (the visible part). You could line those concepts up with the following example (this is a classic example for HMMs):

- **States**: Let us say the hidden states are **sunny** and **rainy**.

- **Observations**: The observations are whether people are **carrying an umbrella** or **not carrying an umbrella**.

- **Transition probabilities**: For example, if it is **sunny** today, there is a 90% chance it will be **sunny** tomorrow and a 10% chance it will be **rainy**. Similarly, if it is rainy today, there is a 50% chance it will be rainy tomorrow and a 50% chance it will be sunny.

- **Emission probabilities**: When it is sunny, there is a 20% chance people will carry umbrellas (maybe for shade), and an 80% chance they will not. When it is rainy, there is a 90% chance people will carry umbrellas and a 10% chance they will not.

- **Initial probabilities**: These could be something like a 50% chance, starting with sunny and a 50% chance of starting in rainy.

As HMMs are particularly powerful when you have sequences of data, you suspect there is an underlying process influencing this data that you cannot directly observe. They are widely used in fields, such as speech recognition, bioinformatics, and finance:

- There are mathematical models used here, using a forward algorithm helps in calculating the probability of a particular sequence of observations given the model. For example, it can answer questions like, *given our HMM, what is the probability of seeing a sequence of observations (like a week of umbrella observations)?*

- The Viterbi algorithm finds the most likely sequence of hidden states that could have generated the observed sequence. For example, it can tell us the most likely sequence of weather conditions.

- The Baum-Welch HMM algorithm is used to train the HMM. It helps in estimating the transition and emission probabilities given a set of observations.

You can see that the HMM is a powerful statistical tool for modeling sequences of data where the underlying processes are hidden. By understanding and applying HMMs, we can make better predictions and uncover the hidden structures within complex datasets. Whether it is predicting weather, recognizing speech, or analyzing financial markets, HMMs are an invaluable tool in the data scientist's toolkit.

HMMs present several challenges and limitations that can impact their effectiveness in certain applications. One major challenge is determining the optimal number of hidden states, as too many states can cause overfitting, especially with limited data, while too few states may not capture the complexity of the data accurately. HMMs operate under the assumption of the Markovian property, where the future state depends only on the current state. This assumption might oversimplify many real-world processes where past states influence future outcomes. Additionally, the algorithms used for training HMMs, like the Baum-Welch algorithm, are computationally demanding, which can be a barrier when working with large datasets or models with many states. Data sparsity also poses a problem for HMMs; when data is limited, or the number of observable states is large compared to the data, accurately estimating transition and emission probabilities becomes challenging. Furthermore, HMMs are sensitive to how their parameters are initialized, which can significantly influence their performance and the convergence of the training process.

Boltzmann machines

Energy-based models that learn the probability distribution over the input data are a powerful concept in the realm of generative models and neural networks. Let us break down what Boltzmann machines are, how they work, and their applications in a way that is accessible to everyone, even if you are only semi-technical.

A Boltzmann machine is a type of stochastic recurrent neural network. It is designed to learn patterns in data by modeling the complex dependencies between variables. Think of it as a network of interconnected neurons (or nodes) where each connection has a weight, and the network learns by adjusting these weights to represent the underlying structure of the data.

The key concepts for Boltzmann machines center around four major concepts. These speak to how we describe and interact with Boltzmann machines. The key concepts are as follows:

- **Neurons (Nodes)**: These are the basic units of the network, you will recall we spoke to them when discussing neural networks, this is a specific way they are applied. In a Boltzmann machine, neurons are usually binary, meaning they can be in one of two states: on or off (represented as 1 or 0).

- **Weights**: These are the connections between neurons. Each weight represents the strength and direction of the interaction between two neurons.

- **Energy function**: This is a measure of the overall state of the network. The network learns by minimizing this energy, which corresponds to finding the most probable configurations of neurons that explain the data.

- **Stochasticity**: This refers to the probabilistic nature of neuron states. Instead of being deterministically on or off, neurons in a Boltzmann machine switch states based on certain probabilities.

An example of when to use a Boltzmann machine is to imagine you have a dataset of users and their movie preferences. The visible layer represents whether a user has watched (or liked) a particular movie. The hidden layer captures patterns like *user likes action movies* or *user prefers romantic comedies*. Let us look at the steps which occur in a Boltzmann:

- **Initialization**: Start with random weights and states.

- **Energy calculation**: Compute the energy based on the current states of movie preferences and hidden patterns.

- **State updating**: Update the states of hidden neurons based on the probabilities influenced by the visible neurons (movie preferences).

- **Learning**: Adjust the weights to better capture the patterns in movie preferences.

Over time, the Boltzmann machines learn to represent user preferences and can predict which movies a user is likely to enjoy, even if they have not rated those movies yet.

So, you now know that Boltzmann machines, particularly restricted Boltzmann machines, are powerful tools for modeling complex data distributions. By learning the underlying structure of data, they can perform tasks like dimensionality reduction, feature learning, and recommendation. While the concept involves advanced mathematics and probabilistic models, the core idea is about finding patterns and dependencies in data.

Boltzmann machines have several downsides and risks associated with their use. One significant issue is their computational complexity; training Boltzmann machines involves calculating the partition function, which is computationally expensive and often intractable for large networks. This makes them less scalable to very large datasets or complex models compared to other deep learning techniques. Another challenge is the difficulty in training, as Boltzmann machines require careful tuning of learning parameters and may converge slowly or get stuck in local minima. Additionally, they can be sensitive to initial conditions and the specific configuration of their architecture. Despite their theoretical appeal, these practical challenges limit their widespread adoption in problems where simpler, more efficient alternatives can achieve comparable or better performance.

Variational autoencoders

VAEs are a type of generative model that combines principles from neural networks and probability theory to create a powerful tool for generating and understanding complex data. They use neural networks to learn a latent space representation of the data, allowing for the generation of new data points by sampling from this latent space. They are specifically designed to generate new data points similar to the ones in your training set. VAEs are particularly useful because they allow us to learn a compact representation of our data (called the latent space) and then generate new data points by sampling from this latent space.

The key concepts for VAEs focus on the encoder, which is the part of the network that compresses the input data into a smaller, latent representation. Think of it as summarizing the essential information from the input. Another concept is using latent space which is a lower-dimensional space where the encoder maps the input data. Each point in this space represents a compressed version of the original data. The decoder is part of the network that reconstructs the original data from the latent representation. It is like taking the summary and trying to recreate the full original data from it. Lastly, the variational aspect encodes it as a distribution over the latent space instead of encoding a data point into a single point in the latent space. This helps in generating more varied and realistic new data points.

The VAE works by following four major steps. They are as follows:

- **Encoding**: The encoder takes an input data point (For example, an image) and maps it to a distribution in the latent space, typically a Gaussian distribution with a mean and a variance. This step is probabilistic, meaning each input is represented not just as a single point but as a region in the latent space.

- **Sampling**: From this latent distribution, we sample a point. This sampled point is then used to generate new data. This sampling introduces variability, which is crucial for generating diverse outputs.

- **Decoding**: The sampled point from the latent space is passed through the decoder, which tries to reconstruct the original data point from it. The goal is to make the reconstructed data as close as possible to the original input.

- **Loss function**: VAEs use a special loss function that has the following two parts:

  - **Reconstruction loss**: This measures how well the decoder can reconstruct the input data from the latent representation.

  - **Kullback-Leibler divergence**: This term measures how close the encoded latent distribution is to a standard Gaussian distribution. This regularizes the latent space and ensures smooth sampling. It is a measure of how dissimilar discrete probability distributions are.

The use and application of VAEs focus on scenarios, such as being able to generate realistic images by learning the distribution of the training images, they can fill in missing parts of data by sampling from the latent space. Another area of use is bioinformatics. VAEs can generate new molecular structures with desired properties by learning from existing molecules. They can identify anomalies via the process of learning the distribution of normal data, VAEs can then effectively detect anomalies that deviate from this distribution.

So, we have covered off on how VAEs are a powerful type of generative model that combines neural networks with probabilistic methods to create new data points similar to the training data. They are versatile tools used for data generation, dimensionality reduction, and anomaly detection, among other applications. By learning a smooth and compact representation of data, VAEs open up new possibilities in various fields, from computer vision to bioinformatics.

VAEs have several limitations and risks. One of the primary challenges with VAEs is the balance between the latent space's complexity and the model's ability to generalize. If the latent space is too constrained, the model may not capture the full complexity of the data, leading to underfitting. Conversely, too complex a latent space can cause overfitting, where the model learns noise instead of the underlying data distribution.

Another significant issue is the assumption of a specific prior distribution (often Gaussian) for the latent variables. This assumption can be limiting if the true underlying distribution of the data is significantly different, potentially leading to suboptimal performance. Moreover, VAEs can suffer from **posterior collapse** where the model ignores the latent variables altogether if the decoder is too powerful, effectively reducing the model to a standard autoencoder.

Training VAEs also presents computational challenges, particularly in balancing the reconstruction loss with the KL divergence term in the loss function, which requires careful tuning of hyperparameters. Additionally, VAEs might produce blurred or less sharp outputs compared to other generative models like GANs, which can be a drawback in applications where high-quality, detailed generation is crucial.

Generative adversarial networks

GANs consist of two neural networks (a generator and a discriminator) that compete against each other, with the generator creating synthetic data and the discriminator evaluating its authenticity.

What does the **Adversarial** mean in a GAN? Adversarial training is a pivotal concept in the field of AI, particularly within the framework of GANs. Introduced in the last decade, adversarial training involves two neural networks working together, giving it the ability to produce high-quality, realistic data that was previously unattainable with other methods. This technique has revolutionized various fields, including image and video synthesis, data augmentation for training robust models, and creating art and music. The continuous feedback loop between the generator and discriminator drives innovation and enhances the performance of AI systems, making adversarial training a cornerstone in the advancement of generative models and their applications. As technology systems grow more and more, their hunger for data also increases, driving the need for high quality, reliable data that is generated. Why would someone want to use generated data? Think of an example of a financial institution with millions and millions of real transactions a day, with potentially hundreds of millions of customer/client records. You really do not want to test with real data in this situation, so high-quality data is important.

GANs have revolutionized the way we generate data and are used in a variety of applications. GANs consist of two neural networks, the **generator**, and the **discriminator**, that are trained simultaneously through a process of competition. The idea is to have these two networks play a game where the generator tries to create data that is indistinguishable from real data while the discriminator tries to tell the difference between real and generated data.

A key concept to keep in mind for a GAN, is that it focuses on generating new data points. It takes random noise as input and transforms it into data that resembles the training data. Think of it as a creative artist trying to paint a picture that looks like a real photograph; this is the generator. The network evaluates the data. It takes input data (real or generated) and tries to classify it as real or fake. Imagine it as an art critic who determines whether a painting is an authentic masterpiece or a forgery; this is the discriminator. The third concept is that the two networks are trained together in a zero-sum game. The generator tries to fool the discriminator by creating more realistic data while the discriminator gets better at detecting fake data. This competition continues until the generator produces data that is so realistic that the discriminator can no longer distinguish it from real data.

The general process of running a GAN is to start with random weights for both the generator and the discriminator, which is the initiation phase. This is followed by the generator which creates a batch of fake data from random noise, known as generator training. Then the discriminator itself is trained on a batch of real data and a batch of fake data from the generator. It learns to output a probability indicating whether each input is real or fake. A feedback loop is then created as the generator receives feedback from the discriminator's performance. If the discriminator correctly identifies the fake data, the generator adjusts its weights to create more realistic data in the next iteration. To make the quality better over time, iterative improvement occurs as the training steps are repeated, alternating between training the discriminator and the generator. Over time, both networks improve: the generator produces more realistic data, and the discriminator becomes a more accurate judge. Let us look at this in action with examples of a GAN in practice:

- **The generator**: The generator starts with random noise and generates images of faces. Initially, these images are just random patterns.

- **The discriminator**: The discriminator is trained on a set of real human face images and the generated images. Its job is to classify each image as real or fake.

- **The training**: The discriminator provides feedback to the generator. If the generated faces are easily detected as fake, the generator adjusts its parameters to create more realistic faces in the next round.

- **The competition**: This process continues, with the generator getting better at producing realistic faces and the discriminator getting better at detecting fakes. Eventually, the generator creates faces that are so realistic that even humans cannot easily tell they are generated.

GANs are a groundbreaking approach to generating realistic data. By pitting two neural networks against each other in a competitive game, GANs can produce high-quality, diverse data that can be used in a multitude of applications. Whether it is creating stunning images, enhancing photo quality, or aiding in creative endeavors, GANs have opened up new possibilities in the field of AI.

GANs come with their own set of challenges and risks. One of the main difficulties with GANs is the stability of training; the adversarial setup, involving a generator and a discriminator competing against each other, can lead to training instability and convergence issues. This is often manifested as **mode collapse**, where the generator starts producing a limited variety of outputs, or **vanishing gradients**, which can occur when the discriminator becomes too effective, making it difficult for the generator to improve.

Another risk with GANs is their sensitivity to hyperparameter settings, including learning rates and the architecture of both the generator and discriminator. Finding the right balance requires extensive experimentation and tuning, which can be quite resource intensive. So, if you are an IT system owner using AI, just be aware that your costs could drive up depending on the model you use. GANs require a significant amount of data to train effectively, and they can be prone to overfitting if the dataset is not large or diverse enough.

GANs can be computationally expensive to train, requiring substantial **graphic processing unit (GPU)** resources, which might not be feasible for all projects or researchers. Despite these challenges, the potential of GANs to generate high-fidelity, diverse outputs makes them a popular choice in fields, such as image generation, style transfer, and more, where visual quality is pertinent.

Conclusion

In this chapter, we discussed generative models, a fundamental pillar in the realm of AI, which has undergone a remarkable evolution, significantly influencing various domains. This chapter delves into the historical development, core concepts, and contemporary applications of generative models, shedding light on their transformative impact. We spoke about how mathematics and statistics drove various models tracing back to the mid-20th century, with early statistical methods laying the groundwork. Initially, these models were simplistic, often constrained by limited computational power and rudimentary algorithms. We learned that the advent of more sophisticated mathematical frameworks and advancements in computing technology catalyzed their development.

Generative models, from their humble beginnings to their current prominence, have profoundly reshaped numerous industries. Their ability to learn and replicate the intricacies of data offers boundless opportunities yet also demands careful consideration of ethical and practical implications. As technology advances, the role of generative models will undoubtedly expand, continuing to influence and inspire innovation across the globe.

We now have a foundation to begin to move into the rise of GPT. In the next chapter, we will talk to transformers and start our long discussion about the many GPT options out there, where they came from, and begin to delve into how you can leverage them for work, school, or test.

Join our book's Discord space

Join the book's Discord Workspace for Latest updates, Offers, Tech happenings around the world, New Release and Sessions with the Authors:

https://discord.bpbonline.com

CHAPTER 4
Rise of GPT and Transformer-Based Models

Introduction

The chapter reviews the evolution and significance of Transformer-based models in the field of AI, particularly in prompt engineering. It begins with a background on the development of machine learning models, leading up to the groundbreaking advent of Transformer-based architectures. This section includes an exploration of the self-attention mechanism, which is pivotal to understanding the efficiency and effectiveness of these models.

The chapter provides a concise overview of major models like BERT and GPT, detailing the key breakthroughs and milestones that have marked their development. It explains the core concepts of the Transformer architecture, such as scaled dot-product attention and multi-head attention, position-wise feed-forward networks, and positional encoding. The discussion goes into the advantages of the self-attention mechanism, demonstrating how it allows for better handling of dependencies in data compared to previous approaches.

This chapter not only offers a detailed account of the technological advancements in AI but also highlights the importance and relevance of these models in enhancing the capabilities and applications of prompt engineering, making it a crucial read for those interested in the latest AI technologies.

Structure

This chapter will cover the following topics:

- Overview of Transformer-based models
- History of Transformer-based models

Objectives

When you complete this chapter, you will have a strong understanding of how Transformer models are leveraged in **artificial intelligence** (**AI**). You will understand how neural networks are used for data to be input into AI systems. You will also develop and understand how vectors are used for statistical purposes by converting input into a numeric representation of the text.

Overview of Transformer-based models

Machine learning has experienced a remarkable evolution over the past few decades, transitioning from basic statistical methods to advanced neural network architectures. We will provide an overview of the milestones in this evolution, focusing on how these developments set the stage for the emergence of Transformer-based models. Understanding this progression is crucial for appreciating the transformative impact of Transformers in modern AI.

Before Transformers, sequence models like **recurrent neural networks** (**RNNs**) and **long short-term memory** (**LSTM**) were the backbone of **natural language processing (NLP)** tasks. These models, while effective, had limitations in handling long-range dependencies due to issues like vanishing gradients and sequential processing constraints.

Transformer-based models have fundamentally altered the landscape of AI, especially in NLP. We will focus on a historical overview of the development and evolution of Transformer models from their inception to recent advancements. It discusses key innovations, such as self-attention mechanisms and bidirectional processing, highlights significant models that we will dive into, including BERT and GPT (usually written as *GPT-X* where *x* is the version number=), and explores the broader implications and future directions of Transformer-based technologies- we will spend more time on BERT and GPT shortly.

Importance and relevance of Transformer-based models

Transformer-based models have become central to the practice of prompt engineering, a technique that involves crafting specific input prompts to guide AI models towards generating desired outputs. Prompt engineering leverages the nuanced understanding and contextual awareness of large Transformer models, such as GPT-3 and beyond, to perform a wide array of tasks by simply altering the input text provided to the model. This has opened new avenues for utilizing AI without extensive retraining or fine-tuning, making AI more accessible and versatile.

The sophistication of Transformer models allows them to understand and generate human-like text based on the context provided by the prompts. This capability is rooted in the self-attention mechanism, which enables the models to weigh the importance of each word in the input sequence relative to others, thereby capturing intricate patterns and relationships. As a result, well-crafted prompts can elicit highly specific and contextually appropriate responses from these models. For instance, a prompt that begins with `tell me a happy children's story about...` can lead the model to generate an engaging narrative that aligns with the initial setup.

Prompt engineering has proven particularly valuable in scenarios where quick adaptability is essential. By adjusting the prompts, users can tailor the output for different applications without the need to modify the underlying model. This flexibility is crucial in industry-like customer service, content creation, and educational technology, where the ability to generate relevant and context-sensitive content dynamically can significantly enhance user experience. The use of prompts also mitigates some of the challenges associated with deploying AI, such as the need for extensive labeled data and the time-consuming process of retraining models.

Keeping all this in mind, the iterative nature of prompt engineering allows for continuous refinement and improvement. Users can experiment with different phrasings, formats, and structures to discover which prompts yield the best results for their specific needs. This process of trial and error is facilitated by the model's ability to handle diverse inputs and generate coherent outputs across a broad range of topics. Communities and platforms dedicated to sharing and discussing prompt strategies have emerged, fostering collaborative advancements in the field and democratizing access to effective AI utilization techniques.

Transformer-based models have fundamentally transformed the landscape of prompt engineering, making it a powerful tool for leveraging AI in diverse applications. The ability to guide model behavior through carefully designed prompts has expanded the practical utility of these models, allowing for rapid adaptation and deployment in various contexts. As research and experimentation in prompt engineering continue to evolve, it is likely that even more innovative uses and best practices will emerge, further enhancing the capabilities and accessibility of AI technologies.

History of Transformer-based models

As we discussed, the field of AI has witnessed rapid advancements over the past decade, with a significant portion of these improvements attributable to Transformer-based models.

Prior to their introduction, sequence models like RNNs and LSTM networks dominated NLP tasks but faced inherent limitations. We will provide a detailed historical overview of Transformer models, their impact on AI, and future research directions.

The evolution of machine learning models, from early statistical methods to deep learning architectures, set the stage for the development of Transformer-based models. Each phase of this progression addresses the limitations of the previous generation, leading to increasingly powerful and versatile models. The advent of Transformers, with their ability to handle long-range dependencies and parallel processing, represents a culmination of these advancements. As research continues to build on these foundations, Transformer-based models are likely to play an even more central role in the future of AI.

Before moving deeper into Transformers, we need to understand the landscape they disrupted. Early sequence models, such as RNNs and LSTMs, were pivotal in processing sequential data. These models could, in theory, handle long-range dependencies through mechanisms designed to combat issues like vanishing gradients. However, their sequential nature resulted in inefficiencies and difficulties in capturing long-term dependencies effectively. In 2017, a group of researchers led by *Ashish Vaswani* et al. introduced the Transformer model through their seminal paper, *Attention is All You Need*. This section will explore the following key components and innovations of the Transformer model:

- **Self-attention mechanism**: The self-attention mechanism allows the model to weigh the importance of different words in a sentence relative to each other. This mechanism enables the model to capture contextual relationships more effectively than RNNs and LSTMs. We will talk more about this later in detail.

- **Positional encoding:** Transformers process data in parallel, unlike their sequential predecessors. Positional encoding was introduced to provide the model with information about the position of words in a sentence, compensating for the lack of inherent sequential processing.

- **Layered architecture**: Transformers employ a layered architecture, stacking multiple layers of self-attention and FFNNs. This design allows for deep hierarchical representations of the input data, enhancing the model's capacity to understand complex relationships.

We will learn more about the technology behind these transformer models in with the next section so we can hon our understanding of the technical underpinnings of AI and prompts.

Technical background for Transformer-based models

The Transformer architecture consists of an encoder-decoder structure, although many applications, especially in NLP, use only the encoder (for example, BERT) or the decoder (for example, GPT). The encoder's role is to convert an input sequence into a sequence of continuous representations, while the decoder transforms these representations back into an output sequence. Each encoder and decoder comprises of multiple identical layers, typically including a self-attention mechanism and a **feed-forward neural network** (**FFNN**). We are going to quickly revisit the self-attention mechanism on a bit of a technical level versus historical as well as many other mechanisms.

Feed-forward neural networks

Each layer in the Transformer architecture includes a FFNN applied independently to each position. The FFNN typically consists of two linear transformations with a rectified linear activation function in between. This component helps the model to capture complex patterns and non-linear relationships within the data, complementing the self-attention mechanism. The outputs of the self-attention sub-layer and the feed-forward sub-layer are combined through residual connections and layer normalization, enhancing training stability and efficiency.

Self-attention mechanism

At the heart of the Transformer is the self-attention mechanism, which allows the model to weigh the relevance of different words in a sequence relative to each other. This mechanism computes a set of attention scores that represent the amount of focus each word should receive when producing an output. The calculation involves three matrices: **Query (Q)**, **Key (K)**, and **Value (V)**. The attention scores are derived by taking the dot product of the Query and Key matrices, applying a scaling factor, and then using a function to normalize these scores. The resulting scores are then used to weight the Value matrix, effectively enabling the model to attend to relevant parts of the input sequence. We will get more into what you can do these numbers when we discuss vectors.

The introduction of attention mechanisms addressed several limitations of RNNs. Attention mechanisms allowed models to dynamically focus on different parts of the input sequence, regardless of their position. This innovation was first applied in sequence-to-sequence models for tasks like machine translation, where it significantly improved performance by enabling the model to attend to relevant parts of the source sequence when generating each part of the target sequence.

Let us use a real example to explain what is going on in the following short example of the generated text:

Once upon a time, a happy giant lived in the forest. His best friends were the animals there. His friends were Laughing Deer and Smiling Rabbit.

Here, the first sentence, **Once upon a time, a happy giant lived in the forest** sets the foundation that the following text will have relevance to. In this case, we will talk about **Happy** being the word that is **attended** to. So, the model generates words that align to the meaning. In this case, **Laughing** and **Smiling**.

Then, the second sentence, **His best friends were the animals there** is generated with **Animals** the word that is attended to, leading to **Deer** and **Rabbit** in the third sentence. The attention mechanism, therefore, does not forget but tracks (remembers) previously generated data.

Let us look at this in *Figure 4.1*. You can see words in the first two sentences are remembered to generate relevant text in the third sentence. RNNs do not have the ability to remember details as the story gets longer since they are unable to recall (attend) text generated from before. Assuming one has sufficient computing power with equal storage and money to pay for it, this method could theoretically never forget anything. This is why the attention-based encoder/decoder architecture was identified:

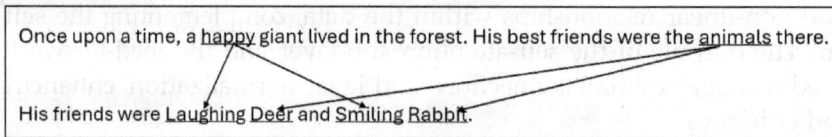

Once upon a time, a happy giant lived in the forest. His best friends were the animals there.

His friends were Laughing Deer and Smiling Rabbit.

Figure 4.1: An attenuator at work

Input tokenization

Input tokenization in AI involves converting text into smaller units called tokens, which can be words, sub-words, or even individual characters. The process starts by breaking down the input text into these tokens using predefined rules or algorithms. Each token is then mapped to a unique numerical value using a vocabulary or dictionary that the model understands. This transformation allows the AI to process and analyze the text in a structured and quantifiable manner. Tokenization is essential for models to handle the input efficiently, as it translates human language into a form that computational systems can work with effectively. This data is stored for speedy retrieval in the future. *Figure 4.2* shows the text being inputted, in our case, it is **Tell me a happy children's story**. That data is then converted, via the tokenization process, into a mathematical representation, as shown in the following figure:

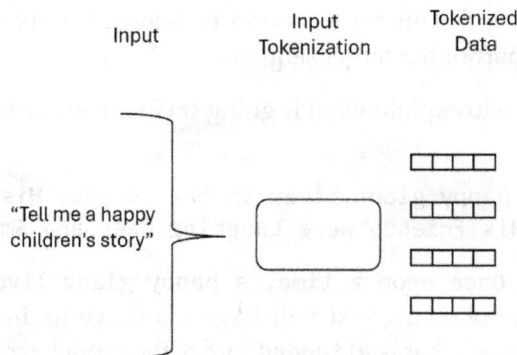

Input   Input Tokenization   Tokenized Data

"Tell me a happy children's story"

Figure 4.2: Input tokenization

Vectors in tokenization

When talking about vectors, the quick description is **converting words to a numerical representation of them**. Although, it is a bit more complicated than that. A vector is a mathematical representation of a token (such as a word or sub-word) in a continuous, high-dimensional space. Essentially it is an array of numbers (or components) that represents the position of the token in a high-dimensional space. Each number in the vector corresponds to a specific dimension in this space, made up of multiple dimensions.

The number of dimensions (components) of the vector is typically fixed and is a hyperparameter chosen during the design of the model. Common dimensionalities include 50, 100, 300, or even 768 or more, depending on the complexity and requirements of the model. Vectors usually have non-zero values in most of their components. This density allows the vector to capture more nuanced information about the token. Vectors are then used in the embedding space to capture semantic relationships between tokens. So, the vectors for words with similar meanings or that appear in similar contexts will be close to each other in the high-dimensional space. This property is achieved by training on large datasets where the model learns these relationships from training.

Then, the vectors serve as the input to the AI model. By converting tokens to vectors, the model can process the text more effectively, using the numerical relationships to perform tasks like translation, sentiment analysis, and more.

Let us consider a simplified real-world example of what the vector for the word **Tell** might look like in a sentence like **Tell me a happy children's story**.

For illustration, we will use a five-dimensional vector space. In practice, vectors typically have higher dimensions (that is, 300, 768), but a 5-dimensional vector will help illustrate the concept clearly.

Let us use our example sentence again. Let us also assume that we have trained an embedding model, a Transformer model like BERT, on a large corpus of text. This model assigns a unique vector to each word based on its context and semantic meaning.

Here is a hypothetical five-dimensional vector for the word **Tell**, the first word in our sentence is as follows:

```
[0.35, -0.12, 0.88, 0.45, -0.67]
```

How do we get this? Each number in this vector represents a different dimension of the embedding space, capturing various aspects of the word's meaning based on its usage in the corpus.

To give more context, look at the following:

- **0.35** might capture some aspect of verbal communication.

- **-0.12** might capture some aspect of the imperative mood or command form.

- **0.88** might relate to the position of **Tell** within typical sentences (for example, often at the beginning of commands).

- **0.45** could relate to the positivity or neutrality of the word (for example, `Tell` is neutral).

- **-0.67** might capture some contextual relationship to pronouns like **me** that often follow it.

In reality, you would use more complicated data. We would use a real pre-trained model with 50 dimensions, and the vector would be a list of 50 floating-point numbers representing the word's position in the embedding space based on semantic and contextual similarity.

These embeddings help the model understand that `Tell` in the sentence `Tell me a happy children's story` has a similar context to other communicative actions and commands in different sentences, allowing the AI to process and understand the text more effectively.

Encoder and decoder layers

The encoder layer in a Transformer consists of two main components: multi-head self-attention and a position-wise FFNN. Each of these components is followed by residual connections and layer normalization. The decoder layer includes an additional multi-head attention mechanism that performs attention over the encoder's output, enabling the model to consider the entire input sequence when generating each part of the output. This structure allows the decoder to iteratively refine its output based on both the encoded input and the previously generated tokens.

Connected network

A **fully connected network** (or fully connected layer) in the context of encoding, particularly in neural networks, refers to a layer where every neuron (node) is connected to every neuron in the next layer. Here is a breakdown of what this means and its significance.

If you recall our example from chapter two, *Figure 2.1*, when we were discussing the layout of a neural network, every one of the neurons in one layer is connected to the networks in adjacent layers. That is what is referred to as *Connected Network*, it means that the neural network is functioning and configured as it should be.

Positional encoding

Unlike RNNs, Transformers do not inherently process sequences in a specific order due to their parallel architecture. To retain positional information, Transformers introduce positional encodings. These encodings are added to the input embeddings and contain information about the position of each token in the sequence. Typically, sine and cosine functions of different frequencies are used to generate these encodings, ensuring that each position has a unique representation. This addition allows the model to consider both the content and the order of the tokens in the sequence.

Multi-head attention

To capture different types of relationships and dependencies, Transformers employ multi-head attention. Instead of performing a single self-attention operation, the model executes multiple self-attention operations in parallel, each with different learned projections of Q, K, and V matrices. The outputs from these operations are concatenated and linearly transformed to produce the final result. This approach allows the model to simultaneously focus on different positions and aspects of the input sequence, enriching its understanding and representation of the data.

Training and optimization

Training Transformer models involves minimizing a loss function that measures the difference between the predicted outputs and the actual target sequences. Typically, cross-entropy loss is used for this purpose. Transformers are trained using variants of stochastic gradient descent, such as Adam, which are well-suited for handling large-scale datasets and complex optimization landscapes associated with these models. Due to the high computational demands of training Transformers, techniques like mixed-precision training and distributed computing are often employed to improve efficiency and scalability.

Scalability and efficiency

One of the key advantages of the Transformer architecture is its scalability. The parallel processing capabilities of self-attention allow Transformers to leverage modern hardware, such as **graphic process units (GPU)** and **tensor processing units (TPUs)**, more effectively than sequential models like RNNs. However, the quadratic complexity of self-attention with respect to the sequence length poses challenges for very long sequences. Recent research has introduced various modifications, such as sparse attention mechanisms and memory-efficient Transformers, to address these scalability issues and extend the applicability of Transformer models to longer sequences and larger datasets.

You can see the technical foundation of Transformer-based models, characterized by self-attention, multi-head attention, positional encoding, and a robust layered architecture, has enabled significant advancements in AI. These models excel in capturing complex dependencies and contextual relationships, making them highly effective for a wide range of tasks beyond NLP, including computer vision, reinforcement learning, and scientific research. The ongoing improvements in efficiency and scalability continue to expand their impact, solidifying their role as a cornerstone of modern AI technology.

The first step is that text is first broken down through an input tokenizer, which converts the text to numeric values that can have multiple statistical models run on it. The data is then encoded so that the whole of it can be used.

In *Figure 4.3*, we see a basic encoder and decoder architecture and the Transformer encoder and decoder work together to handle tasks, such as language translation, text summarization, and more.

A summary of the Transformer encoder is as follows:

- **Input embedding**: The input text is tokenized, and each token is converted into a dense vector (embedding).

- **Positional encoding**: Since Transformers do not inherently understand the order of tokens, positional encodings are added to the embeddings to inject information about the position of each token in the sequence.

- **Multi-head self-attention**: The encoder processes the embeddings through multiple self-attention heads, which allow the model to weigh the importance of different tokens relative to each other. This helps the model capture relationships between words in a context-aware manner.

- **FFNN**: The output from the self-attention layers is passed through a series of FFNNs, which apply transformations to the data.

- **Stacking layers**: Multiple layers of self-attention and feed-forward networks are stacked to build a deep model that can capture complex patterns in the input data.

A summary of the Transformer decoder is as follows:

- **Masked multi-head self-attention**: The decoder starts with masked self-attention layers that prevent the model from looking ahead at future tokens during training, ensuring that the prediction of each token only depends on the tokens that come before it.

- **Encoder-decoder attention**: The decoder includes attention layers that focus on the encoder's output, allowing it to align its generation with the relevant parts of the input sequence.

- **FFNN**: Similar to the encoder, the decoder uses FFNNs to transform the data.

- **Output generation**: Finally, the decoder produces an output sequence, token by token, based on the processed data.

In the following figure, we will look at the self-attention model, which is the model to consider the entire input sequence at once, understanding relationships between tokens regardless of their position by assigning weights to tokens in the input. We also see positional encoding helping maintain the order of tokens. With the encoder-decoder attention occurring, it allows the decoder to focus on relevant parts of the input sequence while generating the output, as seen in the following figure:

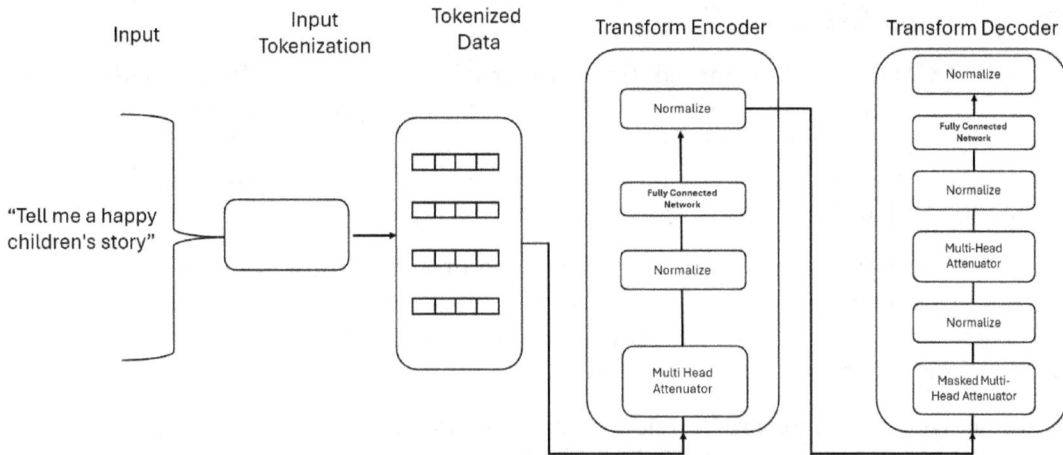

Figure 4.3: *Basic encoder and decoder architecture*

Evolution of machine learning models

The late 2000s and early 2010s saw a resurgence of interest in neural networks, driven by advancements in computational power and the availability of large datasets. Deep learning, characterized by deep neural networks with many layers, emerged as a powerful paradigm for machine learning. **Convolutional neural networks** (**CNN**) and RNNs became popular architectures for tasks involving image and sequential data, respectively.

CNNs revolutionized computer vision by introducing convolutional layers that could capture spatial hierarchies in images. RNNs, on the other hand, were designed to handle sequential data by maintaining hidden states that captured temporal dependencies. **LSTM** networks and **gated recurrent units** (**GRUs**) were developed to address the limitations of vanilla RNNs, such as vanishing and exploding gradients, enabling more effective modeling of long-term dependencies.

Key breakthroughs and milestones

As stated, the work by *Vaswani et al*, introduced the notion of a Transformer model with its self-attention mechanisms to process input sequences in parallel rather than sequentially addressing gaps in RNNs and LSTMs.

We spoke about Google's **Bidirectional Encoder Representations from Transformers** (**BERT**) earlier. It was introduced in 2018 as a bidirectional approach to understanding text, allowing the model to consider context from both directions. BERT's pre-training tasks, **masked language modeling** (**MLM**) and **next sentence prediction** (**NSP**), significantly improved performance on various NLP benchmarks and tasks.

BERT and GPT

BERT and **Generative Pre-trained Transformer (GPT)** are two landmark models in the evolution of Transformer-based architectures. This section provides a exploration of their development, unique features, and contributions to the field of NLP. It examines the innovations introduced by these models, their training methodologies, and their impact on various NLP tasks.

BERT is a Transformer-based model designed to understand the context of a word in a sentence by looking at both its left and right context simultaneously. This bidirectional approach marked a significant departure from previous models, which typically processed text in a unidirectional manner (left-to-right or right-to-left).

BERT utilizes the Transformer encoder architecture. It consists of multiple layers of bidirectional self-attention and FFNNs. The key innovation in BERT is its ability to pre-train a deep bidirectional representation by jointly conditioning both left and right context in all layers.

BERT leverages pre-training, focusing on the following two areas:

- **MLM:** In this task, 15% of the words in the input sequence are randomly masked, and the model is trained to predict these masked words based on the surrounding context. This enables BERT to learn bidirectional representations.

- **NSP:** This task involves predicting whether a given sentence B follows sentence A in the original text. This helps the model understand the relationship between sentences, which is crucial for tasks like question answering and natural language inference.

After pre-training, BERT is fine-tuned on specific downstream tasks by adding a simple classification layer on top. This allows BERT to achieve state-of-the-art results on various of NLP tasks with minimal task-specific modifications. BERT's introduction significantly advanced the state of NLP, setting new benchmarks on numerous tasks, such as question answering, sentiment analysis, and named entity recognition. Its bidirectional approach enabled a deeper understanding of context, improving performance across a variety of applications.

GPT, which was developed by OpenAI, represents a series of Transformer-based models designed for text generation and understanding. The first model, GPT-1, was introduced in 2018, followed by GPT-2 in 2019, GPT-3 in 2020, and GPT- 4.0 being released in March of 2023. Unlike BERT, which focuses on understanding text, GPT is designed to generate coherent and contextually relevant text. You will see that these are updated often, so do not get too used to any one version, it will soon be yesterday's news. GPT models utilize the Transformer decoder architecture. They process text in a unidirectional manner (left-to-right), which is suited for generation tasks where the prediction of the next word in a sequence is essential.

GPT models follow a two-stage training process, which is as follows:

- **Unsupervised pre-training**: The model is trained on a large corpus of text to predict the next word in a sequence. This involves learning to generate text that is coherent and contextually appropriate based on the preceding words.

- **Supervised fine-tuning**: After pre-training, GPT models can be fine-tuned on specific tasks with labeled data, though they often perform well without extensive fine-tuning due to the vast amount of knowledge acquired during pre-training.

Regarding the GPT-2 model, it significantly increased the number of variables used, called parameters (1.5 billion), and demonstrated the ability to generate high-quality text across various domains. It raised important discussions about the ethical implications of powerful text generation models.

As for GPT-3, it uses up to 175 billion parameters. It further pushed the boundaries of what language models can achieve. It demonstrated remarkable capabilities in zero-shot, one-shot, and few-shot learning, where the model performs tasks with little to no task-specific training data.

More recently, we saw the release of the GPT-4 model. It is beginning to achieve a human-level performance in testing, in *Chapter 1, A Brief Overview of ML and AI*, we spoke about how there is a *Turbo* variant which has a faster time to respond and deeper prompt understanding.

With their massive parameter counts, they have demonstrated remarkable capabilities in generating coherent, contextually relevant text, making them powerful tools for tasks ranging from dialogue systems to creative writing. Both models' architectures and training methodologies highlight their complementary strengths, with BERT excelling in understanding text and GPT in generating it, collectively driving significant advancements in AI and NLP applications.

GPT models excel in a wide range of text generation tasks, including writing essays, creating dialogue systems, translating text, and even programming assistance. Their ability to generate human-like text has opened up new possibilities for creative and practical applications in various industries.

BERT's bidirectional approach allows it to capture context from both directions, making it highly effective for understanding and interpreting text. In contrast, GPT's unidirectional approach is optimized for text generation, focusing on predicting the next word based on the preceding context. BERT's MLM and NSP tasks enable it to learn deep contextual representations, while GPT's autoregressive objective focuses on generating coherent text. These different objectives highlight the complementary strengths of each model in understanding versus generating text.

Both BERT and GPT have scaled up in subsequent iterations, with models like BERT-Large and GPT-4 showcasing the benefits of increased parameters and training data. This scalability has been crucial in achieving state-of-the-art performance across a wide range of tasks.

The introduction of BERT and GPT has spurred a wave of research into pre-trained language models, leading to numerous variants and improvements. Their success has also driven the adoption of Transformer-based models in various practical applications, from chatbots to automated content creation.

BERT and GPT represent two significant milestones in the evolution of Transformer-based models. Their unique architectures, training methodologies, and applications have advanced the field of NLP, setting new benchmarks and opening up new possibilities for AI-driven language understanding and generation. As research continues to build on these foundations, BERT and GPT will likely remain central to the ongoing development and innovation in NLP.

There are other models increasingly being used now, which are being leveraged across industries:

- **Multimodal Transformers:** The adaptation of Transformer models to handle multiple data modalities (for example, Vision Transformers for image processing) marked a significant extension of their applicability. These models demonstrated the ability to handle complex tasks involving different types of data inputs.

- **Efficiency improvements:** Ongoing research has focused on making Transformers more efficient and scalable. Innovations, such as sparse attention, model pruning, knowledge distillation, and memory-efficient Transformers, have addressed the high computational and memory demands of these models, making them more accessible and practical for various applications.

- **Ethical and societal impact:** The powerful capabilities of Transformer-based models have sparked important discussions about their ethical use, including issues of bias, data privacy, and the environmental impact of large-scale training. These considerations have influenced research directions and policies around the deployment and development of AI technologies.

- **AlphaFold:** In 2020, *DeepMind's* AlphaFold utilized Transformer-based architectures to predict protein folding with high accuracy, showcasing the versatility of Transformers in scientific research and their potential impact on fields beyond traditional NLP.

The progress has been driven by a series of groundbreaking innovations and milestones that have expanded their capabilities, improved their efficiency, and broadened their applicability across various domains. If anything, it is not slowing down but speeding up as more people begin to work and interact with AI.

Looking back

Transformer-based models represent a significant advancement in the field of machine learning, fundamentally changing how computers process and understand human language. The journey began with simple algorithms that could perform basic tasks like recognizing handwritten digits or sorting spam emails, relying heavily on human intervention for improvement. The introduction of deep learning in the 2010s marked a pivotal moment, drawing inspiration from the human brain to develop neural networks capable of learning complex patterns in large datasets. This shift enabled breakthroughs in image recognition, speech processing, and more.

The real revolution came in 2017 with the advent of Transformer models. Unlike their predecessors, Transformers analyze multiple pieces of information simultaneously, allowing them to understand context and handle larger datasets more efficiently. This approach significantly enhances the accuracy of language-related tasks, leading to more reliable virtual assistants, better translation services, and more precise content recommendations.

Transformers are highly scalable, making them ideal for large-scale applications, such as analyzing social media trends or processing vast numbers of customer queries. Their versatility extends beyond language processing, as they are being adapted for various fields, including healthcare, finance, and scientific research. In essence, Transformer-based models have opened new frontiers in machine learning, providing powerful tools for businesses to leverage data in innovative and impactful ways.

Conclusion

This chapter has covered the background, history, and technology behind the Transformer-based models. This becomes the basis for how prompt engineering interacts with modern AI models. This chapter reviewed, in detail, the major steps from the Input to the tokenization process to how the data works through the Transform encoder and the Transform decoder. You should now have a solid base for beginning to delve deep into the world of prompt engineering.

In the next chapter, we will begin to pivot to how prompt engineering interacts with AI via Transformer modules and how you can better leverage those skills.

Join our book's Discord space

Join the book's Discord Workspace for Latest updates, Offers, Tech happenings around the world, New Release and Sessions with the Authors:

https://discord.bpbonline.com

CHAPTER 5

Transformer-based Models in Prompt Engineering

Introduction

Alongside other useful talents, one of the most important advancements made possible by Transformer-based models is for text to have long-range dependencies. A long-range dependency refers to relationships between words or phrases that are far apart in a series of texts. Sequential processing architectures, such as **recurrent neural network (RNNs)** and **long short-term memories (LSTMs)**, networks where one step of processing on the outcome of the previous step, often had trouble encoding long-range dependencies because they could not keep track of important information all the way back from the start of the text to the point in the sequence where they were making predictions. At long enough distances in the text, they would forget almost everything. While we can add memory mechanisms to RNNs that can help to mitigate this issue, these architectures still could generally handle only relatively short sequences before your text started to break down into meaninglessness.

Where recurrent networks previously had to use clever tricks to handle long-distance dependencies, Transformers' use of a self-attention mechanism lets the model consider how important each word is, relative to every other word in the text, no matter how many words away the one may be from the other. This process enables Transformers to maintain and use context over long stretches of text, ensuring that what was said early in a sequence is used appropriately in the later sections of that sequence. This is necessary in machine translation, for example, where a sentence's meaning may depend on words many lines apart, or in text summarization, where a summary requires the model to remember the key points throughout the document when figuring out what to put in the summary and where.

Perhaps even more important for prompt engineering of this kind is that this new ability at handling long-range dependencies helps to drastically expand the model's responsiveness to more sophisticated prompts. With these earlier iterations, one can design a prompt that is highly sensitive to a reference or quotation as long as one puts the relevant information carefully scattered in the text, as we saw with BERT. However, what Transformers now allow is more sophisticated prompts that break whatever constraints might have been in place, such as length limits, because they can handle very long sequences without losing track of the context. The result is not just a greater accuracy in response from AI to tasks that require an intricate understanding of or reasoning from long texts but also expanding what might be thought of as the more general scope of AI-generated responses in more sophisticated applications that business, the law, and society, in general, will one day embrace. Handling long-range dependencies, then, shows the potential for a new direction in AI and what it means for us in the world today: to empower models to perform more complex and contextualized tasks with greater accuracy and confidence.

Structure

In this chapter, you will learn about the following topics:

- Evolution of prompt engineering
- Advancements enabled by Transformers
- Sentiment analysis and text classification
- Customizing Transformers for specific tasks
- Methodologies in prompt engineering
- Specific applications to use in prompt engineering

Objectives

You will have a strong overview of the significance of Transformer-based models in prompt engineering, emphasizing their transformative impact on the development and optimization of AI interactions. You should feel well grounded in the advancements enabled by Transformers and how to apply them, along with understanding the methodologies in prompt engineering and identifying some very specific applications within prompt engineering.

Evolution of prompt engineering

As we saw in previous chapters, the main selling point for Transformer-based models like, BERT, **Generative Pre-trained Transformer** (**GPT**), T5, and so on is that they achieve state-of-the-art performance for a diverse set of **natural language processing (NLP)** tasks, ranging from basic machine translation and text summarization to much more intricate tasks such as long-form question answering and dialogues.

Defining the scope and significance

Prompt engineering is paramount to Transformer-based models because of their human-sounding results in response to input prompts. Prompt engineering works because of the Transformer model's inherent ability to internalize context, syntax, and semantics and provide responses accordingly. Depending upon the type of prompt engineering required, users can compel Transformer-based models to exhibit their capabilities by altering the syntax, paraphrasing the phrasing or targeting a different genre or potential outcome. With prompt engineering, users can shape the responses to support non-ideal cultural outcomes and diminish undesirable responses to specific prompts.

Transformer-based models are applicable to different tasks, such as content creation, producing human sounding automated response in customer service, and even highly regulated fields such as law and medicine, where contextual appropriateness must be at play in the generated answers. Additionally, with each model improvement – whether it is the growth of model size or the recently popular model fine-tuning approach – Transformer can generate the longest and most nuanced output text. This is why Transformer-based models are all over prompt engineering, as they set the course of AI application efficacy and enable users to flexibly control AI in enhanced and more sophisticated ways. This co-evolutionary relationship between Transformer models and prompt engineering is a step in humanity's pursuit of AI capability in understanding how humans produce and communicate in everyday language, a key research and practical domain.

Enhancing AI creativity via the use of Transformer-based models represents a leap in how artificial intelligence can generate novel and imaginative content. Transformers, with their self-attention mechanisms and deep contextual understanding, excel not just in processing language but also in generating creative outputs. When applied to contextual prompt design, Transformers enable the crafting of prompts that lead to more original and diverse responses.

Transformers in contextual prompt design

Creating more creative AI, in turn, means encouraging more creative and possibly strange replies. Transformer-based models are an important step forward in encouraging weirdness by helping synthetic creativity overcome the limitation of recursion networks. The self-attention mechanism allows Transformers to process deep contextual information more effectively, which enables them not just to process language but to generate creative language. Indeed, one of the most important ways in which we can empower generative models to be creative is by prompting them in more creative ways. By optimizing prompt context to be more creative, it is possible to scale and improve creative AI in a way that is simply not possible with modeling algorithms restricted to working with strictly defined and bounded inputs. The scale and spread of creativity, for example, in the realm of creative writing, notable possible applications of contextual prompt optimization with Transformers would be creating potentially unlimited numbers of prompts for story generation or enhancing trip-generating apps, so that they would be able to produce more attractive and original descriptions of places rather than the dull networks that humans tend to use when discussing sights. Similarly, Transformers could be employed to generate more creative AI-written ad copy for the multi-billion-dollar creative copywriting market, which has become one of the last refuges for the dwindling ranks of human English-language writers. For art, the same logic could be applied in perhaps unexpected ways. Architecture exhibitions showing mockups are vastly more eye-catching than mere advertisements. We could also utilize Transformers to generate realistic CGI renderings of the architectural commissions that result from this new algorithm-led wave of creativity.

Conversely, models utilized for prompt engineering tend to optimize responses mainly for accuracy and relevance relative to a given prompt and task. While such models regularly produce fine-grained, contextually appropriate responses, their creativity is often clipped by the rigid demands of the prompts they are provided with. Traditional prompt engineering tends to marginalize the impact of ambiguity in responses, aiming to direct the AI to generate the most factually accurate and useful response possible. This type of approach might be appropriate for many applications, but it often tends to limit the level of creativity we see in generated responses. This is because, in many instances, the focus on accuracy and clear response means clipping the AI model's wings and limiting imaginative – and potentially useful – outputs.

 Putting these approaches side by side, it is not hard to see that they can go quite differently and that traditional prompt engineering – useful as it is for systems that require great accuracy and reliability – is inherently limited when it comes to letting AI be creative. The inherent contextual sensitivity of Transformers – their ability to generate complex, context-rich language – means that AI can, when given contextual prompts, be essentially coaxed into outputs that – unlike what was apparently able in these human-grade prompt engineering systems – provide correct text and creative text. The ability of Transformers to be sensitive both to creativity and context and hence the apparent tradeoff between them, has so far been absent in the comparatively blunt world of AI models. Importantly, that means it is a unique strength in the particular systems where we want to nudge AI as far as it can go.

Advancements enabled by Transformers

The emergence of Transformer-based models brought about some truly impressive changes. One of the most striking improvements you will find is in the model's ability to understand. How does this work? Well, to demonstrate the model's sense of context, we can have it paraphrase the text it has been trained on while retaining citations and quotes. Already, we are seeing contextual awareness spilling over to the generation. For instance, the powerful self-attention mechanism in the Transformer gives the model the ability to generate explanations that have a better sense of logic, structure, and complexity than previous RNN based models. This is particularly true when we shift to task-based evaluation, as in the case of paraphrasing. RNN models were notoriously bad at retaining long-term dependencies since they process inputs sequentially, and as the input sequence grows longer, the processing time lengthens. The upside to this issue was their ability to learn directly from raw text, so they were favored for monolingual applications like spam filtering.

Improved contextual understanding

Increased contextual understanding offered by Transformers has been important to a wide variety of applications, including in many natural language processing tasks, such as translation, summarization, and question answering, where the influence of structure and increased ability to maintain and track over longer passages translates to more accurate and coherent outputs. Creative applications benefit from improved contextual understanding since it allows AI to generate text that is not only semantically consistent but also contextually appropriate. This ability was also key in systems with dialogue, such as conversational AI, which require maintaining context across many exchanges to produce salient human-sounding responses.

Another way to put it is that Transformers, unlike naive models that were used in prior prompt-engineering work, are better at modeling context and better at exploiting it than previous models. Prompts that steer text generation are tinkering with context: a really good prompt is one that helps the AI keep the most productive contextual information intact throughout the task. Transformers do not care whether a prompt is good or bad– their innate modeling context means they can still do a passable job. What Transformers give us is an enormously powerful new ability for designers to semantically guide AI to solutions in a new way without creating overly rigid rules. With these new models that understand context easily, the prompt creator – the person writing new prompts for AI to follow – can begin to think more flexibly and wonderfully, letting go of some of the burdensome chokehold constraints they may have been putting on their prompts in the past. Engineers describe this leap in context as increasing the **generalization** of AI systems and the leap in reliability as increasing their **quality**. However, these names do not capture what is happening. The jump lends itself to two – and better – interpretations. One obvious one is that better knowledge of context means fewer errors. However, the second, because context shapes the possible paths of response, these new Transformer models give us a glimpse at what AI will be able to do when granted these new tools. Since context influences what actually fits together and what does not, a leap in the ability to model that context is a leap in the range of things that AI can be steered towards. A Transformer model can effectively say: Input is not high definition, but the result will be as good as possible.

Handling long-range dependencies

Alongside their other useful talents, one of the most important advancements made possible by Transformer-based models is for text to have long-range dependencies. A long-range dependency refers to relationships between words or phrases that are far apart in a series of texts. Sequential processing architectures such as RNNs and LSTMs, where one step of processing relies on the outcome of the previous step, often had trouble encoding long-range dependencies because they could not keep track of important information all the way back from the start of the text to the point in the sequence where they were making predictions. At long enough distances in the text, they would forget almost everything. Where recurrent networks previously had to use clever tricks to handle long-distance dependencies, Transformers' use of a self-attention mechanism lets the model consider how important each word is relative to every other word in the text, no matter how many words away the one may be from the other. This process enables Transformers to maintain and use context over long stretches of text, ensuring that what was said early in a sequence is used appropriately in the later sections of that sequence. A sentence's meaning may depend on words many lines apart, or in text summarization, and in the 1980s, a summary requires the model to remember the key points throughout the document when figuring out what to put in the summary and where.

Perhaps even more important for prompt engineering of this kind is that this new ability to handle long-range dependencies helps to drastically expand the model's responsiveness to more sophisticated prompts. With these earlier iterations, one can design a prompt that is highly sensitive to a reference or quotation as long as one puts the relevant information carefully scattered in the text, as we saw with BERT. However, what Transformers now allow is more sophisticated prompts that break whatever constraints might have been in place, such as length limits, because they can handle very long sequences without losing track of the context. The result is not just greater accuracy in response from AI to tasks that require intricate understanding of or reasoning from long texts, but also expanding what might be thought of as the more general scope of AI-generated responses in more sophisticated applications that business, the law, and society in general will one day embrace. Handling long-range dependencies, then, shows the potential for a new direction in AI and what it means for us today: to empower models to perform more complex and contextualized tasks with greater accuracy and confidence.

Scalability and parallelization

One of the main aspects of the models made possible by Transformer-based models is our ability to scale these systems and efficiently paralyze them. As discussed earlier, RNNs process sequences of data in a stepwise manner. This sequential processing, in turn, limits scalability, both in terms of speeding up the system and, most importantly, training on large datasets, where each step highly depends on the completion of the step before it. Our ability to scale such models to systems that can handle larger or more complex datasets can be extremely costly, both computationally and in time.

Transformers brought in a genuinely different paradigm because their architecture is inherently **parallelizable**. The computational self-attention core of Transformers allows them to compute over whole sequences in parallel rather than step-by-step, significantly speeding up both training and inference. Further, by being able to distribute the computations across many processors or GPUs in parallel, they can scale to much larger datasets and some larger, but still relatively shallow, models than was possible with computational bottlenecks arising from necessary sequential methods (hence, the migration to more massive models, leading from GPT-4o to GPT-4 and beyond that).

Eager to exploit the scale and parallelism that made Transformer models possible, researchers started to devise models that could support more complex, longer inputs. With previous models, the complexity of the prompt was constrained by the computational budget, and therefore, asks the required enormous amounts of information to inform responses or that needed to gather evidence to inform these responses in more ways and from more knowledge sources was often unfeasible. Transformers can handle prompts that are much richer and more complex. This can be used by researchers to devise more sophisticated AI applications that can process increasingly more information at speed and produced ever longer responses within a computing environment, that in itself, can take in additional information and evidence. This both improves the performance of AI in existing applications, as well as spurring further creativity by researchers and practitioners, who now have the freedom to explore new applications at the forefront of AI capabilities.

 This, in turn, means that even non-expert players can compete on equal footing with the best in the world. On the flip side, the huge scalability and parallelization enabled by the Transformers brought a new realm of possibilities to the technical side of AI and accelerated its progress on various fronts.

The ability to summarize is a second way that Transformers exhibit the power of contextual learning at scale. Writing a summary of a text includes retaining the most relevant information from a source while compressing it into a shorter version that still makes sense. Early trained systems struggled with this task. Often, they copied a lot of the original text while leaving out important information. The Transformer's ability to manipulate context to find the right words makes it well-suited for summaries. It is skilled at identifying relevant information and structure. In single-document summary, for instance, it excels at finding the most crucial information and abstracting it into a smaller, yet still meaningful, version of the original text. It does this while retaining quotes, quotes within quotes, complex paragraphs, and other important linguistic and contextual features tracked by earlier models. Transformers have demonstrated the same success in multi-document analysis, taking information from multiple texts and condensing it into one concise summary. Such capability would be useful for newsfeeds, scholarly articles or legal opinions on complex matters.

Better language translation and summing will have important effects on how we interact with the world with languages in a globalized world. In language translation, where cultures communicate with one another, language translation reduces the barrier when people communicate in a variety of languages. For summarization, where large amounts of data are produced, they can pass the information faster and more efficiently. Overall, with improved accuracy and fluency, Transformer-based models have important implications for NLP, helping to make AI-powered natural language processing an efficient and simulated human-sounding tool.

Sentiment analysis and text classification

It goes as far as making discernment in sentiment analysis, which is the act of determining the sentiment of virtual text, that is, whether the text expresses a positive, negative or neutral emotion. In these discussions, sentiments usually refer to the emotion that someone is trying to express through text. This can range from something like: **I failed, and I feel so sorry for myself**, which is clearly negative, to **I failed, I'm sorry**, - which is considered sarcasm. Previous models were simply not equipped to deal with all these complex emotions. BERT-like models have a more human-like understanding of how emotions are expressed in text and the extent to which those emotions can quickly change. For example, in the last sentence, came one of the most hated examples that readers have come across in their sentiment analysis work, and it helped choose a more accurate tone. Now, this analysis would be fairly useless if you were trying to understand a scathing tweet or a conversation among friends after someone lied about going on vacation to get out of a bad dinner date. The thing that gives Transformers the ability to do these things is called a deep contextual awareness. Essentially, these models can incorporate more words and phrases when they try to understand a certain element of text. This enables them to perform analysis precisely like a human interpreter. This makes them uniquely valuable for tasks in which understanding human sentiment, such as social media monitoring, customer feedback analysis, and market research, is paramount.

Transformer-based models have also helped another text task called text classification – assigning text a pre-defined category based on its content. Regardless of the task, it could typically be done reliably with traditional classifiers, either incapable of working on entire text sequences or forced to observe mega-buckets of text to discern the features that set them apart. With Transformers – and their ability to compare entire text sequences to each other all at once – it became much easier to identify these Tell-Tale signs, because subtle but contextually coherent features by which to distinguish categories, can be ignored by traditional classifiers who, even if fed extremely large amounts of training data, will focus only on text by-items to find the key to the task at hand. This meant that researchers could flow endless amounts of text through a Transformer – tagging each text item with a reference category – and the model would quickly master the task because these features became so easily visible to it. Text classification is now a leading auto-tagging application known for its speed and accuracy. It is used to tag content for automated moderation, as well as indexing mega-arsenals of data, such as mammoth corporate databases.

Positive sentiment – the optimistic stance, Transformers did not just improve the accuracy of models on text classification and sentiment analysis tasks. They also introduce added flexibility, where models can be finetuned for greater context-specific use – say, within a narrow domain of law or medicine or in financial markets containing specific terminological or stylistic variations. In these domains, meaning can be highly dependent on context, and slight variations of words or sentences can carry drastically different meanings. Transformers can provide more fine-grained, context-relevant analysis, enabling companies to get more accurate with their decisions or communication strategies.

The introduction of Transformer-based models into sentiment analysis and text classification marks a real shift in how to extract information from texts and classify it. Not only do they make it more accurate and reliable, but also offer new ways in which they can be used in different directions and further establish the Transformer as the central technology of modern NLP.

Customizing Transformers for specific tasks

Fine-tuning Transformer-based models for task-specific applications is quite common nowadays and has become a central focus of maximizing their utility.

Fine-tuning techniques

Fine-tuning involves training a large pre-trained Transformer model on a general-purpose, broad-coverage dataset to capture some level of skill in representing language. The fine-tuning step involves an additional bout of training – sometimes very brief – on a smaller task-specific data set, with the aim of helping it adapt the knowledge and skills it picked up in pre-training to suit the details of this new task.

What makes fine-tuning so efficient is that it takes advantage of the vast linguistic knowledge that a Transformer model, such as BERT or GPT, acquires during pretraining on large corpora, such as Wikipedia or Common Crawl. The model learns many general patterns about language, its structure, and relationships, which can be applied to any task. Fine-tuning specializes in this general knowledge of the language for a new task, whether sentiment analysis, text classification, or more complex uses like summarizing legal documents or predicting the outcome of a medical diagnosis.

If we are attempting to get a pre-trained Transformer to do a task, such as sentiment analysis – predicting whether the customer review text is politely favorable, politely negative, or indifferent – we would fine-tune the model on a dataset of similarly labeled customer reviews. In doing so, the model tweaks its internal state to better predict the sentiment of new reviews based on what it has learned from the words it sees in the dataset (the distribution of linguistic patterns). Not only does this training improve the model's performance on the target task, but, ideally, it also makes it more robust to specific challenges related to the dataset – its slang, dialectal expressions, and industry jargon.

Also, fine-tuning is required for any task that needs to involve domain-specific knowledge. Fine-tuning a Transformer on a medical records dataset allows the model to focus more on attunement to the specific technical language, abbreviations, and concerns of medical records. Specialized models are a necessity when the stakes are high, and there is little room for error.

Additionally, it can be done pretty rapidly and is relative to training a model from scratch, using much fewer computational resources and less data. So, fine-tuning can be an attractive option for third parties seeking to deploy AI tailored to their own uses without needing to fund extensive computational infrastructure or massive datasets themselves. Even more importantly, it lends itself to iterative improvement. A fine-tuned model may be refined as it accumulates a more task-specific dataset or as the contours of the real-life task change.

Fine-tuning is central to making Transformer-based models work well on any number of different tasks to make the most of their pre-trained expertise while adjusting for the nuances of a specific task. This makes them effective for all kinds of useful applications, from niche industrial tasks all the way to highly specialized ones. Fine-tuning not only allows Transformers to perform well but makes sophisticated AI available to all kinds of domains.

Transfer learning in NLP

Transfer learning is a widely important technique: speeding up research and decreasing costs through learning in one task to help in another. One of the most momentous developments in NLP in the last couple of years is that transfer learning is now possible to do extremely well with Transformer-based models, whose size and computational requirements had come to be seen as prohibitive. This means that we can take a model that has been pre-trained on a very large, diverse dataset and then **transfer** that model – in both parameter weights and understanding of how it works – to a new, related task that we want to solve, even with little or no data for that task (the so-called **target** or **downstream** task).

A model that was previously trained on a quite general objective, such as BERT or GPT, and that has experienced a very large amount of language patterns, structures, and semantics during its pre-training phase – such a model has learned a rather general understanding of language that could be applied to many different types of tasks. Then, when we apply transfer learning, we fine-tune this previous model on a smaller number of examples relevant to our new task. Practically, this contributes to adapting its quite general language understanding to the new task.

Another major advantage of transfer learning in NLP is that it allows building models for specific tasks with far less labeled data. Since the Transformer has learned core representations of language during pre-training, it needs only a few task-specific instances to fine-tune its parameters and get good accuracy. This is particularly helpful in domains where gathering labeled data is expensive or scarce, such as in medical or legal domains where expert annotations are usually required.

Furthermore, the benefits of transfer learning might speed up the transition of NLP models into customer use. If the pre-trained Transformers are already endowed with a general, high-level sense of the workings of language, it should be much faster to fine-tune them to fulfill more specific tasks. So, a correctly calibrated model, network, or other tool that has been fine-tuned to fit your organization should be able developed and deployed on your systems in a matter of days rather than months. This benefit could be a real boon in situations where the flexibility to deploy new tools to meet new tasks or changing conditions is an urgent necessity.

Similarly, transfer learning encourages researchers to spread the benefits of expertise across NLP tasks and domains. A Transformer model trained on generic language data can be transferred to sentiment analysis and then fine-tuned again on text summarization. Benefits from previous training can be carried over to the new task. Such flexibility not only boosts the utility of NLP models but also fosters wider innovation by allowing researchers to apply powerful AI properties and techniques to a wider range of problems.

Transfer learning for NLP based on Transformer-style models is an advancement in the way language models are brought to bear on new tasks. While the massive pre-training done on Transformers gives them strong abilities for general language processing, transfer learning can be a fit between that pre-training and a new task – a way of using the prior knowledge that the model already possesses. Instead, the model is not trained from scratch for each task and can even make do with much less fully annotated data than before – hence the greatly increased deployment speed and the ability to work with far smaller datasets. Transfer learning both improves the performance and consistency of NLP models, as well as vastly increasing the range of applications to which they can be put. The use of advanced AI tools, such as automated language understanding, is now possible in a far wider range of fields and industries.

Methodologies in prompt engineering

Crafting effective prompts is a crucial methodology in prompt engineering, particularly when working with Transformer-based models like GPT-4. The prompt serves as the initial input or query that guides the model's output, and its design can influence the relevance, accuracy, and creativity of the response generated by the AI. Crafting effective prompts requires a deep understanding of both the model's capabilities and the specific task or goal at hand, as the quality of the prompt directly impacts the quality of the output. Once more, crafting the prompt properly – designing the first input or query that becomes the cornerstone of a catchphrase response – is a major methodology of prompt engineering, especially when working with Transformer-based models like GPT-4. To be a skilled prompt writer one needs to grasp the model and the outcome trying to be achieved.

Crafting effective prompts

Context is the *guardrails* prompts are built on by providing the right amount of information in the right way. The more information we give a model, the better it will perform. Overly vague or ambiguous prompts can lead to off-target or nonsensical outputs. If the model cannot figure out what you want it to do, it would not be able to do it.

Iterative refinement is also integral to the process of creating good prompts. If a user's first attempt to get a desired result from the model does not work, prompt finetuning is an excellent option. Depending on the desired outcome, users might have to experiment with different phrasing, levels of detail, or contextual cues. Figuring out what works often involves trial and error, as users learn how to shape their inputs in ways that reliably elicit the highest quality content from the model. Thus, iterating over prompt design is key to crafting effective prompts.

Beyond that, it is important to have an appreciation of the limits of the model, and to formulate prompts accordingly. The top-performing Transformer-based models also have points of failure, for example, where they are dealing with specialized jargon or a set of instructions that is too long and complex. Prompts that anticipate these points of failure, for instance by splitting a complex task into lower-level steps, or providing additional context, can help avoid pitfalls and diminish the possibility of unusable AI outputs.

Clear, specific, well-constructed and iteratively refined prompts form an indispensable methodology for prompt engineering. Getting it right makes good use of Transformer-based models, which work well, by helping them to generate thoughtful, relevant and contextual responses. It is crucial to good, tailored writing – and to life.

Measuring prompt efficacy

Efficacy measurement, in particular, is a vital tool in prompt engineering as it provides a systematic means for assessing how effectively a given prompt prompts a Transformer-based model to provide an output that is relevant, accurate and of high quality, in relation to the task at hand. Since the way that prompting affects efficacy, finding ways systematically to measure it, provides a clear way of how one can tweak their prompt, and therefore, be sure that the AI model is achieving its full capacity.

A popular measurement method of prompt efficacy is qualitative assessment, essentially comparing or measuring two outputs created from two different prompts, against a checklist of certain criteria, such as coherence, surprise, on-topic, creativity, factual accuracy, etc. To do so often means appealing to human judgment – lay readers or a panel of evaluators, for example, to assess the output from the system as to how the model works towards the desired result. For example, in a text generation task, the evaluators might ask, **Do you like the model's style?** ; or **Was the key idea expressed?**

Quantitative metrics can also be used to grade prompt efficacy. Where the endpoint of the task is ostensibly simple, and lends itself to objective metrics – for example, information retrieval where **precision** (the portion of relevant documents actually retrieved) and **recall** (the portion of retrieved documents that were actually relevant) can be used to compare how well a system does its job independently – precision, recall and F1 score can all be used to quantify the effect of a prompt. Other more robust metrics, such as perplexity (a measure of how well a probability model predicts a probability distribution in a hold-out sample) or **bilingual evaluation understudy** (**BLEU**) score (a metric for evaluating the quality of machine-translated text) can also be reduced to numbers, bringing clarity to how well a prompt guides the model along the desired path.

The other essential way to assess whether prompting is working is through A/B testing – a side-by-side comparison of two or more prompts. This method becomes vital when trying to understand the effectiveness of minute changes in wording or even the ordering of sentences to achieve the final outputs. By assessing the results of different versions of a prompt, the prompt engineer can determine which variation gives rise to better – and potentially even more accurate – outputs.

Feedback from users in other applications, especially those where the AI-generated content is made available to the public or to customers, can also serve as an indicator of prompt efficacy. For instance, if AI-sounding text, that is meant to convince readers of its human origins, fails to improve users' perceived credibility or relevance, that could be an indication that there is room for improvement in the model's prompts. In other words, users' verdicts on the outcomes generated by AI can create a feedback loop for prompt learning and signal to users that the AI output is meeting their expectations over time.

There is also the matter of contextual efficacy; some prompts might work well in one context but not in another, depending on the task's complexity, domain specificity or language characteristics, such as complexity and density. In such a case, the prompt performance depends on the task context. Prompts should be measured on robustness and flexibility (contextual efficacy) since prompts will inevitably have specific and narrow conditions in which they function.

Efficacy is something that clearly needs to be taken into account; no single stakeholder would miss it as a crucial aspect of prompt evaluation. As we have seen in this digest, prompt efficacy can never be **just** a simple, quantitative metric: measuring it demands multiple forms of input (qualitative judgment, quantitative metrics, A/B testing, user feedback, contextual analysis, etc.). Nonetheless, as prompts are evaluated and tweaked through such processes, the outputs of AI systems will tap into ever-deeper and sophisticated facets of the world.

Comparison with other models used in prompt engineering

For parallelism and long-range dependencies, Transformers have rewritten the rules in AI (as well as prompt engineering) because they have the architecture to perform parallel computing and long-range dependency of data. Transformers are computationally faster and more efficient than older algorithms such as **recurrent neural networks** (**RNNs**) and **long short-term memory networks** (**LSTMs**), and they are particularly good at contextual understanding in large datasets. While RNNs and LSTMs each analyze data in order, which takes time and does not necessarily add context to long text strings, Transformers analyze whole blocks of text at once and offer a better view of language structures. However, that is a higher-cost capability with a high computational overhead, so typically more powerful hardware and bigger data to train on. However, given these requirements, Transformers are more scalable and more effective at producing coherent and contextual text than they are often the preferred choice for more challenging prompt engineering.

Specific applications in prompt engineering

In the realm of specific applications within prompt engineering, generative tasks, such as text completion and story generation, stand out as particularly impactful. These tasks involve guiding Transformer-based models to produce coherent and contextually appropriate content based on an initial input, or prompt. The effectiveness of these generative tasks hinges on the ability of the prompt to elicit responses that not only follow logically from the input but also display creativity and fluency, making the results useful for a variety of purposes, from creative writing to automated content generation.

Generative tasks

For text completion, prompts are crafted to give the model a good starting point, after which the model would be expected to generate text that completes an input sentence, paragraph or (in the case of this essay) a much fuller document. In a creative writing context, a prompt that introduces a character or setting in a vivid, open-ended way can encourage the model to generate a continuation that is imaginative and richly detailed.

Generating stories is another generative task where thoughtful prompts can make a big difference. Here, the prompt could set up the initial context, characters and conflict, and then let the model spin out an engaging story that remains coherent as it progresses. The hard part of story generation is keeping things coherent while also allowing for creative divergence, forcing prompts to straddle the continuum between structure and flexibility. For instance, a good prompt could outline the opening of a story while leaving a lot of room for the model to explore new narrative directions, in order to come up with something consistent and also creative.

Another area where modern Transformers give a big advantage over their predecessors, is in tasks to know how actions in a distant part of the later on. These are called generative tasks: you provide the model with some constraints, and it generates text for you. In the case of computer-generated, it is pronouncing words in a way that still sounds plausible within a meaningful sentence. In a video game, automated plot generation needs to be enabled when the player does something different on devices and platforms. It is crucial for the model to maintain when the player is in. The character in the game should still be aware of what the player has done so far, and any written content should still make sense in a week's time, and potentially drift.

The extent of success in both text completion and story generation seems to be strongly correlated to a prompt's ability to provide a strong, clear structure while still allowing the model great freedom to be interesting material. This tension between structure and creativity is perhaps the most exciting thing about generative tasks in prompt engineering – getting a prompt just right is a challenging but satisfying task. With a bit of practice, users can take full advantage of the potential of Transformer-based models to produce high-quality, contextually rich, and well-sounding text in a wide variety of creative and practical use.

Conversational AI

Conversational AI, including products such as chatbots and virtual assistants, is one of the most vibrant and important areas for applying prompt engineering today. The quality and success of a conversational AI system is often determined by the design of the prompts that control its responses. Unlike the prompt engineering needed for responses to individual prompts, the prompt engineering of conversational AI needs to not just produce fluent (human-sounding) responses, but also control the context of the interaction to be appropriate for the user, and address the specific success criteria of the conversation, whether it is customer service, information retrieval or personal assistance.

Good prompt engineering ensures that a chatbot can handle a large variety of user inputs, going from simple questions (**What time does this restaurant close?**) to more elaborate, multistep conversations (**I need to check on the status of my order in San Francisco, but I woulld like to also ask a few additional questions**). With the customer service example in mind, prompts can be designed to help the AI understand common needs and scenarios that users might have. A prompt could frame the context of the conversation (The user is probably enquiring about the status of their order in San Francisco, so please retrieve the information from that order and proceed), enabling the AI to retrieve what they need in the shortest time, and eliciting a smoother, more satisfactory experience for the customer. Prompts can also be designed for **off-script** user inputs that could catch the AI off guard, or be ambiguous in nature. Rather than blowing up or just ignoring the input, prompts can be designed to compel the AI to ask for clarifications or gently guide the conversation to a more helpful direction.

More recently, the rise of models built on the Transformer architecture have brought a new depth to conversational AI capabilities, including the ability to track context from earlier utterances and to capture richer flow from actual human conversation, such as better understanding the motive for a user's query, or the direction in which they are headed with what they want to say over many turns of a conversation, even to the point where they can handle conversational pranks, such as pivoting the topic or the tone. This has helped to give chatbots and virtual assistants more nuanced user responses – one that feels more in sync with human speech.

Prompt engineering for conversational AI is highly iterative. As humans use these systems, their responses and behaviors reveal valuable information about prompt design that can be used to refine and re-engineer prompts as the AI improves itself in usage, thereby becoming more capable of serving user needs over time. This iterative process of prompt engineering, from design to experimentation, testing, and refinement, is part of the roadmap to creating conversational AI that performs at a high level and adapts and improves itself in response to real-world usage. As it stands, many successful conversational AI applications – such as many chatbots and virtual assistants – rely on highly complex prompt engineering to yield meaningful interactions and behavior.

Language translation and summarization

Particularly important applications within prompt engineering are commonly referenced in its name – namely, language translation and summarization – both of which have benefited from having their arguably most important parameters being given precisely to the model through the prompt, facilitating improvements that make them more strongly *contextualized*, *accurate* and *frugal*, to borrow some of the terms we use in linguistics to describe the nature of human communication. Tasks. such as translation and summarization, need to be designed carefully as prompts, such that the model is perfectly positioned to say the right thing in exactly the right way.

Prompt engineering can help us prepare prompts for language translation to guide the AI toward producing texts that are idiomatically correct in terms of cultural and contextual sensitivity rather than just grammatically correct. A well-designed prompt must provide the AI with proper context surrounding the domain of the source text, such as the topic, target audience, or any particular linguistic intricacies that might need to be transferred. For example, when translating technical manuals, a prompt could emphasize accuracy and precision in the translation, so that the text is not only correct but also accessible to the audience. Translating literary works, on the other hand, could involve prompts that encourage the model to preserve or enhance the stylistic features and affective tone of the original text, oracular in nature, thus a translation that is not mere correct content delivery but an expressive and appreciative performance.

Prompt engineering has another, related aspect, specific to translation. In addition to flagging when a specific word should not be changed, the prompts have to steer the linguistic model, often sentence by sentence, through idiomatic expressions, cultural references and language-specific syntax, the absence or presence of which are not identical in all languages. For example, good prompts would signal to the AI: this phrase would not come through right in the translation because in English it means die, but because it is slang and socially improper in that context. We need the translation to come through as an equivalent idiomatic expression in the other language, not literally. Kick the bucket might be part of the prompt, to drag the AI away from the literal meaning, or from inadvertently perpetuating offensive speech in the target language.

Another common use of prompt engineering is in summarization – the process of reducing a larger body of text to a shorter, coherent version while preserving citations and quotes, and still retaining the most important points, themes and conclusions of the original. In this use, prompts must encourage AI models to focus more on distilling key points, themes and conclusions from the input, and less on features such as citations, quotes and claims. Summarization is a particularly relevant, but different use of prompt engineering. The challenge of summarization lies in steering the right balance between brevity and accuracy. A prompt that is too vague might result in a summary that is just too bland, or perhaps omits important points, while a detailed prompt might result in a summary that is just a lengthy regurgitation of the original.

Good prompt engineering for summarization also requires considering the use envisioned for the purpose: if a summary is being created for the general reader, the prompt might guide the AI to rephrase abstract concepts and remove jargon – making the content more digestible. By contrast, if the summary is written for experts in a field, the prompt might guide the AI to keep more jargon and nuance – increasing the likelihood that the summary would address the informational needs of a specialized audience.

In both the tasks of translation and summarization, Transformer-based models that are good at accounting for long-range dependencies and maintaining contextual coherence over long spans of text can benefit from paraphrases that exploit these qualities by retaining the text's original structure and lengths. In these cases, effective prompt engineering involves helping the AI to avoid frustrated behavior by encouraging it to stay on topic, while also leveraging the model's inherent strengths to improve the quality of its translations and summaries.

Prompt engineering serves an important role in making these AI models work within the context of language translation and summarization so that, for example, an AI model trained on all existing scientific literature can produce an intelligible output for a summary, without a background in general relativity and quantum theory. By designing prompts in a task-specific manner with proper consideration of the model's audience, engineers can tune the model so that the outputs are both informative and as context-appropriate as possible, which makes these models extremely useful to a wide variety of applications.

Sentiment analysis and text classification

The most important applications in prompt engineering benefiting from Transformer-based models are sentiment analysis and text classification, where models are trained to classify text according to its emotional tone or thematic content. These applications are based on the proper design of prompts that are able to guide the model in understanding and classifying the input at hand.

Sentiment analysis is where prompt engineering helps the AI decide if a given piece of text is positive, negative or neutral. Good prompt-writing for sentiment analysis involves giving the AI the right context to understand the expressed sentiments. By including examples of linguistic tricks like sarcasm or irony – words that express sentiments counter to their literal meaning – the prompt is designed to help the general AI model better understand that the sentiments themselves are the real key, not the linguistic flourishes. As *Wolpert and Loy* so succinctly put it, it is not **I am feeling happy towards** dinner but rather **I am feeling hungry**. Such specific cues help the AI better identify the real source of the sentiments.

This greater fidelity could be a crucial thing in **Point-Of-Sale** (**POS**) applications for social media analytics, for example, where knowing exactly what the public is saying – and feeling – in real-time could be a make-or-break element for many businesses and other organizations.

In the case of text classification, the input is text that is assigned to a set of predefined categories on the basis of what it is about. In this context, the goal of prompt engineering is to specify these categories and the distinctive features that can be used to best characterize the categories. Proper prompts, therefore, help the system focus on these distinctive features of the input and, consequently, assign the input to the proper category. Going back to the news classification example, prompts might need to direct the modelling to focus on keywords, topics, or the source to correctly assign an article to politics, sports, or entertainment. The challenge here is how to craft prompts that help the system attend to the relevant information without also being inundated by irrelevant information.

Both sentiment analysis and text classification benefit from the contextual reasoning of Transformer-based models and produce highly accurate results from the perspective of standard metrics. At the same time, these powerful models still defer to the quality of the prompts used to guide them. When poorly specified, models can misclassify text categories or misjudge sentiment, especially in cases where meanings or sentiments are ambiguous or mixed.

Furthermore, the iterative nature of prompt engineering for sentiment analysis and text classification can be crucial for creative success. Prompt design can be a process of trial and error as engineers experiment with what phrasing, what structure, what specificity of prompt design will work best, and then iterate those designs continuously until the AI model delivers the desired accuracy in its task performance. That iterative quality is even more critical to successful applications of text enhancement that require sensitive and nuanced outputs.

Conclusion

This chapter has covered the evolution of prompt engineering, focusing on how AI interacts with the Transformers we have covered off on. We talked about how critical Transformers are in contextual design for prompts and then turned our attention to the many advancements enabled by Transformers and how we can leverage them. We focused on prompt engineering methodologies and then went into detail on very specific applications that you can focus on in prompt engineering. In the next chapter, we will now take what we learned and look at architecture concepts in Transformers before digging into the prompt ecosystem itself as we dig into the transfer architecture concepts.

CHAPTER 6

Transformer Architecture Concepts

Introduction

This chapter provides a comprehensive examination of the advancements in transformer architecture, emphasizing the development and impact of **Generative Pre-trained Transformers (GPT)** introduced by OpenAI. Beginning with an introduction to the basic concept and architecture of the original GPT model, the chapter progresses through the subsequent iterations—GPT-2 with GPT-3 and the new GPT-4 and GPT 4o—highlighting their scaled-up capabilities and the massive scope of their applications. The discussion looks into the technical details of GPT models, including their architecture, training methodologies, and the use of language modeling and transfer learning. It further explores a range of applications from natural language processing to creative endeavors like writing and art, and practical industry uses, such as customer service automation. The narrative underscores the transformative impact of these models on various sectors, providing a nuanced understanding of their potential and the technological innovation they represent.

Structure

In this chapter, we will learn about the following topics:

- Transformer models
- Technical details of GPT models
- Comparison with other AI models

Objectives

By the end of this chapter, you will understand where OpenAI came from and the critical evolutions from GPT-1 up to and including the current GPT-4o. You will know the architecture behind GPT and be able to relate the transformers you learned about in previous chapters. You will understand the architecture of OpenAI's GPT and identify the myriad applications using GPT.

Transformer models

At the core of all AI systems is the transformer model, which consists of algorithms used in converting speech/typed-in text into something a computer system can apply deep learning. Transformer models vary for the type of AI work they are created to focus on but all modern AI systems use them.

The advent of GPT by OpenAI

We have covered OpenAI and Chat GPT in the previous chapters, but we will devote a few pages to look back at ChatGPT and what has happened in the past two and a half years. In December 2015, *Sam Altman, Greg Brockman, Ilya Sutskever, Wojciech Zaremba* and *John Schulman,* and others formed an organization called OpenAI, a pioneering AI research organization made up of renowned research teams dedicated to ensuring that **artificial general intelligence** (**AGI**) benefits all of humanity, by default. This was a non-profit organization initially set up to build AI safely and transparently while keeping it aligned with human values.

Concept and architecture

A defining characteristic of OpenAI's approach has been pushing the art of AI system-design forward, putting particular emphasis on **reinforcement learning** (**RL**) and **natural language processing** (**NLP**). The GPT series of models, which quickly became one of OpenAI's most prominent products, was intended to be a response to **nudging beyond the edge of what was currently possible in text-generating AI**. The Transformer differs from other models (such as **recurrent neural networks** (**RNNs**)) in that it is much lighter weight, allowing for models to process and generate language more efficiently.

The next generation models, GPT-2 and GPT-3 (released in 2019 and 2020), would also exhibit aspects of larger scaling and greater power, especially with GPT-2 sparking notice over the fact that the model could produce more convincing text, fitting into a wider narrative – so much so that OpenAI chose to initially hold back on the release of GPT-2 out of fears of misuse. However, GPT-3 further expanded on this, increasing parameters up to 175 billion, making it the largest and most powerful language model at the time. Following the release of GPT-3, a new type of critique began to emerge on the heels of advanced language models, one that explores the impact on wellbeing. Chat GPT-3 was considered the next landmark in the AI realm; as it demonstrated the most impressive capabilities ever achieved across a wide range of tasks, including machine translation, summarization and generative creative writing. Chat GPT-3 was released in March of 2023. Its successor, GPT-4o (where the O stands for Omni), is extremely new, at the time of writing May of 2024.

OpenAI's path, from the creation of its first bots to the development of the GPT series, thus helps illustrate its long-term ambitions in pushing the frontiers of AI in an innovative and ethically conscious fashion.

Contextual reference to detailed Transformer model exploration

We have spent a lot of time with transformer models, but there are many advances to discuss which led to the creation of OpenAI's toolset, the beginning of a new era in the study of NLP. As you remember, the ability to leverage parallel processing of the Transformer enabled and scalable training of models on larger datasets (which were required to train ever-larger models, such as new NLP models increased the accuracy of language models, but also paved the way for the rapid progress in AI-based understanding and generation of it.

Start of GPT

The last few chapters were all focused on transformers leading to the GPT. That work gave us many LLMs, who were both pre-trained and not yet pre-trained.

OpenAI's most important introduction to date was GPT-1, which appeared in 2018, followed by the GPT series of models, ushering in a new era of NLP. This model was built upon the Transformer architecture, which received attention at that time due to efficiency and effectiveness of dealing with sequential data, without using RNNs. GPT-1 was trained on a large dataset of text using an unsupervised learning approach, meaning the text was unlabeled data from which the model was trained. The size of GPT-1 was 117 million parameters.

The major innovation in GPT-1 was devising a two-staged training process: unsupervised pre-training followed by supervised fine-tuning. In pre-training, the model was trained to predict the next word in a sequence, capturing a very general understanding of linguistic patterns and the distributions of words in human text. This factored in essential contextual information and was critical in allowing the model to generalize across a large set of linguistic tasks. Fine-tuning occurred after the pre-training stage, in which the pre-trained model was adapted to specific tasks with the use of labelled datasets.

 With this, we showed that the recent success of pre-training in NLP had generalized to fine-tuning: transfer learning could work with generative pre-training as well. Of course,

GPT-1 was a fairly modest model by today's standards. GPT-2 and GPT-3 certainly take this first step further; they proceed to then pre-train these models on increasingly more human-sounding text until they can generate it at basically any length.

Scaling up and improved performance with GPT-2

GPT-2, released by OpenAI in 2019, was a leap in scale and sophistication over its predecessor. It incorporated 1.5 billion parameters trained on an immensely varied and large corpus of text, generating its outputs in a manner that seemed both logically contextual and coherent, an approximation for human-sounding text.

Text produced by GPT-2 was sometimes indistinguishable from authentic human text – and, at times, sufficiently plausible to deceive human readers. This technique of first pre-training the model on a large dataset and then fine-tuning it for a specific task was new to GPT-2.

Capitalizing on this architecture, it could handle a vast array of linguistic tasks without needing to be trained on task-specific data sets that were specially collected. A toy that could absorb humans and write back to the prompt, while simultaneously modelling human-sounding text, would invite experiments running all the way from the fanciful to the empirical.

At the fanciful end was text produced by GPT-2 that was, at times, indistinguishable from authentic human text – and, at times, sufficiently plausible to dupe human readers. There was delight at the sudden appearance of the narrative. At the more serious end, GPT-2 had the ability to answer questions authoritatively, sometimes even with a touch of flair.

GPT-2 was controversial because of fears that the full model might be used to create disinformation or misinformation leading to harm. This led OpenAI to not to release the full model to the public and to rely upon editors and fact-checkers, who are much harder to create than text-generating models. In contrast to GPT-2's release, the military and defense sectors have been predominantly closed: what scientists do in these fields is closely guarded information, and there are concerns among journal editors and publishers about publishing work that might reveal **dual-use** technologies, especially in cases where its military applications are deemed to be harmful When OpenAI did release GPT-2 (in stages that were fortuitously aligned with journalists' schedules), it demonstrated that the developers of advanced AI models have a responsibility to protect their work from dangerous and fake-news uses.

GPT-2's realization became the de facto NLP implementation standard, and its success paved the way for what was afterward dubbed GPT-3. However, perhaps its true significance lies in how it set technical and ethical considerations of AI research and deployment side by side, demonstrating on a large scale that the quest for increasingly human sounding yet seemingly inhuman computers was both possible and morally ambiguous.

Large scale and broad capabilities with GPT-3

GPT-3, unveiled in 2020 by OpenAI, was a major milestone in the growth of language models by both scale and capacity. GPT-3 was the third model in the GPT series of systems, but, with 175 billion parameters, was an order of magnitude larger than its predecessors, GPT-2 and GPT-1. The scale of GPT-3 allowed it to capture language statistics that achieved a remarkable level of linguistic fidelity in its text outputs, across a wide spectrum of tasks.

Going from GPT-2 to GPT-3 represents one of the largest leaps in scale and capacity throughout the history of OpenAI's language models. This is because GPT-2 is an impressive model in its own right, which showed us how a million-dollar investment in large-scale unsupervised learning can generate text that sounds coherent and appropriate. The introduction of GPT-3 then took this to a new level, increasing the number of parameters more than 100-fold to 175 billion.

This linear scale up from GPT-2 to GPT-3 could not be solely the exploration of what one could do with a language model of this scale. Increasing the capacity of the model (the parameter count) meant that GPT-3 can be trained to capture vastly more complex patterns in language. Compared with GPT-2, this superior language modelling ability led to improvements in the quality, coherence and diversity of the text it could produce. The scale of GPT-3 allowed it to perform a wide range of tasks with little or no prior fine-tuning, known as few-shot or even zero-shot learning. The success of GPT-3, in terms of quality of output but also in terms of its performance on a wide variety of tasks zero-shot or few-shot, represents a departure from **narrow task** fine-tuning.

They executed GPT-3 by training it on a heterogeneous, large corpus of text from books, articles, websites, and more. This meant, for instance, that GPT-3 could complete translation, summarization, question-answering and creative writing tasks with impressive fluidity, coherence and fidelity to human writing as its main output. In this way, GPT-3 was able to complete many tasks with little zero-shot or few-shot fine-tuning, that is, without explicitly training a model on how to do said tasks, but rather giving it a few examples of how to do something in order to complete a new task.

Generating human-sounding text that could be parleyed into conversation – writing essays and code alongside minimal human inputs – attracted a hefty wave of attention to the possible use-cases for GPT-3. Prominent visionaries envisioned the use of the model in providing automated customer service, and many publishers exhibited growing interest in its budding applications for content creation. Besides, the ethical dilemmas of deploying such a powerful model awoke fears over the consequences of GPT-3's widely acknowledged capacity to generate misinformation, bias and more.

By all measures, it marked a significant milestone in the development of language models, attesting to the power of large-scale neural networks in advancing the field of NLP, and to the work still needed in research and ethics surrounding the development and deployment of AI technologies worldwide.

Popularity and scale improvements with GPT 4

In 2023, OpenAI announced GPT-4, the fourth incarnation of their large-scale human-sounding language model. It built on architectural and operational decisions of GPT-1 and GPT-3, adding complexity and nuance to NLP tasks. To date, OpenAI has not announced just how complex GPT-4 is, though representatives say that GPT-4 is significantly more capable than GPT-3. The expected trend continues: bigger models to do a better job.

The technologies that went into creating GPT-4 included several innovations that differentiate it from its predecessors. These innovations include RL to improve fine-tuning and improved performance across the lossy-training space. This has made the model more effective both at responding to large prompts and generating contextually appropriate text. GPT-4 also has better multi-modal processing. It can perform tasks that require the integration of different types of input data into natural-sounding final outputs. For example, in combination with a visual foundation network, GPT-4 can incorporate text, images, and other data types to produce useful text outputs. GPT-3's use of 175 billion parameters was a leap from the previous 12 billion parameters.

The increase in scale alone would not have been significant had it just been a matter of adding more parameters. It was an expansion of all levels of the underlying data, training processes, and model architecture. The increased scale enabled GPT-4 to better capture subtler patterns in language (and, as OpenAI admits, reproduced its adversarial behavior on text labels), more capably capture context, respond to queries with greater accuracy and coherence, engage in more sophisticated reasoning tasks, engage with a wider variety of input types, and hold themselves together more consistently over longer runs of text-generation.

Another important part of the rollout of GPT-4 has been to allow users to customize their experience to minimize the potential for causing harm by providing more robust ways of avoiding biases and reducing the risk of the model generating content that might be harmful or lead people astray. The financial success of both GPT-3 and GPT-4 is a reflection of the demand for AI models of this capacity and points to the need for ongoing monitoring of the ways in which such potent resources are taken up, especially if we want to be able to harness it in safe and appropriate ways.

GPT-4 represents an important step forward for the field of AI by providing improved functionality and applicability while overcoming some of the shortcomings and ethical debates that were raised with previous versions – and this attempt to emulate the human brain will continue to change the world around us.

GPT-4o as the latest innovation

This model was seen as a version of GPT-4 designed for real-time language processing and adapting to conduct in conversational AI tasks. While GPT-4 itself marked a leap in scale and capability of these models, we decided to develop a sub-model of GPT-4, called

GPT-4o, for large-scale acceleration and optimization to confront the focused challenges of online and real-time, time/response-sensitive and interactive tasks. The models are intended for deployment in time-sensitive, high-latency tasks, such as conversations.

To put GPT-4o into action, the developers made a series of tweaks that were targeted towards its use cases, including the following:

- They optimized the model to be run efficiently without compromising on quality of output by leveraging modelling pruning, and architecture changes that together reduce the computational footprint of the model.

- They implemented improved techniques for contextual awareness that retain the coherence and relevance of extended interactions even when run on compressed devices with limited processing ability or bandwidth.

The second key aspect in the implementation of GPT-4o was its robustness. This model was both trained and fine-tuned on many datasets, including training over human-sounding text and further training over real-time conversations. This means that the model has been trained to handle inputs in an interruption-prone, semi-complete, and dynamically changing conversational context, which makes it ideal for use cases, like customer service, virtual assistant, or bot training applications as well as use cases related to real-time content generation.

GPT-4o, for example, deliberately refers to a change in scale after producing models to mimic the nuances of writing. For example, hypothetically, we make an explicit tradeoff from optimization for a specific real-time application to inscrutably massive-scale in order to maximize the power of these models to process natural language in a human-sounding way. GPT-4o was created with **primacy of speed and generality in a constrained** environment, but GPT-4, with its scale-up, had **primacy of raw power and depth**.

Optimized for execution speed and efficiency while maintaining strong performance across a wide range of use cases (GPT-4 flies first class; GPT-4o takes the bus), GPT-4o uses a smaller set of parameters than GPT-4 – but still enough to produce some darn good text Decisions to prune the model intuitively embed trade-offs at inference time into the training process. Here, training goals are balanced relative to constraints. Here, compromise is that tightrope one must walk, balancing competing forces while maintaining stability.

By contrast, the scale leap from GPT-4o represents a retreat from the efficiency of its predecessors, and a return to maximizing the specific model's ability to process data with high dimensionality and complexity. The sheer growth in parameters and data points, that increased GPT-4's scale, served to improve GPT-4's sophistication, eclipsing the efficiency of its predecessors. However, GPT-4 displays increased sophistication in language generation scenarios that required more reasoning and processing of information. The user interface for all the previous GPT version is accessible via the OpenAI website for Chat GPT: **https://chatgpt.com**. You can see it in the following figure, it is a simple text entry. You simply click on the text box and begin typing your prompt. In the upper left you have a drop-down menu to select the model to use. Today's available models are GPT-4-o. GPT-4o mini, and GPT-4. These are updated as new versions come out which is quite often. See *Figure 6.1* for the interface to the most current ChatGPT as of this writing:

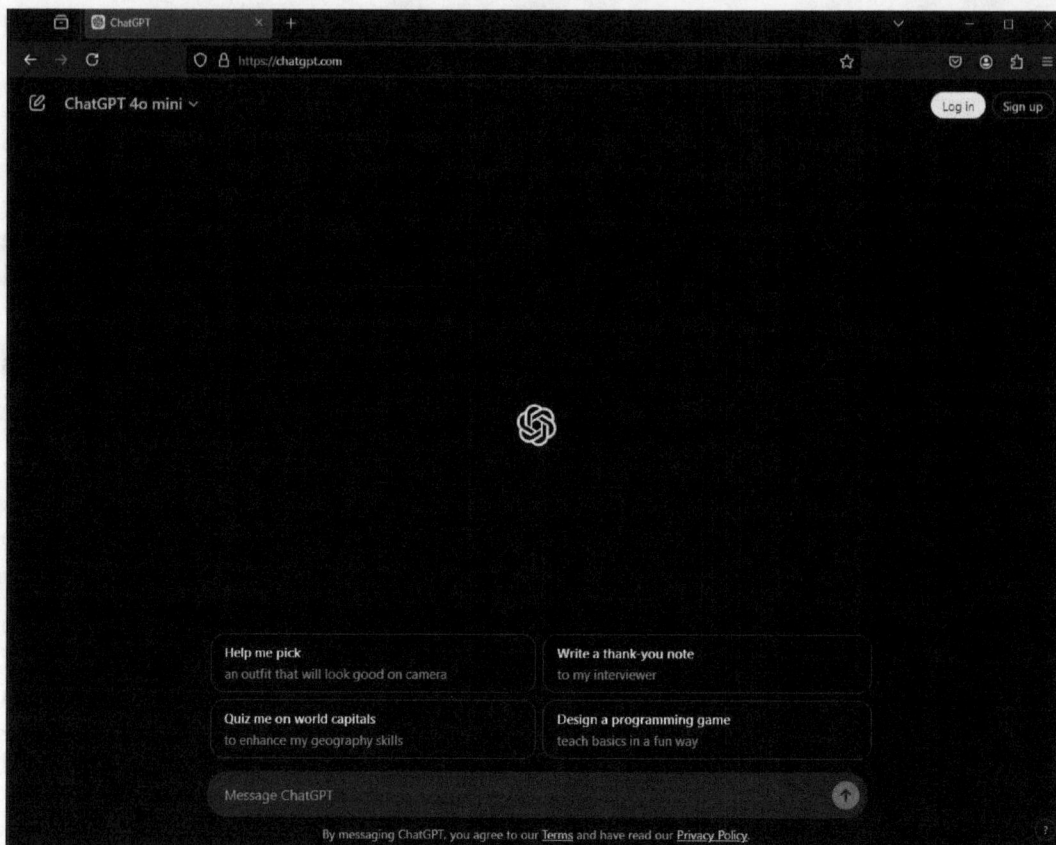

Figure 6.1: The default ChatGPT interface

GPT-4o was implemented as a highly optimized variant of GPT-4, designed to deliver high-quality language processing in environments where speed, efficiency, and adaptability are critical. Its development highlights the ongoing efforts to tailor AI models to specific operational requirements, ensuring that the benefits of advanced language models can be realized across a broader range of practical applications.

Technical details of GPT models

What are the architectures and training schemes that lie beneath the phenomenon of making a body move while calculating a model that can read like a human, and yet having all those different functions? GPT models hinge on architecture and training abilities in an essential way. They deploy the Transformer that we previously discussed; as we know, it forms an alternative approach to sequences by using self-attention, in contrast to RNNs, which compute a scalar representation based on nearby words in local processing units. The attention mechanism comes in handy to measure words' relations over long distances.

Architecture and training

Recapitulating rapidly, the attention mechanism at the core of the Transformer architecture computes attention between all pairs of words in the sequence involved; each word produces an attention score for every other word, and these scores are used to decide how much attention the model should pay to which word while generating the output. Crucially, the architecture makes use of multi-head attention, which allows the model to capture different kinds of relationships between words all at once. The output of the attention block is fed through a feedforward neural network, followed by layer normalization and residual connections that stabilize and speed up training.

The two-phase process these models are trained on – pre-training and fine-tuning – involves first exposing the model to an unlabeled corpus of text data (pre-training, which is an unsupervised training process) to learn to predict the next word, given the context of previous words, through a specific training objective known as language modelling. Models pre-trained in this manner learn robust notions of linguistic structure, syntax and semantics via their sheer exposure to text. Pre-training involves minimizing the cross-entropy loss – a measure that calculates how distant the probabilities assigned to predicted words are to the actual word in the sequence. Fine-tuning uses and adjusts the language knowledge learned in pre-training, allowing the model to perform its specific task while retaining general linguistic knowledge as much as possible.

GPT models strike a balance between over-engineered complexity and straight-up brute-force efficiency in today's AI. The winning combination in these models is the Transformer architecture itself, which excels at parallelizing across multiple points in a text and incorporating broad context as each unit is evaluated. However, that is not the end of the story. When used together properly with dedicated specialized components, large-scale language models like GPT prove effective at many real-world, large-scale natural language processing tasks. For broad and practical applications, large-scale, pre-trained models seem to be the key to modern AI.

Learning GPT's architecture

The architecture of GPT models has been finely tuned to the specific task of NLP. GPT models typically use decoder-only architecture, rather than the encoder-decoder architecture of the original Transformer, which was designed to handle both encoding and decoding as needed in translation tasks, for example decoder-only transformers are used for language modelling, where the goal is to predict the next word in the sequence, based on the sequence of words already generated. First, we are going to talk about how transformers, which we discussed in the last few chapters, are put together to get the architecture of Chat GPT.

The network architecture of a GPT is based on multiple layers of a Transformer decoder. A GPT's architecture consists of many identical decoder layers, which themselves are made up of two main components: a masked multi-head self-attention mechanism and a position-wise fully connected feed-forward network. The layers are **stacked** and, for GPT-1, there are 12 layers (for GPT-4, 48 layers and a number of layers that increased in later versions of GPTs to support larger parameter counts and more sophisticated modelling capabilities).

Key components of GPT architecture:

- **Masked multi-head self-attention:** The self-attention mechanism allows GPT to attend to different words in the input sequence for encoding and decoding text. The attention mechanism in GPT is the masked version – it only attends to earlier tokens in the sequence during training, ensuring that the model predicts the next token according to the entire context without **cheating** by looking ahead. This is essential to the autoregressive nature of the model – text is generated one token at a time. Multi-head attention comprises multiple independent attention mechanisms each feeding into the same model. Each head captures a different form or dependency between the words in the sequence, and these are then concatenated and then passed through a linear transformation – a process that allows the model to capture multiple relationships between the tokens of the sequence simultaneously.

- **Feed-forward networks:** The attention mechanism in each layer is a feed-forward neural network comprising two linear transformations separated by a non-linear activation function, typically **Gaussian Error Linear Unit (GELU)** for later versions of GPT. These networks are applied using a separate parameter set to each position in the sequence receiving attention, so the model can both refine the attended information and transform it into a more abstract representation.

- **Positional encoding:** Because the Transformer architecture itself does not have any notion of sequential processing, GPT models have to add something called positional encodings to indicate where each word in the sequence is located. The positional encodings are added as additional dimensions to the input embeddings, and they help the model understand that this word, for instance, is the third word in the sequence, and not the fifth.

- **Layer normalization and residual connections:** Every sub-layer (the attention mechanism, and the feed-forward network) is followed by layer normalization and a residual connection. Layer normalization, by scaling the output of each layer using the information about the distribution of the inputs to the layer (more precisely, it normalizes the inputs so that its feature-space direction and norm are similar across layers), mitigates the issue of exploding or vanishing gradients, and puts the inputs to each layer on a similar scale.

Architectural evolution summary across GPT versions is as follows:

- **GPT-1:** The initial model, with 12 layers and 117 million parameters, demonstrated the feasibility of the Transformer decoder architecture for text generation.

- **GPT-2:** This version expanded the architecture to 48 layers with 1.5 billion parameters, introducing improvements in both depth and scale, which seriously enhanced the model's text generation capabilities.

- **GPT-3:** Evolved to have 96 layers (compare this with 12, 18 or 24 in the previous models) and a 175 billion parameters – enough that virtually any prompt can be given to this model and have it produce a (mostly) coherent response with only a few lines of fine-tuning functions. Deepening the model and, more importantly, widening its parameter depth, allowed GPT-3 to capture more nuanced linguistic forms and generate more believable, context-rich text.

- **GPT-4/4o:** Though some features of GPT-4's architecture are currently a corporate secret, we do know that it is scored gains over GPT-3 by increasing the number of layers and parameters, continuing to push the GPT-3 performance curve up for still larger and more complex challenges.

Architecturally speaking, we should really refer to GPT-specific architecture as its own unique architecture, consisting of an extensively distilled Transformer decoder optimized to this precision task in autoregressive text generation, systematically arranged and appended in four stages of computation: processing the input; transforming it into condensed internal states; generating its output; optimizing and fine-tuning language. GPT models, therefore, embody one of the world's most powerful NLP agents.

Training GPT and the need for computational power

Training of GPT models is a computationally expensive process where a huge number of parameters across multiple layers in a deep neural network are optimized. Following standard practice, a large corpus of text data is used to train these models unsupervised. Unsupervised methods involve training a language model based on large amounts of text data coming from a wide mix of domains, such as books, articles and websites. They can help predict the next word in a sequence given its context (words immediately preceding). Such tasks of predicting text are repeated millions of times, whereby parameters of the models are gradually fine-tuned to minimize the difference between predicted and the actual words.

The magnitude of GPT models (which can consist of hundreds of billions of parameters) demands computational resources on a similar scale. Training is done on large hardware, frequently using cluster configurations of **graphics processing units (GPUs)** or **tensor processing units (TPUs)**. These are custom hardware designed to handle the massive parallel computations necessary to process large datasets and to update the parameters of the model in order to reduce its error over time by way of backpropagation. This process, for models of the scale of GPT, demands not only vast quantities of computing hardware but also vast amounts of time – and not just days or weeks, but the repetitive computation can easily pile into months upon the clusters of these very pricey processors.

Demand for computational power also increases due to the need for a high level of exploration and experimentation. All language models are still subject to calibration, and researchers often try different configurations of the model – for example, adjusting the learning rate, adjusting the batch size or the number of layers, etc. This raises demand for more computational resources because between different models, size matters because their evaluation scores are so noisy. It takes many iterations to train a GPT model, and each consumes more computational resources. In summary, training a cutting-edge language model involves lots of computational resources, and it is a costly experiment. This gives us a sense of the challenges in creating cutting-edge language models, as well as the importance of the widely available high-performance computing facilities.

Language modelling and transfer learning

These GPT models learn language patterns using an approach in machine learning, known as unsupervised learning, through a technique commonly called language modelling. Training involves making a model capable of predicting which word will come next in a sequence given the words that have come before in the text, a task that involves trying to distill the patterns and structures of the language.

GPT models learning language patterns

The first thing to do is saturate the model with a massive and very varied corpus of text data, covering every imaginable topic, style and grammatical structure you could think of. In this text, however, no labels are attached to any elements, such as key words or topics to classify into labels. The model learns by guessing the next word in a given sequence, and correcting its parameters accordingly, so each time the model gets a prediction wrong, it redefines its parameters in such a way as to reduce the prediction error. All that is repeated over millions of examples, and the model tends to internalize complex linguistic patterns related to grammar, syntax and semantics, as well as more subtle features, for example, tone and style, and context.

Through the interaction of self-attention mechanisms that weight where to look across the text relative to itself, and the cross-attention mechanisms that weigh where to look across the text relative to a prompt, the architecture of the Transformer model drives a process of learned reading, steering the model to depend appropriately on far-away bits of text, while suturing sentence knife-points together over long textual distances, thereby enabling coherent and context-appropriate text.

As it processes more text, the model can form an ever-richer picture of how words relate to one another in context, and in turn produce text that is syntactically and semantically accurate – which is to say, indistinguishable from how humans might respond. By the completion of training, the model will have learned how to complete a wide range of natural language processing tasks, from text completion to conversation simulation.

This form of exposure-driven learning, thus empowers GPT models to generalize across different natural language tasks without explicit training for each of them, highlighting the potential of unsupervised learning in the AI realm.

Transfer learning and its benefits

Transfer learning – namely, training an ML model on a large, general-purpose atomic dataset initially and fine-tuning it on an atomic task-specific dataset later – is central to the development and use of GPT models.

Within the context of the GPT models, this comes in the form of pre-training, when the model is presented with very large amounts of data in an unsupervised manner, so that the general patterns, structures, and abstract relationships in the data, such as frequency profiles of words or phrases, sentences of varying lengths and structures, relationships between sentences in the text, or connections between the content word of a sentence and the rest of the sentence content, can be internalized. The pre-trained model will already have some broad-based knowledge about the text.

The second phase, fine-tuning, comes afterward when a model pre-trained on a general-purpose corpus is further trained (on the same model architecture) on a more specific task-oriented corpus with fewer examples. As a result of pre-training, the fine-tuning process involves fewer steps, less data and compute to reach a comparable performance to standard supervised training on the task-specific corpus.

This means the usefulness of transfer learning is threefold:

- **Saves on computational resources**: It significantly lowers the amount of data and time that models require to train on, by learning from already pre-trained models.

- **Improvement in performance**: Training on a broad range of language tasks means that the model gains a greater understanding of the language, which can be applied more generally in specific tasks, even when we only have limited labelled data to know exactly how to perform well on them.

- **Increased flexibility:** As the same pre-trained model can be adapted to many different tasks, we do not need to re-train our models to transfer the knowledge of the task to another.

Transfer learning, thus, plays a central role in the success of GPT models in achieving – often the best – results on a huge array of natural language processing tasks while using the least resources and being the most flexible.

Comparison with other AI models

The typical GPT model contains hundreds of billions of parameters, which means that it can produce very fluent text with consistently sound contextual choices that outperform much smaller models in assessments of human likeness. It also means that the GPT scales up dramatically in computational expense to gather training examples and make inferences.

GPT models stand out due to their large-scale, multi-purpose architecture and generation prowess. Other powerful models, such as BERT, often perform better on tasks that require more deep contextual understanding. The choice between GPT and other language models depends on the specific need of the task, whether contextual generation or comprehension is required, and available resources and desired trade-offs in performance. We anticipate seeing more integration and hybridization of the models we have introduced in this essay as AI continues to evolve, yielding more powerful solutions to complex language-processing tasks.

Applications and impact of GPT models

The arrival of GPT models in NLP has made it possible to improve the ability of chatbots or virtual assistants, enhance the process of language translation and summarization, as well as improve sentiment analysis and text classification and detection. All these areas have been helped by GPT's language understanding and generation skills.

These models will be used for generally improving chatbots and virtual assistants, improving translation and summarizations, sentiment analysis and text classification among other things. GPT has set a new benchmark in leveraging human-sounding text, moving AI within NLP tasks towards being orders of magnitude better than human performance.

Enhancing chatbots and virtual assistants

Since GPT models can capture the aspects of human conversation, they take the chatbot idea – a machine simulating an agreeable conversational partner, and really maximize it. Old-school chatbots were limited to canned responses and rule-based systems that were ok for simple queries or giving out basic information but failed when asked questions outside the predefined training datasets or when users trailed off mid-utterance.

Language translation and summarization

GPT models have contributed to text summarization and language translation. Older translation systems sometimes struggled to preserve the finer details of source-language nuance (for example, idiomatic expressions or context-specific meanings), because older systems were not equipped to handle this type of contextual specificity. GPT models are now trained on tens of billions of words from many diverse languages, and as a result, they have improved translation quality. They can create paraphrases that stay true to the source-language nuance and context while avoiding the jarring style of older machine translation systems that served as our benchmarks a decade ago.

Sentiment analysis and text classification

Moreover, GPT models have also improved the accuracy and efficiency of other tasks related to text classification, such as sentiment analysis. Since sentiment analysis algorithms must assess or recognize opinions about subjects that arise in text, a GPT model that demonstrates an improved understanding of context is likely to also increase the accuracy of sentiment analysis. These improvements take into account situations where emotion is coded implicitly and where the primary syntax and terminology are expressing a wide range of meaning, as in the case of irony. At other times, these models help to sense the abstract themes of a text and to classify what has been written, helping to increase the precision of text classification. For example, they enable the detection of the intent behind text, the recognition of slang and stereotypes, and the categorizing of text into predetermined labels. The ability to recognize intent is useful in content moderation on social media, while improvements in general text classification can boost market analysis, recommendation systems, and more.

Creative applications

Importantly for creative writing (and storytelling more broadly), GPT models can be used to generate ideas, formulate plots, and write character dialogue; they can even generate storylines, indicate plot twists, or even write entire passages in a variety of styles to help writers through writers' block and find new creative pathways. If a writer is stuck for a storyline, GPT models can often generate one. However, GPT models can also reproduce known genres, tones or voices, opening up new avenues of creative experimentation with various narrative genres or styles. Writers can use GPT models to hone different forms of narrative through mimicry and can even co-create content with GPT models by having a model write a draft that they then refine for publication.

Marketing opportunities

GPT models have become an invaluable asset in the task of creating content for marketing purposes. They can quickly generate well-written content that is engaging for the intended readership. Marketers and content creators can reduce the amount of effort they put into producing articles, blog posts, social media updates, and advertisements targeted at different audiences. GPT models will be the hardest workers in this field. All they require is to be trained to understand the trends among the target demographic, cultural sensibilities and how to adapt language according to the context. Second, they can produce a number of different variations for the same content. For example, a small team can create five different versions of an article and feed them into the GPT model. The model can then identify which one works best in getting the reader's attention. This works well for digital marketing purposes as the content needs to be continually refreshed to maintain interest.

Educational content creation

As part of educational content, GPT models create interactive learning scenarios and educational games. For personalized learning experiences where content can be adapted to the learner's level, tastes, and interests, GPT models can create self-adjusting quizzes, explanatory texts, or even fictional scenarios. Tapping into the entertainment value of learning content, edutainment editorial applications can harness the power of creativity of GPT models to create information that can be entertaining and educational at the same time, bringing complex or risky topics to the masses in an attractive way.

The ultimate chatbot

In *Chapter 1, A Brief Overview of ML and AI*, we considered the Turning test, the benchmark for artificial intelligence, proposed in 1950 by *Alan Turing*, according to which an entity can be considered as intelligent as a human if it cannot be distinguished from a person in conversation. The ability of modern GPT models to generate human-sounding text is remarkable – they are able to produce coherent, relevant and often insightful responses to a wide range of prompts, frequently engaging in conversation that is virtually indistinguishable from that of a person over the human-seeming text he produces. It is difficult to get a true sense over a single conversation, it is really the test of time that will determine when AI achieves that state.

To strictly pass the Turing Test in the literal sense, something more than just producing text that looks like a human is required: it must understand meta-communicative norms, such as the contexts in which indirect speech acts are appropriate, as well as a whole range of human experiences. While state-of-the-art GPT models are enormously impressive feats of technology, they remain essentially pattern-recognition systems that communicate by responding to probabilities – rather than actual comprehension. Genuine understanding, reasoning and consciousness are key aspects of human intelligence that are fundamentally absent in generative models such as GPTs. These models can occasionally serve up answers that, even though they superficially make sense, expose their shortcomings by demonstrating their inability to reason, discern context, be sensitive to ethical considerations, or any of a multitude of other human attributes.

Although, they have come much closer to mimicking the textual output that Turing's original idea for running the test entailed – in other words, most GPT models today pass what we might call the textual Turing Test – it is definitely not yet true that a GPT model also passes what could be called the thinking Turing Test; that is, that GPT models are really emulating human understanding or real human intelligence. In other words, although GPT models might have come very close to passing Turing's original idea of the test, it is still definitely not true that they have passed the fuller, richer, multi-faceted Turing Test in its more modern and robust sense.

Conclusion

This chapter dealt with some of the details of prompt engineering, which is becoming an essential skill for harnessing the power of generative AI models – especially those sub-branches of a probably approach among AI researchers, such as the GPT series of OpenAI. Over the past decade, as AI models have grown in scale and complexity and now include humans in the world-building efforts – we are essentially training the AI model on data that includes, among many other things, people like Musk and you, there is a drive for prompt engineering as a crucial skillset for using these sophisticated and massive models, whose outputs can be leveraged if prompted appropriately. This chapter gave the reader a historical and theoretical perspective on the evolution of GPT models followed by some best practices on prompt engineering.

In the next chapter, we will specifically go deep into the prompt ecosystem. The simplest prompt of all was one of the first ones ever `What is ChatGPT?` Of course, there are other GPT models and we will talk to them too.

Join our book's Discord space

Join the book's Discord Workspace for Latest updates, Offers, Tech happenings around the world, New Release and Sessions with the Authors:

https://discord.bpbonline.com

CHAPTER 7

The Prompt Ecosystem

Introduction

This chapter will truly begin to delve deep into the mechanics of an excellent prompt. It offers an insightful exploration into the field of prompt engineering, a crucial aspect of working with transformer-based models in **artificial intelligence (AI)** and **machine learning (ML)**. It starts by defining prompt engineering and detailing its objectives, explaining the significance of crafting effective prompts to enhance the functionality and accuracy of AI systems.

Structure

In this chapter, you will learn about the following topics:

- The prompt ecosystem
- Components of the prompt ecosystem
- Dynamics of prompt creation

Objectives

This chapter will walk us through the results components of what makes a good prompt, and how to understand the interplay between the sections of a prompt. By understanding the elements of a prompt, you will have a foundation of what you need to build any prompt in the future. This is effectively learning the structure and process to follow for all future prompts.

The prompt ecosystem

The prompt ecosystem involves the complex and dynamic system that surrounds the interaction between human input and AI models, specifically those based on transformer architectures. More precisely, a prompt is a structured input that can be used to guide the behavior of an AI model, which may be understood as an input to both a question and a directive that is interpreted by the AI model to produce an answer. The prompt ecosystem, therefore, is about the complete ecology of prompts – their creation, iteration and use; the feedback mechanisms that feed into continuous optimization; and more.

Conceptual overview

We will speak about the anatomy of a prompt, what makes a good one, what to think about, and how to improve yours. You are most likely reading this book to learn and then increase your skill set to be a prompt engineer. Let us use a prompt to ask about a prompt. The most basic prompt is a short question. So, let us use the Bing Copilot AI at **https:// www.bing.com/chat.** We will ask it **what is a prompt for AI?** and look at its answer in *Figure 7.1*. We will also learn why a prompt this short is missing a large amount of helpful information to get the answer you want. While this will work well now, recall that simple prompts get simple and basic answers:

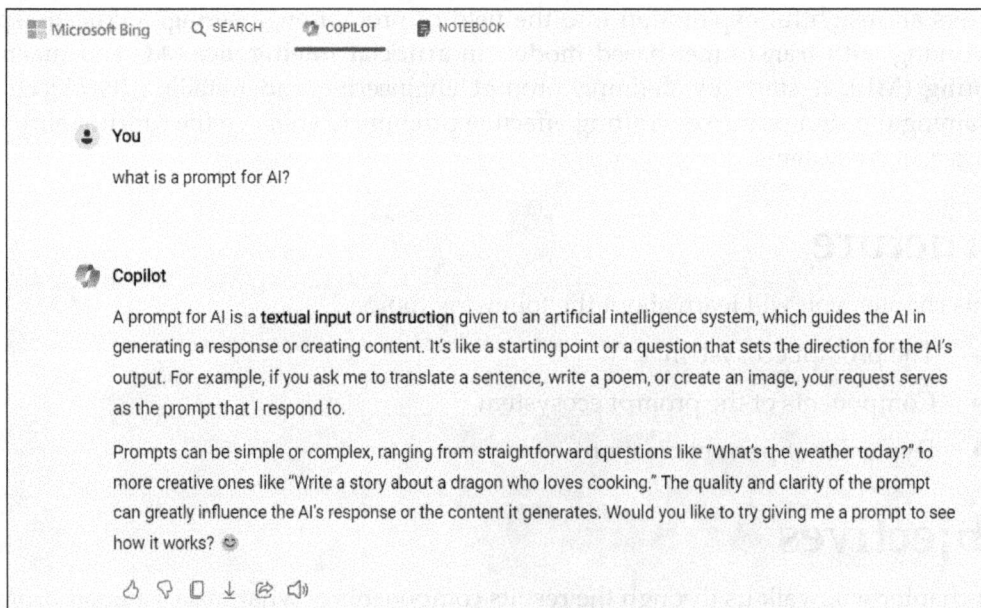

Figure 7.1: *What you use a prompt to ask about a prompt*

Prompt ecosystem's role in AI-driven models

By prompt ecosystem, we refer to the complex system that encompasses how human inputs influence AI models – especially models using transformer architectures – and how these models are able to develop insights regarding human input and create an output from it. A prompt can be thought of as a properly constructed input that influences AI models in specific ways – it is essentially a question and command that an AI model is told to read and answer. The prompt ecosystem then entails the entire lifecycle of a prompt – how they are created, tweaked, and deployed, as well as the feedback systems that help to improve them iteratively.

However, in AI models based on techniques such as **natural language processing** (**NLP**), prompts are not so many inputs to the model as inputs to the human operating the model: they are the fundamental mechanism by which human intent is translated into machine action. The nomenclature committees are currently hard at work and are not to be dismissed: around prompts, as around any other technology, thrives an ecosystem, encompassing not only prompts but also the means and tools for generating, testing, and refining them. The more sophisticated and capable AI models become, the more the upstream elements of this ecosystem begin to act as constraints on their behavior, and the more central the prompt engineering becomes. A well-designed prompt can influence the way an AI system formulates an answer, shifting its direction and usefulness.

Differentiating from other artificial intelligence subsystems

Although it is important for the prompt ecosystem, it is structurally distinct from other AI systems that make up the AI architecture, such as traditional AI subsystems: the model architecture itself (such as transformers, neural networks, and so on), data preprocessing modules, training pipeline, and evaluation modules. Those subsystems naturally worry about the internal mechanics of what the AI can do – how it takes in data, how it learns and generalizes from examples, and so on.

In contrast, the prompt ecosystem spans the interaction layer: the pathway by which external intent travels from the user to the model and through which it encourages the model's internal workings to return a desired, contextually relevant output. Whereas the model architecture is largely invariant upon the task, the prompt ecosystem is highly volatile. The shape of the prompt ecosystem is constantly liquid and ever responsive to the fluctuating needs of the user, as well as the specific demands of a particular task over time. The prompt ecosystem is a fundamentally unique and important subsystem of AI.

Shaping model outputs

The prompt is at the core of how an AI model works because the prompt defines what kind of response the model will generate. The prompt is the lens that the AI looks through to understand the task – you need to tell the model not only what it should attend by telling it what you want it to look for but also how it should do that by defining how you want it to think about the problem. A poorly written prompt can produce outputs that are irrelevant, misleading, or nonsense, no matter how powerful a model is at its core. Similarly, a well-crafted prompt can apply all the power of that model in order to produce a precise and insightful output that is exactly what the user was asking for.

The prominence of prompts is further underscored by the fact that they form the primary operational frontier between non-expert users and a complicated range of AI systems. As AI continues to expand into numerous domains – from healthcare and finance to the creative arts – the potential to use prompts to make AI increasingly accessible and effective is an urgent and rapidly expanding area of endeavor.

Importance of the prompt ecosystem

In the field of text-to-text translation, a model is prompted with a human-sounding input and returns a human-sounding response. Since transformer-based models are highly sensitive to input phrasing, structure, and context, small changes to the phrasing can yield major changes in the resulting text. This is a major reason why specialized focus on learning how to create prompts is so important today.

Significance of prompts in artificial intelligence

The prompt is the genesis of interacting with AI, it is super-important. The reason for this is that transformer-based models, perhaps the most impactful architecture in NLP of the current decade, involving widely known architectures like **Generative Pre-trained Transformer** (**GPT**) and others, are designed to generate text that sounds like a human wrote it based on the prompt you feed it. Think about how central the form and shape of your prompts are to their success.

The value of the prompt regime is further highlighted by its impact on model behavior at a more granular level – for example, in tasks such as text generation, summarization, or translation, the prompt can determine the register, style, length, and depth of the response; and in more complex applications, such as coding or decision-making, prompts can determine the logic, accuracy and moral values encoded in the model outputs. Given its growing use in sensitive areas, the importance of learning how to engineer prompts in AI systems cannot be overstated – it will directly shape the trustworthiness of how we build AI.

Implications on artificial intelligence applications

The prompt ecosystem also points to much greater stakes than mere text generation. NLP applications, such as machine translation, sentiment analysis, and question answering would be impossible without prompts that nudge AI systems toward more accurate responses. In these applications, the prompt can affect not only the correctness of the AI response but also its relevance and cultural relativism. In machine translation, an imprecise prompt could result in technically correct but culturally off-putting translations. Similarly, prompt framing could influence the sentiment that an AI system detects in a piece of text, such as anger, sadness or happiness, leading to different results.

The prompt ecosystem is key to providing users with outputs from decision-making algorithms that are not merely correct but ethically justifiable and otherwise satisfactory. Consider, for instance, an automated system used for credit scoring, evaluation of job candidates, or medical diagnosis. In such contexts, the prompt sets the parameters and variables that a model will use when making a decision. A well-designed prompt will allow a model to make a judgment unbiased, considering all relevant factors – while a poorly designed prompt risks decisions that perpetuate bias or ignore variables that should be taken into account.

We can already see this in creative forward-projection uses of AI, such as text generation, image creation, and game design. Here, too, prompts can spark inventions, direct creative endeavors, and even define the scope of what is deemed novel and allowable. The entire domain of the prompt ecosystem, then, not just its constituent models and data, also impacts both the formal and creative outputs of AI applications on human users. It even influences their ethical and ethical-creative implications.

With the continual growth of the capabilities of AI, and the expansion of its uses, the prompt ecosystem will continue to play a crucial role in determining the success or failure of AI systems. The ability to navigate and manipulate it will be an indispensable key for anyone engaged in building, deploying or using AI technologies. By doing so, they can prevent the missteps that have often marred the development of AI and allow its critics to gain an advantage.

Components of the prompt ecosystem

The prompt objective is the cornerstone – it defines the aim of the prompt. The prompt objective dictates what the AI model is supposed to achieve – its guiding function. Clearly specifying the objective will ensure that the model generates a response targeted towards the correct aspect of the request. If the objective is to generate a technical explanation, then the prompt also needs to explicitly specify it as such – directing the model to produce an explanation that is the most technical, detailed and lowest-level, but also one that is specific to a technical audience. A prompt with a poor specification of the objective may produce responses that are off-target or miss the mark of the user.

Structural elements

Understanding the structural elements of a prompt is fundamental to effective, prompt engineering. A prompt is not merely a query or statement; it is a carefully constructed tool that guides the AI model toward producing a specific and relevant output. Each prompt has four high-level components. Those components are objective, the context of the prompt, the instructions to the AI model, and any constraints put upon it.

Anatomy of a prompt

A context provides a model with additional information about the task as represented by the prompt that might not be explicitly stated. It can use this information to help generate a meaningful, likely response that relates to the prompt. This element serves to frame the prompt within a specific context by providing it with various contextual details, assumptions, or constraints that are relevant to the model's task:

- Instructions are the bits of the prompt that tell the model how to get to that goal. They create parameters around the kinds of formatting, tone, and structure the requested output should follow. They might tell the model to **Keep it short!** or to publish the output as bullet points instead of paragraphs when possible. When done effectively, instructions can help limit what the model does to the output that best approximates what the user expects in response to what the input means and how it should be delivered. Instructions are especially helpful for tasks in which the user has very specific parameters around how the output should be afforded, such as writing code snippets, formal reports, or more creative writing.

- Constraints are the limitations baked into the prompt that constrain the scope and reach of model responses. Constraints can refer to exclusions – for example, when a prompt asserts that the model should not mention X or should not use stylistic feature Y. Constraints can also limit the length or complexity of model responses. Constraints help us control the scope and reach of a model's responses. For example, consider an instruction like: **Provide a technical explanation of X – but don't mention ethical considerations.** Or consider a prompt that places a constraint by directing a model to discuss just one feature of the assigned topic, thus limiting the model's agenda from branching out to cover everything under the sun.

Types of prompts

Writers can generate prompts of three broad types: informative, interrogative, and directive. Each of these different types is associated with a different purpose and a different model behavior or output.

The goal of informative prompts is information extraction from the model. They are often used to query the model for facts, explanations or descriptions. Compared with directive prompts, informative prompts provide a more specific goal and context, as the prompt asks the model to provide detailed information on a specific topic. Like directive prompts, the goal and context of informative prompts also indicate what is required. For example, the prompt **Tell me about photosynthesis in plants** – the counterpart of the previously mentioned directive prompt – requires the model to describe the process of photosynthesis in a comprehensive and accurate way. The understanding of human behavior implied by informative prompts is that the model should gather and deliver relevant knowledge in an accurate and comprehensive way.

Since an interrogative prompt is phrased as a question, the model already knows that it is being asked to give a very limited answer: it needs to provide information that answers the question (hence the interrogative nature of this kind of prompt). This narrowing of the request to deal with direct answers means there is a substantially lower likelihood that it will stray into unnecessary details. With the prompt **What is the capital of France?**, there is less likelihood that the model will talk about the weather in the south or the color of its rivers. The meaning of interrogative prompts is that information provided through these prompts will be specific and (caveats notwithstanding) expected to be directly relevant to the prompt rather than covering general information.

A tells the model to do a certain thing or to generate some kind of output. It is action-oriented, often containing more than one instruction and detailing the how of the task. For example: Directive: **Paraphrase this input into sounding natural while retaining quotes and citations.** With directive prompts, there is a greater degree of control over the model's behavior, and the user can fashion the output according to their specifications.

Different types of prompts will generate the response in a different way – which gives prompt engineers different tools to work with so they can understand the implications of different types of prompts, and tailor their prompts accordingly, ensuring their AI output is pertinent and effective.

Dynamics of prompt creation

One key strategy is clarity: the prompt needs to be clear, well-stated and overt, leaning on discrete ends. This means practicing with a particular language over general language or, over prompt-openings that invite a potentially indeterminate result: **Please explain a concept in a three-paragraph essay** should become: **Please explain the concept of blockchain technology in three paragraphs - with particular regard to financial services.**

Crafting effective prompts

Being good at prompt crafting is both an art and a science. It demands an intimate understanding of a prompt's role in an AI model, as well as its relationship to humans – what it is used for, how it helps, why it facilitates the achievement of a task's goal over an alternative task's goal, and why that matters. In general, well-crafted prompts achieve an alignment between the external structure of the prompt itself, its semantic content, and the user's distal goals. That is because the prompt sits at the narrowest interface of human meaning and machine output. Several key techniques exist for developing good prompts.

Context is how parts of the prompt relate to one another and the broader ask. Sufficient context within the prompt can greatly improve the relevance and accuracy of the model's output. This might mean providing background information, explicitly specifying the audience, or imposing constraints that focus the model's efforts. Contextualized prompts help the model to better understand the ecological context in which a task has emerged and, therefore, make more finely-tuned responses.

Case studies of good and bad prompt design enable us to illustrate how these techniques work. A good prompt might ask the model to paraphrase a technical summary for people who do not read the original paper, perhaps specifying its ideal length, tone, and what you want the model to cover. A good prompt might then produce a short, structured summary for a non-technical audience. In contrast, a bad prompt might simply ask the model to `Talk about Medical ethics`, providing no focus or constraints and producing something that is, at best, a little too generic for practical use and, at worst, potentially creating output that could be improper or very inaccurate.

Prompt iteration and refinement

Effective prompts are rarely a one-off, instant achievement; instead, they often come to be only through iterations over time. Each step of user interaction can help indicate to them what sort of model they are dealing with. When users see the outputs that their prompts generate, they start to get a sense of what kinds of instructions they respond to, in what ways, and how it does so.

One critical strategy for prompt iteration is iterative testing, where the user assigns a rating to each of their prompts to gauge which versions lead to more factual and relevant outputs. They might try each prompt with different variations – a higher level of detail, simpler wording, or a change in constraints. With each rerun, they learn how the model responds to specific changes and can tweak their prompt until they get their desired outcome. If the first set of prompts sounds overly technical, they might try to simplify the language or add other constraints to zero in on tangible applications.

A second method is feedback incorporation: upon receiving feedback on the outputs produced based on a user's prompt (by the model itself using self-evaluation mechanisms or by peers or domain experts), a user may not only evaluate the usefulness of the prompt, but also detect specific ways in which it could be improved the next time (for example, to better describe the context or alter the scope of the request). Figuring out effective feedback mechanisms is core to this second direction.

Trial and error is another important ingredient in prompt engineering. Due to the dynamics of how AI models behave, it is not always straightforward to design an optimal prompt. We believe that users experimenting with a model end up discovering how to craft the best prompt. Along the way, they gain knowledge about the tendencies of that model for that specific task. They might accidentally try different variations before finding what seems most effective. Through this iterative process, users can uncover subtleties in prompt-design decision-making: You may ask the question `does it matter exactly which words you use`? In general, as long as the words in the prompt are generally accepted words, you will find (in this case) that day to day English should be fine. Avoid slang and other hyper-local language, however.

At an extreme, iterative prompting essentially means continual learning. As data sets increase in size, as the equations and connections between physical entities or metaphoric neural nets become more sophisticated, so too must the methods of engineering prompts. For this reason, the iterative nature of prompt engineering must be dynamic and ongoing if users of the individualized emotional landscape that is model prompting are to get what they want from it, and to do so reliably.

Detailed elements of a prompt

We will take what we discussed in the previous sections and go into the specifics of a prompt. The very beginning of every good prompt is a clear goal. In the world of prompt engineering, setting goals is not a (mere) best practice, it is a foundational component of a good interaction that should help make the output from the AI model both straightforward and useful. A prompt without clear goals is like a car ride without knowing the destination: what do you care about most, because it does not matter which way you go! So, let us learn about prompt design to understand the importance of clear goals and why this aspect of prompts is so important.

Setting clear objectives

A central function of such well-defined objectives is to tighten the focus and processing power of the AI model in a particular direction. With a well-defined objective, what the AI model **knows** becomes narrower in scope, and it focuses in on the subset of facts and examples that are most relevant to the task at hand. For example, if the objective of the prompt is to generate a paraphrased summary of a research paper, the objective of the prompt should indicate this. This will then inform the AI model to set aside all other information and hone in on the most important findings of the paper. If this well-defined objective is absent, the response may simply be much too broad or miss the mark entirely.

However, perhaps most importantly, clear objectives help determine whether or not the model was successful at fulfilling its directive. Unambiguous and measurable goals allow a comparison between the prompt and what the AI produces. For users, this means knowing if the model has been successful, that is if the AI has delivered on what you asked for, and if it is still possible to recalibrate the prompt next time. If you are asking an AI to produce a 200-word summary of a long and intricate legal case, you should have a baseline with which you can compare the result as a summary document. If the response tends to be off target, it might be a sign that the prompt needs to be recalibrated.

To create goals that are specific and measurable, prompt engineers have several tools in their kit. One such technique is the use of SMART criteria. SMART goals are specific, measurable, achievable, relevant, and time-bound. Framing goals within this framework ensures clarity and actionability. For example, in place of: **Explain blockchain**. You could have: **Paraphrase a 300-word summary of how blockchain technology improves cybersecurity in financial transactions**' So, by default, a SMART objective is specific (it is about cybersecurity in financial transactions), measurable (300 words), achievable (given that natural-language models can paraphrase 300 words), relevant (again, given that cybersecurity in finance probably intersects with the area of dialogue), and time-bound (immediate output – **You can have your answer now**). Notice how, adding more and more context to what you are asking results directly in a focus answer. Prompts are the AI analog of asking the right question to create the answer you are seeking.

Another is to break down complex objectives into bite-sized chunks. If a prompt relates to a complex topic, it can be difficult for a model to tackle the objective all at once. In these cases, you can partition the objective into several sub-objectives, which the model can process serially. For example, if the overall objective was: **Paraphrase the human-sounding text while retaining citations and quotes,** the prompt might be broken down into sub-objectives such as: **First, paraphrase the text while retaining original word count and quotes and citations**. Then, **Second, retain the article structure and title**. Then: **Third, retain special characters like dashes and quotes**, and so on. Beyond clarifying the objective, this strategy also helps the model to generate a more ordered output.

Setting objectives is an essential part of directive massaging, not only to make the skill of the prompt engineer explicit, but also to ensure response calibration to the user's intent. SMART criteria and objective decomposition are some ways to optimize prompt quality over prototypes, leading to more relevant and trustworthy AI responses.

Contextualization and background information

Contextualization is one of the most important features of good prompt writing, because often the model does not have enough details to grasp the exact nuances of what you are asking for. Without additional contextual detail, a prompt can be open to multiple interpretations, and there is no guarantee that the model will choose the one relevant to your question. In addition, without further context, the model might understand the prompt but choose a very general response and sometimes even give you something completely disconnected from what you are asking. Adding the context to the prompt prevents these miscommunications in a way that a simple prompt alone could not.

Providing context

Contextualizing involves giving a model some background information about the task or question at hand. For example, if that task or question involves generating text about a certain topic, the AI might be provided the following information The nature of the task, that is, educational, persuasive or entertaining., the particular or general time period or location it might relate to, the requirement of humor, and information regarding a specific audience. This contextualization confers some knowledge of the task's **world** to the AI and helps it to generate a more appropriate response (one that is informed by an understanding of its own context).

If you want your prompt to effectively embed this context, you will first need to frame the task that you want it to complete. If your model needs to generate an appropriate response to a prompt asking it to write a report about applications of ML in healthcare, for example, your prompt could include the following context: You are an AI system, and your task is to generate a report on applications of ML in healthcare for the benefit of healthcare professionals who do not have much technical knowledge but would like to learn more about these applications. The goals of the assignment are to summarize the applications of ML in healthcare, explain how ML models are used in each application, and describe how these models are classified according to their approach and output. (While this exact task would be challenging because healthcare providers can use ML models for diagnostics, personalized treatment, and other purposes, the example shows that prompts incorporating context can help address systematic over-generality.) This information about the audience and applications might help the model understand what it needs to do, improving the quality of the model's response to the prompt by making it audience-appropriate and tailored to the objectives of the report.

A further means of embedding context is via domain-specific knowledge (literary, scenario) directions. For example, **here's some context about the current state of the industry in question, common challenges it faces, and relevant regulatory considerations**, which the model can then bring to bear in its response, potentially producing an answer that will be both contextually relevant –pertaining to the specific industry mentioned in the prompt – and be insightful, informed and relevant given the domains cited.

Context additionally has a drastic effect on how well content produced in response to a prompt aligns with what a user expects when reading the prompt. When context is appropriately defined and known, an AI model can draw from a vast array of supporting training data to generate a response that appropriately meets the needs of the user. On the flip side, if context is lacking, the system can make mistakes or otherwise produce outputs that do not meet the needs of the prompt. For example, if a prompt says something like: **Paraphrase this input into text that still sounds human while retaining citations and quotes**, but lacks context, the resulting output may range from a technical discussion of neural networks to illuminating the philosophical debates in AI ethics – depending on what the AI model decides seems most closely related to the meaning of the prompt. Providing good context is in some sense, like pointing at what the user needs out of the response.

Managing prior knowledge

A second critical element of contextualization in prompt design involves managing pre-existing knowledge. AI models that use transformer architectures have acquired vast amounts of let us say, pre-existing knowledge from their training data. This pre-existing knowledge is both a blessing and a curse when it comes to prompt engineering. On the one hand, it can enable a model to craft a response that draws from worldly knowledge and is thus informed and sophisticated.

Using **Retrieval-Augmented Generation**, or **RAG** applies here. It is a method used by data and computer scientists to ensure the data is more accurate and the reliability of what is generated from the AI model is more accurate. It is done by fetching data from sources outside of what it has been trained specifically on. It is the AI version of looking something up with a search engine to enhance your knowledge about it.

Dealing with pre-trained model assumptions on your existing knowledge base can be tricky. Users should not assume that the model knows what matters or is important when it comes to achieving the goals of the task. Instead, they should design prompts in such a way that they clarify the possible ambiguities and, at the same time, guide the application of the model's prior knowledge accordingly. Without this specification, the model might respond based on outdated information or generalizations for which the user did not intend it. Explicit instruction and contextual framing are ways that prompt engineers can help a model accommodate for prior knowledge explicitly.

Good prompt engineering involves mastering the resources an AI model brings to the interaction to ensure that it deploys its prior knowledge in service of the given prompt, whether the goal is to increase model relevance, accuracy or efficacy, including avoiding breaches of privacy by engineering privacy-enhancing prompts. Explicit training and contextualization through instruction and framing can help manage user assumptions and cull ambiguity in a prompt by informing the AI model of users' intended meaning and, thus, regulating the model's application of its prior knowledge.

Specificity and precision in instructions

Eliminating ambiguity is an important element of instructional clarity. An ambiguous prompt can be read in multiple ways by the model, with outputs that may or may not be useful for the user. To guard against that possibility, prompt-engineering teams use precise language to convey exactly what they want the model to do. You could say something like `maintain the format of this document, but sound like a regular human versus a clear retain the citations and official quotes and speak to a non-subject matter audience`.

The second instruction is much less open to interpretation. For example, `List and explain three key economic benefits of solar energy adoption in developing countries` leaves little wiggle room. It specifies that the model should focus only on solar energy, in only one context, and on only a specific number of economic benefits.

Instructional clarity

Providing clear, explicit instructions is, arguably, the most basic tenet of good prompt engineering. Without clear instructions, it is impossible to determine exactly what response the model is focusing on, which will ultimately be returned as the output of the AI system. Do not be unclear or too broad in your request; you can also get too specific, which will miss some details. Building skills to create good and consistent prompts is a must-have skill. This will allow the model to give the best possible chance it has. There is a huge difference between a `Summarize this` to `Give bullet points on this`. The output will match the question. Flexibility in how you build the prompt is worth a bit of forethought to get clear asks; a prompt that you can iterate on multiple times is a good step to take, as there is no doubt you will need to iterate. Balancing vague versus prescriptive takes time; the way to strike this balance is to specify clear boundaries within which the model must operate but, at the same time, leave enough constructive room for the model to engage in some discretion in how to go about achieving the desired outcome.

Desired depth and scope

The scope and depth of a prompt influence the level of detail and inclusiveness of the AI model's response. Exploring and refining the parameters of scope and depth can help business users manage the trade-off between thoroughness and brevity. This entails defining the level of detail that the model should reach when developing an answer and its extent of coverage over a topic.

Let us use an example of the expectation of desired depth that will need to scale to different prompt lengths and tasks and different audiences. If the prompt specifies that the task is to give a broad overview of a topic at a generalized level, then the model should not be expected to go into detail. Quality should matter when it comes to holding the engineers of these models accountable. If a model is given a prompt that asks them to deliver a broad overview of some topic for a general audience, the prompt should not instruct the model to go further and deeper. Similarly, a prompt requesting a narrowed-in focused treatment of the same topic but for a more specialized audience should instruct the model to go further/deeper. For instance, `Write a general introduction to quantum computing, suitable for a non-technically oriented audience of students, that highlights the fundamentals and illustrates the potential applications`. The first prompt leaves no doubt about the expectations: the aim is to provide an overview at a high level so that readers will not have to deal with technical terms. Now compare this with the following detailed prompt: `Examine the consequences of quantum entanglement for cryptography, with a discussion of Bell's theorem and its relevance to secure communication.` In this case, the prompt tells us that we can assume that the intended audience is technically minded and will follow our discussion of complex ideas such as Bell's theorem.

Controlling the amount of depth versus length is another way to control the assigning of background detail and context. Often, a prompt will require a trade-off, for example, between the need for detail and brevity. If the prompt asks the model to paraphrase content to make it appear less artificial while retaining quotes and survey responses, its instruction must balance those needs. For example, if the model is producing content for a summary report or other executive-focused content, the prompt would ask it to summarize complex information into a short report without losing soundbites. To accomplish this task, the prompt might include a word limit or request a summary that captures a topic's key points in one paragraph.

For instance, `Paraphrase the study's main finding on the effects of climate change on agriculture in less than 150 words`, where the prompt stacks two expectations – brevity and capturing the study's main finding. Dealing with this balance between brevity and depth is a big challenge for the model since it could either over-simplify its answer and leave out important insights or work harder to condense the information without sacrificing depth. Starting broad and narrowing it down is often a technique that works very well.

Instructional specificity and clarity can make it possible for the model to arrive at outputs that are useful and relevant for a given user query. For example, a prompt engineer could constrain the response to return answers that are nuanced on a given topic but are less likely to stray into tangential and irrelevant territory. Instructional specificity and clarity also allow for managing scope and depth. By changing the boundaries and objectives for the inference task, prompt engineers can create prompts that result in outputs that are sufficiently detailed but not overly long-winded and sufficiently informative but not burdened with unnecessary details.

Examples, analogies and constraints

Writing the prompt comes with the thought of limiting the response; these are the constraints you put on, and you can use analogies with care as well as using the notion of examples. These set up a direction for the AI to respond properly. You can think of them as ways to keep the AI moving in the correct direction with its answer.

Using examples and analogies

Prompts featuring examples and/or analogies were also designed to make the model speak better to the user's world from its own. Adding examples makes responses more circumstantial and relatable, helping people appreciate how the AI is responding to their input. Analogies help build bridges between unfamiliar ideas and more familiar ones, making the model more accessible to its users. We will get deeper into it later, but this is a situation where the model can be trained with ML. **Zero shot** learning is where the AI will generate answers without specific training, but **few shot** is where it will see a few examples, where it will generate the reply from.

Adding examples to a prompt can be particularly valuable where you are trying to explain or illustrate a concept and target a broad audience. Many of the models we have been training so far tend to be chilly and theoretical in their explanation. Adding specific examples can serve as a predicate, instructing the model to shape its discussion towards something more practical and real-world. Applied to the preceding example prompt, this might look like the following: paraphrase: Take this prompt: `Paraphrase the input into human-sounding text while retaining citations and quotes.` Incorporating examples with a prompt like this can be especially valuable when you are seeking to explain or illustrate a concept and want to make that concept feel rooted in the real world and accessible to a general audience. One way to do that is to add specific examples. The use of a potential example from a specific industry focuses on the model's response to a specific application of automation, which results in an answer to the user's query that is unique and on-topic.

Leveraging analogies is another form of prompt engineering, useful in situations where a concept is difficult or abstract, and some users will not have the innate understanding necessary to grasp the new input – for instance, a computer's contents and memory are stored on the hard drive, and the hard drive is an (electronic) collection of spinning disks. You may be familiar with using analogies in real-world contexts, such as likening electricity to water flowing from a tap by saying: *I'm turning the electricity (tap) on.* A prompt may request of the model: **Paraphrase blockchain technology to the analogy of a shared digital ledger in a bank**, which in turn will help users familiar with conventional banking to grasp the decentralized nature of blockchain. Analogies are particularly helpful when the purpose is for the AI's output to be more intuitive or relevant to the reader; for audiences who lack a sophisticated understanding of the relevant technical detail, the report observes. Take a prompt that asks you to describe the concept of quantum computing for a lay audience: The analogy of a multi-lane highway where cars (data) can simultaneously travel in different lanes (quantum states) can be helpful in explaining the notion of superposition to a lay audience. Recall when we make prompts work as examples or analogies, they increase the familiarity and, hence, the readability of the model's answer. From the perspective of prompt engineering, this is an ideal outcome.

Defining constraints and limitations

Constraints provide important structure for prompt design; they direct the model's focus and limit or exclude irrelevant and off-topic content. Specifying what a user does not want to hear in the response and asking the model to refrain from doing so can narrow the scope of the output to deliver distinct value for a user with specific informational goals.

One way to establish boundaries within prompts is by adding constraints describing the boundaries of the model's answer and what should or should not be included in the response. This can be especially helpful when the prompt aims to discuss a broad or complex topic, which otherwise leaves the model free to give a wider or tangential response.

Constraints can also be employed to control the depth of response. For example, a prompt could direct the model to **Describe the economic benefits of renewable energy in brief terms**, while a constraint might read: **Maintain your response to under 200 words and keep it free of specialist jargon**. Such a constraint would not only apply a length limit but also tailor the language of the response for a non-specialist audience, depending on the user's needs. One use is to configure the prompt in a way where you would specifically try to prevent getting off-color or inflammatory remarks. In 2016, a very early chatbot based on Twitter by Microsoft called *Tay* was pointed at Twitter itself to learn. Unfortunately, it began to give fairly horrible responses and was taken offline permanently on its first day. It is not a bad idea to try to add **Verbal Guardrails** as a constraint, but the models of today should have them built in. The case study of Tay continues to be both fascinating and horrible at the same time.

Tone, style and edge cases

Tailoring tone and style to an audience and purpose can be achieved by modifying the prompt to match the context in which the AI's output might be published or used. For example, the prompt used for a report for an academic audience might include the directive: `Write in a formal tone`, while the prompt for a marketing effort might include the custom: `Use a conversational and persuasive tone`. This contributes to another important challenge when using text: a formal style of writing often feels alienating and distant, while a conversational and familiar style tends to come off as insincere.

Specifying tone and style

The tone and style of any prompt and any desired answer matter quite a lot. The prompt that generates a response is the model's lexical input, and the tone and style of the prompt can be used to manipulate and tweak the model's response to match an intended audience and purpose so that the output is not just informative but also pleasingly presented.

The degree of formality is also important in tone specification. For instance, you would want to lean towards a formal tone for pieces written for academic, legal or technical use, where exactness and professionalism take precedence, compared with a more informal or conversational tone that is more suitable for content written for general audiences, such as blog posts or social media updates. Explicitly specifying what kind of tone you would like the piece to have prevents a piece that is written for an academic audience, for instance, from having an overly conversational tone. The technicality of the model's response is another important dimension. A more sophisticated audience may require a prompt like: `Please provide a full technical explanation of neural networks, including all needed mathematical formulas`. The explanations need to be tailored to suit the intended audience.

The other equally important step is setting the right tone and style in a prompt design. Not because the AI model will have actual sensibility, but because the human prompt engineer can insist that the AI model's response be forced into line with the audience's expectations for its level of formality and technicality.

Addressing edge cases

The science of prompt design involves anticipating edge cases and formulating guidelines that allow the model to effectively work around vague or unusual inputs. The process of preemptively identifying potential edge cases is an important aspect of edge case design. A third key strategy uses edge cases to clarify ambiguous terms in the prompt. Some prompts involve prompt-specific technical terms, cultural references, or local idioms that risk causing confusion for the model. This can lead the model to interpret these terms in a conceptually or linguistically inappropriate way or in a manner unrelated to the prompt.

Handling edge cases by providing contingencies also includes instructions for abnormal or unexpected cases. In addition to the request, for instance, we might include the contingency instruction: `When faced with conflicting pieces of information, source data from peer-reviewed sources` or `When faced with a situation where requested information is not available, provide an alternative analysis to the request subject based on a related topic` to ensure that the model can handle edge cases.

By proactively pinpointing ambiguous scenarios and providing specific explanations on how to handle weird cases, prompt engineers can steer the model towards generating human-sounding responses – referring both to their quality and to robustness across diverse situations – irrespective of how challenging and convoluted user inputs are.

Conclusion

In this chapter, we learned about the granular elements in the prompt ecosystem. Overall, several insights surfaced, merging together to generate a nuanced understanding of how to engineer effective and robust prompts for AI-powered model services. A complex interplay between lucidity, granularity, and flexibility needs to be captured in prompt engineering to create a prompt that instructs the response it dictates but also provides flexibility to cope with the bombshells presented by varying inputs to the model. The value of specificity and precision in instructions was then considered. We saw how specific and unambiguous instructions guide sthe model's output, creating a trade-off between specificity and the flexibility required for the AI to generate creative, nuanced responses. The trade-off between brevity and depth followed, emphasizing the need for prompt engineers to carefully balance the breadth of the scope of the AI's response so as to create lucid prompts that both encapsulate depth as well as brevity.

In the next chapter, we will take what we have learned and start building prompts for the different AI services, leveraging insights from this chapter.

Join our book's Discord space

Join the book's Discord Workspace for Latest updates, Offers, Tech happenings around the world, New Release and Sessions with the Authors:

https://discord.bpbonline.com

CHAPTER 8

Prompt Types In-Depth

Introduction

This chapter details a walk-through of prompt types as employed by computational systems (for example, artificial intelligence and machine learning), dividing them into open-ended, closed-ended, exploratory, multi-modal, and contextual. Open-ended is a prompt that generates more expansive and imaginative responses, while closed-ended is a prompt that is best suited to solicit more specific and concise responses. Exploratory prompts are especially helpful in digging deeper into datasets. Multi-modal prompts include a combination of text, imagery, and sound as well as other data states; often, these prompts can be the most convoluted and complex. Contextual prompts are leveraged to help systems provide more context-relevant or situational responses; for example, commenting on an article can guide how bots and algorithms curate responses for the readers. It also briefly touches upon other less-used but still impactful less common prompt types.

Structure

In this chapter, you will learn the following topics:

- Creative potential of open-ended prompts
- Precision and clarity with closed-ended prompts

- Discovery with exploratory prompts
- Diverse data inputs with multi-modal prompts
- Enhancing accurate responses with contextual prompts
- Sequenced prompting with procedural prompts
- Dynamic interactions with adaptive prompts

Objectives

In this chapter, you will learn different uses of prompt types and how they can inform humans using AI-driven systems to strategically use these prompts to improve interaction, engagement, and output quality. There are a variety of prompt types you could use, asking the AI in a way where you are matching the situation to the prompt type you choose. Understanding those scenarios and prompt types will help you get the right results. We will also talk to some of the challenges with each of the prompt types.

Creative potential of open-ended prompts

An open-ended prompt gives an AI model much more freedom to explore. While closed-ended prompts typically ask for a single, somewhat short response, an open-ended prompt can allow the AI substantial freedom in its response.

Nature of open-ended prompts

This means the AI can interpret the prompt in any way it wants, and that in turn, will lead to a diversity of responses. This makes them great for tasks that we think of as creative, like story generation, brainstorming and exploring complex, multi-faceted topics.

Let us see an example: In answer to the prompt **What might AI mean to our society?**, you might expect the AI to respond with an ethical, moral discussion of AI, an essay on AI and the job market, an essay on AI and medicine, its effects and consequences; or how AI might affect human social status. Here is an open-ended prompt that allows AI to run the gamut of responses from multiple points of view and in detail.

Open-ended gives you maximum flexibility, as most synthesis tasks are likely to involve producing original material in unconventional ways. It encourages a broader span of generative responses because an open-ended prompt allows for a broader range of possible responses. It helps foster and encourage a broader range of generative responses. The machine is not constrained by anything; it is free to come up with outputs that can be generative, novel, or surprising. Open-ended prompts are also good for exploration and ideation tasks where the goal is an open-ended prompt for a new technology with this prompt: **What might we use the AI might come back with some wild ideas that thought of.**

Be aware, however, that a response that is too open, broad, or general (also described as free-floating or naked) is more likely to move in unhelpful directions or be too vague. Narrowing (or framing) the context closely will help to make a response fit for purpose but, in all likelihood, **open enough** to prompt a creative response.

Use cases for open-ended prompts

There are several major use cases for using open-ended prompts. One is in creative writing. Think of an open-ended prompt as a rock that sets off an avalanche; there are many apparently random twists and turns that can happen. This open-ended prompt encourages the AI to imagine a world and then develop the plot to an extent that encompasses a large set of creative possibilities.

In **research and development** (**RD**), open-ended prompts could be used in a company environment like RD to inspire brainstorming sessions and ideas. Another example could be an engineering team working on how to improve its tech products in terms of the environmental dimension, which could presumably be asked: `What are some possible ideas to improve the tech related to renewable energies?` Possible answers could include a list of new projects (such as for solar power or energy storage).

You can also benefit in educational environments where open-ended prompts are especially useful in educational contexts, where debate and deliberation are encouraged. In a classroom environment, for example, the prompt `Discuss how climate change will impact food security globally` might be used to facilitate a nuanced and multifaceted discussion between students. The AI's response could be used to guide debate and argumentation, eliciting deeper critical thinking from students.

Challenges and considerations

While open-ended prompts have many advantages for AI-generated output, there are many challenges that come with using them. Perhaps the most salient for AI-generated output is that of scope. If no context or constraint is provided with an extremely open-ended prompt, the AI can easily end up with an output that is far-ranging or topics-wise irrelevant than what was desired. For example, a prompt asking, `What are the consequences of AI?` risks an output on the order of magnitude of what is described previously. To avoid this, you can provide explicit context or constraints in the prompt itself. For example, you might refine an open-ended prompt to: `What are some of the ethical implications of AI in healthcare?` This prompt is sufficiently broad to allow for a diverse range of responses but now carefully confines would-be answers to a mapped area of interest.

A second constraint is the risk of information overload. Open-ended prompts can sometimes generate responses that are just too voluminous or detailed to be of much use. To handle this, it is sometimes possible to ask the human-sounding AI for summary responses too, effectively specifying the desired depth and scope within the prompt itself. For example, we can say **Give me a rounded summary** or **Just tell me five of the main points**.

Precision and clarity with closed-ended prompts

Closed-ended prompts, one of the basic types of interfaces for AI interaction, are intended to cause the agent to return a specific, often short binary answer. Most open-ended prompts provide free form text with little structure, but closed-ended prompts provide structured answers specifically intended to have high-accuracy and short and specific text that is highly solution-relevant. Closed-ended prompts can be useful in any situation when accuracy, clarity and brevity of text are desirable.

The nature of closed-ended prompts

What distinguishes closed-ended prompts is that they forcefully focus the AI's attention to a specific question or issue and elicit a direct, unambiguous answer. The prompt could actually be binary, that is, a yes or no answer. In many decision-making tasks, particularly those that lend themselves to high and/or equal-precision results, a binary, closed-ended prompt yields the best increase in the AI's precision and cost-effectiveness. Examples of closed-ended prompts include: **Should the loan be approved? Did Maria attend chemistry? What was the high in Salem on 13 July 2013? Were passenger schedules for Amtrak trains person-coded or machine-coded? How many passengers rode with Sean on the Chicago to Dallas Amtrak train?**

Here is an example: **Does AI do health care?,** a question that would strike you as needing a yes or no, since the AI can expound afterward if it wants to. This sort of question-answer structure is especially useful if the information you are pursuing is straightforward or calls for little in the way of probing other possibilities.

Key characteristics of closed-ended prompts are that they force granular responses, having to click on a response from the AI, focuses the mind and ensures that your answer is granular and targeted to the question at hand, which is useful for some narrow tasks. Additionally, when accuracy truly matters – asking questions, documenting facts, or making decisions – closed-ended prompting alone is both safe and effective in any form of communication practice. Also, close-ended questions limit the scope of the AI's answer to your request. Closed-ended prompts, by their nature, limit the scope or the degree to which the AI will return an answer to the query. The AI is doing exactly what was requested of it, which is to give all and only the answer to that one question. In some cases, this limitation is good, allowing the AI to answer as narrowly as possible and to be well-tailored to that one, isolated question. Hopefully, that tailoring means that it includes only information that is relevant to the ability of the asker to meet their needs.

Use cases for closed-ended prompts

Use cases are examples, like questionnaires and surveys. The essence of the closed-ended prompt, not unlike a questionnaire, is written, it has highly formatted data. A survey might ask something like: **Do you use AI in your daily work? (Yes/No).** Due to the automatic nature of this type of question, it lends itself very easily to data gathering, allowing the respondent to quickly provide the data that the surveyor is after, as well as to mobilize lots of people for this data-gathering effort, which might be hard to do through the open-ended prompt. Another use is for decision-support processes that require decision-making, that is, processes where it is crucial that the result be definite and represent a choice between two binary options. This is where closed-ended queries are needed. For example, should the company develop AI-based customer service solutions? Yes/No

Additionally, another strong use case is for closed-ended factual situations where prompts can also be closed-ended when the AI is dealing with situations that require the confirmation or accuracy of certain facts. For example, the AI for fact-checking: **Is Japan's population more than 125 millions? (Y/N).** In this case, closed-ended prompts allow for simple validation, allowing the answer to check out – even if not with a very low error rate. Keep in mind that fact-checking with AI needs to have the broad data needed to check against or you will risk having incorrect facts reported by the AI, known as hallucinations.

Challenges and considerations

By their nature, overly structured prompts can prevent broader responses from the AI. If you are presented with a situation where you need to add in more details or context, this might not be the best way to go. Something to keep in mind is that AI may not interpret the prompt correctly if you do not word it exactly so precision is critical here.

To maximize the effectiveness of closed-ended prompts, several best practices can be employed. Obviously, do not be vague; be clear. Using vernacular terms also is not likely to work for you. Stay on point, and do not add more than you need. You also might need follow-ups. Close-ended questions tend to get terse answers, so you should not expect to get all the information you need; follow-up questions are the way to add. Something you can do is a bit of both, with open-ended prompts being used for more exploration and then getting down to the precision of closed-ended prompts.

We all use closed-ended prompts any time we send a text, fill in a worksheet, take an exam or survey, or translate a quote to fact-check. When a machine needs to answer a specific question, it needs a prompt that delivers a similar result: it must prompt a focused and relevant answer; it must communicate for usefulness and not be open to misinterpretation; and it must pin down an answer, ideally with precision. Ideal closed-ended prompts should pin down a thought with brevity and efficiency. Not all routine AI applications demand the strict clarity of closed-ended prompts, however, the answer can always be specific and thinking-out.

Discovery with exploratory prompts

Exploratory prompts are a dynamic and discursive approach to teaching AI that tends to be open-ended, comparative, and interrogative. In contrast to closed-ended prompts, which ask for specific information in a straightforward manner, and open-ended prompts, which encourage the model to exercise imagination and creativity, exploratory prompts are designed to guide AI through a process of discovery. They are especially helpful in contexts that need AI to engage in careful investigation, comparison and analysis.

Nature of exploratory prompts

Exploratory prompts are designed to promote the AI's fact-finding skills. Accordingly, if you need the AI to dig up information, weigh the pros and cons of a decision, or drill down into a specific topic, provide it with a relevant exploratory prompt that will enhance the overall quality of its response.

Some key characteristics of exploratory prompts are to encourage deeper forms of analysis and investigation, since they are exploratory. This class of prompts is inherently investigative of the input. It asks the AI to examine something in a way that is designed to capture all sides of the matter. For example, making comparisons between two or more disparate aspects of some topic or collating data to offer multiple perspectives in the response. This investigative inclination makes this class of prompt especially suited to tasks requiring detailed, involved investigations of a topic. Also, it is okay to let the AI a bit on a topic via exploratory prompts that give the AI the leeway to examine a topic from various perspectives. It allows the AI to examine the topic from different factors, variables, and perspectives, giving the AI the latitude to wander in many ways.

Use cases for exploratory prompts

Use cases for exploratory prompts would be something like a **Eureka moment** where you use exploratory prompts to navigate your literature review, as well as being the backbone of shorter writing projects, such as blog posts and articles. Academic research is a key application for exploratory prompts because they can help guide AI through the process of literature review and theoretical exploration. This can help researchers gain a broad picture of the current literature and areas of future research. You could also leverage this approach for product comparison and analysis via exploratory prompts. Those prompts are especially powerful when used in product comparison and analysis. For example, a prompt, such as `Compare the features, speed, and user reviews of the five most competitive smartphones on the market` would lead the AI to understand multiple products in detail, side-by-side, and thereby understand the strengths and weaknesses of each. Such an analysis is useful for consumers looking to make a purchase decision and for vendors trying to do a competitive analysis of their products versus others. One area they are being used today is in investigative journalism as they can be used to instruct an AI journalism bot to conduct investigative research and create rich report pieces. For example, a prompt like `Explore social media on political polarization in the past couple of elections` would ask the AI agent to conduct exploratory research, collect investigative information, examine the data, and finally create a report on this issue of social media and political polarization. When conducting the exploration, the journalism bot can conduct a deep-dive investigation irrespective of the dimension of the issue, which can guarantee a thorough report for the human reader. Of course, the bot has to be trained on the right data with the proper **large language model** (**LLM**) support behind it using the correct transformers, etc. but it is a very exciting area.

Challenges and considerations

Exploratory prompts are strong for guiding AI through long and involved investigations, but they can have drawbacks, specifically, overcoming the challenge of the breadth of scope and comprehensiveness of the reply. Encouraging exploratory thinking in an AI can often lead to much longer and more involved replies, and it is important to understand how helpful they will be.

A related concern is to make sure that it stays on topic. This might sound trivial – surely, if we give it the task of writing an essay on neural networks, that is broadly what it will deliver. However, it can have a tendency to pick up on random information and wander a bit with what appears to be with stray sentences or even small details from previous research. Avoiding this can be a matter of careful phrasing; if the prompt is something like: `Please write an essay on neural networks`.

Enhancing the effectiveness of exploratory prompts

To maximize the effectiveness of exploratory prompts, consider the following best practices. Some examples are to point the AI in a specific direction on scope and focus, whereas exploratory prompts benefit from being broad and open-ended; a specific direction on what dimensions, variables, or perspectives of the topic are to be explored can help the AI remain on track and relevant. Another is to ask for comparative analysis, asking the AI to consider contrasts or parallels between various elements in the discourse, which will often force it to add another level of detail. Anything starting with, `please highlight contrasts between … or please highlight parallels between …` will usually force more subtle, and hence more revealing, answers. Additionally, you could request a synthesis of findings and ask the AI to synthesize the findings of your lengthy exploration into a cogent argument or conclusion – a handy tool for many writing projects, from undergraduate essays and papers to articles for reporters.

Since they assist us in the important task of exploring and critically evaluating large data sets, they offer significant value in contexts such as academic research, education, product analysis, and investigative journalism. It remains, however, a scenario that must be used with caution. For exploratory prompts to work well, they must be carefully scaffolded with robust parameters of scope and focus on the kind of information that makes an output worthy of attention. When applied appropriately, exploratory prompts can generate richly contextualized responses that provide salient insights and facilitate informed decision-making across a variety of fields.

Diverse data inputs with multi-modal prompts

Multi-modal prompts allow different input types, such as a JPG or a WAV file, which are different types of media. You will see often an uploaded document as a common item to include in a prompt. Combining different modalities of input allows AI to benefit from more diverse and deeper data, in turn, enabling more nuanced and sophisticated applications than would otherwise be possible using a single data modality alone.

Nature of multi-modal prompts

These simple text inputs place limitations on the complexity and contextual richness of the tasks performed by the AI, since text inputs are passive and single modality in nature. Specifically, text inputs neglect a lot of data that the AI must interpret if she had a way of experiencing it, for example, smells, sounds, and sensations. Multi-modal prompts alleviate these limitations by concurrently providing multiple data modalities for the AI to process simultaneously. This is a particularly useful technique when the input is more complete in combination than its constituent parts. For example, asking an AI to design a vacation destination could lead it to neglect important information if it has to anticipate just textual inputs rather than a combination of text, images, and audio.

For example, one could specify a multimodal instruction, such as paraphrasing human-sounding text while quoting and citing; first-paraphrase the picture and text below; second, analyze in terms of core visual and contextual information from the picture; third, summarize the most important visual attributes found; fourth, explain how the elements fit together with and inform the text. In this case, upon paraphrasing the visual features of the picture and the contextual cues of the text, the AI can process both types of information to arrive at a better, more accurate output than if it had processed only one modality.

For instance, a multi-modal prompt to paraphrase text could look like this: You upload an image and build a prompt to deduce what style of art it is and what the meaning of the piece could be. It is multi-mode as the prompt is made up of both an image and a query.

Multi-modal prompts aid AI's ability to comprehend complex inputs and generate more nuanced responses. The more modes of data we feed an AI, the better it will be at handling complex inputs. An AI analyzing the visual and auditory contents of a video clip can come up with more nuanced responses – for instance, it could describe the important moments of the clip, determine the emotions of the characters based on their facial expressions, or ascertain the tone of the dialogue. This helps with the AI's performance of any task where cross-checking input from multiple sources is especially important.

Since multi-modal prompts are most effective when tuned for a task by incorporating multiple human inputs of different modalities, they are better fitted for the tasks that require a machine learning model trained on knowledge of all three modalities. This makes them well-suited for applications of image and video captioning, multimedia content analysis, and various decision-making applications where multiple types of input data need to be assessed and summed.

Use cases for multi-modal prompts

A notable use case of multi-modal prompts is image and video captioning. In such tasks, the input is the visual content, and the expected output is textual in nature. For example, if we give an instruction like, **Paraphrase the input into human-sounding text while retaining quotes and citations**, the AI will therefore need to analyze the visual elements in the input to come up with a description of what is occurring in the picture. In the case of an image illustrating a sunset over a mountain range, the visual elements can range from the colors and shapes in the frames to the setting. Such prompts can be genuinely useful in digital media, especially for making videos more accessible and searchable. They can also be used for automating content creation.

When it comes to dealing with multimodal content, such as a video, podcast, or presentation, most AI education and entrepreneurs prefer to incorporate multimodal prompts, where both auditory and visual prompts feed information into an AI system. Furthermore, in the preceding situation, the prompt requires the AI to summarize the essence of the video's narration and its visual clues by paying close attention to these combined events and creating an interesting and accurate summary in a timely fashion. The preceding illustrates another human-sounding application of AI that should be developed in the field of journalism, education, and media production, where summarizing and understanding complex information at rapid speeds becomes essential.

Multi-source data synthesis

For decision-making processes that involve multiple input data types, including visual, textual, and numerical data, multi-modal prompts are a useful tool for synthesizing the decision and analysis. For example, such a prompt can include directions like: **Compare the performance metrics listed in the attached chart with the trends depicted in the accompanying video presentation and recommend the optimal course of action.** As a response to this prompt, the bot needs to evaluate both the able of quantitative data and a video presentation to generate a well-rounded and informed recommendation. This is very useful in business, finance, and planning settings, which regularly depend upon the analysis and recommendations resulting from the use of multiple forms of information.

Challenges and considerations

While multi-modal prompts are a powerful qualitative addition to states enabling context, they also need to navigate the same structures as those for inaccurate responses. A huge problem is that the input becomes more complicated. Since there are multiple modalities involved in multi-modal prompts, it needs to know how to parse and ground multiple modalities. On top of that, sophisticated underlying AI models will be needed and assured knowledge of how to combine different forms of data, for the AI to be able to cross-reference all of this and compose a reply. A related problem is that the prompt can sometimes leave room for ambiguity, especially in cases where you are asking the AI to process modalities of data (like both text and video). A question to ask yourself is how you want to break your multi-modal prompt down. Think of what you will link with the *and* it is implied or directly in the prompt.

To fully leverage the capabilities of multi-modal prompts, consider some of the following approaches:

Set the expectations – specify what each modality does: In a multi-modal prompt, when the spatial information is not abundant enough for the AI to decide the great-start instruction itself, it is important to set clear expectations: which modality is more important; what each modality does; if necessary, how much each modality should be used. For example, the prompt could say: **AI, regarding this topic, please focus on the text while the image should be used to provide more context.**

Contextual links between modalities, often increasing the effectiveness of a multi-sensory prompt, necessitates making explicit links between modalities. This might be as simple as connecting the image text citations, creating an obvious visual breakdown of the text or other data type, which allows the AI to put two and two together more effectively. For example, a prompt might ask for a **Paraphrase while retaining citations and quotes with a combination of human-sounding text and citations while still retaining citations and quotes**: The following is an instruction that describes a task, paired with an input that provides further context. Write a response that appropriately completes the request. Paraphrase the input into human-sounding text while retaining citations and quotes: The process by which AI models can create human-sounding text through citations and quotes can be divided into a series of steps. First, you must paraphrase the input by recognizing its main ideas and important elements. Next, you need to insert familiar citations and quotes. Finally, all the supporting content must be removed. In a similar vein, a prompt might ask for an **Explanation of how the image's visuals support the messaging inherent in the accompanying text.**

Multi-modal prompts represent an important step forward in how machines can interact with human users on more challenging inference tasks. Equipped with input data of different modalities, such as text, images, audio and video, AI systems can provide more contextual, nuanced, and accurate responses. Multi-modal prompts enable AI systems to move from simpler tasks, like fact-checking, to much more complex and fuzzy tasks, such as image and video captioning, multimedia content analysis, and decision-making.

In order to better leverage multi-modal prompts to train AI systems for more sophisticated tasks, users should thoughtfully design their prompts as a structured set of instructions, contextual links, and stratified use of different modalities to highlight system strengths and capabilities. With more user-attuned prompt design strategies, multi-modal prompts enable AI systems to provide more sensitive, nuanced, and contextualized responses than ever before.

Enhancing accurate responses with contextual prompts

Contextual prompts represent a sophisticated approach to AI interaction by incorporating relevant external or prior context to generate more accurate, coherent, and relevant responses. These prompts are particularly valuable in applications where understanding the ongoing context is crucial, such as conversational AI systems, customer service platforms, and personalized content delivery. By leveraging the context from previous interactions or external sources, contextual prompts allow AI to deliver responses that are more aligned with the specific needs and expectations of the user.

The nature of contextual prompts

Contextual prompts help AI take the surrounding context of a task (from somewhere within a conversation it has so far been involved with, in a related document, or another place it might access as an external source) and learn to direct the AI response better towards output that is more consistent with the general context in which the action is happening. This means that AI is programmed more towards a view of each action as next in a series of what was previously already happening, rather than to view each interaction as if it is lodged like an island:

- Say the conversational AI providing an answer to a customer-service request receives preceding inputs such as this: **Paraphrased to sound more conversational: what should we tell this customer about his billing issues?** The AI must remember information from the preceding exchanges about what the billing problem is, who the customer is (name, location, purchase, and contact history), what past attempts have been made to resolve it, etc. to provide any kind of useful response to the prompt. Contextual prompts are prompts where the context from outside or before the prompt guides an AI's responses. The nature of the context can be context from prior utterances in a coherent conversational context, context from the users' profile data, or context from another source of external knowledge databases.

- **Helps better maintain a coherent and on-topic conversation**: Contextual prompts are critical to a coherent conversationalist. An AI that remains discussed thus far can maintain topicality and cheapen gaps by drawing upon citations to the previous parts of the conversation.

Use cases for contextual prompts

Now, let us investigate some contextual prompts by using a few potential real-world examples:

- **Conversational AI and chatbots:** Contextual prompts in conversational AI systems and chatbots are essential for maintaining the natural flow and continuity of the conversation. In the example of a customer support chatbot, a prompt could ask the AI system to `Keep the conversation going on the basis of the customer's last service request (Q: How long will the product be delivered?).` The system will then base its answer on this particular context, take into account the previous interaction, and respond in a way that ensures the flow and support of the customer's query.

- **Customer service and support systems**: As in customer service environments, contextual prompts are tremendously effective where understanding the history and past interactions of the customer/patient is of paramount importance for the efficient and satisfactory provision of support.

Challenges and considerations

While contextual prompts have many advantages for interactional sensitivity and coherence, they pose a number of risks, and we need to proceed cautiously to manage these issues.

What this amounts to, among other things, is that even if the AI's instructions are to attend to context, it could still go wrong by making incorrect inferences about context, for instance, by assuming too much about what is going on or by applying context to the wrong places. This could lead to a response that has nothing to do with the original context. Dealing with the challenge of memorability requires thinking of prompts that tell the AI exactly what context is relevant and how. Another is the amount of work required to track and retrieve relevant context – especially for systems with extensive archives or systems that must be able to hold multiple conversations simultaneously. Ensuring that the system has access to the most germane and up-to-date context could be critical to maintaining proper performance and responses. Such a system might require sophisticated context management systems that can efficiently store, retrieve, and apply context when and how it is needed. Also, be aware that another risk you might face is limited context causing challenges.

To maximize the benefits of contextual prompts, consider the following best practices:

- Try to give clear instructions about context usage; when developing instructions for a contextual prompt, be explicit on how context should be used, such as `Give weight to the synonym extracted from the preceding utterance or Consider both of the credit card on file.` This (hopefully) will lead your AI to focus on the most relevant context and apply it to your intended task.

- Provide accurate context retrieval; contextual prompts should only prompt a response if the AI can accurately retrieve relevant context. Strong systems for context management and storage are, therefore, key to allowing the AI to apply those most relevant to the situation at hand. Simply keeping those systems updated and well-maintained can minimize errors and help ensure contextual interactions are probable and reliable.

Make sure that you balance contextual depth with simplicity: Although contextual prompts benefit from fine-grained, deep context, they can become overly complex when you give the AI too many details that it does not need to solve the contextual situation at hand.

Using contextual prompts can dramatically impact the accuracy, relevance, and coherence of a response: by providing a question, paraphrase, or small prompt from previous input in the interaction, an AI system can do a lot more with much less data. Contextual prompts can be immensely valuable in applications such as conversational AI (chatbots), customer service, personalized text or content generation, or even providing suggested actions or resolution steps to a user. A design challenge is to minimize the input needed for these systems while still incorporating their full skillset; for example, a company that recommends new orders for its clients might want to prompt its chatbot with an intention, such as asking for the best price on a given good, but also consider the client's context of a slowdown in production at their factory. So, here is how you might make use of contextual prompts in a problem-solving dialogue with a system providing remediations:

- We suggest training focused on expanding production capacity, staff training and wellness, or redesigning products with customer needs in mind;

- Alternatively, we could suggest implementing production improvement software, training in agile manufacturing practices and reduce barriers across department silos. In the previous version, we see that the new suggested HR remediation (that is, reducing barriers within departments) was inspired by the contextual prior prompt that was provided to the system. Contextual prompts can help give the impression that the AI system is thinking **outside** the scope of the original problem-solving task. Overall, if well-designed, contextual prompts can dramatically improve user experience and bring more value across a variety of language-based scenarios where the AI needs to be more aligned with its user.

Procedural prompts are a specific class of prompt where humans guide the AI through a step-by-step process (often with the AI having to generate extensive new instructions, detailed workflows or sequences). These prompts appear most useful in situations where linear, logical, and structured output is essential, for example, in technical literature, content creation for classrooms, or workforce productivity. It also helps us develop software that emulates oiliness and stickiness. In the development of business processes, procedural prompts serve as a means to limit ambiguity, minimize side-tracking, and ensure the completion of necessary steps.

Sequenced prompting with procedural prompts

Procedural prompts seek to break down high-level commands into a series of procedures or steps to guide the AI through the process of generating a list of instructions or sequences in a sequence-specific way.

This prompt prompts it to catalog an entire sequence of steps in sequential order: the first steps are the preparatory steps (such as identifying security needs), the middle steps are the actual steps (such as setting up firewalls, encrypting data), and the final steps end in a very clear instruction that sounds like it came straight out of an instruction manual. Anyone with the right kind of technical expertise could perform this exact task.

Nature of procedural prompts

Several key characteristics of procedural prompts give the advantage of paying attention to sequence and steps to the outcome. Perhaps in response to the `paraphrase while retaining citations and quotes` prompt, it tends to focus on procedural tasks that require list-like output in sequential steps with interlocking elements. Fit for long-form content with stepped instructions or workflows, procedural prompts hold a distinct advantage for tasks with vastly detailed stepped instructions or workflows, such as technical writing, instructional content, or operational workflows.

Use cases for procedural prompts

Procedural prompts are indispensable in the creation of technical documentation and manuals. For example, one can request: `Paraphrase the input into human-sounding text while retaining citations and quotes.` or: `Paraphrase into human-sounding text while retaining all headings, quotes and quotes within quotes` A human paraphraser would take this request seriously and quote parts of the input, while retaining quotes within quotes. An AI, however, would take this request literally, in some instances resulting in hilarious or even nonsensical results. By demanding that the AI follow the customer's request to the letter, users make the AIs behave in unexpected and strange ways that humans almost never do. These error messages could be a disconcerting way to start a day, but this gets even funnier and more discomforting. Imagine asking an AI to create technical documentation (for example, a user manual on how to install and configure a home wireless router) by giving it a specific request, such as `Create a user manual for installing and configuring a home wireless router`. The AI could then paraphrase the input while retaining all quotes and quotes within quotes.: As well as being entertaining, all these examples show that the way a human requests something already determines its outcome, even if AI could provide a human-sounding paraphrased input, the humans would still not be satisfied.

Procedural prompts encourage the creation of highly targeted instructions for learning to achieve a specific process or skill. For example, the prompt **Paraphrase the input into human-sounding text while retaining citations and quotes.** can clear direction to the AI in an educational content creation environment towards the *context* so that the instructional text that it generates will better assist learners in following what they should be doing within the educational context. Similarly, a prompt such as **Develop a lesson plan for teaching students how to conduct a scientific experiment** could help the AI to assemble the learning content in a logical manner, outlining the steps of a scientific experiment in a learner-friendly manner, all the way from defining a hypothesis to recording and analyzing the results. Such an instruction from an AI is greatly beneficial to students engaged in learning scientific experiments. Procedural prompts are also useful for generating operational workflows and processes, particularly in business or industrial environments. The formatting of the answer provided by an AI would ensure the workflow is well-ordered and structured to make it easier for the business to carry out and as fluent as possible, ultimately saving time and labor costs.

Challenges and considerations

Although procedural prompts are powerful tools for reducing ambiguity and encouraging clear, logical instructions, the downside of procedural behavior is that it is dependent on careful management of the communicative environment.

A major challenge is encoding and maintaining the procedural knowledge needed to interpret the prompt correctly and execute each step in the correct order. For example, if the prompt is underspecified or if the AI does not have access to sufficient procedural knowledge about the task, the output result could be incomplete or missing steps, out-of-order, or otherwise inaccurate. To mitigate such risks, procedural prompts must be designed both clearly and precisely, eliminating ambiguity by specifying each step through an intelligible interface.

Another factor of concern is the possibility that procedural prompts over-simplify what someone would say about a task. Sometimes, procedures can be a little too prescriptive and leave out nuances of how to do something. Another possible approach to this is to offer a balance between clarity and detail. One could ask the AI to be clear about what to do yet include enough detail to convey complexity without overwhelming the user with unnecessary information.

To maximize the effectiveness of procedural prompts, consider the following best practices, such as:

- Making language clear and specific, making sure your language is specific and pertains to the end user when creating procedural prompts.

  Keeping it simple is the best way forward. This way, the machine can understand what it needs to do to help human operatives through the process.

- Chunk large tasks that are complicated into bite-sized nuggets. Not only does this make the prompt easier for the AI to follow, but it also creates some coherence in the output it creates. Any additional sub-steps or sections within your prompt will help the AI understand the process you want it to follow. Then, thoroughly test your results to ensure they are hitting the target.

When it comes to tools that instruct AI how to create step-by-step instructions, workflows, or processes, procedural prompts play an important role. Since such outputs have a distinct sequential and logical quality, it is easier to get prompt responses from AI when it is asked to provide clear, detailed, and methodical answers to your prompts– in contexts that include technical documentation, educational content creation, and operational workflows. Examples include instructions for doing laundry, constructing a deck, or walking your dog. Supporting technologies for procedural prompts include clear and specific language citations, more granular sub-task instructions, and accuracy and completeness tests. Used effectively, AI systems that respond to procedural prompts are sometimes clearer, more precise, and more user-friendly than available human-authored alternatives.

Dynamic interactions with adaptive prompts

Adaptive prompts are the most flexible and responsive form of AI interaction. They evolve as the AI responds to or the user provides more information over time within an interaction. While static prompts remain fixed and unchanging, adaptive prompts alter on the fly as the AI adapts to the changing context of interactions based on what happens within that interaction. This dynamic range of interaction is particularly helpful for interactive applications, such as tutors, adaptive learning systems, and real-time decision support systems, where evolution within an interaction is key.

Nature of adaptive prompts

An adaptive prompt allows the AI to iterate, updating the response if new facts emerge or if a user's needs develop over time. The term adaptive prompt was coined by *James Faizollahi*, a student of *Barnden's* at the 2011 New Scientist Minds Meet conference, to capture our attempts to achieve this kind of iteration. Adaptive prompts suit iterative processes because it is often necessary to provide only part of an answer at a time and update as things develop. This form of prompt is particularly well-suited for situations that require you to get feedback before moving on.

For example, a replotted chart of world population change with an explanatory annotation might be followed by an adaptive prompt such as **Paraphrase photosynthesis into human-sounding text while keeping quotes and citations intact. If unsure, explain it using simple terms or an example.** The system might start with a standard description that is primed to respond to the student's confusion with something less complex and more accessible.

The key characteristics of adaptive prompts span several areas:

- **Being dynamic and its responsiveness to the AI's outputs or user's inputs**: The central defining feature of adaptive prompts is responsiveness to the AI's output (or its responses, or its paraphrases) or the user's input. Thus, if you think of a prompt as instructing or directing the AI's response, the adaptation of the prompt in response to the AI's output or the user's input means that the prompt can direct the AI's responses as the interaction unfolds, in real-time, to track changes in context and requirements as they arise. Situations where the context or requirements are likely to change as an AI interaction proceeds are well-suited to adaptive prompts.

- **Well-suited for interactive or iterative applications**: Adaptive prompts are designed to work best with applications that are intended to be continuous or exploratory in nature, where the prompt itself can be adjusted as part of an iterative process based on learnings of how the AI instantiating the system is performing, or how the use of the system is going overall.

Use cases for adaptive prompts

Adaptive prompts can be used to dynamically adapt what is taught to an educational system, based on where a student is in their holistic learning journey, specifically providing the student with helpful scaffolding wherever they are. For instance, an adaptive learning system might use an adaptive prompt to ask questions about a topic, such as: (Basic prompt) `What is the importance of the water cycle to ecosystems?` If a student is `not yet` or unable to answer this sort of question at their learning level, a common occurrence with many questions at their learning level, the prompt can dynamically adapt to provide scaffolding, such as hints, topic-to-question mappings (for example, providing specific questions that paraphrase the prompt), or explanations and rewordings for a student to absorb. If a student understands it, the system can confidently de-escalate. One can readily see how this would help a student on his journey.

Adaptive prompts are excellent for interactive storytelling and games. The preceding system can also be used to generate dynamic stories/gameplay that is responsive to player actions and choices. In an introductory bout of interactive storytelling that could be used as a role-playing game, a prompt for a dungeon crawl might be: `What direction from the town will you take through the forest?` and in the next prompt, the story might throw some new obstacles (for example, a monster in the woods!), new characters (for example, a friendly hooded figure!), or new twists (for example, tiny frogs that can talk!) as a result of your player avatar's new action. Your game is more real to you as it requires responsiveness. You are through the looking glass; now you are in the game! Player engagement, therefore, increases so that the story, or game, still appears more compelling or, at minimum, more interesting because it is evolving around you.

In a related use, tools that offer adaptive dynamic decision guidance can help users make a complex sequential choice in real-time by adapting the decision support to changing context. For example, in a financial decision support system, an adaptive prompt might start by **Do you want me to tell you about investing in low-risk vs high-risk assets?** It might then ask for more granular advice, update its suggestions based on changing market conditions, or might suggest switching to a completely different strategy when the current one will not get the user to achieve their goal.

Challenges and considerations

While adaptive prompts offer many advantages over relying on overt verbal language, they are not without some issues that need careful management. One of the primary challenges will be keeping the adaptive system on track without making it hard for the user to understand what the AI is up to. With the wrong kind of adaptive logic, the AI might begin digressing in unexpected ways or become unclear and erratic. For this reason, it is important to ensure the AI's adjustments are based on a coherent adaptive pathway – a well-thought-out roadmap for taking the conversation wherever it needs to go.

Another consideration is the additional complexity of creating and managing adaptive prompts, particularly in cases where an approach involves adaptive layers. The creation of prompts that can handle a wide variety of possible inputs and outputs and the sampling of those prompts with the AI external environment often necessitates a carefully developed taxonomy of expected inputs and outputs and an iterative plan for how the AI will navigate the landscape of possibilities without becoming inundated or misfiring.

To maximize the effectiveness of adaptive prompts, consider the following best practices, such as:

- Design clear and logical adaptive pathways. When designing adaptive prompts, it becomes essential to design clear and logical paths of adaptation that allow an AI to traverse through all the possible adaptive variation space that could emerge in the course of the interaction. So, a crucial aspect of designing adaptive prompts is deciding upon the space of possible adaptations, which forms the basis of the prompt itself. This entails **frontloading** the space of possible inputs or responses and devising a set of instructions for the AI on how it should tweak, shape, and reframe its response in light of what it receives.

- Designing the space of qualitative adaptations in this fashion helps to ensure smoother qualitative convergence and coherence of the responses that the AI generates in bringing the interaction towards the desired goals. Based on your tests, you will want to modify the flex prompts.

- Balance flexibility with structure to get the right output. Although the flexibility of these prompts is a real virtue, keeping the AI on track – by providing a frame or structure – is equally important. Although we always want the interaction to be flexible, it is a fine balance between bending too much and breaking. If you are on a lederhosen-wearing version of Google, suddenly asking, **What is a dancing** `platform with shoelaces attached to the front called?` might be too much of a departure to stay on topic.

Adaptive prompts reflect a fundamental design principle: the more a computer diagnoses and responds to the particulars of the interaction with the user (or, more broadly, the environment) in real-time, the more likely it can produce more meaningful, contextually appropriate responses. In applications where the AI system must react to real-time changes, such as the next move in an adaptive learning system, the choices made within a story, or how to prioritize tasks over others in a real-time decision support application, adaptive prompts can go a long way toward creating scripts that reflect the varying goals of different users in different stages of their interactions with the system. To keep things on track, AI designers will need to create adaptive prompts with clear, logical pathways, test for consistency and coherence, and manage the ideal balance between flexibility and structure. This will allow us to reap the fullest benefits of the adaptive prompts approach for enriching the user experience and making interactions with AI-driven applications more engaging, effective, and personalized.

Conclusion

In this chapter, you learned about the multitude of prompt types, be it open-ended or close-ended, etc. You learned what the prompt types do well and what their gaps are. You also learned when to use the prompt types and considerations to take when writing them. The ability to leverage these subtle but important prompts will continue to be valuable as AI expands and evolves over time into ever more impressive domains and applications. In the next chapter, we will start our discussion of tokens, what they are, and how they impact prompts.

Join our book's Discord space

Join the book's Discord Workspace for Latest updates, Offers, Tech happenings around the world, New Release and Sessions with the Authors:

https://discord.bpbonline.com

CHAPTER 9

Understanding
Tokens

Introduction

This chapter explains what tokens are and sketches the function they play, conceptually and practically, in machine-learning environments for processing and producing responses. Then it describes the process of tokenizing text and illustrates it with examples in different languages to convey the degree of that versatility but also how tokens relate to processor load.

The chapter also elaborates on the constraints of tokens, such as the token limitations of any given AI model, including GPT-4, and outlines the implications of such constraints on prompt design and the efficiency of AI systems in general. Talking to the details of tokens at the core of AI models provides readers with a structured framework for developing a further-reaching, more granular understanding of how these powerful AI models actually *think* and how we can course-correct when we do (not) like AI's solution. Tokens also will eventually tie into the cost of running AI systems for those eventually working towards a buy vs buy solution. Tokenization is done as a function of the LLM, so while you do not need to manually perform the process, it is good to have insight as to how it works.

Structure

In this chapter, you will learn about the following topics:

- Introduction to tokens
- Using tokens in processing and generating responses
- Tokenization process
- Token limitations
- Implications for artificial intelligence system design
- Future of tokenization in artificial intelligence

Objectives

You will learn in this chapter how tokens work at a detailed level. Tokens directly drive both effective and efficient prompts. Understanding them saves you time and helps keep costs down. You will learn how the tokens are actually extracted from a prompt and how they are broken down into constituent linguistic elements, which are then analyzed. You will learn how they affect memory and processing, and also get a view into system design for AI models, with a view as to what evolution may occur for AI tokens.

Introduction to tokens

Tokens are the building blocks of a prompt in terms of an AI model. They take in language, process it, and respond in language, but the process of converting the input language into pieces of data, which can be worked on by the AI model, is at the core of all human interaction with AI systems. When we flip complicated text into small chunks (either words or sub-words), we make them approachable for modeling. We help AI break tracing its structure and meaning and use it for **natural language processing (NLP)** tasks.

Definition and role of tokens in artificial intelligence

In contemporary AI systems, especially those employed in NLP, the term **token** is used to describe an atomic unit of text. Consider a sentence like: **The quick brown fox jumps over the lazy dog**. An AI model tasked with understanding and operating on this sentence will break the text down into smaller constituent parts. It is somewhat analogous to breaking a larger word down into its sub-elements. Let us look at the word **Cheeseburger** as a very simple example. It is really made up of two words: **Cheese** and **Burger** each one has a distinct meaning. AI breaks all input down into small chunks- words or parts of words- potentially even down into individual characters. For example, **I** can be a letter in a word or a word by itself. So, what happens is the models receive those small chunks, not as a paragraph or a sentence but as a stream of tokens.

Natural language is ingested in the form of text through characters, etc., and these characters or groups of them are immediately processed with tokenization, a linguistic strategy to convert a string of text into a data structure that machine can better handle. As with our cheeseburger example, the transformer models will break the data into the small-sized bites (and ironically **bytes** at the same time) before taking action (while this is a joke, note that in actuality one token equals one byte).

Overview of tokenization in artificial intelligence models

These early NLP models (pre-GPT-4) treated tokens in a much blunter way than current models, usually seeing every word as a separate token, with the semantic value of each word being purely independent of the others. This caused problems with unseen words, misspellings, and languages with large inflections, where one word can have a whole range of forms depending on context.

Modern systems use more nuanced tokenization, employing a method called sub-word tokenization. Models, such as BERT, GPT-4, and other transformers, have recently begun to use this approach. Again, this is where words and sentences are broken down into smaller units, which are tokenized. It is not unlike how the human mind breaks streams of words down into manageable chunks to gain an understanding from words we have not come across before. As with humans, the reason these systems are flexible and can handle any novel words they have not seen before.

In expressing the meaning of the word unhappiness, it might tokenize it as **un-**, **happy**, and **-ness** (and then link those three elements together into a higher-level unit, let us call it **unhappy-ness**, which in turn will cascade into further units, ad infinitum). With a small number of tokens and with a few extras to indicate links between words, this approach offers flexibility: the model can parse new words by building up from the element that is familiar to it. In contrast, the previous passage includes no state-changing utterances at all. Oversimplifying a bit but not terribly so, GPT-4 has become such a high-performing machine-language translator because it generates a highly coherent response by building up those token units into a very efficient collection of non-state-changing units in **intelligible** order.

Tokens central to artificial intelligence communication

At the center of AI communication is the translation from human language to something a machine can **understand**. Tokens are paramount because they are what AI is directly manipulating, querying, and generating. After feeding it text, one of the first things an AI model does is convert the text into a stream of tokens and then translate that into numbers by mapping all the tokens into an embedding space – a mathematical model in the form of a vast, multidimensional landscape in which words that are semantically similar to one another are placed next to each other.

By converting tokens into these mathematical forms, the AI can manipulate them as meaningful, contextual, and relational assemblies of words and thus **understand** and **speak** human prose.

Using tokens in processing and generating responses

Flow of text input to token output: When you interact with an AI model, your input goes through a systematic process that starts with tokenization. For instance, if you type, **What's the weather today?** the AI will break this input into tokens—likely something like: **What**, **s**, **the**, **weather**, **today**, **?**. In truth it is more granular than that usually.

The tokens are processed and are ingested by the model, which then performs the analysis on the sequence. It is effectively doing analysis on each token with different filters based on what has already been entered to help form context but also looking at potential alternate meanings. These create AI-generated insights used to formulate a response.

In our example, you may get a tokenized response akin to: **It's sunny**, **in your area**, **today**. When assembled into human-like communication, again leveraging NLP, it is human-readable.

This flow—from tokenizing the input to generating the output—is at the core of how language models interact with us. It shows how machines can convert human language into structured, computable data and then back into something we can read and understand.

Importance of tokens for efficient computation

A challenge of NLP is the sheer volume of data it needs to ingest, analyze and act upon. Each text that the AI reads and processes must be tokenized, categorized, and stored in a way that enables fast retrieval and manipulation. That is where tokens come in handy, saving valuable computation time.

This process essentially tokenizes language, which means that AI models do not have to assimilate each document as one long string of data. Instead, they work directly with smaller portions, which saves on computation. That means models can now process extremely large data sets – such as books, articles, or social media posts – rapidly and easily.

For instance, one of the models we referenced previously, GPT-4, can deal with as many as 100,000 input tokens in a single input, which is why searches on large texts can be done so promptly. If it were not for tokenization, human language would be so computationally complex that even our current range of interactions with artificial intelligence would not be possible in real-time.

GPT-4 and token optimization case study

Time to take a real-world example. Recall something that makes GPT-4 powerful is because of how it manages and optimizes tokens. Every time you interact with GPT-4, it is not just the words you are typing that matter—it is how the model converts those words into tokens and how it prioritizes them during processing.

Imagine you are working with a limit of 8,000 tokens (a common limit in language models). If your input is 2,000 tokens long, GPT-4 has 6,000 tokens available for generating a response. The model carefully analyzes which tokens are most important, deciding which ones carry the most meaning and how they relate to the overall context. This enables it to generate coherent, detailed responses that feel natural and aligned with your input.

Moreover, token optimization is critical for managing response quality and speed. The fewer tokens a model needs to process, the faster it can deliver a response. GPT-4's ability to process tokens with high efficiency ensures that it can maintain performance even when handling complex queries or vast datasets. In fact, a well-optimized token sequence often leads to a more relevant and higher-quality response because the model spends less time on irrelevant information.

Today, tokens are at the core of every modern AI model now used to process, understand, and generate human language, from breaking text into manageable chunks to quickly and efficiently generating a reply while handling petabytes of data, which powers NLP systems like GPT-4 and BERT. Both computer and data scientists will continue to refine the process to make token injection and action more efficient to reduce the in/out cycle; the semantic analysis, which has to be done rapidly, is substantial.

Tokenization process

When we talk about AI and how it processes text, one of its foundational steps is tokenization. We now know tokenization is the process of **cutting** text up into smaller pieces (known as tokens) for a machine learning model to work with. Let us start with how this works today and then run through the process step-by-step at a bit more technical depth than in the previous section.

Breaking down text into tokens

Tokenization algorithms are how text is split into tokens. There are many algorithmic approaches, but two in particular – **Byte Pair Encoding** (**BPE**) and WordPiece – are the most commonly used in AI. They both convert raw text into smaller pieces we can work with, but they do so differently:

- **BPE**: BPE starts with a basic set of characters via iteration that merges the most common pairs of characters into new, larger tokens. For instance, if **t** and **h** frequently appear together in the text, BPE might merge them into the token **th**. What happens next is that statistical analysis is done to identify pairs that often occur along with one another. As **th** begins, many words in English would be the likely ones to be identified. BPE works well when working on a large vocabulary due to the flexibility you gain using it with the representation of sub-words and words.

- **WordPiece**: The other popular option is WordPiece, which we saw was used in BERT. WordPiece is very similar to BPE and usually appears as a subcomponent of BERT. It begins with a vocabulary of subwords that are known a priori, and then iteratively builds up tokens by combining the subwords so as to cover the full vocabulary.

Detailed steps in the tokenization process

Tokenization is not just about splitting text; it is a structured process:

1. **Input normalization:** Firstly, the input needs to standardize which is done via normalization. In this process, all of the punctuation could be removed, as well as making all capital letters lowercase. This is done so there is consistent input into the tokenization process.

2. **Splitting by spaces:** This process is where words are broken apart based on the spaces, which is a natural place to separate input elements. An example is a phrase such as **peanutbutter and jelly** would be broken into **peanutbutter**, and **jelly**.

3. **Further splitting into subwords or characters:** This occurs after splitting by spaces. Here any subwords which can be created are. In the preceding **peanutbutter** would be split into **peanut** and **butter**, the word **peanut** itself could be split into **pea** and **nut** potentially. This step is crucial for handling complex words and ensuring that tokens are manageable for the model.

Role of vocabulary in tokenization

The vocabulary is basically a list of all possible tokens that a model has learned to recognize. During training, we build a vocabulary for the model based on the tokens it has seen; for example, a model trained on English text might wind up with a vocabulary of individual words and sub-words such as: cat chat ting. When it comes time to process new text, the model consults this list to determine what tokens it should use.

Efficient tokenization – that is, breaking the input into words – and a well-designed vocabulary enable the model to cope with new and unseen words by decomposing them into known sub-word units or by relying on context.

Examples of tokenization in various languages

Performing tokenization in many languages, such as English, is a rather direct exercise as words have clear separators between them- a space. This does not, however, apply to all languages. Remember, AI needs to exist in non-Latin alphabet-based languages as well. Let us look at several non-English languages and see how they are treated via tokenization:

- **Chinese:** Chinese text does not use spaces to separate words, which makes tokenization more challenging. A sentence like 我爱人工智能 (**I love artificial intelligence** in simplified Chinese) needs to be tokenized into meaningful units. AI models have specific tokenizers designed to handle Chinese by using dictionaries of known characters and words.

- **Japanese:** Japanese may or may not use spaces as a separator and/or employ three different scripts (Hiragana, Katakana, and Kanji) that compose the Japanese writing system. This can really make tokenization a challenge, thus driving more complexity into the algorithms for tokenization.

Challenges in tokenizing morphologically rich languages

It is even harder with morphologically rich languages such as Turkish or Finnish, or morphological languages, where words can consist of several morphemes (the smallest individually meaningful units of language). Take the word **lentokonesuojeluskuntamuseo** that exists in Finnish; it loosely means **aviation museum**, but it literally translates into its three component words. It is a word with a translation in English for sure, but some of the subtle meaning is lost, as it literally translates into **airplane attack-protect organization-museum**.

How do AI models handle such challenges? They optimize the tokenization of sub-words, which will build a stronger model of tokens with greater individual meaning.

Tokenization of programming languages

When it comes to ingesting programming languages for AI, syntax is an absolute must. In the case of programming languages, like Python, a syntax and sentence structure exists which needs to be assimilated by models trained for coding understanding.

Tokenization refers to breaking down code into meaningful components, such as keywords, operators, identifiers, symbols, and whitespaces. Let us take a very short look at a real-world example. The Python code snippet **`for i in range(10):`** would be tokenized to tokens such as **for, i, in,** and **10**. Tokenization is what lets the model understand the sequence and purpose of code when solving tasks like code completion or bug checking.

Understanding tokenization is key to understanding how AI models work with text and code. It forms the foundation of most NLP and machine learning applications, allowing models to take in, handle, and interpret the large mass of data without getting overwhelmed. Understanding tokenization gives us insight into how AI models interpret and work with text and code. It is a fundamental aspect of NLP and machine learning, enabling models to handle and make sense of the vast amount of data they encounter.

Token limitations

The way that AI models today perform is very much due to the limitations of the use of tokens. Token limits are just that the maximum count of tokens (therefore text) that an AI model can ingest and process in a single request. Think of it as the size of the bite of data that can be taken at once.

The limits are driven by the model's architecture and how well it can perform. Each new model does a better job, but a limit still exists for each one. Each token a model processes uses computer memory and demands computational resources. The longer the input, the more memory you need to store and process it, which could lead to a significant drop in performance. So, each model has a set limit, which you cannot exceed to keep the model as efficient as possible. One of the drivers of vast speed increases of AI models in the last few years has been a great focus on increasing the token limits. Clearly, if a model cannot look far past a few hundred tokens (words) at any given point in time, it would not be able to retain context over sentences and paragraphs. As a result, these models tend to work best on short stretches of text or reduced versions of longer texts.

Effect on memory and processing power

The link between token limits and model memory footprint is direct: the more tokens, the more memory. Each token incurs a load, and when we are talking about sufficiently large pieces of text, the model needs to bring that load under control if it is not to degrade in performance. You might want to use a model with features for handling thousands of tokens. Although this means it needs greater memory to save context and more processing time as the model parses and generates pieces of text. If the input is too large, it might trim text to come under the token limit, and the model will lack critical context to produce a coherent response.

Given these constraints, several strategies have emerged to handle token limits effectively:

- **Text truncation**: Cut off the text that exceeds the limit of tokens. Though it is easy to do, important information might be lost. So clearly, knowing what to truncate needs to be identified with a high degree of care.

- **Summarization**: Summarization is just that, taking a larger body of work but ensuring to emphasize the salient points. For example, one could summarize a lengthy article into bullet points, such that the model would have to process the gist of what the article says rather than all of it.

- **Splitting**: You can chop up your long text inputs into sections or chunks of text less than the token limit, each of which you can process one by one. However, remember to work on the continuity between the chunks to ensure coherence and context when processing them.

Designing effective prompts within token constraints

Writing prompts that fit within its token limit requires careful thinking about what will be relevant since there is little space for extraneous information. At the same time, a good prompt should read like full-length text so that the AI responds in a similar way to a person. Suppose your instruction is asking a model to paraphrase a long document into human-sounding text while retaining citations. In that case, the prompt should specify the length of the summary and highlight which sections are most important to address. Stripping the prompt of irrelevant aspects helps to make the most out of the allotted tokens and make the AI's response more relevant.

Example scenarios of prompt optimization

Consider the following two prompts for a model with a token limit:

- **Verbose prompt**: Let us use an example of a rather wordy prompt: `Provide analysis of the impact of hydropower on US States with large river systems. Include historical insights as to their total electrical generation mix over the last decade and how it affected the cost of each kilowatt-hour generated.`

- **Concise prompt**: Now let us take a look at that prompt but refine it: `...in the last five years, what percentage of hydro-electric power was generated in Washington State and analyze the cost of electricity in Washington in that time`

Although, the verbose provides more context, the concise version is less likely to take the model over the token limit and is thus, more conducive to keeping the model on topic. The verbose prompt, while more helpful in terms of providing context, is also more likely to be rejected by the model due to its token limit or might force the model to cut off or truncate useful information.

Long context handling allows for the retention of context that will extend beyond the token limit. For this, AI systems use several methods like the following:

- **Memory-based model:** The focus here is all about retaining information from previous prompts would allow it to refer back to previous prompts and answers to give a better setting. This can keep contextual information over longer dialogues or documents. One can think of this as how session variables are used for HTTP requests.

- **Context windows:** These involve sliding windows of tokens that move over the text, making sure that every segment of the text is meaningfully considered in context with the segments surrounding it. This way, models can cope with longer contexts by processing sub-segments sequentially and maintaining coherence in doing so.

For technical writers, a token limit could influence the length or detail of the response. Explanations or analyses would have to be abbreviated to leave room for follow-up questions, potentially affecting the quality of their answers.

Knowing how to apply token limits is important for how AI models are used. This could include strategies for coping with prompt, input, and output limitations, combined with an understanding of how to design prompts in a way that enhances human-sounding text rather than detracting from it.

Implications for artificial intelligence system design

When we think about AI, particularly the models that handle language, code, or images, one of the key concepts we need to understand is **tokenization**. Tokenization is the process of breaking down a piece of data—whether it is text, code, or even images—into smaller units called **tokens** that a machine can process. These tokens are like building blocks, and the way we choose and manage them has a big impact on the architecture of AI systems.

Tokenization and model architecture

The impact of tokenization on model design has implications for model design and is particularly relevant for large language models like GPT, where transformers have their biggest use so far. Think of it like constructing a house – if you are working with a brick building, we want the bricks to be as similar as possible so it is easier to manage. Now, if you are dumping a massive pile of raw stones at the construction site, that can be a messy situation to work with and a difficult and inefficient to process. So, instead, we turn that squishy pile of raw stones into segments – that can be handled by the AI model in an efficient way.

When we consider transformers, the architecture behind many of the current state-of-the-art models, including GPT, models like them operate on token sequences, hinging on the fact that we can represent input data in a format that the model can work with. How we tokenize input data, therefore, fundamentally determines how a model learns to find patterns and relationships in it.

In the case of near-context-free tokenization, like breaking down text into words or sub-words, is used to construct training data from an unprocessed text stream. Sub-word tokenization is often preferred because it allows the model to better handle complex, inhibited, or out-of-vocabulary words that it has never seen before by breaking them up into constituent sub-words. This, in turn, affects what kind of architecture the AI can legitimately estimate. A model using word tokenization runs into the problem of having to account for a vast vocabulary, which involves training much slower and less parsimoniously than some algorithms allow when built otherwise, such as through sub-word, and near-context-free tokenization, among other alternatives.

Role of tokens in scaling artificial intelligence models

As AI models scale—getting bigger and more powerful—the importance of tokenization becomes even more critical. When training models on massive datasets that span multiple domains like language, programming code, or even images, the tokenization scheme has to balance between granularity and efficiency.

Let us take an example from NLP. If you are training a model like GPT on vast datasets with millions of sentences, word-level tokenization quickly becomes unmanageable because the vocabulary becomes too large. However, if you break down those words into sub-word tokens, you end up with fewer unique tokens and the model can generalize better across different languages and domains. That efficiency is how it is able to perform equally well on data from different domains – whether that is text from legal documents, medical records, or images.

For models that work in multimodal domains (like **Contrastive Language-Image Pre-Training** (**CLIP**), which maps text to images), tokenization allows the same model to work well for textual as well as visual input; here, tokens can also be patches of an image. Toy-like sighted agents that share their experience, leading to multiple toy-like minds in computer novel systems modeled on the mimicry of human brains, are being constructed scaled up in both model size and dataset size by tokenization. Since the output of these AI models is determined by how well they learn to process their input, the ability of tokenization to allow this across different kinds of data is crucial to their scalability.

Custom tokenization for domain-specific tasks

In certain fields where sentence structure, abbreviations, terms, and more are pathological or domain-specific (for example, in medicine or law), generic tokenization is not sufficient. Here, NLP needs domain-specific tokenization to model that pathology.

Let us use an example of the medical industry. Medicine has an extraordinarily broad and specific language. Any AI system trained and deployed to work in medical contexts requires a bespoke tokenization scheme, as medical language is often highly specialized, inherently complex, and often domain-specific. Generic tokenization, optimized for every day, everyday language, tends to fall apart when confronted with unfamiliar constructs in text, such as medical and technical terms, abbreviations, and shorthand notations, as well as largely syntactically structured data, such as diagnostic or toxicology coding systems that enable concise, machine-consumable capture of medical events, drug names, laboratory tests, vital signs, and other medical information. Some technical terms present specific challenges with respect to processing; for example, the term **hypertension** might be tokenized as a list of sub-words (**hyper** and **tension**) or even **broken apart** and treated as distinct, independent words). This could lead to data loss or ambiguity, as the absolute and medical context will be lost on the AI if **pressure** is treated, for example, in the same way as *press*. While in common English, they could have generally similar meanings, in medical terms, they do not. In this case, a custom tokenization scheme will maintain *hypertension* as a single, unified sub-word, allowing the model to process it correctly.

Case histories in medical texts also often consist of highly structured data – numbers from lab results, dosages of drugs, and aspects of treatment protocols produced in a tabular format – intermixed with natural language. In the current vocabulary of NLP, pre-trained tokenizers could be applied in a **generic** fashion that lumps all text into the *more or less meaningless* category and fails to recognize subtle types. Those who want to design the interfaces of a clinical decision-making system should opt for custom-built tokenization approaches that identify and handle numerical and categorical data (also when presented in human-sounding text, for example, dosages: 500mg; lab results: HbA1c: 7.5%) in a way preserving their context and semantics.

Imagine that we are considering medical text processing that is based on using diagnosis jargon. Medical terms such as **hypertension** or **cardiomegaly** will not appear frequently in general-purpose data that would be used to train a language model. Worse, though, general tokenization might fragment **cardiomegaly** into **cardio**, **mega**, and **ly**, where they are no longer some significant part of speech. Custom tokenization can instead identify such specialist terms, treating them as single tokens and retaining the integrity of the term so that the domain model will have a better sense of its specialist meaning. We can be confident that AI diagnostic tools are being created at some of the best universities with both excellent medical schools and computer science or data science departments, let alone start-up companies seeing a huge potential for such a tool.

In addition to the preceding issues mentioned, AI systems used to assist legal professionals must adopt a bespoke approach to tokenization due to the highly technical and precise nature of legal language. The vocabulary used in laws and judgments – think of phrases like **habeas corpus** and **force majeure** – is not necessarily found anywhere else and can be fragmented or misunderstood by general-purpose approaches to tokenization. In such cases, it makes sense to treat these terms as single units, particularly as many of these phrases are coined to carry a particular legal significance, which general-purpose tokenization models cannot account for. It would be impossible for an AI system to parse legal documents and complete legal tasks, such as sentencing proposals or contract analysis, without a bespoke tokenization strategy that captures the nuances of the legal vocabulary. When a legal term is broken down incorrectly, or first-order representations of legal documents lose meaning as a result of contracted tokenization, key legal concepts are lost or warped and come out flawed – facts that, if overlooked, can lead to incorrect verdicts and consequential miscarriages of justice.

A rationale that led us to design our own custom-coded tokenization was the nature of legal writing, which can be highly structured and repetitive. Legal documents, like contracts, statutes, and case law, can have rigid syntax suggested by their structure, making them amenable to automation; legal writing also typically employs a specific set of phrases that recur but vary in important specific and legal ways. Generic tokenization techniques would miss some or all these patterns or fail to capture the hierarchical and generative structure of legal writing. With a custom tokenization method that is tailored to those recurring legal patterns of phrasing and syntax, AI models can become more aware of the generative or hierarchical structures of legal writing – clauses, provisions, or legal precedent – and when doing contract-review or legal-document-drafting work areas, can make better predictions.

Moreover, legal systems differ considerably from place to place. At the state level, provisions have different sets of rules with their own choice of terminology, quotations from precedential cases, or legal standards. Customized tokenization permits AI systems to tokenize legal documents in a manner that is appropriate to the jurisdiction and consistent with the regional or local tradition of practice. A specialized tokenizer can achieve better results in this domain by making sure terms such as **writ of habeas corpus** or **amicus curiae** are handled as cohesive terms rather than dissolved into their basic component sub-words, giving the law profession a custom AI tool. One can assume that this is being worked on by multiple companies today to identify a tool to help build legal briefs and documents or prep legal teams for trial.

Future of tokenization in artificial intelligence

As AI models become more sophisticated, so do the tokenization methods we employ to tokenize input data – today, we are seeing ever more fine-grained sub-word models that we already discussed, such as the sub-word models discussed previously, like BPE and SentencePiece, that are halfway between word-based and character-based tokenization, allowing models to efficiently process large vocabularies. The future of tokenization might expand modularity even further into much smaller pieces. Select researchers are already prototyping character-level modeling where instead of being tokenized at the word or sub-word level, we tokenize at the character level, granting even finer control over our data processing. This might prove especially beneficial to tasks where a word means little and a character means everything – for instance, in code generation or particularly technical use cases.

The other is continuous token streams. With indefinite tokenization, there is no separate algorithm to recognize where one token ends and another begins. It is an interesting evolution in the way AI systems can handle and process language. In a world where AI systems operate on streams of discrete, working with continuous streams of tokens means changing the way data can be filtered and processed in an inherently fluid, streaming way. This could make it easier for a computer system to maintain a flowing conversation informationally rather than making it react to isolated, finite token distribution.

One of the major potential benefits of the token stream is that it provides a better way of managing more live, extended contexts. The token stream alleviates the tight constraint on the number of tokens in many models, providing more flow and, therefore, hopefully, more contextual accuracy in modeling, like in applications for real-time conversation, lengthy content curation, and analysis, for instance.

A constant stream of tokens has the potential to offer more context-sensitive real-time processing of language and systems, giving more efficient handling of large amounts of information involved in complex contextual and time-dependent tasks and the capacity to deliver richer outputs for the user of the AI model. Today's IT infrastructure is replete with systems to manage huge volumes of real-time data; this could potentially be leveraged as a foundational architecture for AI systems.

Potential developments

You might pose the question, Are we looking at a scenario in which all AI models will eventually dispense with tokens altogether? Some have argued that we will progress to AI systems that operate on continuous representations of language, image or sound, rather than those based on tokens.

Neural-symbolic models are a focal point for efforts to pioneer new models of AI that can escape some of the constraints of token-based systems. Unlike token-based models, which tend to flag or ignore symbols only based on extensive experience with them (like unusually long sentences, for example), neural-symbolic systems are supposed to integrate more power of both neural networks and symbolic reasoning. They could end up changing how AI systems see the world and how we interact with them. A neural-symbolic model combines the ability of neural networks to recognize patterns in large amounts of data and the ability of symbolic systems to reason explicitly about complex relations.

By bringing these two approaches together, neural-symbolic models might be able to escape the token trap altogether. Rather than tokenize language, based as it is on relationships, these models might draw on a broader understanding of language and concepts – for example, symbolic representations of knowledge and relationships, which enable the model to have a more nuanced and context-aware concept of the world and what it is doing with it. This would allow the model to get to work. The AI Model will work to move from more vague responses to more specific responses. Humans are good at making leaps, but AI systems need to do it systematically.

Neural-symbolic models could help enhance how AI systems cope with longer-range continuity and context in text. Token-based models struggle as they cannot simultaneously track a huge number of tokens; neural-symbolic systems, by contrast, could potentially maintain and reason about wider contexts, allowing for better performance in applications that require longer-term understanding and coherence in extremely long texts or complex actions. Taken together, these types of neural-symbolic models promise to be token-independent, taking AI out of the realm of pink-slime parodies and closer to a new type of AI capability. The combination of neural and symbolic approaches in a single model could ultimately alter how AI systems understand and produce language, setting the stage for more context-sensitive, versatile applications.

There is still another approach that could be taken towards neural embeddings that represent data directly as dense, continuous vectors. If this embedding can encode rich relationships between different data types (for example, words, phrases, or even images), then tokenization as we know it could become unnecessary – in theory, anyway. This would change the paradigm of how AI models are built and trained, which could make tokenization irrelevant.

Neural embeddings are an important next step in the evolution of AI toward information-rich deep representations. In token-level approaches, tokens are abstracted out as discrete entities in respective slots of an AI production rule and then interpreted as discrete tuples of information in memory. In neural embeddings, the token information is dense and continuous, embedded in vectors of continuous information.

Neural embeddings represent data points (usually words, phrases or entire documents) in continuous vector spaces in which semantically similar items are positioned close to one another. They excel at representing complex patterns and relationships. Since they are learned from our data and re-trained as the models are used, the embeddings can represent subtle semantic nuances and contextual variation that might otherwise be flattened by a token-based approach. Each representation is a moving target that, as we produce text, gradually updates until it settles on the most appropriate linguistic meaning. This mechanism allows a model to handle synonyms and polysemy (that is, words that have multiple meanings, such as *cover*) and other linguistic phenomena better than many past methods and to accomplish it without complex coding.

They are not subject to token constraints. In token-based models, the lengths of texts captured (or the scales of context that can be held across long passages) are limited by predetermined token bounds. Embeddings provide a more elastic representation of information that can grow and shrink at the same rate as the information itself. This allows for larger, more coherent, and well-contextualized outputs in tasks such as translation, summarization or contextualization of language.

Neural embeddings are a major leap forward in data representation for AI models. The added dimension of continuous dense space allows a more nuanced capture of semantic relationships and context, compared with the original sparse token-based representation, which can make all the difference. Hopefully, this improvement will lead to more complex and accurate AI applications as well. Just imagine new possibilities in automated natural language understanding and generation.

Conclusion

In this chapter, we learned about tokenization, which is essential to the design, scaling, and specialization of AI models. We learned about the make-up of tokens, and how they are actually used during the input of prompts to break broad information down into manageable pieces. We reviewed examples of tokens and focused on critical guidelines to keep in mind when creating your own custom prompts.

In the next chapter, we will take what we have learned and start to craft prompts with a focus on efficiency. Efficient prompts give us an overall lower cost basis when managing AI systems at scale, or even if you have a subscription to an AI service and want to maximize your spend.

Join our book's Discord space

Join the book's Discord Workspace for Latest updates, Offers, Tech happenings around the world, New Release and Sessions with the Authors:

https://discord.bpbonline.com

CHAPTER 10

Efficiency in Prompt Engineering

Introduction

In this chapter, we present a thorough examination of the argument that efficiency is of fundamental concern in prompt engineering – **artificial intelligence** (**AI**) and **machine learning** (**ML**) development that utilizes training data with specific sets of instructions (prompts) to generate outputs that fulfill various goals. We begin by explaining why efficiency is a consideration of importance in prompt engineering, emphasizing the fact that the increase in accuracy of responses and system performance that well-designed prompts yield hold immense utility.

It then pivots to providing information on different types of prompts that enable greater efficiency and the importance of wording them clearly and succinctly. Along with some practical tools for readers to use, this section offers a selection of metrics to assess prompt quality, as well as some examples (optimized and non-optimized) to illustrate the benefits of adopting more efficient ways of engineering prompts. With this material, the chapter seeks to help readers grasp the methods needed to improve their engineering of prompts and, by extension, to increase their AI applications' functionality.

Structure

In this chapter, you will learn about the following topics:

- Introduction to prompt efficiency

- Impact of efficiency on computational costs
- Benefits of efficient prompts
- Strategies for efficient prompt design
- Measuring and optimizing efficiency
- Future considerations for efficient prompt engineering

Objectives

In this chapter, you will learn how to consider efficiency in prompt engineering as efficiency not only gets the answer you are looking for faster, but it is also less expensive. We will learn about efficiency from an architectural perspective and the real-world benefits of efficiency in prompts, as well as move into the best strategies for you to consider.

Introduction to prompt efficiency

Efficiency is about the ability to specify and generate prompts that elicit the best performance in AI models while also minimizing cost. Put another way, the ability to write efficient prompts is the ability to provide AI models with the right amount of information that leads to the best interpretation and processing of the prompt without any wasted or noisy information. Prompt efficiency is not the same as short prompts, although prompt brevity is part of the picture. For example, a prompt for an instruction-following AI might ensure that the model gives the right answer by providing auxiliary information about the context, but a more efficient prompt would accomplish the same result with fewer words. Efficient prompts matter because, in principle, they would allow us to maximize performance while minimizing computational costs in a wide range of AI applications. The design space for AI systems is rich, especially for systems that perform a combination of complex tasks, such as machines that can both process text and visual data.

Scope of efficiency in prompt engineering

The reach of efficiency in prompt engineering becomes clear when we look at its ubiquity. Whether you are training a conversational AI chatbot, requesting an AI assistant to generate a code snippet, or running a query through a business intelligence system, there is a crucial role for efficiency in the prompt. Namely, it determines whether the system can respond fast and accurately or if it will produce a response that falls short of user expectations and is, therefore, computationally wasteful (for the AI system) or frustrating (for the user). When prompts are not effective, they can produce ambiguous, partial, or even incorrect responses, wasting more computational effort and user frustration. So again, we see that efficiency is not only about reducing computational strain – its relevance to the quality of AI outputs also makes it a key goal in building reliable AI systems.

Role of prompt engineering in AI performance

Without an understanding of prompt efficiency, we cannot fully comprehend how efficacy is impacted in the larger AI ecosystem. Even the most sophisticated AI models, such as language models with 100 billion parameters, represent a black-box system that must extrapolate vast quantities of information based on a sparse input metric. The AI's ability to do this accurately is contingent upon the prompt being of sufficient quality and being understood correctly. In other words, the interface between the user's meaning and the AI's representation of that meaning is crucial to the relationship. It follows that if the interface is vague, overly complicated, or simply outside the model's reach, the very essence of the communication will be unclear to the system, and its ability to return an accurate or useful answer will be seriously undermined. Efficient prompts, on the other hand, retain the AI's capacity for versatility and precision in execution. They embed signals within the text that communicate to the model what is likely to be the most relevant factors in addressing or completing the given task and minimize the risk of the model responding with an irrelevant or erroneous output. In cases where response time or speed of decision is crucial, the efficacy of prompt engineering can be the critical distinction between a successful interaction and a failure.

Efficiency impacts resource utilization

Prompt engineering efficiency is highly significant as well: it is a factor that directly influences the quality of responses outputted by the AI and the number of resources required to compute those responses. When you optimize your prompts, you tend to elicit more accurate, concise, or coherent responses from the AI. As a result, you are less likely to have to repeat or clarify your query. This matters in minimizing cognitive overhead when the AI is being used in real-time interactions with humans, such as in customer service bots, shopping assistants used for reading reviews, or some virtual assistants. Inefficient prompts often yield responses that are either verbose, redundant, or irrelevant. Such responses waste both the user's time and require the system itself to expend more computational resources than necessary. For instance, every prompt processed by an AI model consumes computational power and memory; larger language models are linear in computational cost per token, which means that additional words in the prompt or response serve as an overhead cost. Efficient prompts reduce this overhead by ensuring that what the AI focuses on is a relevant subset of information, which can entail faster throughput times, less energy use, and larger and faster systems that can handle more users without compromising the user experience.

Examples of efficiency leading to better outcomes

Each of the following real-world cases highlights the real, tangible benefits of this prompt-honing strategy. Let us look at customer support-related AI systems. The expectation here is for a prompt that is efficient, asking only for seminal bites of information from its users while retaining its bandwidth for more complex cognitive activities. In this scenario, redundancy from added queuing questions that only serve to inflate communication overhead will hinder the desirable outcome and delay the resolution of the query. Thinking more like a human agent for humans, a well-crafted support prompt should strike a delicate balance between specificity and brevity. A favorable result: every interaction with the support AI would elicit a more targeted response if it had to collect information in an incremental fashion, increasing user satisfaction and reducing the number of tickets that need to be addressed physically by support agents at a lower operational cost, and lowering server load since fewer API calls are required to solve the problem.

Prompts should be as informative as possible so that the model generates relevant, good-quality content. In these cases, efficacy depends on the prompt, clearly informing the model of what type of content (a recipe, a book review, a biography, etc.), in what tone (formal, casual, academic), and of what length (50 words, five paragraphs) the user wants the content to be. Conversely, inefficient prompts could result in boring, irrelevant, incoherent outputs. When users need AI-generated content for work, it is important that they can rely on the model to provide something good, quickly, and with minimal editing, which highlights the importance of keeping the prompt structure in check. This way, organizations can save much time editing the AI's work and get on with their next task much more quickly.

In more advanced prompts for AI data-science/code-generating systems, the leaner the prompt, the less computationally taxing it will be for it to fulfill the request. For instance, a code-writing AI can deliver insights to a user if prompted appropriately. For example, AI might generate clarifying insights about trends within a given data set upon efficient prompting. A lean prompt that provides the AI with the bare essentials for the nature of the task (enough to execute the process without offering it unnecessary information or computational loads), can allow it to deliver human-sounding snippets of insights or relevant data summaries to the user, as opposed to serving up pages of data onto which the reader needs to do search-and-rescue computations.

An important takeaway from the discussion of efficiency is that writing an efficient prompt can be as essential for the performance of an AI system from an engineering perspective as it can be for the AI-user experience. Efficient prompts not only make it easier for an AI system and user to interact with each other but also accelerate response accuracy, minimize resource expenditure, and ultimately make the system more scalable, responsive, and less costly to operate. As AI continues to develop and mature over time, the ability to engineer prompts that are optimized for engineer-definable degrees of efficiency will be more important than ever since it serves as a key lever in exploiting the full potential of these systems into more viable and reliable tools for increasingly demanding real-world use.

Impact of efficiency on computational costs

There is a clear connection to computational costs: each time a user enters a prompt into an AI model, it costs something. Modern AI models, especially many of those determining language, are very computationally expensive. At each timestep (another word for an internal iteration or step through the program), the model takes a single input prompt and runs it through a vast sea of parameters it has learned early in its training – predicting and generating a possible response for every input. For particularly long prompts or difficult tasks, this will spend more timesteps exploring possibilities, all of which boosts the demand for infrastructure for these systems, uses more power, and requires more upkeep. By being as efficient as possible with our prompts, we pump the most out of each dollar spent on infrastructure in these current models. Efficiency also becomes important for organizations deploying AI at scale. When it comes to companies paying for a service of AI systems, you generally pay for tokens that you both send and receive, as the AI system has to receive a token, then responds in kind.

Resource optimization to reducing API calls

Getting the prompt in and out efficiently gets the answer fast and keeps costs down. For end users of an AI system, it gives them a better experience, so they are more likely to continue to use the system. Prompts might need a fair bit of analysis, depending on the complexity. At this stage, the backend servers are fully stressed, and this stress is what takes a toll on speed. A well-crafted prompt allows the AI model to focus on scoring the task quickly, which means that there are fewer quotes processed at the back end. In purely technical terms, fewer queries mean less external interaction. Accordingly, this shows up directly as a reduction in the number of API calls, which in turn translates to less server load during the execution of each query, impacting the overall performance of the system (which ultimately means that we can process more queries at the same time). As mentioned earlier, this directly translates into better scalability since a service is based on size/scale. All these factors are directly related to another dimension: energy usage and cooling. Companies trying to be more energy-conscious and operationally efficient are concerned about these factors.

Lowering operational expenses

Although it is not an immediately obvious advantage, one of the most clear-cut benefits is the potential for reduced business costs for any company implementing a large-scale AI. Any company that uses an AI customer service bot, a data-analysis tool, or a content-generation system will see reduced maintenance costs often linked with computational overhead. The longer it takes for a system to process data or the slower it responds to requests, the higher the costs – in terms of cloud infrastructure maintenance as well as usage charges. A prompt that produces quick, efficient responses can reduce maintenance costs for companies dealing with high request volumes. Large language models are charged per token (a character or word in a prompt), and so any prompt that produces the same efficiency with fewer tokens reduces usage costs directly.

Improving response times and user experience

Practically, the faster an AI can generate a plausible and relevant answer, the more satisfying and useful that experience can be. If prompt architecture encourages an AI agent to arrive at a crisp and focused answer to a user query as quickly as possible, it will include information that both the system and the user are interested in and will deliver that information faster than otherwise. If every system could do that, it would greatly benefit user experience. There are many examples of this: in e-commerce, where purchasing decisions can hinge on small latencies, a slow response can lead to a user abandoning the cart; in customer support, where wait time is associated with increased irascibility and systems are frustrated by this, a slow response is likely to lead to a user becoming angry. Prompt efficiency is a race against latency.

AI in customer support

How quick, accurate responses drive satisfaction. A well-written prompt makes quick service and correct responses easier in customer-support environments, too. Because AI systems are often the first contact for customer issues, resolution times vary significantly, depending on the prompt and how much actionable information it takes to resolve the issue. A poorly written prompt might ask for information that the AI already has, or it might ask for something completely irrelevant to the problem – that is, the interaction will take more steps, requiring, at some point, more costly human intervention. By contrast, a well-written prompt allows the AI to find the information it needs in the fewest steps, so the query gets resolved more quickly, freeing up human agents in those routine issues and avoiding escalation. This level of efficiency can save a company time and money by allowing human agents to tackle more complex problems. As a rule, these routine queries could happen autonomously since the AI is built to handle them.

Real-time AI applications

How efficiency enables smoother interactions. Once AI is applied to automated trading or emergency services – as well as in other scenarios in which the system offers, say, real-time transcription – prompt efficiency might be of the utmost importance. In financial market dynamics, there is a quick interplay among many automated systems eyeing the market and reacting to changes in milliseconds. In such contexts, an instantaneous but inefficient prompt that delayed the AI's response by a fraction of a second could result in millions of dollars of losses. In emergency response systems, which rely on AI for real-time analysis or to dispatch help, a prompt that takes no time, leading to smoother, more assured interactions, could mean prompt and promptly effective assistance – and conversely, delayed action. Any error made by poorly functioning systems that are not able to fulfill their purpose effectively can easily lead to disaster.

Enhancing model performance with well-designed prompts

Getting the best out of AI often depends on writing prompts as effectively as possible to boost the robustness of the model. Poorly formulated prompts lead the model to produce sensible-looking text that is simply irrelevant, long-winded, or ambiguous. Using too many tokens or offering unclear instructions forces the model to devote resources to extraneous processing, which can lead to a bloated response that roams more widely (and less relevantly) – a worse outcome from the user's perspective, and from the model's viewpoint because it has to work harder. Writing prompts that nudge the model toward the information needed or the specific task to accomplish reduces the chances of disjointed outputs and expensive, wasteful token usage. Minimizing token usage overlooks not only computational costs but also the AI's strongest capacity, which is to concentrate on the bare bones of the task at hand. The consequence is cleaner, more actionable data.

Efficient prompt design also requires making sure that the prompt sticks to the bare essentials of a task. For instance, if the use case is to have an AI summarize a lengthy document, an efficient prompt is one that is clear and directive. It would say something to the effect of: `Paraphrase the input into human-sounding text while retaining citations and quotes`. By contrast, an inefficient prompt in this case might be: `Paraphrase the input while retaining its length and quotes`. The least efficient prompt would be something like: `Paraphrase the input while retaining its citations and quotes` – which might result in something like: `Paraphrase the input whilst retaining citations and quotes`. This does not even make sense! In all three cases, the result is an AI model that spends more computing power on the task simply because the user has not been sufficiently precise with their request. Similarly, a prompt for code generation that is too verbose might result in the AI writing needlessly long and convoluted code, while an efficiently calibrated prompt will help the AI code short, understandable, and functional code that just does the job.

Aggregate efficiency-versus-inefficiency case studies show concrete differences in the cost of computation and model performance. Once, a simple judgment call helped a customer service AI identify a better way to prompt input from a user. All sensors were green. Two different design patterns for prompts were utilized to achieve the same objective: the inefficient version was verbose and prone to ambiguity. It required multiple QA steps from the AI to the user in order to validate intent; this led to both a greater count of QA steps in total and also a longer total time spent in interaction. Both scenarios frustrated the user and escalated cheque counts, sparking more expense in larger businesses running the AI in parallel. Once prompts were rewritten for efficiency, the needed QA steps went down by half; response times were better; the AI was able to resolve queries in fewer steps; as misclassification is expensive, the model saved costs with improved efficiency. Reduced server load translated into reduced friction in processing and, therefore, a clear financial benefit to the business running the AI system. At another time, an automated content generator, using an AI, communicated with users through prompts. Optimizing prompts to emphasize both clarity and brevity improved both costs of output and quality since the system was able to compile requests in fewer words (lower token count), trimming the costs to feed the model with input.

Efficiency trickles down to influence computational costs at every level of an AI system's functional layers. Optimizing prompt design can directly reduce the resources required to deploy APIs, as well as improve response times and output quality, both of which incrementally decrease computational costs and improve user quality of experience and system performance, all at the same time. As we see AI systems continue to grow in complexity and scale, the importance of efficiency in prompt design will likely remain central to ensuring their ability to remain an affordable, responsive and highly useful set of technologies for a large number of applications.

Benefits of efficient prompts

Beyond saving instruction time, proper prompt engineering offers a number of benefits. Being efficient benefits those who receive the prompt, both AI models and the humans giving them direction. So why do prompts get so convoluted? Just like tangled instructions given to a human worker can cause stress and cognitive overload, inefficient prompts given to an AI model can also cause unnecessary confusion and slow down an AI model's ability to focus on the words that matter.

Reducing cognitive overload

When a prompt is given to an AI model, the model has to read, range, and contextualize the text to orient itself in a way that is relevant to the requested action. This all requires computation, and inefficient prompts can cause unnecessary cognitive overload. Now, imagine you work at a factory that makes pens, and one day, a new boss is recruited to improve efficiency at your company. To start, she has a clear goal – increase productivity. With this clear direction in mind, she makes a number of changes – perhaps more radio breaks, decreased lighting, and revamped onboarding for new hires. After a few months, the company is working efficiently and everyone is happy. However, what exactly prompted this efficiency boost? Now, imagine this story applied to a prompt engineer trying to help a company train an AI system that performs a process like recognizing and classifying images.

Let us look at how to ensure a prompt is concise to focus on your core task. This economy of focus is particularly important because short prompts are the ones that truly focus the AI on the ask. Long, inefficient prompts might imply a meandering and verbose response that the AI might try to provide as it loops around every possible task interpretation in the input. In contrast, a short, efficient prompt shows the AI exactly what the user means, so it can narrow its focus to the pinpointedly requested information or action. Beyond efficiency, relevant AI use depends on relevance. The core task might be writing an efficient 300-word essay about the dangers of climate change. Fortunately, a user can ask for exactly that in the prompt. A concise prompt, for example, might say: `,create a table of contents and a 300 word essay with references on the mathematical model behind climate change`. This is clearly giving the AI too much to do, even though the larger length is ultimately irrelevant. The AI could respond with a written narrative that stretches beyond 8,000 words, creating a wasted workload for the user. A robust content generation API should not waste words while pulling content out or time when inserting words back in. The best economy of focus will still create something relevant, timely, and usable. A concise prompt allows the user to specify exactly what the AI must deliver and nothing more. The best prompts deliver an economy of focus, concision, and clarity in one.

Let us look at designing prompts to give focused more relevant responses. An AI model informed with a well-designed prompt is far likelier to respond to the query with fewer, more relevant candidate responses. A prompt that is too open-ended often leaves an AI model with too many possible interpretations, which in turn manifests as a large number of candidate answers, few or none of which are actually what the user wants. One way that careful prompt design reduces this ambiguity is by making explicit the scope of the task. Consider this task on data analysis: `Paraphrase this table into human-sounding text while retaining quotes and citations`. The model tackling this query will flood the query with numerous datasets. However, by giving it clear guidelines, such as `Identify the top three growth trajectories in Q1 revenue`, we can instead give the AI model a narrower and more useful scope, likely resulting in prompting responses that are more in tune with the user's expectation. In doing so, the prompt helps to reduce additional queries from the user (for example, *What about Q2?*) or inputs to correct the results produced by the model, ultimately reducing the computational cost from generating redundant results.

Scaling AI systems efficiency to managing workloads

Efficient prompt design becomes more important as large workloads are distributed across exponentially more sophisticated AI systems. AI applications on large scales might include services, such as automated customer service text systems for a large company or web chatbots for a major tech firm. In either case, the sheer amount of input the AI must work through presents a massive scaling challenge. Efficient prompts contribute to meeting that challenge. The more concise and shorter the prompts, the more effectively an AI system can impact the outcome. This supports scale by allowing the AI to wade through more queries and more responses and do it faster. This is especially important in high-traffic environments, where inefficiency in prompt design can quickly compound. As users submit more queries, which take more resources to process, response times become slower, and the load on the server(s) increases. In this setting, an inefficient prompt can contribute to delays, while an efficient prompt can be more effective in driving outcomes. The better an AI can process information at scale, the faster it can perform its assigned tasks, using fewer computational resources.

Beyond balancing a workload, timely efficiency can save time and resources in any interaction that tends to be continuous and prompt-driven. For companies or applications that heavily rely on AI interactions, such as automated customer service systems or AI marketing bots, each query increases the overall computational cost. If the prompts are not efficient, the interaction might be longer, with the AI conversational model asking more clarification questions or generating longer responses – all of which wastes time and computing power. Prompt efficiency allows interaction to be shorter, with AI responding to user queries in fewer steps, saving time and reducing the overall number of API calls. This can also save money since interaction with these APIs costs running the system. For businesses that operate at scale, these small savings can accumulate.

Efficient prompts are not only accessible to a greater range of users, they are also essential to making AI usable. Generally speaking, users who have less experience in dealing with AI tend to encounter more errors when using complex, convoluted or jargon-filled prompts. This means that hidden or inconvenient entries in the prompts can create problems for less experienced users. This is a point where efficiency intersects most directly with accessibility and inclusivity. The more concise and accessible the prompts, the simpler it is for people of all abilities, skills and backgrounds to use AI. Consequently, usable and accessible AIs are easier to distribute throughout society at large, meaning that more people can benefit from the use of AI technologies, including those from different linguistic and cultural backgrounds.

Enhancing accessibility and inclusivity

Efficient prompts also enable communication across language divides, further facilitating inclusion. For non-natives or users who struggle to comprehend complex syntax, shorter prompts decrease the cognitive load needed to parse and engage with the AI. Going back to our room service example, users should receive messages from the AI that are easy to digest – the shorter the input, the better. In multilingual environments, users might interact with an AI system in more than one language. Concise prompts decrease the margin of error, corresponding to more appropriate responses on the part of the AI across different languages.

In practice, this means that it manifests across many settings. For instance, in customer service, it turns into faster satisfaction and shorter resolution times as users get answers to questions in a prompt and appropriate way. For creative industries, it implies that an AI model will end up doing its job faster – it will have more freedom to be imaginative and create more versatile and quality-sounding content. For data scientists, it means more effective technical environments as AI is now driven towards the most relevant part of the data faster. Generally, the concept of efficient prompt engineering emerges as a way to transform AI systems into more optimal ones in either user-facing or technical/product settings. Overall, the combination of efficiency and prompt engineering should be seen as a way to **optimize** AI as a whole – for more organic and better interactions and experiences at scale.

This might seem trivial, but well-designed, efficient prompts can offer a whole lot more than increased speed and accuracy of text. They can also prime less efficient but fully human **behavior, making AI systems more useful and usable to a wider audience by reducing the cognitive and computational load on both users and models**, or offer more time and space to AI models and users alike, enabling applications in more far-flung, remote or non-English speaking contexts. Moving forward, we believe efficiency in prompt design could come to serve the crucial work of scaling up and empowering AI across diverse and far-flung contexts.

Strategies for efficient prompt design

Efficient prompt engineering brings a range of critical benefits, both for AI models and the users who interact with them. One of the primary advantages is the reduction of cognitive overload, both for the AI systems and the humans directing them.

Balancing detail and brevity

In multilingual environments, users might interact with an AI system in more than one language. Concise prompts decrease the margin of error, corresponding to more appropriate responses on the part of the AI across different languages. **This can drive linguistic challenges, so ensuring the prompt is right, short, and on target, is a strong best practice to ensure a good initial response to iterate on**. For creative industries, it implies that an AI model will end up doing its job faster – it will have more freedom to be imaginative and create more versatile and quality-sounding content. For data scientists, it means more effective technical environments as AI is now driven towards the most relevant part of the data faster. Generally, the concept of an efficient prompt engineering emerges as a way to transform AI systems into more optimal ones in either user-facing or technical/product settings. Overall, the combination of efficiency and prompt engineering should be seen as a way to **optimize** AI as a whole – for more organic and better interactions and experiences at scale.

While it might seem trivial, a well-designed and efficient prompt can offer a whole lot more than mere speed and accuracy of text. They can also prime less efficient but fully human **behavior, making AI systems more useful and usable to a wider audience by reducing the cognitive and computational load on both users and models** or offer more time and space to AI models and users alike, enabling applications in more far-flung, remote or non-English speaking contexts. Moving forward, we believe efficiency in prompt design could come to serve the crucial work of scaling up and empowering AI across diverse and far-flung contexts.

To look at a very practical example of a prompt, you could ask it to limit the response to a sentence or a paragraph, that is a way to get efficiency out of the AI system. To have a very efficient prompt that you write, use straightforward prompts initially, before you go on to remind them, and not create an overly complex prompt from the start.

Measuring and optimizing efficiency

Tools and metrics for evaluating prompt efficiency: Efficiency in prompt engineering cannot be merely an abstract objective – we need to have clear metrics that allow us to measure efficiency, analyze it, and continue to improve it so that AI systems work as efficiently as possible. Measuring and optimizing efficiency involves looking at a slew of metrics that will directly reflect on the quality of outputs of an AI system, as well as the computational resources required for its performance. Metrics, such as token usage, latency and accuracy of the response, will directly convey how efficiently a prompt runs through an AI model. These metrics can tell you if you are being too verbose, if it is not conveying what you want, or if it is taking up too many resources.

Prompt accuracy is also directly related to prompt efficiency. A prompt is efficient when its outputs are correct and relevant to the user's request. If the prompt is poorly structured or ambiguous, the AI will produce inaccurate, incomplete or irrelevant outputs that require follow-up queries or reprocessing, increasing computational overhead and frustrating users. Taking the time to do that analysis on the logs will allow your engineers to make adjustments in the models as needed. For instance, if a poor prompt has led the AI to produce off-topic or unclear outputs, it can be re-crafted to be more specific so the AI produces responses that are closer to the user's intent.

A particularly sensitive and tangible way to evaluate prompt efficiency is token usage. (For large language models, cost crucially correlates to the number of tokens processed; every word, punctuation mark, and space counts toward a model's token limit.) The length of a prompt can quickly add up: an overly wordy or abstract prompt is likely to drive up overall resource usage. However, token usage represents not only cost but also speed and focus. An overly long prompt about, say, the banking crisis of 2008 might focus the model's attentive resources on unessential background details. That could result in an overly long or diffuse response when it would have served the purpose of the prompt equally well – if not better – to give a pithy outline of the essentials of the case. A token analyzer or similar tool might reveal to the prompt engineer that the prompt writer has waffled a little, and she adjusts it to get better results.

Latency is another key metric for understanding prompt efficiency – it measures how long the prompt takes to elicit input from the AI. Intuitively, high latency is often associated with poor prompt engineering. If the task is unclear or the prompt is excessively wordy or convoluted, the AI may struggle more to understand what it is supposed to do. In applications that require immediate responses, like customer service or conversational agents, this can have a noticeable impact on user experience. Faster experiences and shorter response times are preferable, of course. Since prompt engineering introduces the human element into models that are otherwise computerized and objective, such maneuvering can be tricky to optimize. Performance dashboards and latency trackers can help prompt engineers gauge how long their prompts are taking to elicit responses and identify what part of the task is taking the longest, enabling timelier interactions.

We have tools to quantify each of these metrics on a prompt efficiency chart. A token analyzer can help engineers count the number of tokens that each prompt uses. Using the number of tokens as a benchmark for efficiency, additional tech, such as a prompt efficiency matrix, can help prompt engineers to recognize and reduce unnecessary token use. Similarly, new data analysis tools, like performance dashboards, can provide real-time data on latency and response times to help the prompt engineer identify sluggish parts of the prompt that lead to latency and sluggish overall system response. There are also logging and analytics tools to help precisely quantify prompt accuracy to see how well the AI is performing on a prompt-by-prompt basis. We can already see a feedback loop forming, prompt engineers can use these tools to track and quantify the prompt efficiency in real-time, and can use the resulting insights to inform ongoing improvements in prompt engineering.

This data-driven approach can inform best practices for prompt improvement. Prompt engineers should review their own performance logs on a regular schedule, so as to uncover systemic trends or recurring issues with respect to prompt design. For example, if an engineer were to find prompts exhibits, a pattern where they take longer than others to respond to or have a lower accuracy, this data can be used to redesign the troublesome prompts. Continuous A/B testing, which involves comparing the performance of two variations of the same prompt, is another powerful method. By identifying the components of a prompt that can be toggled individually, prompt engineers can evaluate different prompt structures that lead to the most efficient and accurate AI outputs. The case studies offer guidance and encouragement to those designing prompts: for each one, measurable improvements in AI performance stem from better ways of focusing the AI system through prompt engineering. For example, a customer service app improved speed by reducing the token count and removing superfluous context from user queries, allowing the AI to focus on only what was important, likewise, for a content generation tool that responded more accurately and quickly when prompts were reorganized for greater clarity and brevity. Across all four case studies, incremental improvements in prompt engineering resulted in decidedly non-incremental gains in AI system performance.

Examples of optimized versus non-optimized prompts

Writing concrete examples of optimized and non-optimized prompts also highlights the difference in what an optimized prompt allows the AI to achieve versus a sub-optimized prompt. The most common reasons why these prompts fail to succeed fall into a few general buckets: lacking clarity, meaning too much, and suffering from *paralysis by analysis*, or lacking it. Prompts, where meanings are not clear, confuse the AI and can result in outputs that are irrelevant to user needs. For example, asking the AI to **explain the results of the report** may lead to scattered or incomplete responses, as the AI does not know exactly which aspect of the report is desired. This could be avoided by specifying the section of the report in question or the type of analysis needed (for example, explain the financial implications of the report's conclusions). Inefficient prompts also tend to burden the model with too much information.

Optimizing those for different tasks requires thinking about what a given use case is trying to achieve and modifying the prompts accordingly. In technical use cases, precision and clarity could matter much more than open-endedness: for instance, the prompt for a code generation task might need to be very specific to allow only one correct output, such as: `Paraphrase the input into human-sounding text while retaining citations and quotes.` This kind of drill can also help with making prompts more effective. Let us take a previous example and re-work the prompt to be more efficient. We could recast it : `Paraphrase the key events that led to the beginning of the war.` In that way, we are constantly reminding ourselves of the importance of parsimony, restating the problem, and tailoring the prompt to the desired end. Over months and years, systematic practice at paraphrasing low-effort prompts into high-effort ones will build proficiency in such skills. By following the path of least effort, prompt engineers are able to craft more efficient designs for AI, thereby building more effective AI applications.

Prompt efficiency is an important matter to measure, track, and optimize to improve AI performance, reduce computational costs on backends, and ultimately improve user experiences. We can develop various response token and accuracy metrics and tools to track token usage and latency and put that knowledge to practical use in prompt design. By refining prompts to better-fit tasks, borrowing best practices through case studies, and encouraging knowledge exchange via data-sharing, prompt engineers can have a substantial impact on the efficiency of AI systems. Ultimately, we can all witness the value of optimizing prompt efficiency through real-world applications and prompt-engineering exercises. It is clear that prompt engineers have a crucial role in improving what state-of-the-art AI systems can achieve.

Future considerations for efficient prompt engineering

Of course, prompt engineering will likely evolve along with the AI that it shapes. Even if it is impossible to predict what this future will look like, one thing is certain: complexity will be the name of the game. Evolutions of prompt engineering for generative AI are likely to run parallel to evolutions in generative AI models, with both becoming more complex and nuanced together.

Future evolution of prompts in generative AI

As AI models continue to improve, prompts will likewise have to grow in complexity to achieve the same goal they do now – the extrapolation from human prompts to AI-generated output. With greater complexity in model prowess comes a greater complexity in what goes into prompt engineering, with significantly more integer variables comprising the final equation. As time goes on, prompt engineers will likely have to strike a balance between greater precision in wording, stylistic direction and intent, and greater flexibility and nuance, allowing them to harness an AI model's expanded creative repertoire and increased problem-solving capacity. We may see prompts that are both more finely honed and less specific – capable of conveying more complex human intent within a broader spectrum of choices. While at the same time minimizing ambiguity and opacity to a model with a superior ability to resolve them.

Automation and efficiency

There is also a focus on using AI to help create prompts for AI. One area being seen quite a bit is to use something like ChatGPT to create a strong prompt for an image in MidJourney to get an image created for you, many of the AI systems are trained on how to best work with AI systems generally so an AI system can actually be a great interface into AI systems—for the computer scientists out there yes it feels a bit recursive.

Prompt-building tools could be further refined by making them more accessible to AI-assisted users with a much lower cognitive load, and with far greater efficiency in their interactions with the underlying complex models. A user might say: **Please analyze market trends over the past 10 years.** The system would create a super-optimized, highly specific prompt of considerable complexity, informed by the initial request. The most efficient and effective prompts are increasingly likely to be used for corresponding tasks since syntax offers a much more pliable structure for AI applicability than data types. Without prompt engineering, users need not understand the intricate science behind it. AI will enable users to do better and do less. With the continuation of this trajectory, access to complex AI systems will be democratized, reducing the reliance on deep technical expertise.

However, as AI models become more complicated and versatile at handling multimodal inputs – such as combining text, images, and other types of data all within one interaction – prompt efficiency strategies will need to keep pace with these iterations of emerging technology. This could include instructing the model on whatever task it was designed for, such as generating text, classifying images, extracting quotes, summarizing documents, or something different.

Adapting prompt efficiency strategies

Future developments in AI architecture and training techniques will require iterative adaptation – even redefinition – of what it means for a prompt to be **efficient**. As AI models scale and grow in capability, concepts of prompt efficiency at a given level of sophistication could become insufficient or even simplistic in the age of larger or more capable systems. Future models might require prompts developed with an anticipated capacity to handle more nuanced ways of parsing context, intent, and expertise in the question at hand. Engineers would need to keep up with these developments by both creating more advanced metrics for evaluating prompt performance as well as deriving new best practices for optimizing interactions.

Since prompt efficiency depends on AI models with specific capabilities, we will need to retain some flexibility in our approaches to keep up with future generations of systems. As models get better, prompts that perform well for one iteration might not for the next – and with each iteration, AI will learn new tricks: better ability to understand natural language, smarter handling of ambiguity and incomplete instruction, and most importantly, generations of models that are better able to create outputs that mimic creativity. So, we as individuals working in prompt engineering also need to continue to grow and evolve while we use efficiency as a **north star** to guide us. Likely, we will see more new and interesting ways to create prompts balanced by efficiencies built into those approaches. One would not doubt that prompt generation systems are being worked on today to help move forward here.

Prompts used in future AI apps might shift away from the highly static, one-way instruction model towards a more dynamic interactive model where the AI system is expected to initiate clarification, refinement – even correction – of its understanding of the task in response to verbal (and perhaps non-verbal) cues from the human user. In that case, efficiency will not only be a matter of writing clearly, but of creating prompts that can handle more complex, multistep types of exchange where the initial prompt serves as a launching point for a more open-ended dialogue between humans and machines. In such an environment, efficiency will depend on how well the prompt **truly gets things started**, as it were, allowing the AI to improve its output a step at a time.

The introduction of new types of AI models and technologies is bound to shift the focus to thinking in terms of prompt scaling – prompt efficiency at the scale of thousands or millions of interactions versus prompt efficiency applied to one interaction at a time. Whether for enterprise applications, customer-facing apps, or decision-support systems that act in real-time, as AI becomes embedded in critical systems, promoting models will need to process an increasing volume and variety of inputs. Prompt engineers will need tools and methodologies to help search and generate prompts that are efficient at these scales – which is very different from focusing on the efficiency of individual prompts. For instance, look at the performance of a prompt fare across thousands or millions of interactions. Also consider how we can optimize prompt structures for environments where small inefficiencies might lead to millions of dollars of resource expenditure or performance bottlenecks across a system.

The future of efficient, prompt engineering will be heavily influenced by the continuous advancements of AI models as well as the increasing role of AI in optimizing these interactions. Going forward, prompt engineers must adapt with the times, fine-tuning their intentions and systems on the go to effectively cope with increasingly powerful and sophisticated system architectures. Novel tools to assist prompt engineering and optimization will likely be needed to automate some of the effort required to compose efficient prompts while enabling more users to leverage the power of AI. Furthermore, in concert with the ongoing AI explosion and AI-optimizing AI, the cognitive and inference-level strategies for achieving interconnected AI architectures range from different usage contexts and applications. AI will increasingly be embedded in everyday life and work, and novel paradigms for making AI systems effective, responsive and resource-efficient will need to follow suit. In other words, the AI revolution will endure.

Conclusion

In this chapter, we went deep into the effects of prompts, why you should structure the best prompt you should, and how it helps you in the end. We build on the foundations of previous chapters, allowing you to take the system architecture of AI systems into account when considering prompts. In the next chapter, we will move into tying syntax with some of the current major systems, ChatGPT, Gemini, Copilot, etc. As prompt syntax is derived from language, we will start with English syntax (as this is a book in English), but it applies to every other language.

Join our book's Discord space

Join the book's Discord Workspace for Latest updates, Offers, Tech happenings around the world, New Release and Sessions with the Authors:

https://discord.bpbonline.com

CHAPTER 11

Critical Role of Syntax

Introduction

This chapter gives a detailed account of how syntax can affect the efficiency of prompts in AI systems: It is shown that **Its effects** is a better prompt than **The effects are** for the AI to make human-sounding completions. Syntactic variations can lead to completely different outputs of the AI.

This discussion leads into another section, *Best practices for syntactical clarity*, which encourages users to be clear; be unambiguous and to structure requests in ways that will provide the clearest response. You will review the overall importance of syntax but also focus on how the importance of precision in syntax affects your outcome.

The chapter also covers deeper syntactical techniques. It describes how defined keywords and phrases can be used to prompt desired effects in different responses and how certain syntactical constructions can guide an AI's reactions more purposefully. We will look at some syntactical prompt approaches, explaining their potential impacts and advantages – offering optimization techniques and principles for prompt engineering in the context of AI applications.

Structure

In this chapter, we will cover the following topics:

- Importance of syntax in prompts
- Best practices for syntactical precision
- Advanced syntactical techniques
- Implications for efficiency in prompt engineering
- Future trends in syntax-driven prompt engineering

Objectives

Language, we all share it; it is how we communicate. Each human language has a set of rules, or syntax, to follow. Syntax matters crucially in prompt engineering – and truly matters on many fronts as AI systems emerge as the engines for ever more text production, question-answering, and interrogating amounts of unstructured data at a massive scale. You will learn how to construct prompts to be efficient in getting the right answer as soon as possible. You will learn about how to handle greater degrees of complexity in your prompting. You will also learn about how to prepare for the future trends being brought about by current work in AI service engineering.

Importance of syntax in prompts

Syntax in prompt engineering, where a system **perceives** and decodes what a query or text is **asking** it to do, is part of the fabric of how AI is currently being built to interact with humans. Unlike human cognition, where lifelong contextual and experiential learning support attempts to encode understanding and action, AI models can rely only on the syntactical rules of its task-oriented training data to arrive at the purported meaning of a query or to assess the apparent intent behind the query's syntax.

Effect of syntax on artificial intelligence

Human syntactical understanding relies on a multilayered integration of mastery of grammar, semantics, great flexibility and ambiguity when we communicate every day. However, an AI-powered parser that runs on a more mechanical-like software system will work in a far more rigid space. Machine learning models, the most common form of AI modeling, especially the models that have been, work through statistical patterns gleaned from large datasets. They have become remarkably capable of understanding, and good at remembering and have the depth we need them to have. The previous chapters of the book speak to the progress which has been made here.

A distinction between declarative versus interrogative syntax can have the effect of changing how an AI understands a prompt by prompting it to focus its attention on different aspects of the content before making a response. In a simple declarative structure such as *Paraphrasing is a useful skill because it helps you condense your thoughts and communicate them more concisely*, an AI could easily be fooled into thinking that it should provide additional justification or expand further on an already perfectly satisfactory explanation. A different interrogative structure will normally interpret the cues as indicating that a tighter, more economical response is appropriate. What this means in practice is that once we understand how the interpretive mechanisms of AI models themselves operate, learning the syntax of prompts is not necessarily just about learning how to write grammatically.

Meta prompting

Meta-prompting in AI and prompt engineering is about making prompts that can enhance or refine how prompts are designed or applied. Not necessarily directed at the AI to produce an answer, but a meta-prompt is a prompt about prompts: a call to let the AI interpret, test or modify prompt techniques for improved results. Whether that is to ask the AI for feedback on a prompt's grammatical accuracy, suggest new phrases, or create a new prompt all together in order to fill in certain details in a task. Meta-prompts can also help you understand prompt optimization and design more specific, dependable, or original answers.

Meta-prompting is especially useful in real-world situations, when a single prompt is not always enough. With a meta-prompt, prompt engineers can leverage AI to tailor prompt language or logic to user needs. It allows for an iterative design that is able to be designed in an iterative manner, in which AI helps prompt the design, making the interfaces with AI systems much more productive and robust.

An example is if you are using an AI Art program and are trying to come up with an idea for what you will like, you could create a prompt using MidJourney AI art generation, create a prompt to use to create a 1930 style travel poster for New York city in 1938.

Examples of syntactical variations and their impacts

As per the focus of this chapter, syntax is one of the most important factors to consider when performing prompt engineering because small syntactical tweaks can drastically change how AI systems behave. The prompt **paraphrase that like a human** will probably elicit a very high-level, broad summary. The system interprets the sentence as a request for an explanation. However, syntactically tweaking the sentence into **Paraphrase the input into human-sounding text while retaining citations and quotes** transforms it into a more targeted interrogation, prompting a much more specific, facts-driven response from the AI.

The choice of syntactical form in the prompt can make quite a difference to task performance across every AI application of this type. In summary transformers and other applications where the exact task outcome is hard to specify precisely, `Summarize this article`' leads to point extraction and paraphrasing, whereas `What are the main points of this article?` could lead the AI to create a different list of points from the human one.

Structural prompts in question-answering systems

If we ask a question-answering system in general terms – that is, with no specification of answer format, such as open- or closed-ended questions – or formulating the question as a query, as in the case of digital assistants like Claude, that will lead to one outcome. If we use multiple-choice options, that will lead to something entirely different.

When creating a prompt, rhetorical choices related to syntax are even more striking. If you want the AI to answer the prompt clearly with instructions about style, tone, and length, you will get a different text if you leave that out of the instruction, as shown in the following example, which goes from `Write a short, formal letter` to `Can you write a quick letter?` An AI would probably write a more precise structural and tonal sentence in the first one than in the second, which would probably be more conversational. An approach to getting more clarity on a prompt about an article is to not be vague, like, `What are the main points of this article?` but to frame it up with constraints and context, for example, `As an expert in finance and business, review this article about a company, and it's financial earnings reports to focus on risk in investing in the company` this way the requestor gets what they are really looking for other than a generic summary.

The preceding examples illustrate the interplay between whether it is framed as a question, command or statement – and the architecture of the system, enabling the engineer of prompts to design queries that elicit both a particular type of response and a more predictable and efficient outcome.

Syntax and ambiguity in language

It is not just that language is inherently ambiguous, but the kinds of ambiguities AI systems are going to spot and exploit depends a lot on what kind of syntax is present in the prompt and instruction. Everyday language is full of ambiguity because we invariably leave room to interpret a phrase or a sentence in different ways. Humans, ultimately, are skilled at the use of smart guessing infrastructure, such as context, tone, and prior knowledge, but AI systems lack this smart guessing infrastructure and are forced to navigate ambiguities only through the syntactical clues that we provide for them. For example, consider a prompt such as `Can you list five countries in Africa?` versus `List five countries in Africa.` The first is obviously very different than the second. Got it. Now try rewriting that prompt but without using the modal verb.

Ambiguous referential terms are another source of ambiguity. `What is it?`, for example, leaves little for an AI to grab onto syntactically and, therefore, makes the system's identification of it more open to erroneous monotonic inferences. By contrast, `What is`

the capital of France? guarantees the AI lexically marked information, allowing it to provide a clearer misdirected as it is very unambiguous.

The problem of semantic ambiguity can be helped by prompt engineers helping to refine their syntax. A lot of the fogginess can be removed with clearer, more precise wording. For example, rather than saying: **What should I do about this?** a requester should offer something like, **What should I do about the privacy issue in the third paragraph?** Here, the AI has something more concrete to work with. It can disambiguate and respond more confidently. This comes back to giving the AI more context at every opportunity you can.

Effectively, the prompt tells the AI where to go and how to get there. Good syntax can improve the quality, reliability, and efficiency of an AI model's outputs, causing less confusion, inefficiency, and even outright error in a model's response. As AI technology continues to improve, syntactical competence is going to become even more important to **prompt engineers** who seek to improve AI performance in myriad tasks, and learning how syntax can affect this process could be a significant advance in AI. Context often comes from syntax, and context is king.

Best practices for syntactical precision

Precise syntax, especially when it comes to prompt engineering on the fly, is crucial. Structure also affects and is affected by what the AI is specifically tuned to. For example, Mid-journey is outstanding at creating custom images with a wide variety of input choices but it is not at all tuned at helping a student research accounting rule. Perhaps a little more detail can help with standards regarding syntactical precision in prompt engineering: clarity, structure, and the interface between human syntax and AI reading.

Using clear and unambiguous language

Syntactical precision – a robust handle on the fundamental component-to-sentence particle level of language – is probably one of the most important and essential considerations in prompt engineering. This is because ambiguity is one of the AI system's nemeses. Unlike humans, an AI system cannot infuse which might enable them to choose and deliver contextual *stride*. So, a prompt like **Tell me about this** becomes ambiguous at the surface because there is no way for *this* to be declared (pointed to, specified, etc.). the background context.

The quick fix for them is to make the prompts very specific: cut out the vague framing and jut tell the AI what it is trying to achieve, letting it decide how to do it. After all, if a prompt is **paraphrase into human-sounding text while retaining citations and quotes**, then it should say just that. It is often much easier than the instructions we give to human typists. For instance, instead of paraphrasing while retaining the voice of the original – which is extremely common in academia, it should be specific. **Tell me more**, which is non-specific and leaves a great deal of interpretation up to the typist, the prompt could be: **Elaborate: the causes of climate change.** Now, this prompt is quite specific: the subject of elaboration (causes of climate change) is clear, and if the AI is competent, it is very clear what needs doing. "Keep it Simple Silly" or the "KISS Principle" is always a good guide. Start by avoiding sentences that have ambiguity, like **What are the main drivers** and **What drives growth here?** because **here** is ambiguous. Vague clichés and pronouns dramatically raise the risk that Siri will end up saying something irrelevant and imprecise.

Another mistake that can potentially cost unqualified points is using too much technical language (jargon). Current AI systems can recognize a wide range of technical languages but will have trouble if the syntax contains a high number of undefined terms or if it is too convoluted. This means achieving clarity and precision needs to extend to the choice of vocabulary as well, and complex terms should be simplified wherever possible.

Structuring prompts for maximum clarity

In addition to lexical clarity, the structure of the prompt can influence the nature of a well-organized prompt, which can implicitly instruct in a way that helps the AI generate an answer that is formed. Such a prompt may present information in a logical order that strongly suggests how the train of thought should be structured as the AI composes the text step by step.

You could create a prompt in an ordered or hierarchical way to be successful, like: **First, paraphrase the point made in the article. Then, list three reasons why that point might be wrong. Finally, give me your opinion about whether that point in the article might be wrong.** The AI knows in which order the first prompt, whereas the second one is much more open-ended and runs the risk of generating an unstructured, less informative reply. You are supplying the AI with a specific order of operations effectively. You basically created a multi-tasking prompt in one larger one.

We also want to avoid over- and under-specification in prompts, where over-specification means needlessly restricting the AI, preventing it from giving a more natural response than is necessary to meet the prompt, and under-specification leaves too much inch-square latitude, as already noted. A good prompt will strike the balance of providing the AI with the context it needs to understand the task without encasing it in a too-small square. For example, instead of: **list all environmental factors impact on company X's quarterly earnings in the fourth quarter of 2024?** which is too restrictive, **What environmental factors are likely to affect the earnings of company X in the near future?** is much better.

When humans communicate with others, we depend on a shared model of how language is structured in our minds, as well as through a shared perspective as members of the same culture: when they agree on what a sentence means, this co-reliance fosters predictive alignment that is not present when humans and AI systems communicate. What AI has is a powerful machine, a probabilistic model of language construction that is immensely good at completing inputs, but unlike human speakers, it lacks experiential knowledge, which is something humans excel at. The structure of a prompt will often become a template used by the human. A common structure is to set the persona first. `As an expert in astronomy…` for example, would set a prompt up for scientific answers about stars, etc., and avoid getting pseudo-science or myth-based answers when focusing on something like a constellation.

Avoiding common syntactical pitfalls

There are many common syntactic traps that can interfere with a prompt's effectiveness, leading to responses that are either incorrect or of a lower quality than they might otherwise be. Perhaps the most common one is tense. Many people end up violating the tense of the input question. For instance, if the question is: `What drove the stock market last year?` the question is internally inconsistent (and confusing) from a time perspective. Our AI might think users meant either: What did drive the stock market last year? Or What will drive the stock market next year?. Either way, ambiguities like this one force and reduce the accuracy of its response. These kinds of problems are easy to avoid by making the tense of the prompt consistent.

Another syntactic trap is what they call conjunction/modifier misuse, where a conjunction (such as *and* or *so*, or a modifier) can change the meaning of a sentence in a significant way. An example of conjunction confusion could be `list companies in AI that are making money and doing good.` you really should ask something like `list AI companies which are both profitable and AI companies that are known to be ethical`. This reduces ambiguity in how the model assesses it.

Misplaced modifiers are also sometimes capable of shifting a prompt's focus, making the prompt's intent opaque and opening a path toward irrelevant and off-topic responses. Compare the following two versions of the same prompt: `Identify the most influential books of the past century written by economists.` The first sentence is clear: the prompt is asking for an evaluation of the most influential books published in the past century without regard to who wrote them. The second version is far from clear: `Identify the most influential books written in the past century by economists.` The slippage from `written in the past century` to `written by economists` might seem slight, but when rendered by a syntactically-sensitive AI it does shift a person's focus toward books written by economists in the past century, instead of the most influential books overall, written by economists. Such crimes against syntax can change how an AI interprets a prompt and what sort of response you get.

Influence of human syntax on artificial intelligence responses

There is a fascinating connection between human syntax and responses from some AI models, such as OpenAI's GPT. AI models operate on language based on probabilistic patterns, while human syntax is built from cognitive and experientially evidenced assumptions. Human language is always infused with cultural appreciations and subtleties of context, as well as extending syntax to include regularized social subtexts, asides, and non-conscious nuance and emotion. Statistical AI models compute responses that arise from learned probabilities applied to large corpora, meaning that their responses, even if accurate by statistical standards, are often much more blunt than human speech.

One place where the difference shows up is in the extent to which AI systems tend to get confused by overly human-type input in their response with many colloquialisms, etc. If an informal or poorly structured prompt goes in, then the AI will mimic back a less coherent or more casual reply than it might otherwise generate. This mirroring is a direct consequence of how the AI models parse the syntactical information in the prompt and apply learned word and phrase structures to produce similar kinds of peaks and valleys in the syntax of its response.

Moreover, it highlights the importance of using a more formal and structured approach in prompt writing if you want a reply that is more formal. If the output has to be polished, professional, and precise, then it is all the more important for the prompt to be polished, professional, and precise. Small syntactical shifts, even choosing the passive rather than the active voice, or odd literary language rather than everyday vernacular, can dramatically alter AI outputs. to get the best out.

Syntactic subtlety is the bedrock of careful, prompt construction. Disambiguation of meaning through clarity of syntax creates opportunities for a captivating response, while syntactical care during construction allows us to actively guide how an AI interprets a prompt. We should add that through careful control of modifying clauses, without subtle errors that throw AI off its path, by using correct tenses. With all this in mind, we must learn to speak the language of these engineered systems carefully while avoiding using impenetrable jargon when we speak to humans. More formal and less imaginative language will get a generally better response. By capturing our understanding of this human syntax and translating it to bracket our own expectations about where an AI will stop reading, we unlock ways of learning from the future. In a world where AI is evolving, syntactical clarity is going to become a cornerstone of careful prompt construction. It is worth noting that loose prompts can illicit more imaginative responses.

It might feel like we have been focusing on how to avoid getting an imaginative response. Let us use a fun, real-world example to show a fully imaginative example.

The scenario: You and your friends are playing Dungeons and Dragons, and you go to ChatGPT 4o for an idea. You set up the context, frame it up, and limit the response to keep it short and to the point. Here is your prompt:

```
Answer as an expert in didactic storytelling and Dungeons and Dragons Give
me a very imaginative response to setting up a riddle for a group of wizards
playing "Dungeons and Dragoons" where they have 2 minutes to solve the riddle
or the floor turns to lava". respond in two paragraphs.
```

The answer ChatGPT 4o came up with is as follows:

The stone walls of the ancient chamber tremble as you step into the dimly lit hall, a magical clock ticking down in the distance. Before you, etched into the floor by arcane forces, is a shimmering circle, pulsating with a heat that promises danger. In the center of the room, a pedestal rises, and atop it, a floating scroll. As your party of wizards approaches, a voice, ancient and melodic, reverberates through the air. "Solve this riddle, lest the ground beneath you blaze like the heart of a volcano." The walls flicker with the faintest hint of magma, creeping upwards, threatening to turn the chamber into a fiery abyss. The countdown begins. Two minutes.

The riddle appears, inscribed in glowing runes: "I have a face, but no eyes. I have hands, but no arms. I'm always running, but never walk. What am I?" The tension in the room thickens, as you glance at each other, wands at the ready, minds racing against time. Sweat forms on your brow—not from fear, but from the heat intensifying beneath your feet. The ground begins to hum, a low rumble echoing with each tick of the clock

The following figure shows the prompt answer:

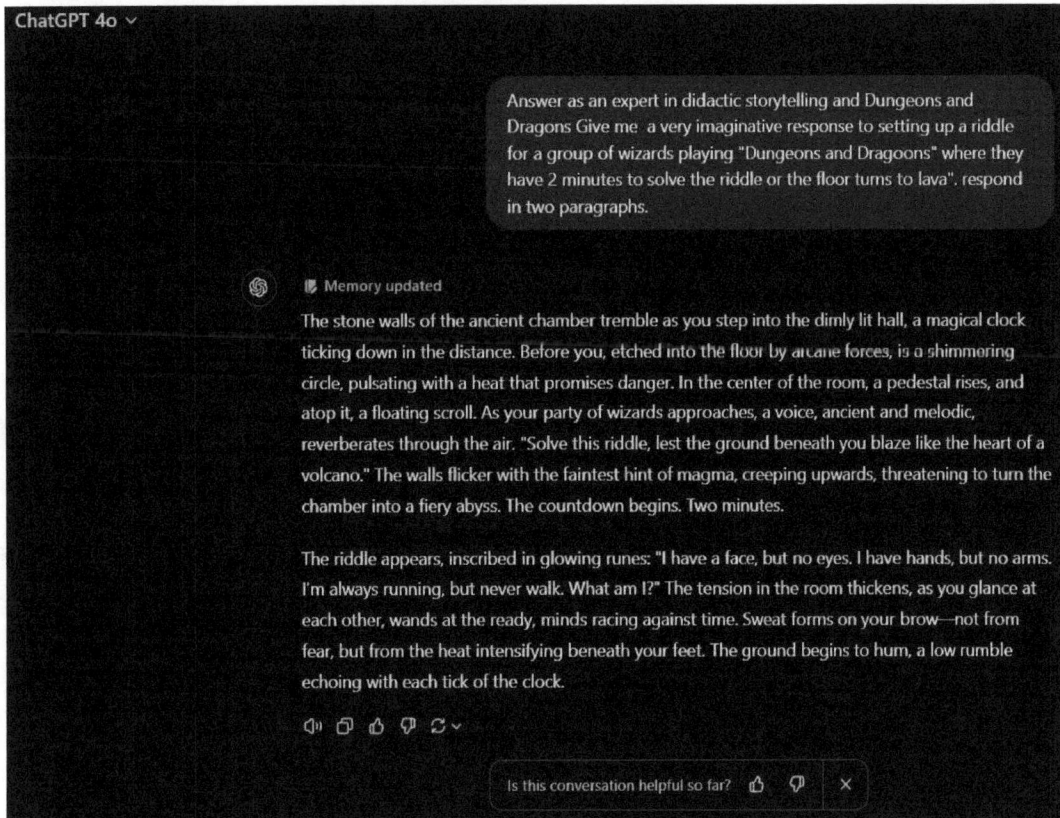

Figure 11.1: Using structured syntax for an imaginative response

Sounds like a fun encounter. The answer to the riddle is *A clock* as it has a face, hands (hour and minute hands—at least on an analog clock) and is always running but it cannot walk.

Advanced syntactical techniques

Advanced prompt engineering relies on gaining mastery over syntax in sharpening and refining the outputs. The growing sophistication of AI systems allows increasingly complex tasks, such as via **natural language processing** (**NLP**) models, have resulted in corresponding sophistication of syntax in prompt tools. Syntax then elevates to determine not just the clarity and arrangement to craft well-structured sentences that define the clarity and specificity of the answer from the AI system. That answer needs to be consumed and understood by the human and only has value if it is a valid language model that the human understands and can extract value from.

Using specific keywords and phrases for desired outcomes

Today, a common method for ensuring the output you get is what you expect from the AI is leveraging specific phrases or individual keywords in your prompt. By choosing your words carefully, the prompt engineer can create strong anchor words to direct the AI linguistic model to a specific idea or concept to get output focused on that area.

We can amplify this approach when we further manipulate strategies for directive language and question forms as well as conditional prompts. For example, directives such as 'explain,' 'list', or 'analyze' can be used to push the AI toward different kinds of outputs. The best benefit of specific keywords or directive language is that it is possible to match the human intent, where it gets translated into keywords that the AI recognizes. In other words, there needs to be an expert understanding of what words, and what coloring of those words will reach into the AI's decision tree and attain the desired category or node.

Employing syntactical structures to guide AI responses

In addition to specific keywords, syntactical structures—how sentences are organized and framed—play a crucial role in influencing AI responses. A declarative sentence – one that states a fact – typically invites further exposition or reframing of the input: **Photosynthesis is how plants make energy.** An interrogative sentence – a question – will typically give a factual response: **What is photosynthesis?** An imperative sentence – an instruction more structured, step-by-step response and the output will likely be more instructional in tone: **Explain how photosynthesis works.**

Techniques, like parallelism, parenthetical phrases, and nested clauses can further refine the response, adding layers of complexity or precision. Parallelism—a method of balancing phrases or clauses—can enforce a structured, orderly response from the AI. A prompt, such as **Compare the benefits and drawbacks of renewable energy and fossil fuels** uses a parallel structure to clearly delineate two areas of focus, guiding the AI to create a similarly balanced response. Using parentheses () can add an additional layer of qualifiers to modify or enhance what is being asked, for example, **describe the effect yeast (in particular Instant rise) has on dough**" adds **Instant rise** to the question to get additional information on it to emphasis while it is a broad question on yeast, there is a request for more information on the instant rise.

You can also use the programmer technique of 'nesting', where you have one structure within another. In this case, you would effectively ask more than one question at once. An example of that would be something like, **If renewable energy sources become cheaper, but fossil fuels remain dominant, how will that affect global energy policies?**. The AI will respond to consider multiple aspects to get a better result, overall, this is faster and more efficient than building prompt after prompt to narrow down the answers.

Leveraging complex syntax for sophisticated outputs

More sophisticated prompt engineering may call for a greater reliance on more complex syntactical structures that can elicit more nuanced responses. This involves subordinate clauses, conditional sentences, and prompt layering, which asks the AI to compare, analyze, or synthesize information. Before going into what some of these structures look like, note that subordinate clauses (or clauses that are dependent on a main clause) allow us to introduce additional information that guides a prompt toward multi-layered responses. For instance, the challenge **Please state the ways in which the industrial revolution which arose at the late 1800s shaped modern economic thought** takes advantage of the subordinate clause to inform the AI's answer with a timestamp and causal connection.

Conditional sentences are also helpful for leading an AI through a sequence of hypothetical reasoning or simply indicating a scenario-based question or instruction. **If temperatures rise by 2 degrees Celsius, what impact will that have on agricultural productivity?** asks the AI to theorize from given premises and returns a reply involving future projections or scenario analysis. By nesting prompts with conditional clauses or compounding them, prompt engineers can coax AI systems along multiple dimensions of a problem, increasing such responses in 'depth' and 'complexity'.

Complex sentences provide us with another way to generate prompts that generate more sophisticated content by forcing an AI to engage in more complex abstract reasoning or more deep-seated forms of reasoning. For example, we could ask an AI to compare two contrary approaches to a topic, like economic theory, within a single input – like, **Compare Keynesian economics with monetarist theory as regards their approaches to the management of inflation** – and this type of prompt would force the AI to weigh up different perspectives on the topic to produce an informative response that draws information from both of the perspectives on economic theory it has been given. At this relatively simple level, complex syntax lets us start moving away from prompt designs that function by simply calling upon an AI to recall basic facts or combine or summarize information and towards prompts that require more complex forms of analytical thinking.

Balancing simplicity and complexity

Even if the more sophisticated, complex syntax can generate complex outputs, the engineering of prompts involves a certain balance between simplicity and complexity. On the one hand, simplicity in syntax brings advantages, as it is easy to understand, thus helping to avoid misunderstanding by the AI and mitigating the time needed for model training. However, when the task involves giving direct, factual replies, prompts can gain efficiency from brevity and clarity. For example, **List three factors that led to the French Revolution** enjoys brevity and clarity in its syntax and can benefit from it: the task offers itself straightforwardly so that interpretation does not need to be subtle.

More convoluted syntax is usually required when more layers of information are demanded by a complex prompt or if the response requires the AI to string together multiple ideas. Complex prompts mean more convoluted syntax, and vice versa. Over-complex prompting will introduce errors, especially if the AI has trouble parsing a complex sentence. Of course, you practice the art of prompt engineering. You also need to know how to determine when a simple approach is the right one, and when a more complicated command will get your AI to produce a deeper analysis, solve a problem, or create something. For basic fact-finding, keep it simple. For finer analysis, more investigation, a problem to solve, or something creative to write, use more complex syntax to guide your AI through the task.

It is not just a technical concern; getting the balance between these two approaches is an issue of strategy. A prompt engineer must consider what the task's goal is and which syntax fits better. For instance, if we are demanding a tough output, we might want to start with a shallow prompt and later engage in iterations through calibrations to generate more complex output. This iterative approach lets us add complexity according to heuristics that do not allow too much information at the start in case the input is more complex than the AI system can handle.

Advanced syntactical strategies for prompt engineering are key to the task of driving AI machines to produce accurate, contextual, and sophisticated outputs. Using specific keywords, command phrases, and other syntactical patterns such as conditional sentences and nested clauses, prompt engineers can manipulate the way an AI processes queries and reacts to them.

Implications for efficiency in prompt engineering

Syntax accuracy drives efficiency in the prompt ecosystem. The more accurate you can get, the fewer iterations you will need to do for the answer you are looking for.

Efficiency-accuracy tradeoff in syntax

Short prompts work best for simple, fact-producing tasks. The instruction `What is the capital of France?` – short, direct, and unambiguous with a definite input-output model – demands and supports clear, immediate, and correct output. In such cases, the simplicity of the prompt is compatible with efficiency. However, for more sophistication, either from the AI or the user – such as when they ask for a nuanced analysis or creative output – a bit of detail is necessary if the response is to satisfy the user.

Syntactically underspecified prompts can lead to an over-broad output – too generic and irrelevant to the task. For example, a prompt that reads `Paraphrase climate change` might be on the short side but is too broad to provide a stream of information that the AI can whittle down. It risks an output that is too open-ended to be truly relevant to climate change – or, as is also possible with long and syntactically rich prompts, it could actually ignore elements of the input that the user deems relevant to climate change. This shows that adding syntactical detail to the prompt can sometimes get the AI back on track to more effectively reduce the superfluous to the pertinent. `Paraphrase the effects of climate change on Arctic ecosystems` is syntactically more specified and ensures that the resulting output focuses on the relevant materials. In both cases, we are trusting an AI to correctly filter and paraphrase a large amount of text while directly addressing only the aspect of climate change or Arctic ecosystems that the human wants it to focus on, all with a single prompt. Hence, prompt engineers must always find a balance between the syntactical detail that is needed to ensure accuracy, while striving to retain some level of efficiency.

A good prompt teaches the AI what the context of the task is and provides just enough detail to do the job well, but not so much more that it drastically increases length – that is, processing time. Efficiency is at its highest when the prompt is sufficiently precise to point the system in the right direction, but not so long that time is wasted on irrelevant details. In other words, in order to work well, prompt engineers must do the exact opposite of what creative writers do. Prompts should be as long as they need to be, and no longer.

Speeding AI task execution with optimized syntax

Optimized syntax helps execute AI tasks in a timely manner. By designing the prompt syntactically, the time taken for the AI system to process and respond to inputs can be significantly reduced. This is especially important in applications that have time-critical constraints in high-capacity environments, such as real-time query answering, usage of AI Bots as customer support, or content creation.

Another important principle of prompt engineering is to use subordinate syntax as little as possible and to avoid ambiguity. AI models are extremely powerful, but they work best with extremely simple languages. Prompts with compound or ambiguous syntax can trip up the model and slow down processing by forcing it to exert additional effort in figuring out what you are asking about precisely. Here is an example of a request that models where many have trouble interpreting (note the abundance of qualifiers slowing it down): `Paraphrase how to put into a layman's terms the steps to starting a small business.` Here is a marginally clearer version: `Paraphrase the steps to setting up your business for beginners.`

One example of the sort of syntax-aided optimization is phrasing sentence forms that are innately more easily processed by AI. Declarative sentences are processed faster than interrogative ones, since they are not asking the AI to interpret or reformulate the question – they simply provide a command that the AI, written accordingly, can respond to. `Explain how photosynthesis works` will likely be answered more quickly than `How does photosynthesis work?` because the latter is phrased as a query, while the former simply states a command.

Advanced grammar also shortens the time to a high-quality output by removing ambiguity and shrinking the search space for error. For example, consider this prompt: `If carbon emissions decrease, what could happen to global temperatures?` This is a perfectly reasonable prompt, but its use of conditional or hypothetical syntax adds an extra dimension of complexity to what the AI has to process. Consider the same prompt, this time without the conditionality: `Describe the potential relationship between carbon emissions and global temperature changes.` That is not as grammatically rich, but the AI might still be able to respond faster, with greater focus. The idea of prompt syntax optimization is that it should strike the right level of specificity: just enough to ensure relevance but not so much that the prompt requires the AI to dedicate extra time to processing all of the intricacies it describes.

Prompt iteration for improved results

The general flow of prompt creation starts with a starter prompt, which is usually quite general and is, over time, refined into its final form. An example would be `explain prompt engineering`. This would illicit an overly broad reply first, but through iteration, it can get honed to something like `Explain the role of machine learning and its effect on prompt engineering`. This more honed prompt acts as a better guide to the AI to get the results needed. Just like iteration is key for any programmer, the experimentation with prompts allows the prompt engineer to quickly test approaches and iterate to something better.

This process can help the prompt engineer get to what they need fast. Tools are being created to measure the quality of the responses to let prompt engineers use those metrics to pinpoint the syntactical elements that need to change to get even better responses.

This iterative approach allows for the prompt engineers to consider both the efficiency and quality of responses from the AI, thus allowing for the computer scientists and data engineers to update the transformer models being used based on potential real-world feedback from the system. This refinement process is a closed loop and continues with each possible.

Future trends in syntax-driven prompt engineering

One of the central challenges in prompt engineering is finding the balance between concise prompts and the effective generation of AI responses. Finding that balance between brevity and detail is challenging. You can imagine that too little detail can lead to incomplete or less accurate responses, as the AI lacks the necessary context to understand the task at hand fully. This balance—the efficiency-accuracy tradeoff—is one of the most critical factors in designing optimal prompts.

Learning and adapting to human syntax

An exciting direction of human-sounding language interaction will be the increasing sophistication of systems responding to more complex syntax. While today's AI systems can parse relatively complex language very efficiently, increasingly, they will be one of the most challenging aspects of human-sounding text, as in lengthy and complex sentences with embedded subordinate clauses with two possible meanings. Current NLP models, especially deep learning-based the models' brain. AI will increasingly have to develop the ability to handle more ambitious questions as not every human plans out the structure of a question where it can be diagramed as a flowchart.

Another needed area of substantial improvement will lie in the ability of models to parse and conditionals to convey fine- reasoning in our human writing styles, which vary. As AI systems acquire the ability to understand these, engineering will evolve to exploit it: future models to engage in more, for instance, instead of impacts of climate change? be: **Given economic impacts of climate change world populations over the next.**

These changes how prompt engineers approach prompt design. While designers currently focus largely on clarity, they will be able to rely on more complex human language patterns, which will be able to process systems in more natural conversational or potentially stilted. This progression has improved the capacity to adapt to human-style syntax, allowing for greater efficiency by enabling faster, more human-like conversations. This will enhance AI interactions with humans, making it feel less obvious that the individual is interacting with an AI, so more 'real'.

Role of multilingual syntax in AI development

An evolving trend will be the increased emphasis on multi-lingual AI systems. The truth is that AI is only truly primed to handle English-language data. The language of technology (that is, computing languages) syntax is English based. This book is written in English for that reason also. The issue is that while that is great for the nearly 2 billion English speakers, it leaves out 5 billion people, and technology should always, first and foremost, be an enabler of people to strive forward and never block them from that goal.

There are also syntactical differences between languages – AI systems will have to learn to negotiate such variations in the input. For example, word order differs quite a bit across languages. In English, sentences tend to be subject-verb-object (he/ it/ her), whereas in it tend to be subject-object-verb. Importantly, many languages such as Arabic, Russian, and others make heavy use of cases and inflections, whereas languages and context to disambiguate. Such cross-linguistic syntactical variation, the target of prompt engineering, will also need to be adapted in order to accommodate multilingual systems. This means being conversant in the language versus simply being an AI translator.

This trend is likely to lead to AI systems that are capable of spanning language divides. To design systems that can parse and respond to prom language with the same facility, and her counterpart in France might also ask for the same system. A related system would understand both prompts accurately, taking into account syntactical structure. Such an AI system would be especially useful in multilingual environments, such as those typical of international business and academia.

The ability to handle cross-language syntax will help AI feel more at home with AIs and enable a far greater degree of naturalism in all conversations. It will allow prompt engineers to design prompts that better account for users' linguistic practices and barrier might be broken in to model the nuanced cultural information that language can convey.

Human-AI collaboration towards more natural prompts

Syntax-driven prompt engineering will also mean that, in the future, human users will interact more intimately with AI models – creating more human-sounding prompts rather than handing over strictly technical instructions. In fact, the more advanced AI models are at grappling with the subtleties of human language, the more prompt engineers must also focus on designing systems that allow for more conversational interactions. In this way, AI will no longer be limited to a tool that needs commands in a certain syntax but will transform into a partner that can understand human intent through more conversational-sounding dialogue.

There will be profound implications for the way that AI systems are used in the real world, as people will no longer have to phrase queries in a proscribed manner, such as **Paraphrase** `the following article and provide three main points,` but will instead be able to ask questions as they would to another person: `What's this article about? Give me the highlights.` The AI will not only have to process meaning in the prompt but will also have to match its own response style to the user's tone and intent.

Another area of AI research that will have an important impact on this trend is the further development of the ability of AI systems to mimic human syntactic communication. When AI systems learn human language more and more, their training enables them to interact more like human beings, at least linguistically. By democratizing access to AI technologies, ordinary individuals with less training in the art will benefit from AI systems' capacity for human-seeming output.

Another exciting avenue of human-AI co-creation could be its own triggers. As the quality of AI systems and models improves, they will begin to propose ways to augment the user's prompt, perhaps by prompting the user with a clarifying question or suggesting a more specific prompt that would provide more informative feedback. A further possibility going forward is interactive prompt refinement, working with AI to help improve and clarify our queries.

We will continue to close the syntax/language gap in both directions with AI. The future of humans interacting with AI, in ways we never could have considered as real, is not too far away. The movie "Her" is a fascinating look at human-AI interaction on a level heretofore unknown; we are potentially approaching the point where a human could potentially begin to misconstrue an AI interaction as an 'it' and anthropomorphize it.

Conclusion

In this chapter, we spoke about how syntax drives prompts and the responses to prompts. Prompt engineers take time to refine and consider the syntactical impacts of their choices. You should feel grounded in your overview of prompt syntax in general, as well as how to follow best practices for syntax, while focusing on advanced syntax techniques, and keeping in mind the syntax and efficiency relationship. Lastly, we looked at the future trends for AI syntax through development. In the next chapter, we will focus on techniques and strategies for prompt engineering by focusing on how to craft good prompts, looking at advanced techniques, and dig into more examples of real-world prompt engineering with different AI systems, GhatGPT, Meta, Claude, Copilot, Gemini, etc.

CHAPTER 12

Techniques and Strategies for Prompt Engineering

Introduction

This chapter explores in detail how to focus on the craft of creating quality prompts which is the defining skill for interacting with AI systems. The reason prompts exist is to be customized; that is how you hone the prompt to get the answer you want. As any craftsman uses tools to create the object they need, the prompts are the tools the prompt engineer uses. The best prompt for you depends on your individual input and the crowd, machine, or system you are communicating with. There are, however, some common best practices. We will speak to heuristics for crafting prompts, but the best heuristics for prompt crafting will come from practice, iteration, and feedback. This chapter exists to equip you with the right tools and resources to craft good prompts when you need them and to develop a sensibility for when you need good prompts.

We will also talk about applications of few-shot and zero-shot learning, where language models can interpret prompts and respond while having too little or no prior examples of that task. It includes prompt tuning and optimization on how to fine-tune a prompt to a specific task and even debates on multi-turn conversations, which are necessary for more natural and engaging AI behaviors.

Structure

In this chapter, we will cover the following topics:

- Major AI players
- Best practices for crafting prompts
- Advanced prompt engineering techniques

Objectives

In this chapter, you will learn about the major players you will interact with as a prompt engineer. You will learn about the general types of prompts that work best with particular AI systems but also learn about the best practices for creating meaningful prompts with them. You will learn about how to ensure your prompts are meaningful and measurable where possible.

Major AI players

Prompt engineering strategies vary significantly across AI systems like Open AI's ChatGPT, Claude, Meta's LLaMA, GitHub Copilot, and Google's Gemini due to the distinct purposes, architectures, and user expectations of each platform. These differences necessitate specific approaches to crafting prompts to ensure optimal performance based on the system's capabilities and use cases. There are a great many to choose from, so this section will only touch on the ones you are most likely to come across.

> **Note: AI players are showing up increasingly. There are some impressive niche solutions (music, video, etc.) that is beyond the scope of this book.**

OpenAI ChatGPT

ChatGPT was the first large-scale, broadly-used AI system using generative pre-trained transformers. Today it is widely used for teaching people about AI, creative content creation, customer support, or concepts like coming up with marketing overview; let us use a real-world example shown in *Figure 12.1*, showing a possible marketing ask and ask
Come up with a marketing hook for the game "Star citizen" aimed at tech savvy players who like sci-fi:

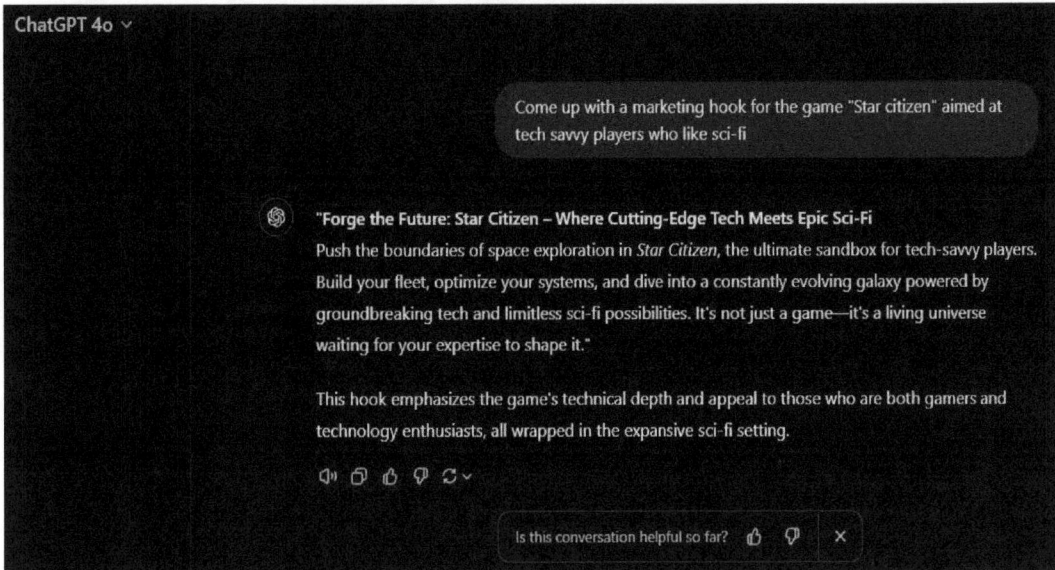

Figure 12.1: Using ChatGPT for a marketing idea

Meta LLaMA

Meta's **Large Language Model Meta AI (LLaMA)** being more research-focused, requires a different prompt engineering strategy. Given that LLaMA is often used in academic or experimental settings, prompts must be more technical and domain-specific. Part of the interest from academia is that LLaMA is open source. The user must supply highly detailed and precise instructions to yield outputs that are aligned with advanced research queries or technical explorations. You might see a researcher input, `Summarize recent advancements in unsupervised learning for medical image classification` with the expectation they will receive a precise, data-driven response. LLaMA's users are typically more familiar with the technical context, so prompts are often longer, more complex, and assume prior knowledge of the topic. See *Figure 12.2* for this example. It gives an excellent summary in bullet form in the answer for the researcher to take the next step, with a few helpful links to help with sources referenced:

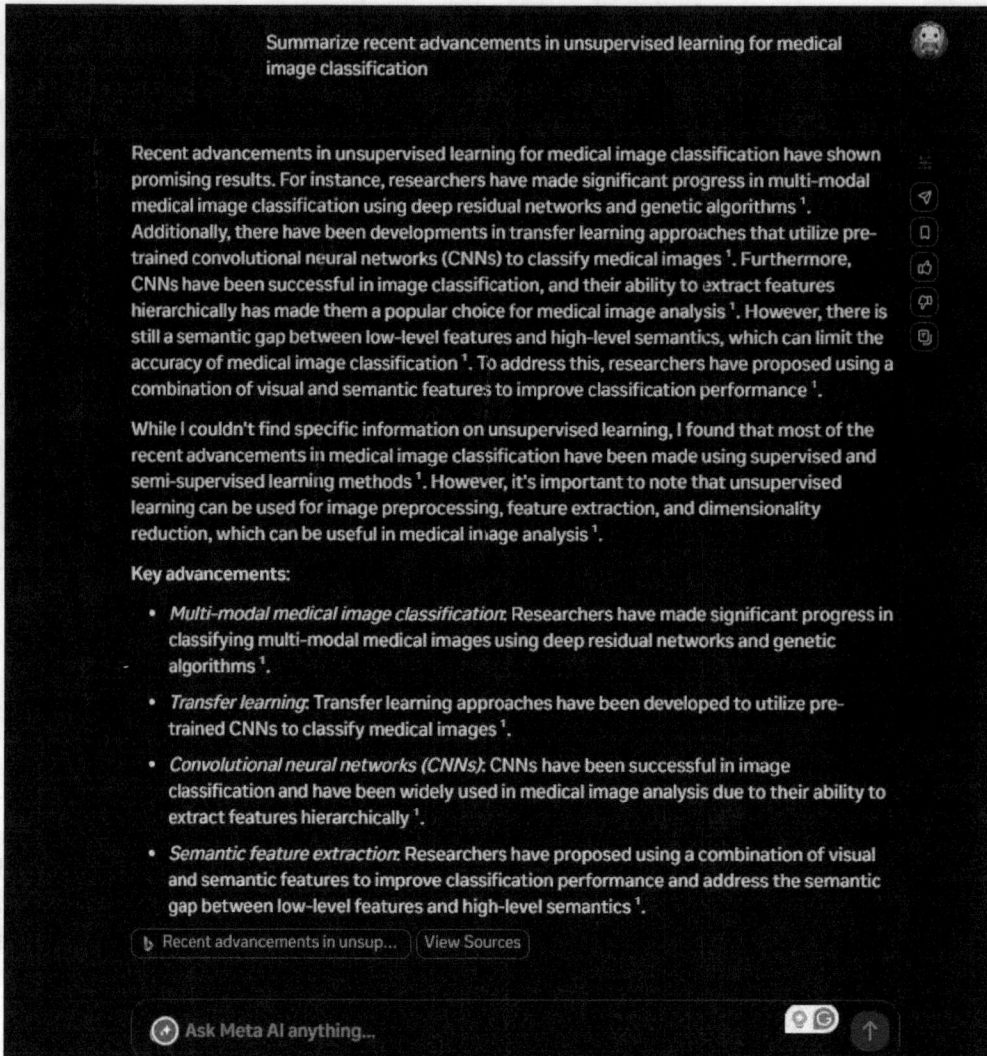

Figure 12.2: Using Meta's LLaMA with results

Google Gemini

Google's Gemini emphasizes knowledge retrieval in high-stakes domains, such as healthcare or finance. Prompt strategies here require an emphasis on precision and domain specificity. Users must provide clear, structured prompts that use the correct industry terminology, such as: `Generate a summary of recent studies on the efficacy of machine learning models in predicting cancer outcomes`. Since Gemini operates in areas where the consequences of inaccurate information are significant, prompts often include constraints to ensure the AI accesses the most reliable and up-to-date information, along with requesting citations or references for further validation:

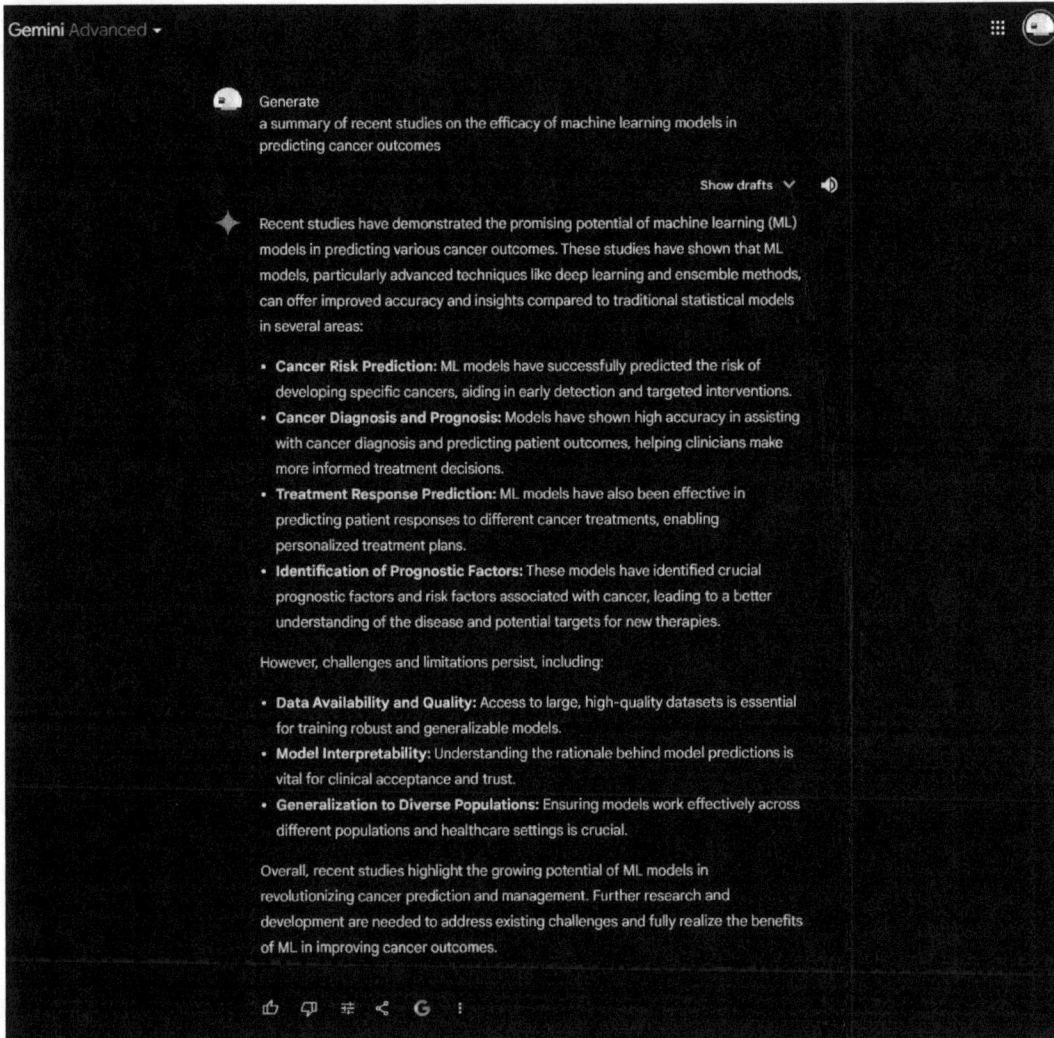

Figure 12.3: Showing Google Gemini Advanced answering questions

Claude

Claude, or Claude.AI, prioritizes being open while focusing on giving consideration to ethics wherever possible, as well as having strong built-in features to support the **why** of an answer. Hence, your approach as a prompt engineer would be to provide a prompt structure that allows Claude to give you an explanation of why it is a series the way it is.

Claude is used in scenarios where the AI's reasoning needs to be transparent and justifiable, so prompts typically include requests for the model to explain its decision-making process and avoid generating harmful or misleading content. Claude is a more recent entrant into the wider AI scene. Let us take an example by asking the following: **Give me advice on**

spending a bit more to buy a house vs rent an apartment? Give me the thought process on pros and cons. You can see from the results in *Figure 12.4*. Claude gives rather an expanded bulleted list exceptional to generate talking points:

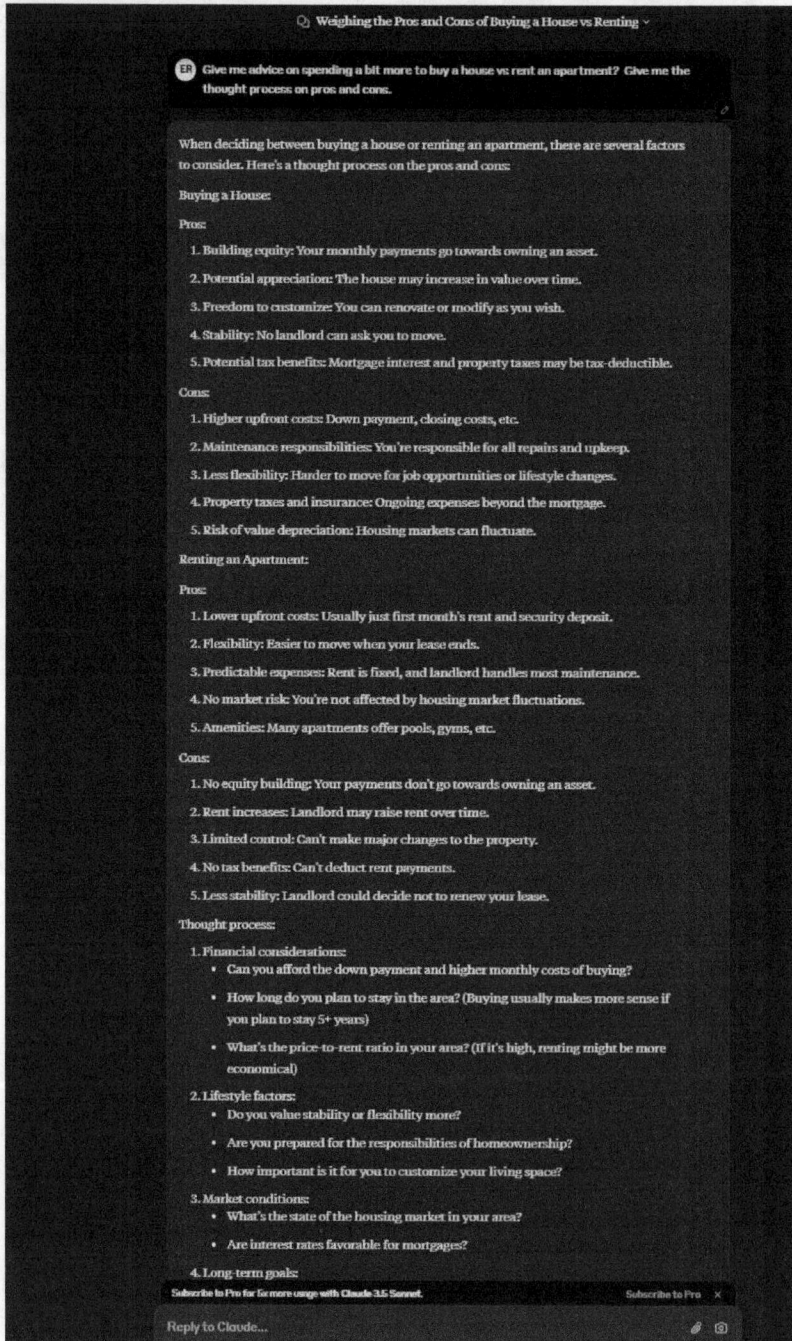

Figure 12.4: Asking Claude to give advice on buy vs buy for housing

Microsoft Copilot

Copilot from Microsoft is an AI Service which comes in several versions. Microsoft has Copilot built into it is GitHub and office suites and can do quite helpful things like come up with a framework in PowerPoint. Let us use a real example of **Create a presentation about how solar storms can affect IoT Devices.** You will actually end up with a very good starter PowePoint deck, in this case 15 slides. It will need updates to be presented but it really does do a huge amount of the work for you. It even generates the images for the deck. *Figure 12.5* shows an example slide in PowerPoint using the built-in Microsoft Copilot:

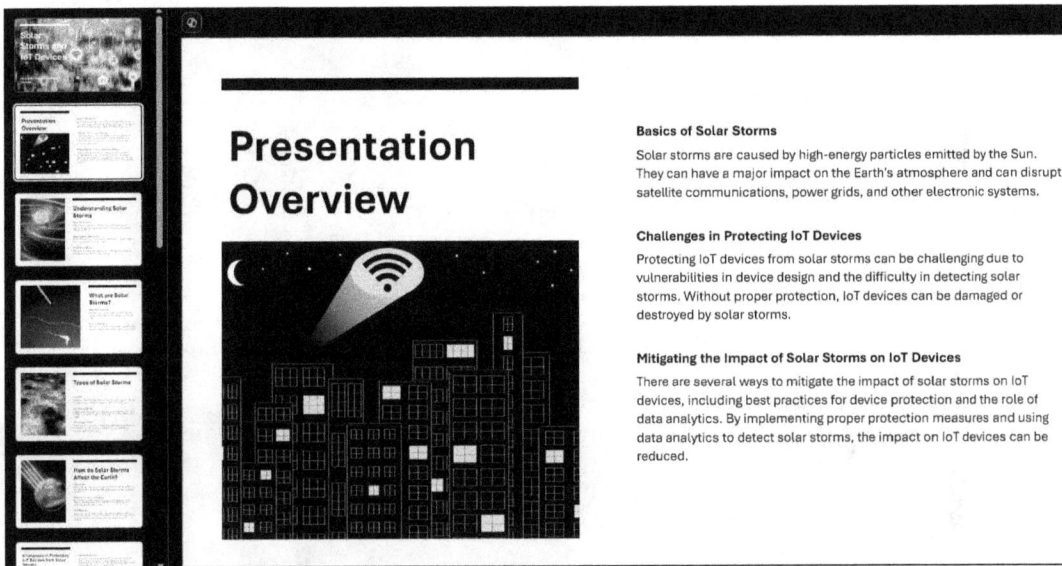

Figure 12.5: Microsoft CoPilot generating an overview PowerPoint automatically

In Microsoft Teams, users with the appropriate licensing will have the ability to have AI-generated meeting summaries with automatic tasks being called out. It is quite useful.

Just like Google does for Gemini, Microsoft has Copilot accessible to ask questions from their Bing search engine user interface. Let us see an example: **write a simple program in python to generate how the engima machine works.** Now, let us see how it works:

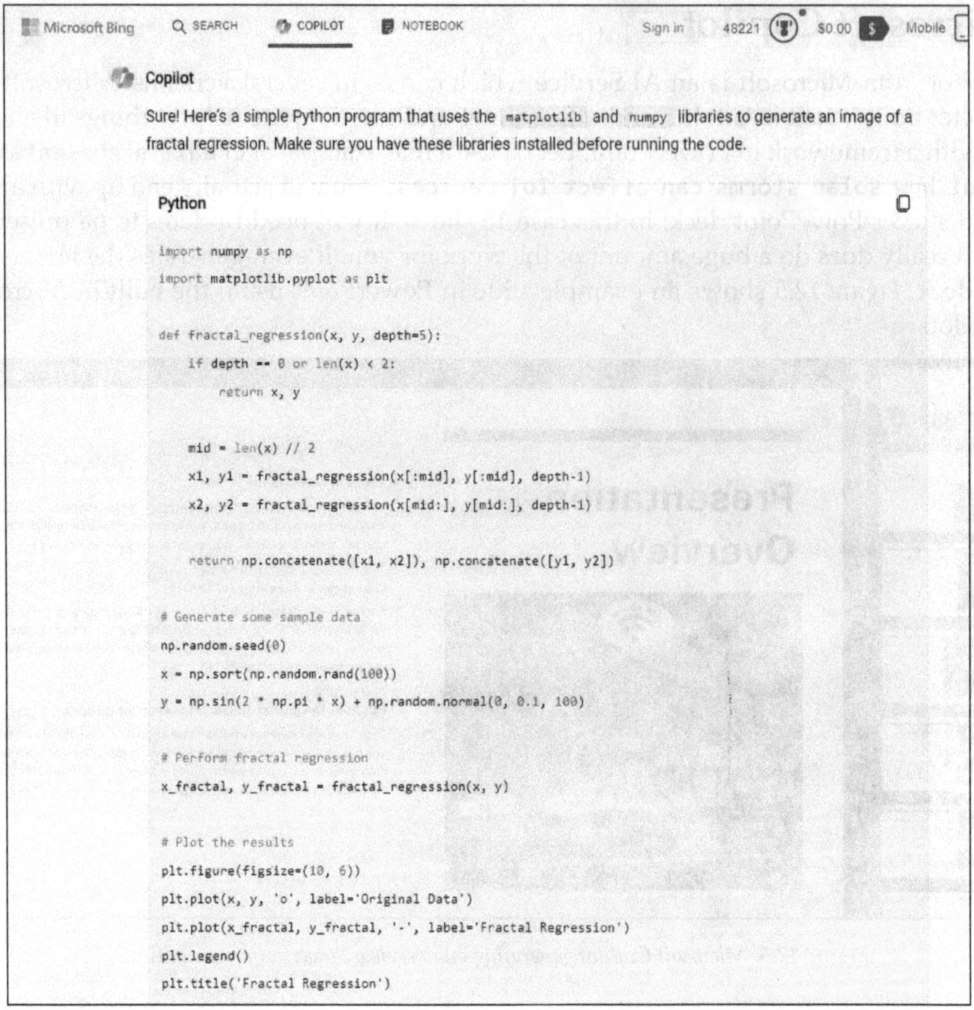

Figure 12.6: Shows Microsoft Copilot generating code in Python

There are other versions of Copilot that can be integrated with GitHub to help a developer. Microsoft markets it as an AI-pair programmer. It goes beyond being simply as a helpful reference on the fly and also generate code examples for you. This is an example which might fit better with GitHub Copilot.

Midjourney

Midjoruney has existed since 2022 and was developed by an independent research lab focused on creating art and visuals through artificial intelligence via human-to-AI text-based interaction. Midjoruney quickly was able to garner attention for its ability to generate highly detailed and creative artwork from text prompts, leveraging advancements in generative AI models, particularly diffusion-based techniques. Midjourney's unique approach allows users to input descriptive language and receive imaginative, often surreal or photorealistic visuals, which has led to its popularity among artists, designers, and creative professionals. The platform stands out for its focus on enabling users to produce visually striking art with minimal technical knowledge, democratizing creative expression, and opening new possibilities for artistic collaboration with AI.

Let us use a prompt to give you a space-themed poster for your room, but make it like an old poster:

Create an image to represent a 1940's style travel poster but for humans flying to the moon in the future.

The result can be seen is in *Figure 12.7*. You get a few examples and can refine, alter, or regenerate:

Figure 12.7: Midjourney generating art via AI

Midjourney also has a very useful interface via Discord. There are other excellent image-generation tools, such as Dall-E and Stable Diffusion, but for the sake of Beverly, we are highlighting only one.

Best practices for crafting prompts

Prompt engineering – writing a prompt to pull out the best response from an AI system – is a key skill for the use of AI. Systems like ChatGPT, Copilot, Midjourney and Gemini that generate everything from text to code to images can still be pretty good at writing a response on their own, but they need to be prompted carefully to do so. However, how should the user prompt an AI model to produce a response that is going to be successful: to pass muster with an editor, to be persuasive to a domain-specific audience or simply to be something that readers might actually want to read? This involves a combination of knowing your audience, honing the prompt through iteration, and getting feedback from your users to see if your work really has the desired effect. Let us look at a guide to prompt engineering that highlights all the insider tips and tricks you need to boost your success rate with quality writing prompts. One is to know who you are writing for. It is important to be cognizant of who you are writing for, whatever result comes out of your AI system. Different readers have different expectations, as well as different valuations of human-sounding versus expert-sounding text.

Understanding the audience

Perhaps the biggest difference in crafting a good prompt is knowing who your audience is or will be. Technical and non-technical users require different prompts and, in turn, get different outputs from AI models. When an AI such as ChatGPT has an exchange with a user, the technical level of that user persona could flip that AI's response from sounding technical to non-technical or from simple to complex and in-depth. An example would be a high-school student interacting with ChatGPT who might need it to sound a lot simpler: **Please explain what a function is in Python using simple examples.** The AI needs to work with an essentially non-technical persona, answering with a human-sounding prompt.

For education, non-technical users who, like a student or content creator, do not expect or need technical resources or jargon, the tone should be more conversational and devoid of complex technical terms, whereas for technical users – such as Copilot's audience of developers – who expect higher technical resources, the outputs should be highly technical and the prompts should include the proper and detailed programming context to output functional code. The key to creating prompts that output the best results is acknowledging this distinction and tailoring prompts to either write schoolwork or code, generate legal resources, or generate educational resources.

For example, compare **Write a contract**' with '**Draft a non-disclosure agreement intellectual property rights and enforceability in the state of California**. The latter provides terminology as well as accurate results. The inclusion of **intellectual property rights**, **enforceability**, and **the state of California** also helps several notches. These will give clues to the AI model and what area of training to draw responses from.

Let us look at a niche areas, such as medicine, and assume a tool such as Copilot built into Word. The AI could help doctors by translating or producing clinical notes or summarizing patient information. However, in order for an AI system to provide the highest-quality response, the prompts must be detailed. The prompt for the physician might then ask: **Paraphrase into human-sounding text while retaining citations and quotes. Create a report summarizing cholesterol and health history, including current medications.** A medical prompt is rich in domain-specific terms, providing the necessary information to arrive at a medical response. Without language-specific content, outputs from AI models might have too little detail or contextual information to the specialized fields given to the AI.

Iterative testing and refinement

Prompt engineering is necessarily iterative: almost always, you are not going to get the most precise or most relevant answer the first time you try a prompt. Iterating allows the user to continually refine the phrasing, specificity, and scope of the prompt, incentivizing increasingly precise and useful responses from the model. Eventually, through this process of iterative testing and refinement, prompting will improve and the AI's output will more and more closely align with what the user is trying to accomplish.

A user might start with a broad prompt: **Paraphrase this text while retaining citations and quotes.** Initial responses might be too broad or gloss over important details that the user wanted to be explored. By iterating a few times with context, like: **Paraphrase this text while retaining citations and quotes but make this focus on the effects of social media on communication among teenagers, with an emphasis on Instagram and TikTok,** the added context results in the following: **In summary, social networking technology has fundamentally transformed communication as compared to traditional alternatives, like phone calls or face-to-face interactions.** Iterative testing can also help users adjust the tone or deepen the analysis, going from general reductions to full expert-level rhetoric as the task or audience changes.

A major component of iterative refinement is changing the output format. If the prompt is too long or unstructured, users can refine it by changing the format. For example, while a prompt such as **Paraphrase the input into human-sounding text while retaining citations and quotes** used earlier could yield perfectly fine text, **Paraphrase the input into human-sounding text while retaining citations and quotes, but keep the text brief and in bullet-point form** might have resulted in a more structured text that is more palatable to read.

Iteration helps calibrate developers track improvements. Success metrics like completion times, user or customer satisfaction scores, or financial outcomes (number of users, training time, conversions, etc.) can be particularly useful. In systems like Gemini, which could be used to inform search results in a search engine, you can use success metrics, such as task completion and quality of search retrievals, to promptly fine-tune your copy. If a prompt consistently results in incomplete or irrelevant responses, you could consider re-wording or restructuring the prompt to hone the model's ability to return more relevant information. Reviewing these metrics will allow you to fine-tune prompt efficiency and ensure your AI's output meets the necessary key performance indicators.

Leveraging feedback and metrics

Feedback is another good thing to add to a rapid engineering process. AI platforms will often have feedback mechanisms like a thumbs-up or thumbs-down (look at the example photos in this chapter to see examples) — in which the users can comment on the output's quality in real-time. These feedback loops are helpful for constantly refining prompts. If a user consistently rates an output as too weak or irrelevant, this is because the prompt is in need of some work or clarification.

Think about an AI-supported support bot for the user. When the bot's answers get rated invariably low, the developers can explore the motivators driving them and adjust them to be more targeted or more appropriate to users. For example, a prompt that gives out too many unrelated details like, `Repair my internet connection`, can be iterated into, `Repair my internet connection is slow on my Wi-Fi network.` By continually adding feedback from users, prompts can become better, more helpful results.

Feedback loops are essential in optimizing AI-generated content as well. Artists are able to comment on the accuracy and imagination of the AI-created images, and influence future versions on platforms such as Midjourney. When an image does not meet the desired standards, users can fine-tune the original call for more descriptive text or references to specific artworks, which further optimizes future results.

Qualitative metrics help measure the efficacy of prompt engines, such as quantitative metrics, include the level of user engagement, click-through rate marketing to compare the efficacy of copy having a good message, etc.

Qualitative metrics usually include user reviews with comments giving a more subjective understanding of prompt performance that can capture nuances that pure quantitative measures. Qualitative feedback from users might suggest that, while an answer is technically correct, it might come across as too formal or less empathetic to a human user in a customer service application.

To do well here requires developing skills in prompt iteration and feedback. It takes practice to get good at. It also requires a willingness to accept what the models tell you, and to apply the measurements to modify your prompts to be as good as possible. Finally, it requires adapting the prompts to your technical experience, theatrical or jargon prompts to the user, and fine-tuning every imaginable type of industry and field to continue to hone prompt engineering practices in order to make sure AI-generated outputs match the ever-evolving needs of users.

Real-world applications and outcomes

Developers can help guide AI models such as ChatGPT, and Midjourney toward more precise, timely, and context-sensitive responses by designing prompts carefully. In customer service, for example, properly written prompts allow AI to offer not only actual answers but also responses that resonate with the brand voice and sensitivity of the organization and thus, provide customers with more satisfaction and engagement. The same can be applied in content development; prompt engineering will enable you to develop creative and unique content following style guides or with specific thematic needs – thus enabling you to become more efficient and save time and resources for content creation.

The tactical implementation of prompt engineering is not limited to more technical domains like software and data. Prompts that developers can customize: AI tools such as GitHub Copilot provide developers with code fragments, debugging, or entire scripts for their projects. Not only does this make development faster, but it reduces human error as well. Data science prompts can be built to teach AI to perform advanced data analysis, visualize data trends, or make accurate predictions about trends. Such applications illustrate how rapid engineering can be a game-changer not just for business efficiency but also for innovation across all sectors by allowing for subtler, smarter engagements with AI.

Lessons learned from successful implementation

Prompt engineering has been successful in many AI applications, and the experiences it teaches are useful for all AI development and deployment practices. An essential lesson is to focus on context and purpose, which is of utmost importance. AI models triggered with a genuine understanding of the end-user's environment, goals, and problems perform better and are more relevant. In healthcare, for instance, AI being asked to read and interpret patient information following clinical rules can make a big difference in diagnosis and patient care. That is due to the prompt being able to add context and, thus, AI is better used in a special environment. These personalized prompting algorithms are not only more functionally useful to AI but also establish trust in users by providing consistently trustworthy and context-appropriate results.

This also illustrates the power of iterative refinement for prompt engineering. A series of feedback loops, in which outputs are analyzed and cues modified, have been key to boosting the AI. It is like agile development — you just adapt and improve. For example, in automated content creation, the incremental adjustment of prompts according to the engagement metrics and editorial feedback can be used to drastically scale the quality and compatibility of the created content with the audience. Iteratively, this ensures that the AI is still responding to changing content norms and user requirements, showing that prompt engineering can and does work. It is not an if-then thing, but an ongoing process responsive to new knowledge and changing conditions.

Advanced prompt engineering techniques

Prompt engineering, while initially a straightforward process of crafting input to guide AI outputs, has evolved into a sophisticated practice that leverages advanced methodologies to optimize the performance of AI systems. As models which we looked at previously in this chapter, like ChatGPT, Copilot, Midjourney, and others grow more capable, prompt engineers must adapt techniques that allow these systems to perform specific, high-quality tasks with minimal input. This involves the integration of concepts like few-shot and zero-shot learning, prompt tuning and optimization, and the effective handling of multi-turn conversations. Together, these techniques push the boundaries of what AI can achieve, enabling it to produce more accurate, relevant, and contextual outputs.

Few-shot and zero-shot learning

Few-shot and zero-shot learning are key innovations in AI, and especially in the use of **large language models** (**LLMs**), which fundamentally changed the way these models process prompts. In classical AI training, models need large amounts of examples in order to learn how to complete a task. These approaches allow those models to make generalizations from minimal input that the model has not yet been trained on; this reduces the need for broader training for an AI model but allows for ways to train the model while actually using the model. It is where **training** comes from in AI terms, as something has some knowledge and then learns more about what it is supposed to know over time, which is very generally how humans work.

Few-shot gives the AI a few examples in the structure of a prompt (thus few-shot) to try to understand the prompt. One could ask a question but qualify it with a few examples of the types of answers being looked for, perhaps answering in haiku or iambic pentameter for poetry when looking for examples. The more iterations through and the higher the specificity, the better the results over time. Again, the learning metaphor is very appropriate here.

In contrast, zero-shot learning asks the AI model to carry out an output task to which it has not been explicitly trained but can still master through generalizing from its massively pre-trained knowledge. This is also useful when the output task has not been seen before – that is, no examples are provided to the AI; it is still asked to analyze or produce something convincing and appropriate. In a zero-shot example, you could ask a prompt with no qualifiers whatsoever. The AI will do its best to relate the context you are asking to the data set the answers are drawn on. In advanced prompt engineering, zero-shot capabilities can actually reduce the burden on the user. The user can prompt AIs to output things over a huge number of domains and can vary the input a great deal without needing to provide many granular examples or preconditions.

There is no rigid rule on how to properly combine few-shot and zero-shot learning with prompt engineering. Rather, the key here is to nuance the approach to familiarize the model with more common inputs for simpler tasks or more general outputs using zero-shot learning and to provide more specific inputs for more precise outputs using few-shot learning. For example, for more common tasks like generating a quick context-independent response, zero-shot learning might be sufficient. However, if the output demands higher precision, such as in the case of creating a legal document or for a much more technical variant of the same task, few-shot learning would be more appropriate. You can adopt this same approach to fine-tune your specific approach to avoid overcomplicating things with additional knowledge and instead focus on the task at hand in order to achieve the best result in terms of quality while also being efficient with your time and compute cycles.

Prompt tuning and optimization

Prompt tuning and other sophisticated prompt engineering techniques are focused on refining a prompt's structure and phrasing, and perhaps also narrowing its scope, in order to steer the AI towards creating better outputs or towards outputs that are more attuned to the input. Picture a dial: we can fine-tune it to align the input more closely with the output. This dial, tuned to the right level – or the correct temperature – results in the AI generating appropriate, coherent, on-topic responses. Prompt tuning is valuable and is employed frequently for models, like the GPT-based ones, Copilot, or Midjourney, exhibiting the highest sensitivity to small changes in phrasing and positioning.

At the heart of prompt tuning is the idea that AI models are incredibly sensitive to **human** linguistic cues. A single word or phrase in a prompt can steer the response in a particular direction. For example, simply tweaking the prompt for ChatGPT from: `Paraphrase the input into human-sounding text while retaining citations and quotes` to: `Paraphrase the input into human-sounding text while retaining citations and quotes, focusing on the importance of linguistic cues in prompt-tuning` changes the answer from generic to more specific and focused on a particular sub-discipline of machine learning: `Below is an instruction that describes a task, paired with an input that provides further context. Write a response that appropriately completes the request.` Understanding what tweaks can improve an AI model's response is critical for good prompt tuning. It can help to align the AI with the user's exact needs and, therefore, produce more useful and better context-matched answers.

Iterative refinement is another vital element of prompt **optimization**. Rarely will a prompt produce an ideal response with just one version, **especially when it comes to more complex tasks, a user might have to tweak, simplify, or clarify instructions or experiment to see how the AI responds to** code: some trial the response meets the desired output. For instance, if you give Copilot the prompt: `Write me a function that handles errors in Python`, it might give me a boilerplate version of something that handles errors. By iterating on that and giving it a sharper prompt – such as: `Write me a Python function that logs errors to a file and retries the operation three times if it fails` – you can get closer to the functionality you want.

Metrics and feedback loops are also a crucial part of prompt optimization. Since outputs can be reviewed against quantified metrics (for example, how long it takes an AI to complete the task, how accurate the response is, or whether users have provided positive feedback about the AI's output), prompt engineers can then experiment with different prompts that optimize for those metrics. For example, if a prompt throws an AI off track by generating an output that veers too much from the topic at hand or that is too wordy, then the prompt can be optimized by constraining the input. A feedback loop could instruct the model to *keep it to 200 words, and stay on-point,* for instance, which ensures that AI stays within these parameters. In Midjourney and similar image-generation systems, prompt optimization can involve tweaking the descriptive terms to achieve a certain aesthetic or style or even experimenting with different words and phrases in combination with other types of constraints that instruct the AI how to produce the chosen artwork (for instance, `give it a dark, moody, Technicolor, three-quarter-lit range silhouette composition in`).

Prompt optimization also takes the form of telling AI tools how to format output. This is especially helpful for producing technical outputs, such as code or structured documents. If you are asking an AI tool to generate such content, then you not only want it to get the content right but also to present it in a way that makes it easy for your user to digest or implement. If you tell ChatGPT to **Paraphrase the input into human-sounding text while retaining citations and quotes**, what you will receive is a full discussion. However, if you tell it to **List the five most common machine learning algorithms and briefly explain each**, what you will receive instead is a list, which is formatted correctly in a concise and easily digestible way.

Experimental prompt tuning can also include tweaking model-specific features such as the temperature of an output (meaning, in certain models, how random or deterministic an output will be). Low temperatures typically give deterministic, narrower results that are useful in many technical contexts – writing a computer program, for example. Higher temperatures can lead to more creative or varied outputs, which can be useful in artistic contexts or brainstorming. Learning how to tweak such temperature settings (or other features of a prompt) enables engineers to further control the tone, creativity and variability of a model's response, offering another layer of optimization for experts.

Handling multi-turn conversations

An area of the current focus is allowing more complex back-and-forth dialogues to occur. Most AI systems have a *memory* approach to this, where it will retain the context of a conversation. That context is usually stored as the whole conversation, thus allowing you to go back to the AI system to pick up where you left off. This is outstanding for developers looking for guidance on code, for example, and they wish to check back at a later date. Keeping track of history is going to be something we all see AI systems doing more and more. This capability is crucial for applications such as customer service bots, technical support or lengthy back-and-forth with conversational agents – like the chatbot ChatGPT.

Multi-turn engineering to retain context between each interaction. Moreover, because one of the major challenges of multi-turn conversations is often the maintenance of context through the length of the back and forth, engineers need to design prompts that forward or reference previous turns. Prompt engineering that effectively asks for more information helps keep context between turns by embedding information from earlier parts of the conversation or by using system tools such as memory functions (if one is built into the AI).

Multi-turn conversations require dynamic prompt tuning as well to handle the different stages of interaction. Early in the conversation, initial prompts will be quite broad and open-ended: **What can I help you with today?** Later in the conversation, prompts need to get more tightly focused as the conversation progresses through the user's responses: **I'm having trouble with my internet connection.** or **Are you having slow speeds or is the connection dropping entirely?** By progressively targeting the conversation with each turn, the AI can provide ever-deeper, more tailored responses.

Ambiguity can still be a challenge as users could potentially give vague or erroneous information. The prompt engineer needs to strive for accuracy where possible, and having an able set of *who, what, why, when,* etc. prompts ready to go is helpful for tools like chatbots. For example, if the user says `I need help with my account`, the AI might reply `Could you clarify whether you're experiencing login issues, difficulties with your billing, or other problems with your account?`

Constraints within prompts can also be to the benefit of multi-turn conversations. By adding context-aware constraints to the system, we can keep a conversation on track and prevent it from going off on a tangent. For example, in a technical support chat, if a user starts veering off-topic about some issue that is not sufficiently related to the problem at hand, the AI might say something like: `Sure, but first let's try to figure out why your internet isn't working. Does it happen with any connected device or just one?`

Finally, applying prompt engineering techniques that involve **utilizing** few-shot and zero-shot learning, refining, and tuning prompts to **optimize** accuracy, and effectively handling multi-turn conversations are key to leveraging the power of AI as much as possible. An understanding of how AI models process text is important for each technique, but learning and using them requires an iterative process of modifying input for the desired outcome. By leveraging these techniques, prompt engineers can unlock all the power of AI and get it to perform complex, human-like, context-aware tasks in multiple domains requiring minimal user input. In the future, as AI progresses, these advanced strategies will become even more important in guiding AI to accurately and intelligently output exactly what a user needs.

Conclusion

In this chapter, we spoke about how syntax drives prompts and the responses to prompts. Prompt engineers take time to refine and consider the syntactical impacts of their choices. You should feel grounded in your overview of prompt syntax in general, as well as how to follow best practices for syntax while focusing on advanced syntax techniques and keeping in mind the syntax and efficiency relationship, and lastly, having an eye on the trends for AI syntax through development. In the next chapter, we will focus on techniques and strategies for prompt engineering by focusing on how to craft good prompts, looking at advanced techniques, and digging into more examples of real-world prompt engineering with different AI systems and the challenges we face for quality prompts.

Join our book's Discord space

Join the book's Discord Workspace for Latest updates, Offers, Tech happenings around the world, New Release and Sessions with the Authors:

https://discord.bpbonline.com

CHAPTER 13

Challenges of Quality Prompts

Introduction

This chapter will cover some of the challenges of creating good prompts for AI. It begins by specifying the key criteria for creating good prompts — clarity, specificity, context, and tone and style. These principles are essential in allowing AI systems to interpret and act on prompts as designed. We will discuss some common problems in prompt engineering, like ambiguity: ambiguous challenges can give rise to indeterminate or unhelpful AI answers. This chapter also tackles the issue of bias in prompt design by emphasizing that human-induced biases can distort AI outputs to the point of ethical concerns. Furthermore, the chapter also considers the difficulties of building prompts with an appropriate balance of detail and concision, neither overtly expansive nor overly restrictive.

Structure

In this chapter, we will cover the following topics:

- Designing effective prompts
- Common challenges in prompt engineering
- Advanced prompt optimization techniques

Objectives

In this chapter, you will learn the pillars of building effective prompts while talking through the common challenges that you may have in prompt engineering due to potential limitations with the model itself. You will also learn more advanced refinement techniques for prompt engineering, and the approach you could use to measure the success of both an AI model and a prompt.

Designing effective prompts

Working with modern computing means working with precision, and working with AI means a critical element of prompt design is clarity. A good prompt brings both clarity and precision together. Ambiguous prompts can often lead you to get unreliable or unexpected outputs, both in human and computer interaction.

Clarity and specificity

In prompt engineering, the AI model might not understand the user's intent with ambiguity. So, you can imagine that clear and specific prompts enhance the accuracy of the generated responses. Let us look at some basic points to keep in mind when creating prompts that focus on good inputs receiving good outputs. We touched on the importance of clarity and specificity before but will expand more here:

- **Defining clear instructions for desired output**s: Clear instructions are key to getting that high-quality response from the AI system that you really want versus a vague answer. Keep in mind when you are defining prompts to consider what you want the AI to do and how you want the output to be structured. The better your clarity via input, the better the input.

  Let us take an example prompt, **Give an explanation of quantum computing**, which is a broad, open-ended prompt that may generate varying responses depending on the context inferred by the model. Now take that and make an update to refine the prompt to something more along the lines of **Explain the principles of quantum computing to a beginner**, which will provide the AI model with more clarity, increasing the likelihood of a suitable response.

- **Common pitfalls in vague or overly general prompt**s: If you give prompts that are vague, you will, of course, get insufficient detail or ambiguity in the language responding to your prompt. For example, a prompt like **What are the benefits of AI?** may result in an answer that is too broad, leaving out important details specific to the user's needs. Now, let us take a look at a prompt which asks, **What are the benefits of AI in healthcare for improving diagnostic accuracy?**. The prompt not only narrows down the scope but also increases the relevance of the response by aligning it with a particular domain.

- **Crafting actionable commands for AI systems**: Always ensure your prompt has a directly actionable outcome. Explicit and direct commands are generally better because they instruct the AI on what to do. For example, `Five reasons why AI can make customer service more efficient` is a straightforward ask that yields a long, specific answer, as opposed to an infinitive question such as `How can AI be helpful for customer service?`.

Context and relevance

Context is essential here so that the AI gets the right answer that will suit the user's request. Invokes should be created so they include the background information needed and keep the question relevant to the exercise.

Let us look at some key points that focus on relevance that come out of a specific set of knowledge of an area to get better outputs:

- **Integrating domain knowledge for enhanced outputs**: The addition of domain-specific expertise helps boost output quality. For instance, an invitation aimed at legal purposes could be "Share what AI does for data privacy law." That gives the AI system context to frame its reply within a legal context rather than creating white papers on data privacy or AI.

- **Maintaining task relevance: Avoiding contextual drift**: Contextual drift occurs when the AI model departs from the answer it was initially giving. It is like someone reminding you of more details when they are giving you an answer, and again reminding you more, to which the answer is muddied. In AI, this often occurs in iterative prompts, where additional information from previous inputs influences later responses. To maintain task relevance, users should provide specific instructions at each step. For example, when asking multiple questions, prompting the AI to `focus only on data protection practices` keeps the response centered on the specified topic, minimizing unrelated outputs.

- **Context preservation in iterative prompting**: We know iterative approaches are how both humans and computer systems learn. We do an initial prompt, refine it, etc. With ease, you can create prompts that are made of several discrete steps. In these cases, with multi-step prompts, preserving context is essential. AI systems tend to generate more consistent outputs when each prompt builds upon the previous one while explicitly maintaining context. An example of context preservation is seen in the following steps:

  1. Prompt: `Explain data encryption in cloud computing.`

  2. Prompt: `Now, compare these methods of encryption to those used in on-premise storage.`

Let us look at real-world answers to these questions to highlight context being preserved. Notice how the context was maintained in the second question, where you do not need to re-ask the first question. This allows you to refer back to the conversation or pick up a previous conversation with some AI modules that keep a history for you. *Figure 13.1* shows this question initially being asked, and the returned answer is a general, good, and high-level overview:

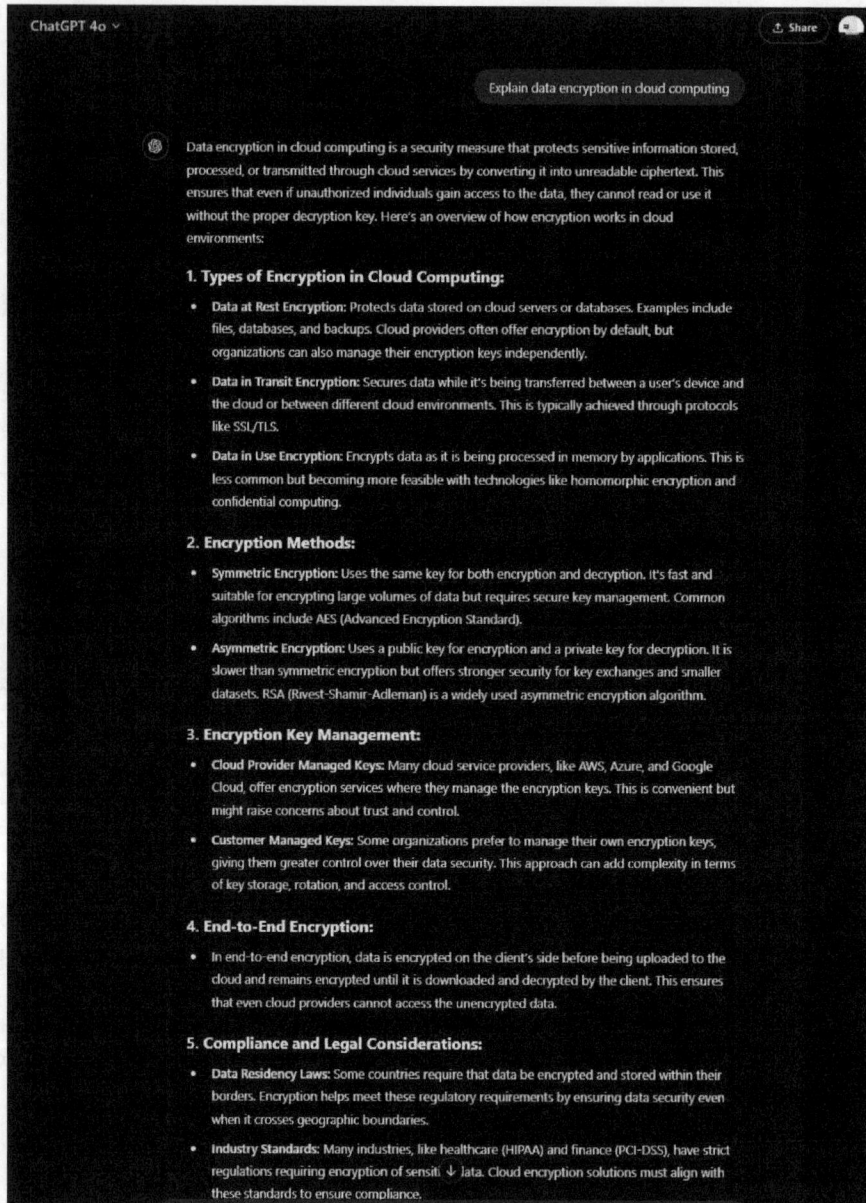

Figure 13.1: *Asking a Question that's a bit vague*

Figure 13.2 shows a follow-up question with context, ensuring AI's subsequent outputs remain aligned with the original prompt:

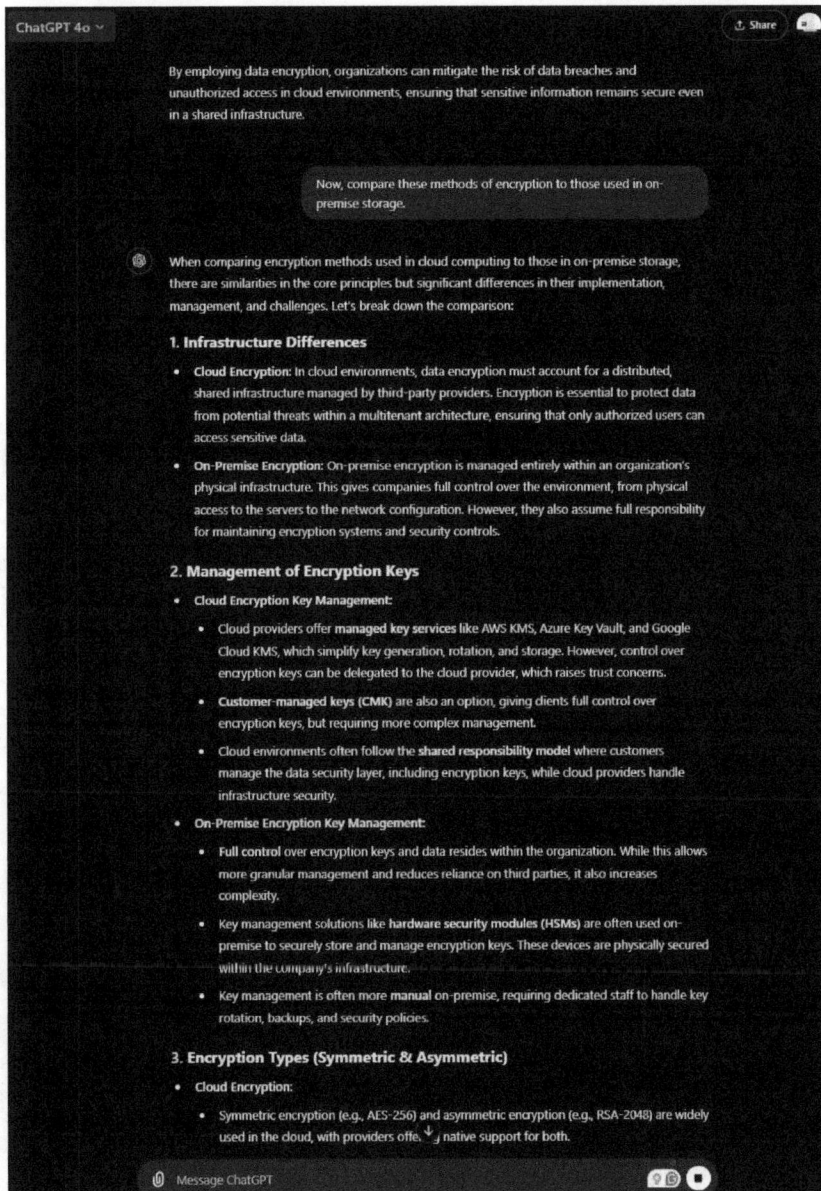

Figure 13.2: Leveraging the AI ability to maintain context

Tone and style considerations

When in the planning stage of prompt creation, one must hold both tone and style as equally important, particularly when the output is intended for specific audiences. The way a prompt engineer sets up a prompt directly influences the response's formality, complexity, and depth:

- **Adapting prompts for different communication goals**: Different communication goals require different prompting strategies. For example, when crafting a prompt aimed at a professional audience, using formal language and including technical jargon may yield more appropriate responses. A prompt such as `Provide a technical analysis of blockchain scalability challenges` is suitable for a specialized audience. Conversely, a prompt like `Explain blockchain scalability to a high school student` would produce a simplified, accessible response.

Let us look at *Figure 13.3*, where the preceding question is asked to Claude. In this case, you get a high-level yet fairly terse response. There is an assumption that the reader is aware of technology in general, as you can see that it responds to block size limits, node synchronization, layer two solutions, etc:

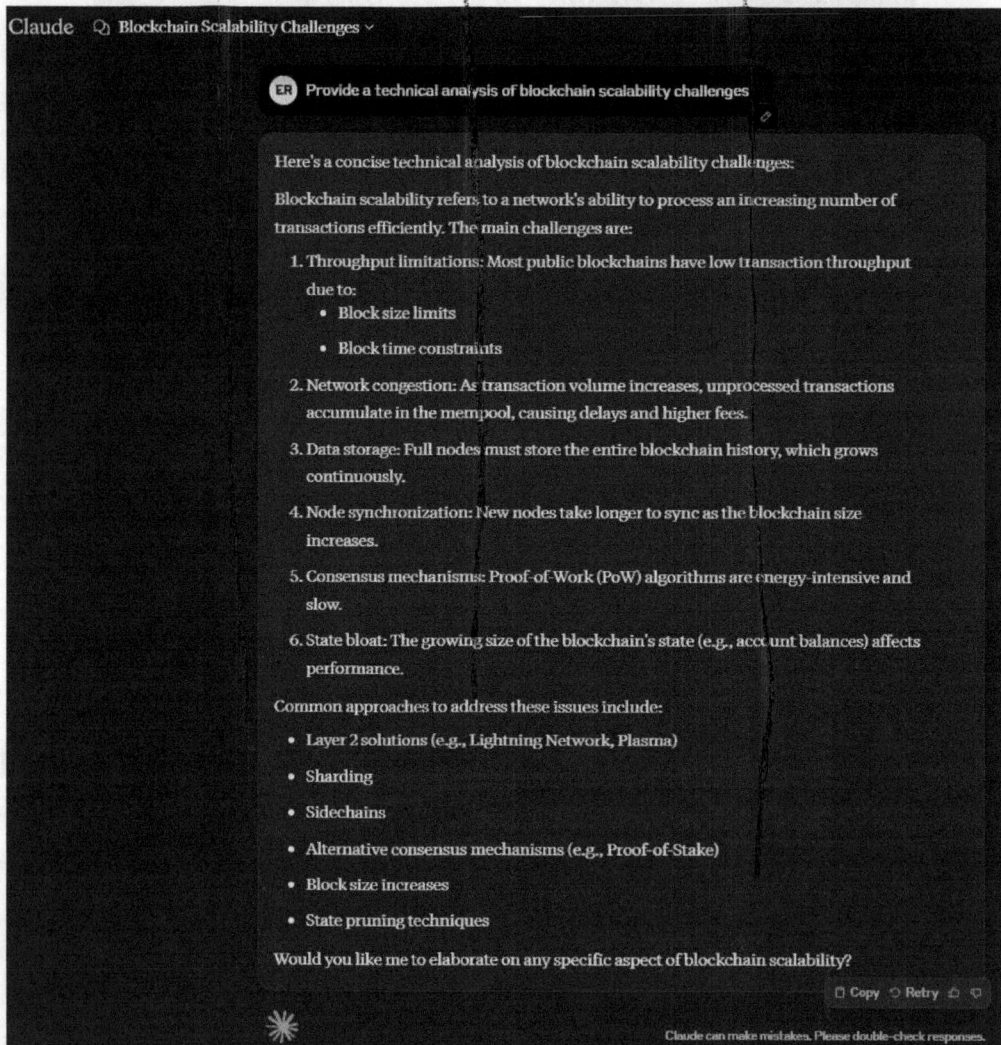

Figure 13.3: Asking Claude a general question about blockchain

Figure 13.4, however, takes the approach that the recipient is a high school student, and as learning is so often accomplished through analogies or metaphors, following is how the answer is presented:

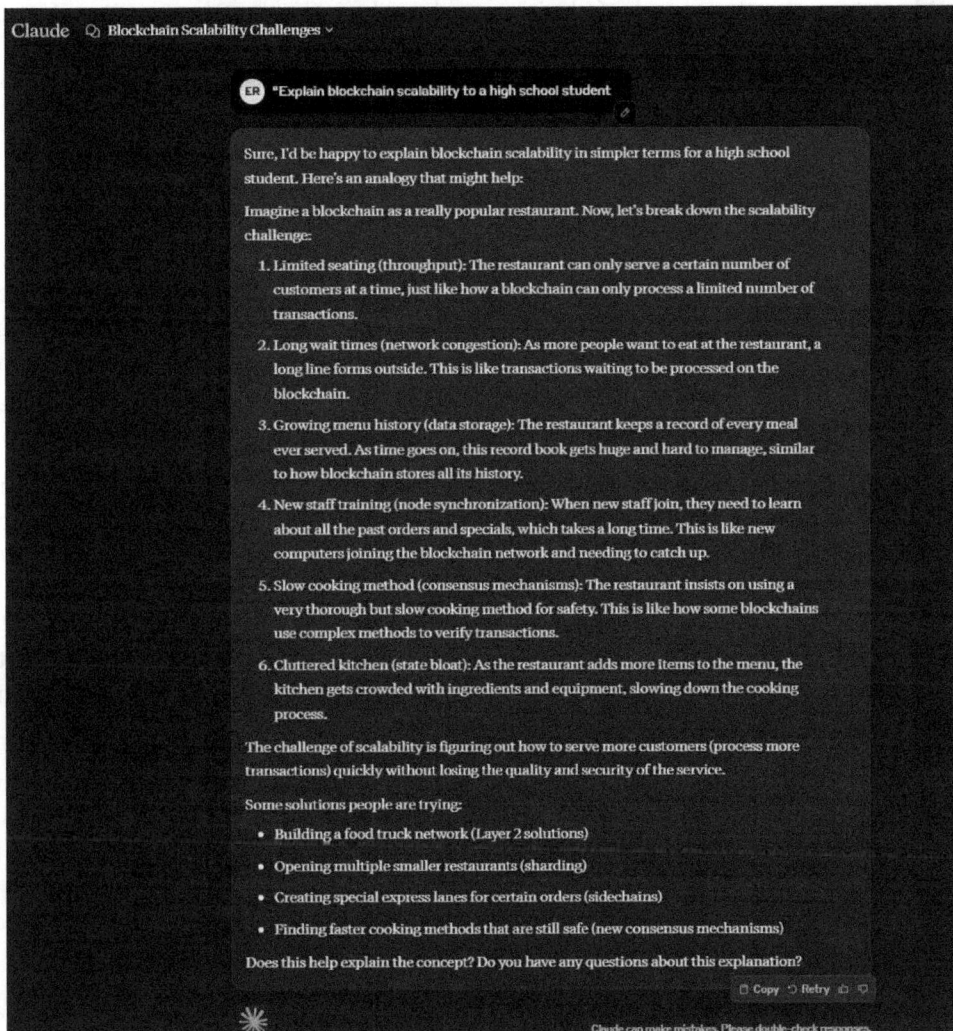

Claude ⟳ Blockchain Scalability Challenges ⌄

ER "Explain blockchain scalability to a high school student

Sure, I'd be happy to explain blockchain scalability in simpler terms for a high school student. Here's an analogy that might help:

Imagine a blockchain as a really popular restaurant. Now, let's break down the scalability challenge:

1. Limited seating (throughput): The restaurant can only serve a certain number of customers at a time, just like how a blockchain can only process a limited number of transactions.

2. Long wait times (network congestion): As more people want to eat at the restaurant, a long line forms outside. This is like transactions waiting to be processed on the blockchain.

3. Growing menu history (data storage): The restaurant keeps a record of every meal ever served. As time goes on, this record book gets huge and hard to manage, similar to how blockchain stores all its history.

4. New staff training (node synchronization): When new staff join, they need to learn about all the past orders and specials, which takes a long time. This is like new computers joining the blockchain network and needing to catch up.

5. Slow cooking method (consensus mechanisms): The restaurant insists on using a very thorough but slow cooking method for safety. This is like how some blockchains use complex methods to verify transactions.

6. Cluttered kitchen (state bloat): As the restaurant adds more items to the menu, the kitchen gets crowded with ingredients and equipment, slowing down the cooking process.

The challenge of scalability is figuring out how to serve more customers (process more transactions) quickly without losing the quality and security of the service.

Some solutions people are trying:

- Building a food truck network (Layer 2 solutions)
- Opening multiple smaller restaurants (sharding)
- Creating special express lanes for certain orders (sidechains)
- Finding faster cooking methods that are still safe (new consensus mechanisms)

Does this help explain the concept? Do you have any questions about this explanation?

🗋 Copy ↺ Retry 👍 👎

Claude can make mistakes. Please double-check responses.

Figure 13.4: Modifying the question to Claude via a persona approach

- **Formal vs. informal tone:** A prompt needs to respond in the same tone in which the input was made. Formal prompts will get a very formal result as the system tries to maintain like-to-like. Interestingly, casual speech could also be used in more casual or creative situations. `Complete a detailed report about climate change policies`, for example, is a formal question that predetermines an organized, data-heavy response. `What's up with climate change and what can we do about it?` is more informal and is probably more likely to generate a dialogue-like answer.

Common challenges in prompt engineering

Prompt engineering involves creating input queries to effectively express a task or request to an AI system. As the speed of design can hugely influence the quality of output, engineers face a wide array of obstacles that prevent optimal functionality. There are three major problem areas: ambiguity, bias, and prompt complexity. Solving these problems is important if you want the AI to react consistently, fairly, and accurately.

Ambiguity

Ambiguity is an ongoing challenge of prompt design. Without a clear prompt, you will have uncertainty, which gives space to many different interpretations of the AI model. Misguided prompts often produce non-conformist or non-useful responses that diminish the utility of the output. In terms of handling ambiguity, three considerations can be: double meaning avoidance, limitation of responses in open-ended prompts, and uniformity of comprehension from model to model. Let us look at them in detail:

- **Recognizing and avoiding double meanings in prompts**: Intuition can throw off AI models since natural language is loaded with homonyms or aphoristic sentences. In particular, a "bank" can mean a bank or a bankside. When designing prompts, you want to have plenty of context in order to clarify your purpose. We can use an example of asking a question `How can a bank be more secure?` but then add some additional context and ask: `How can a financial institution be more secure?`. This additional level of detail means the AI can hone in on the correct meaning and thus provide better answers.

- **Addressing open-ended prompts and controlling response boundaries**: Open-ended prompts can be a real challenge with people not trained in prompt engineering. So, `What are the advantages of AI?`. For instance, you are likely to be greeted with an excruciatingly long list. A more precise call such as `What are the three most important uses for AI in healthcare diagnosis?` lays down tighter constraints, making the AI system give a shorter, more useful answer.

- **Ensuring consistent understanding across different AI models**: The other layer of confusion occurs when different AI models receive the same call differently. That difference might be due to different training data, architecture, or model tuning. This can be minimized by the design of prompts towards a uniformity of layout. The user can set some keywords or examples in the prompt and instruct different models to respond in a similar way. For example, rather than generically asking, `Summarize the data`, adding `Share a one-paragraph summary of the key results of the report attached` guarantees more consistent results from one model to the next.

Bias

Bias in AI systems can come from the data sets they were trained on, giving them an overly narrow viewpoint as they are limited by those data sets. Bias can easily lead to skewed or incorrect outputs. Many systems, for example, are mostly trained on Western data, so the history of parts of the world will have a one-sided perspective. While there are many other examples we can point to, keep in mind how vital it is for prompt engineers to recognize, identify, and mitigate these biases to ensure fair and neutral outputs:

- **Identifying and mitigating implicit bias in language models**: Anticipating such biases means offering neutral language in prompts. To give you an example, asking the question again: **What are some important characteristics of a good leader, both men and women?** allows the AI to provide a more apolitical answer.

- **Handling cultural, gender, and regional bias in prompts:** Cultural, gender, and regional biases can become an issue when prompts involve subjective or value-laden themes. Specifically, AI models developed based on English-language data can lean westward in perspective due to the predominantly English-speaking countries being in the West; thus, texts written in English often represent that perspective, whether deliberate or not.

Best practices for ensuring neutral and fair prompts

Prompt engineers have an ongoing challenge to incorporate a few best practices in order to guarantee AI systems will return objective and just outputs. To start off with, it is less biased if you refrain from lead or loaded questions. Also, to cross-check for potential biases requires checking prompts with different models. Additionally, remember that prompt designers encourage AI to give a range of answers to thorny questions. The prompt, for example, **Share multiple cultures about treatment for mental health** is more welcoming and equal-minded than the one that assumes one.

Complexity

Prompt engineering becomes problematic if prompts are simply too complex or multifaceted for the AI to process coherently. Parsing complexity and striking a balance between both conciseness and completeness while fixing difficult prompts is the way through this problem.

Let us take a look at how a prompt would break down a complex ask into smaller, successive pieces.

- **Deconstructing multi-step prompts for simpler execution**: The multi-step prompts typically introduce too many variables at a time, which causes fuzzy or incomplete outputs. Try to break a complicated prompt around a broad subject, so you would start with something like **Describe blockchain technology and its use cases in supply chains, including how it affects the regulation,** and add a follow-up, `Talk about how it is used in supply chains today` and a final step of `how is it used in compliance today?`. That dissection enables the AI to tackle all the issues directly and correctly and get several back-to-back, on-point answers vs a long, rambling one.

- **Balancing conciseness and completeness**: Along these lines, a challenge in prompt engineering is a matter of how to strike a balance between conciseness and completeness. Shorter commands may fail to deliver the required information, while longer, elaborate commands will overwhelm the AI and possibly cause it to drift.

- **Troubleshooting complex prompts with debugging techniques**: Complex prompts often fail due to misunderstandings or incomplete processing by the AI. Troubleshooting these issues requires the prompt engineer to iterate on the prompt design and refine inputs based on the outputs received. If the AI produces an irrelevant or incomplete response, it is important to analyze whether the prompt was too ambiguous or complex. Techniques such as adding clarifying statements or testing with simpler versions of the prompt can help debug the issue. For example, if the prompt `How do governments use AI in policy-making?` yields an incomplete response, splitting it into `Describe how AI is used by governments` and `Explain how AI influences policy-making decisions` may yield better results.

Ambiguity, bias, and complexity are three core challenges in prompt engineering that can significantly affect the quality of AI-generated outputs. So, the quick points are to focus on clarity while trying to mitigate bias and manage complexity through deconstruction and refinement, prompt engineers can craft more effective prompts. As AI continues to evolve, overcoming these challenges will be essential to maximizing the potential of language models in various applications.

Advanced prompt optimization techniques

As the AI models and especially LLMs have developed further, the need for quality outputs has increased. Prompt engineering plays a crucial role in gaining valuable and timely output from these systems. However, it is not enough to design a single optimal prompt as tasks become more difficult. Developing methods such as iterative refinement, prompt chaining, templates, and automation can provide the potential to optimize prompts for consistency, consistency, and efficiency. Let us look at advanced prompt optimization methods in more detail.

Iterative refinement

Iterative refinement is the process of continuous enhancement of a prompt by observing outputs and tweaking the input accordingly. This will make it possible to scale up and optimize incrementally so that the AI system provides results that satisfy user expectations and demands:

- **Feedback loops (Analyzing outputs to improve prompts):** Feedback loops are the back-and-forth used for the AI output as diagnostic data, measuring areas where the answer delivers or does not. After each output, it is possible to tweak the prompt for individual items that need change. For instance, if a prompt generates too general replies, the user can add further context/instructions to the next generation in order to narrow down the scope.

  Let us look at the following prompt: `Explain quantum computing.`. If the response is too technical for a normal, non-techie audience, the next prompt could be adjusted to: `Explain quantum computing in simple terms for a high school student.` This iterative feedback loop sharpens the quality of responses with each round, making the AI model more likely to provide output that matches the user's intent.

- **Adjusting prompt length and detail for optimal results**: Prompt length and level of detail can really go a long way in determining the quality of an AI's answer. Sometimes, a longer and more precise request will instruct the AI to come up with something more specific and more reliable. Do be sure not to flood the prompt with way too much detail, as the AI model may very well get too much detail to parse well.

  Let us take an example of the prompt `What is the role of AI in modern healthcare?` which may produce a broad response. By refining the prompt to include more specific criteria—`What are the top three applications of AI in diagnostics and patient care in modern healthcare?`—the model is given more direction while avoiding unnecessary complexity. The iterative refinement process involves testing variations of prompt length and detail until the user achieves the desired output.

Prompt chaining

Prompt chaining is a more sophisticated approach to training an AI model using a chain of interacting prompts. That is so the task is not burdened with a single very complicated command but instead is contained into steps. Prompt chaining is particularly helpful for multi-step tasks, where each response feeds back on itself and creates a logical and structured output:

- **Multi-step prompt design for complex tasks**: Problems requiring more than one phase of investigation, such as these, can be mitigated by multiple-step prompt design. As opposed to requiring an AI to give an answer that incorporates all aspects of a problem, each step can be requested one by one, so that the model addresses only one aspect at a time.

For example, a complex task like **Explain how blockchain technology works and how it can be applied in the finance industry** can be broken down into smaller, manageable steps:

1. **Explain the basic principles of blockchain technology.**

2. **How does blockchain ensure security and transparency?**

3. **Discuss specific applications of blockchain in finance, such as cryptocurrency or smart contracts.**

The prompt engineer can take the steps to break the task into several clear and discrete stages. Prompt chaining ensures that the AI can fully explore each aspect of the task without losing track of the overall goal.

- **Sequencing prompts for coherent and structured outputs**: Sequencing prompts reason-wise guarantees the consistency of the AI's output throughout the task. This is crucial, especially when building multi-layered output with all the information nested together. In reality, sequencing entails structuring every ask in such a way that the subsequent one can build upon the previous so that the responses remain consistent and useful.

Prompt templates and automation

For prompt engineering at work, where you use prompts a lot, reusable templates and prompt automation can be very helpful in enhancing efficiency and consistency. You can standardize with templates, where prompts can be formatted differently for repetitive tasks. Even automation can be made to make the work faster by generating prompts based on variables or circumstances.

Creating reusable prompt templates for consistency

Using templates as a boilerplate format to build prompts is really helpful. Prompt templates are templates that have already been defined and could be used on the same kind of task, to keep prompts the same for the AI. Templates are particularly useful for applications where you need to interact with the model many times or follow some pattern. A customer service bot, for example, could use a template that frames prompts such as this:

- **What is the nature of the issue?**
- **Can you provide more details about the problem?**
- **What steps have you already taken to resolve this issue?**

Each time the AI interacts with a customer, the template ensures that the same structured approach is followed, reducing variability in responses. Prompt templates are also useful in educational or technical documentation, where prompts need to follow a consistent format.

Automating prompt generation for efficiency

You can automate the generation of prompts, via writing programming, often leveraging templates. This technique is especially useful for large-scale tasks or environments where prompts must be generated in a big batch. For instance, in a business environment, a system might generate a prompt automatically according to a customer query and context:

- **Input**: Customer reports a billing issue.

- **Automated prompt**: "`A customer is reporting a billing issue regarding an overcharge. Provide instructions for resolving the issue.`"

Automation reduces the need for manual prompt design, especially in high-volume environments, improving both efficiency and response time. Additionally, automation allows users to embed conditional logic into prompt generation, ensuring that the AI model adjusts its output based on real-time data or user inputs.

Modern prompt optimization algorithms, including iterative refinement, prompt chaining, templates, and automation, give us sophisticated instruments to optimize AI-driven outputs. iterative refinement allows to refine the prompts continually, checking and tinkering with the outputs, prompt chaining makes it possible to run larger, multi-step tasks by simplifying them into components. Prompt templates and automation, meanwhile, ensure consistency and scalability, especially in those scenarios where prompt generation is repetitive or high volume.

Using such powerful tools, AI users can hone in on how to respond to language models, giving more accurate, logical, and contextualized results. With AI becoming more advanced, learning to do these kinds of optimizations will be a key step to ensure that prompt engineering can keep up with the new models and applications.

Metrics for quality assessment

Successful prompt input tacitly depends on defining well-defined metrics that indicate the output's success. Knowing what target to hit in terms of operational metrics for the quality of the system is a standard in business for AI systems. These metrics are what enable the AI's actions to live up to the promise. Relevance, accuracy and completeness are commonly used as indices of AI quality. What's more, both humans and machines give different insights into how a prompt is working.

Measuring relevance, accuracy, and completeness

AI model relevance is the degree to which the AI's answer corresponds to the prompt. If the response takes the conversation in the wrong direction or includes redundant content, the prompt needs to be improved. For instance, if the user query, **What can AI be useful for in healthcare?** and the model presents a list of AI uses in different fields, the answer is meaningless. The query could be narrowed by modifying it as: **What are the three**

most significant applications of AI for healthcare diagnostics? to get a more specific answer.

> **Note: In this example, we focused on a healthcare-specific metric but you would need to adapt to your area of focus.**

Accuracy is the measure of how accurate the AI's answer in fact is. This becomes especially useful if the request asks for certain numbers, definitions, or technical information. If the AI is asked, for example, **State what role artificial intelligence plays in automated cybersecurity threat detection**, its answer should have the correct and most recent information about how AI resources such as machine learning models are being applied to this field. False outputs indicate that the AI model has missed the prompt or is lacking the training data.

Completeness measures whether the response fulfills the prompt. It is part of the response when the query is complex, or when the AI system fails to understand parts of the question. For instance, a query like, **Let me explain the mechanics of blockchain and how blockchain can be used in finance** would ask the AI to give an account of both the blockchain and the use case. If the answer addresses only one of these, then it's incomplete.

Relevance, accuracy, and completeness form the holistic measure of how well a prompt does. Any good response should cover all these measures, and the AI output should be laser-like, accurate and complete.

Human versus machine evaluation of prompted outputs

It is also possible to measure the effectiveness of prompts using both human and computer assessment. Both methods have distinct strengths, and each one combined could produce a more complete analysis. The human test includes having professionals or humans manually check the AI's results to see if they are up to scratch and can meet expected quality standards. Assessors are humans who bring context and expertise, and so are perfectly placed to assess tone, relevance, and content-appropriateness. For instance, when considering an AI-generated legal opinion, a human reader would notice mistakes or legal references an automated system might have missed.

Robotic evaluation uses automated parameters and algorithms to evaluate AI results. These methods often use a quantitative statistic such as **Bilingual Evaluation Understudy (BLEU)**, **Recall-Oriented Understudy for Gisting Evaluation (ROUGE)** or cosine similarity to compare an AI's answer to a reference output. This is useful for comparing large-scale outputs and searching for broad trends in precision and content. However, machine judgments lacks the capability to appreciate context or subjectivity. For instance, an automated scoring system could confirm that an AI's answer to **Describe the work of the heart** is technically correct, but it could not identify that the explanation is too technical for a layperson.

The best practice involves a mix of human and machine judgments. We can get context from human reviewers, machine reviews are quick and reliable when it comes to measuring massive amounts of output.

Identifying and resolving failures

Even prompts that you take a great deal of time and effort to create might occasionally misconstrue inputs or return inaccurate answers. Finding these faults and diagnosing them is an essential part of optimizing prompt performance. Knowing where and why an AI system failed can lead prompt engineers to refine their inputs to produce better outcomes.

Troubleshooting misinterpretations and incorrect responses

Incorrectness happens when the AI has no idea what the prompt means and answers the wrong or irrelevant message. This is normally a side-effect of unclear words or lack of detail in the challenge. A prompt such as `Tell me why governance is important,` for instance, could have various meanings: governance in the context of politics, governance in the context of companies. If the answer you are looking for has to do with corporate governance, the question should be clarified as `Talk about corporate governance's role in business management.`

When you get a response returned that isn't accurate, the data scientists and computer scientists monitoring will use diagnostic data to identify the issues to update/change the AI model for the future to prevent incorrect interpretations.

Steps to troubleshoot misinterpretations and incorrect responses:

1. **Clarify ambiguous language**: Refine prompts that leave too much open to interpretation.

2. **Provide more context**: Ensure that the prompt includes the necessary background information for the AI to understand the intended focus.

3. **Simplify complex prompts**: Break down complex queries into smaller, more focused parts, allowing the AI to process each element thoroughly.

4. **Check for model limitations**: Determine whether the AI system is capable of handling the specific domain or topic. If not, adjustments in prompt design or model retraining may be necessary.

Understanding the model's limitations

AI system algorithms and their language models are illusory and subject to certain limitations that should make engineers realize this. There is one limitation, namely, that AI relies on its training data. The model might fail to return meaningful and reliable results if it has not been trained on enough data from one field. This can lead to incoherent, generic or just erroneous results.

For instance, a language model that was trained to an extent on English texts might not do so well in non-trained languages if they are asked for it. Similarly, models that are not continuously updated with new data could be overwhelmed by reminders of recent events, and may give outdated or partial responses. In those cases, prompt engineers should scale expectations and optimize the prompt to better target parts where the model is much more competent.

Also, AI models cannot compute context or deduce meaning if they do not come from training data. They are not **knowing** as humans are, which means they will misrecognize stimulus demands for common sense knowledge or deep contextual knowledge.

In order to circumvent these drawbacks, prompt engineers should identify areas of weakness in the model's training or knowledge base.

Evaluating prompt performance

Prompt engineering, a core area of engagement with AI systems, means building prompts that draw the most accurate and relevant signals from a model. Yet, even designed prompts can generate varied outputs, and a test needs to be conducted to see whether the outputs are efficient.

A language model, for instance, conditioned on a large volume of English-language text will have problems answering when prompted in a non-trained language. Likewise, models that are not continuously refreshed with new data may be weak at answering questions about recent events, returning late or incomplete answers. In those cases, prompt engineers can tweak predictions and tune prompts accordingly in terms of which parts the model is stronger in.

In addition, AI models cannot take into account actual context or make inferences beyond the information presented in the training data. They are not **knowing** in the human sense – that is, they can fall into error at prompts that require common sense explanation or context-sensitive insight.

Conclusion

In this chapter, you will learn about the 'nuts and bolts' of prompts and AI models in terms of how to design prompts that are efficient and get you what you are looking for. You also learned about how to identify challenges in an AI model and what to do about it potentially, as well as consider advanced techniques for prompt engineering. Lastly, you learned about how to best evaluate your model and AI prompts.

In the next chapter, we will look into the tools and platforms for prompt engineering and talk about the many tools that are out there for designing prompts.

CHAPTER 14

Tools and Platforms for Prompt Engineering

Introduction

This chapter will be a guide on creating and optimizing prompts for your AI applications. We will begin with an overview of tools such as OpenAPI Playground and Hugging Face Transformers. We will talk about each tool for its capabilities, interface, and what is unique about that tool for prompt engineering purposes. Now, you are going to be learning the ways to use these tools. It describes the installation and configuration steps for each platform, how to write and test prompts, and how to analyze and understand the output. This chapter seeks to provide users with the information necessary to fully apply these tools, which enhances the quality of interaction with AI. Then, you will be introduced to integrating prompt engineering tools into existing workflows. You will also learn about workflow automation, collaboration version control, and ways to improve and scale prompt engineering operations on a continuous basis.

Structure

In this chapter, we will cover the following topics:

- Developer tools
- Using the tool eventually
- Integrating prompt engineering into workflows

- Advanced use cases and real-world applications
- Challenges and future trends in prompt engineering tools

Objectives

In this chapter, you gain an understanding of several of the popular developer tools and frameworks used in today's modern AI technology ecosystem. You will learn about the tools and how they integrate with your workflows, as well as talk to potential real-world applications of them.

Developer tools

Developers who wish to either leverage AI are plentiful. Many organizations out there are also trying to create their own **artificial intelligence** (**AI**) tools or full AI services for profit. In previous years, this undertaking would have necessitated writing everything from scratch, Today, we have a variety of developer aids and tools, which we will learn about in the coming sections.

The OpenAI Playground

We spoke about the OpenAI Playground as an interface for developers to access the generative models created by OpenAI (which you will really see who is behind GPT-4). We will now actually look at it a bit in detail.

Prompt engineering is now a key competence for all practitioners of AI, helping software developers generate accurate and pertinent responses from linguistic models. Different services and tools make it possible to engineer quickly — OpenAI Playground, Hugging Face Transformers, OpenAI API, and so on. We will look a little deeper into these platforms, including how they operate, the pros and cons of each, and how they can help with certain use cases. It is intended to provide a unified vision of how each tool works for prompt engineering to technical users.

The OpenAI Playground gives you easy access to the very capable GPT-4 model that OpenAI also built. It enables users to test various prompt layouts and model parameters without any heavy coding involved. You can view the OpenAI Playground on the OpenAI Developer Platform webpage here **https://platform.openai.com/docs/overview** shown in *Figure 14.1:*

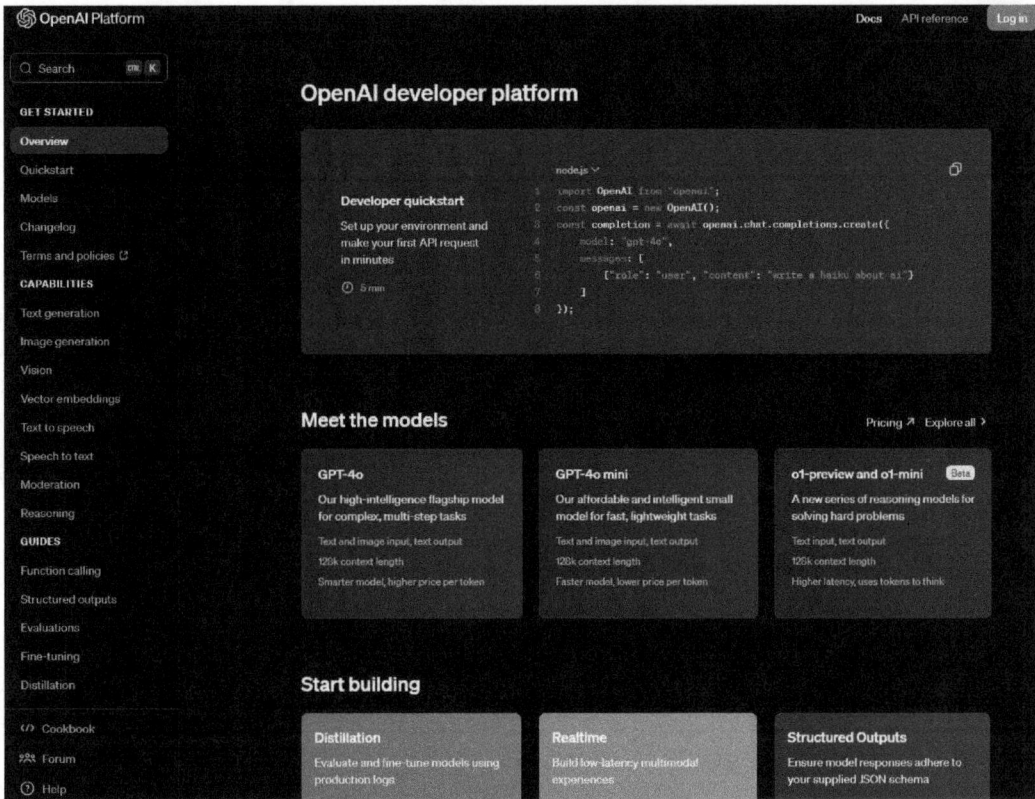

Figure 14.1: showing the OpenAI developer web page

The most attractive aspect of the Playground is the fact that you can adjust things like temperature, which affects the randomness of the result, and max tokens, which determine the duration of responses. You can also set the frequency and presence penalties for influencing the repetition or adventure of the model's outputs. These allow you to essentially try different versions of a prompt and test it until the result you want is achieved. Developers usually work with alternatives — APIs and custom deployments. Regardless, the Playground is great for initial testing, quick debugging, and rapid proof-of-concept.

Hugging Face Transformers

Hugging Face Transformers is an open-source library that provides access to a wide range of pre-trained language models that leverage big players, such as OpenAI as well as Meta, Google, Microsoft, etc. Hugging Face as a platform is highly regarded for its flexibility and is widely used in the **natural language processing (NLP)** community. Developers working with Hugging Face gain access to a growing ecosystem of models, such as BERT, GPT-2, and T5, which are useful for various natural language processing tasks beyond prompt engineering, such as text classification and sentiment analysis. The company Hugging Face, Inc was founded initially in 2016 with the aim of creating chatbots.

One of the benefits of using Hugging Face is its support for both pre-trained and fine-tuned models, giving the developer more flexibility. A pre-trained model is ready to use out of the box, but developers can fine-tune these models on specific datasets to improve performance for niche tasks. For example, if a developer is working on a medical chatbot, fine-tuning the GPT-2 model on a dataset of clinical conversations can yield more accurate and context-aware responses. This flexibility makes Hugging Face Transformers ideal for both general-purpose and specialized AI applications.

Hugging Face is powerful, but it will require some technical skills to set up; the developer will need to manage a variety of Python environments and ensure they install the required dependencies. The developer will also need to configure either local or cloud-based modules. However, as Python is such a powerful and popular language, Hugging Face is well positioned, as the library enables deep customization and powerful integrations.

The Hugging Face web portal for developers can be accessed at this URL: **https://huggingface.co/docs/transformers/en/index**, as shown in *Figure 14.2*:

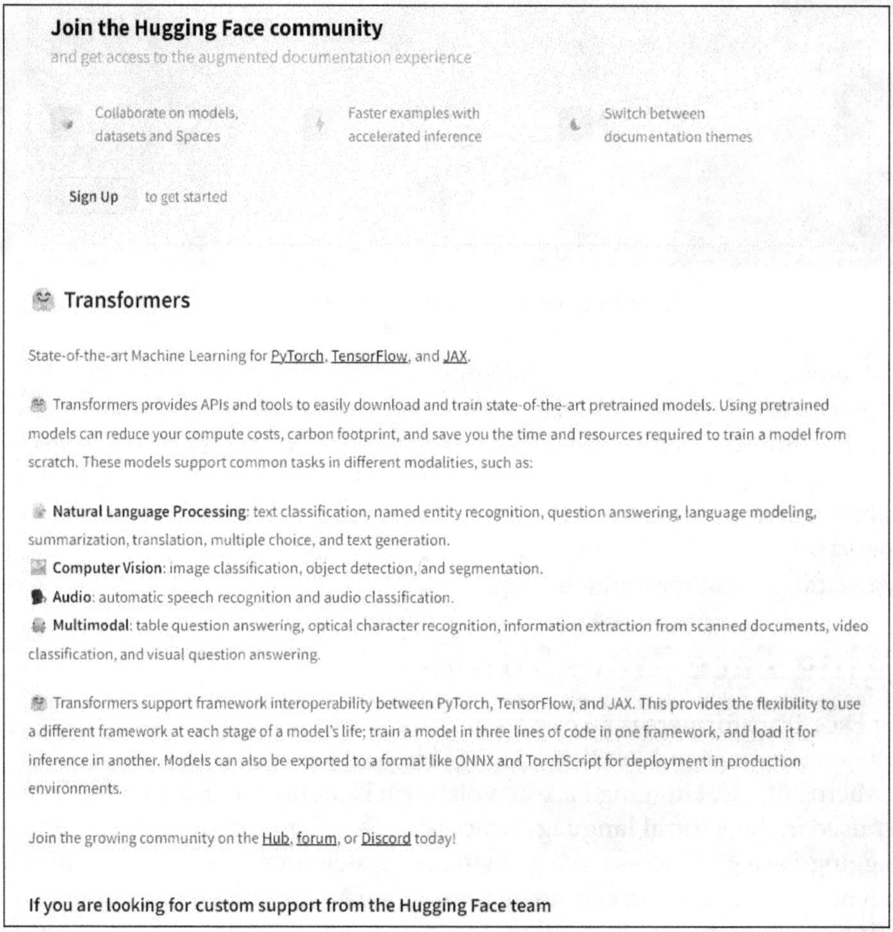

Join the Hugging Face community
and get access to the augmented documentation experience

Collaborate on models, datasets and Spaces

Faster examples with accelerated inference

Switch between documentation themes

Sign Up   to get started

🤗 **Transformers**

State-of-the-art Machine Learning for PyTorch, TensorFlow, and JAX.

🤗 Transformers provides APIs and tools to easily download and train state-of-the-art pretrained models. Using pretrained models can reduce your compute costs, carbon footprint, and save you the time and resources required to train a model from scratch. These models support common tasks in different modalities, such as:

Natural Language Processing: text classification, named entity recognition, question answering, language modeling, summarization, translation, multiple choice, and text generation.
Computer Vision: image classification, object detection, and segmentation.
Audio: automatic speech recognition and audio classification.
Multimodal: table question answering, optical character recognition, information extraction from scanned documents, video classification, and visual question answering.

🤗 Transformers support framework interoperability between PyTorch, TensorFlow, and JAX. This provides the flexibility to use a different framework at each stage of a model's life; train a model in three lines of code in one framework, and load it for inference in another. Models can also be exported to a format like ONNX and TorchScript for deployment in production environments.

Join the growing community on the Hub, forum, or Discord today!

If you are looking for custom support from the Hugging Face team

Figure 14.2: The Hugging Face developer portal

OpenAI API

Open AI created an **application programming interface** (**API**) that allows developers to integrate GPT models directly into their applications. The API provides a developer the **endpoint** they need to make the GPT-4 ecosystem flexible via programming, as the basic interface lacks the scalability and flexibility required for production on anything other than an ad hoc basis. Through arming developers with APIs, they can now make GPT what they need it to be for their own uses. Developers can use the API to create automated workflows, chatbots, content creators, and other AI-driven products that depend on compelling prompts.

API needs a little setup. It requires developers to set up an OpenAI account, build API keys, and perform authentication. Once configured, the API will provide programmatic access to GPT models, which means that a programmer can automatically invoke the model by passing prompts and response codes. The API also has rate caps to manage the demand, so you need to make sure you are maximizing your requests and responses to stay within these limits.

One of the advantages of the API is that it is flexible. Builders can map prompts onto the model, directing it toward something such as summarizing, translating, or creative writing. Programmatically processing the API responses makes it possible to create specialized workflows like multi-step chats and response dynamics. A chatbot created through the API, for instance, can preserve context from multiple conversations, which is a lot more dynamic and conversational.

Other tools and emerging platforms

While OpenAI is a dominant player, there are other platforms offering complementary and innovative features. OpenAI models can be accessed via Microsoft's Azure OpenAI Service, which is ideal for enterprise-level integration and security. This service will also appeal to those companies who already use Microsoft Azure as it integrates with their current cloud services.

Two more companies developing big language models and offering developers APIs are Cohere and Anthropic. The idea of these platforms is to offer a different choice as for OpenAI models (around issues related to model readability and ethical consumption).

Choosing between these platforms often comes down to specific project requirements. For example, some developers may prioritize responsible AI, while others might lean toward specialized NLP models.

Comparing these platforms requires an understanding of each one's strengths. OpenAI's tools excel in versatility and breadth of use, while Hugging Face offers deeper customization options for developers who need fine-tuned models. Azure's service is ideal for enterprises with stringent security requirements, while Cohere and Anthropic are a bit less enterprise-focused. Switching between these platforms can be necessary as projects evolve, particularly when performance or ethical considerations come into play.

Tools for prompt engineering need a lot of careful set-up, prompt design, and meticulous results analysis. Defining the development environment with Python and Visual Studio Code will give the developers access to all the infrastructure that they will require to be productive. Writing and testing prompts is a cycle of iteration, with developers making tweaks to the parameters to achieve the right mix for their purpose. Evaluation is the spotting of patterns and use of evaluation parameters to assess response quality.

When you learn to master these tricks, developers can use AI models to their full potential and create highly secure applications. Rapid engineering is learning by doing — prompt engineering is useful for anyone working with AI, because it is learning and making mistakes constantly. While tools and platforms are constantly changing, staying on top of best practices in configuration, design speed, and testing will be the key to future success in this ever-changing industry.

Using the tool effectively

We will walk through the key steps for enabling the necessary tools, formatting and improving prompts, and reviewing answers for quality and reliability. The goal is to bring real-world development and AI techniques together so that engineers can make the most of their tools and platforms.

Setting up and configuring tools

Any successful prompt engineering effort starts with a clean slate. Typically, this starts by installing the required dependencies, setting up the development environment, and integrating APIs. Python is the programming language of choice for the majority of AI tasks due to its library, community, and flexibility. Installing dependencies like OpenAI and transformers libraries can be done via Python's package manager, pip. The frameworks also allow developers to use OpenAI's models and Hugging Face's set of pre-trained models.

One of the many development environments you can use is Microsoft's Visual Studio Code, which is designed for writing and editing code, with built-in support for JavaScript, TypeScript, and Node.js. You can download the Visual Studio Code from this URL:

https://apps.microsoft.com/detail/xp9khm4bk9fz7q?hl=en-us&gl=US

Figure 14.3 shows the following Visual Studio Code interface:

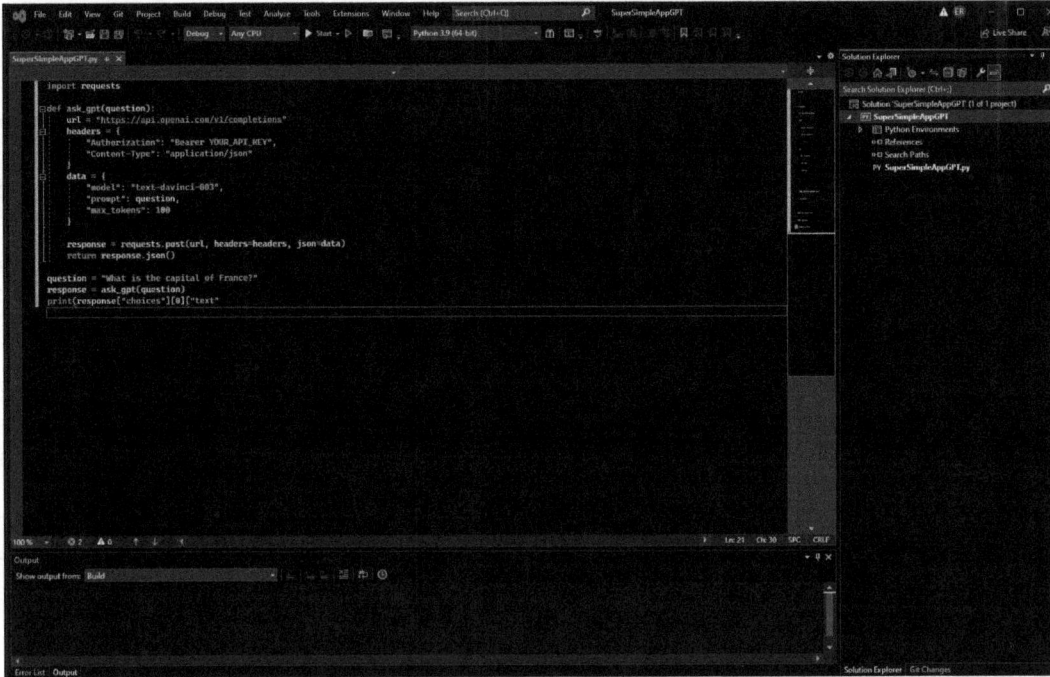

Figure 14.3: Visual Studio Code for using Python to integrate with ChatGPT

Microsoft Visual Studio Code (VS Code) is a very good **integrated development environment (IDE)** for fast engineering processes. Including syntax highlighting, Git integration, and debugging features, VS Code helps you to write, test, and correct code. Extensions such as Python for VS Code streamline the development process, facilitating code browsing and error handling. API integration is also a necessary step in environment preparation. That includes creating API keys, locking them, and handling authentication inside the code. OpenAI's API, for instance, requires developers to pass an authorization token with each model access request. This is because token management is important to keep things seamless and safe while using the platform and preventing request failure or breach of data.

GPT in OpenAI Playground

A website for information on Chat GPT is OpenAI Playground. OpenAI Playground is a web platform OpenAI created to let people play with GPT, its sophisticated language model. It is a friendly interface in which users type texts and get answers from the AI. It is in particular, designed for developers, scientists, and enthusiasts to see what GPT can do in natural language processing and generation. Offering parameters for model behavior — like selecting model versions, customizing style and tone, and setting parameters like response length — OpenAI Playground can be used for applications from education to more advanced explorations of AI text generation.

Writing and testing prompts via tools

After you are done setting up the tools, it is time to write and test useful prompts. A well-structured prompt consists of multiple elements, such as explicit instructions, character types and specific tasks. Directives instruct the model by defining the desired behavior, while personas define the tone or viewpoint of the answer. Workflow instructions also narrow down the scope so the result can be tailored to the user's needs. For instance, in creating a chatbot to help with customer service, you might create a prompt such as **Answer in a polite and professional manner** and further instructions such as **Send quick responses to frequently asked questions**.

Test and debugging alerts are not overnight operations. Developers should fix some key settings to smooth out the results. The temperature variable, for example, governs the model's randomness. The higher the temperature, the more inventive and erratic the output; the lower the temperature, the more targeted. In this case Max tokens specifies the maximum amount of characters to be returned in the response. Counts and presence penalties can also be set to handle repetition and prompt the model to look for new words or concepts. Using this feedback to iteratively test the parameters can allow developers to determine the right combination that delivers the best relevant and quality responses.

Prompt engineering is never a one-off project. Iterative testing is necessary to develop prompts over time. You see, developers tend to play with small versions of the same prompt and measure the output to see which one works best. The approach is patient and imaginative because small changes can make a big difference. Also, iterative testing can be used to detect edge cases where the model might produce an unexpected or unrelated result. By catering to these cases, the last prompt remains robust and repeatable under a variety of scenarios.

Analyzing and interpreting results

Understanding the inner workings of your AI mode is as important as writing the prompt and executing it efficiently. Being able to do analysis on the responses from an AI model, as well as identifying the patterns as well as any aberrations that are associated with the responses, is something you need to do as you scale AI work. You will also need to ensure the output from the model is both relevant and consistent over time; you will do that using metrics to evaluate your results. This is how you tune your model and prompts to avoid potential bias.

For instance, if the model always returns partial solutions, it might be a sign that the prompt is not specific or the maximum token value is too low. The same applies to outliers, which show areas where further refinement is needed.

To assess how coherent, relevant, and innovative these answers are, we need both intuition and statistics. Developers need to determine if the result follows the prompt's intention, is coherent in its place and shows some originality. Creativity is important when it comes to creative writing or thinking. Yet, in technical documentation or customer service settings, simplicity and consistency win over imagination. A proper trade-off between all these means that the output meets the desired quality for the intended use case.

It could also be measured using more quantitative metrics such as **Bilingual Evaluation Understudy (BLEU)** or **Recall-Oriented Understudy for Gisting Evaluation (ROUGE)**. These metrics, developed initially for machine translation and text summarization, sift the model's results through reference works to determine accuracy and relevance. BLEU computes the ratio between how much output and reference phrases overlap, and ROUGE computes the ratio between word or sequence combinations that are in parallel between output and reference texts. These metrics are helpful but should not be used without human judgment to make an accurate assessment.

Effective prompt engineering tools are those whose set-up, prompt design, and analyses of outcomes have been well thought out. Setting up the development environment with Python and Visual Studio Code will ensure that developers are well-equipped with the tools they need to work. The process nature of prompt engineering means that you will continue learning and trying new things — and it is a skill any AI engineer should have. As technologies and platforms develop, educating yourself on best practices in set-up, timely design, and analysis will be crucial to succeeding in this changing landscape.

Integrating prompt engineering into workflows

To gain the most benefit of prompt engineering, prompt engineering needs to be ingrained into existing workflows. Not only will this integrate be productive, but the AI solutions will be standardized and expandable across teams and projects. It talks about three areas in detail — workflow automation, collaboration, and version control, and continuous improvements and scaling. Each is key to ensuring rapid engineering is a fast, collaborative, evolving process.

Workflow automation

Automation is the essence of prompt engineering. Automation allows programmers to get back to fine-tuning the prompts and analyzing the outputs without wasting their time with manual labor. Python's many libraries and ease of use makes Python a favorite programming language for automation scripts. These scripts can also perform common API calls (for example, obtaining responses, logging data, or performing scheduled updates).

Automation to schedule tasks can be performed using the CRON job scheduler on Unix platforms or the Python schedule library. A script, for example, can be scheduled to write daily reports by interacting with a language model, extracting information, and transforming the result into a digestible document. When creating content workflows, you can automate summaries, social media posts, or emails to ensure they are consistent and on time. Similarly, automated data extraction scripts can query data and provide instant answers with AI-driven summaries.

Automation also comes into the picture for edge cases. To provide an example, scripts can track prompt quality and automatically correct it based on metric parameters. This ensures rapid engineering still works well on scale because the repetitive fine-tuning is outsourced to automated processes. These automations cut out the need for human intervention, making processes run more efficiently and free of mistakes.

Collaboration and version control

Prompt engineering tends to be collaborative, meaning that teams need to handle a version of prompts, share best practices, and be consistent. The source-control tools such as GitHub and GitLab are very useful for storing rapid updates. Teams can track prompt changes with repositories and keep only the best versions of them documented and usable later. With branches, other team members can try different versions of prompts and have their workflows not interfered with so that they can work together on improvements.

Also, documentation plays a crucial role in efficient engineering. With every edition of a prompt, you learn what is working, what is not, and why that is the way it went. Note-taking ensures best practices are documented and shared across the team so there is no duplicate work. You can also standardize prompt design with templates to help new team members learn about how prompts work and why they exist.

Using repository tooling such as GitHub and GitLab will allow your team to have proper security/permissions to keep your repository under change control. This ensures prompt integrity during development; this is s also where you can store your API keys or the parameters of your modules. This becomes your intellectual property that sets your work apart from others, so it is worth protecting while allowing you to collaborate.

Continuous improvement and scaling

Prompt engineering is continuous – it should always be monitored and optimized. You want to keep an eye on performance and get user reviews as workflows change and new issues come up. Monitoring can be achieved by logging services or dashboards that measure metrics like response quality, relevancy, and user clicks. Teams can then review these metrics to see where there is room for improvement and revise prompts accordingly.

User input is gold for prompt optimization. Generally speaking, in almost all apps, particularly customer-facing applications, the user provides both explicit and implicit inputs to the AI machine.

An example would be that you can determine if a customer support chatbot works, for example, if it answers a question fast enough or whether your customers complain to a human agent enough. If we have user feedback in the process of prompt engineering, it keeps prompts being created from the user's needs and expectations.

Prompt engineering must be scaled with automated pipelines. Such pipelines make it easy to deploy prompts across multiple platforms or projects to ensure consistency and obviate human work. An online content delivery pipeline, for instance, can stream new requests in real-time to a site or social media network that is always accessible without the need for a constant human interaction. You can also have versioning control for pipelines so that only authenticated prompts are pushed to the production machines.

Scalability also involves adjusting for higher demand or complexity. Companies could process more triggers, or interact with more APIs, or be multilingual when a project grows. Automated pipelines handle this scale with frictionless integration and deployment that enables teams to focus on prompting and capacity expansion instead of infrastructure.

We need to embed quick engineering in processes to ensure maximum efficiency for sharing and continual refinement.

Automated work is less laborious and accelerates the development process, and tools can be used to share code across teams. Monitoring, feedback, and automated pipelines let teams scale up and make good work.

Rapid engineering, especially in a moving market like AI, is an unavoidable competitive edge that can be built into processes. By automating processes, collaborating, and always trying to be better, teams can not only grow but they can also evolve. This is how prompt engineering can become a successful, replicable, stable practice with a predictable impact.

Advanced use cases and real-world applications

As AI models continue to develop, you will observe prompt engineering will be key to taking advantage of AI models in useful and novel ways. Well beyond doing simple tasks, advanced applications such as building custom chatbots, writing code and documents, and augmenting decisions with AI are rich in automation, efficiency, and intelligence. In this part, we see these applications in greater detail to show how prompt engineering can be applied to advanced, real-life problems.

Building custom assistants and chatbots

The most visible use-cases for prompt engineering are the creation of intelligent chatbots and virtual assistants. These systems rely on multiple-turn conversations, wherein the chatbot stores previous conversations and responds contextually. Creating prompts to animate these shifting dynamics is itself a mastery. Prompts need to be designed to predict user intent, take context in multiple interactions, and seamlessly switch between them. The

Python web frameworks Flask and Django are popular Python web frameworks that allow us to easily create and maintain web applications. Flask and Django are open-source web-based frameworks that allow the developer to create a template. From these frameworks, users can construct chat interfaces that communicate directly with AI models via an API, providing real-time answers to their user's queries. Flask, with its light architecture, can be great for a small project, and Django (more robust) can be good for big projects that need to use a database or authentication. Through the integration of AI models into these platforms, chatbots can be personalized for various uses, such as customer care, shopping assistants, and even narrative interactive conversations. *Figure 14.4* shows the Django framework portal, which you can reach at: **https://www.djangoproject.com/start/**

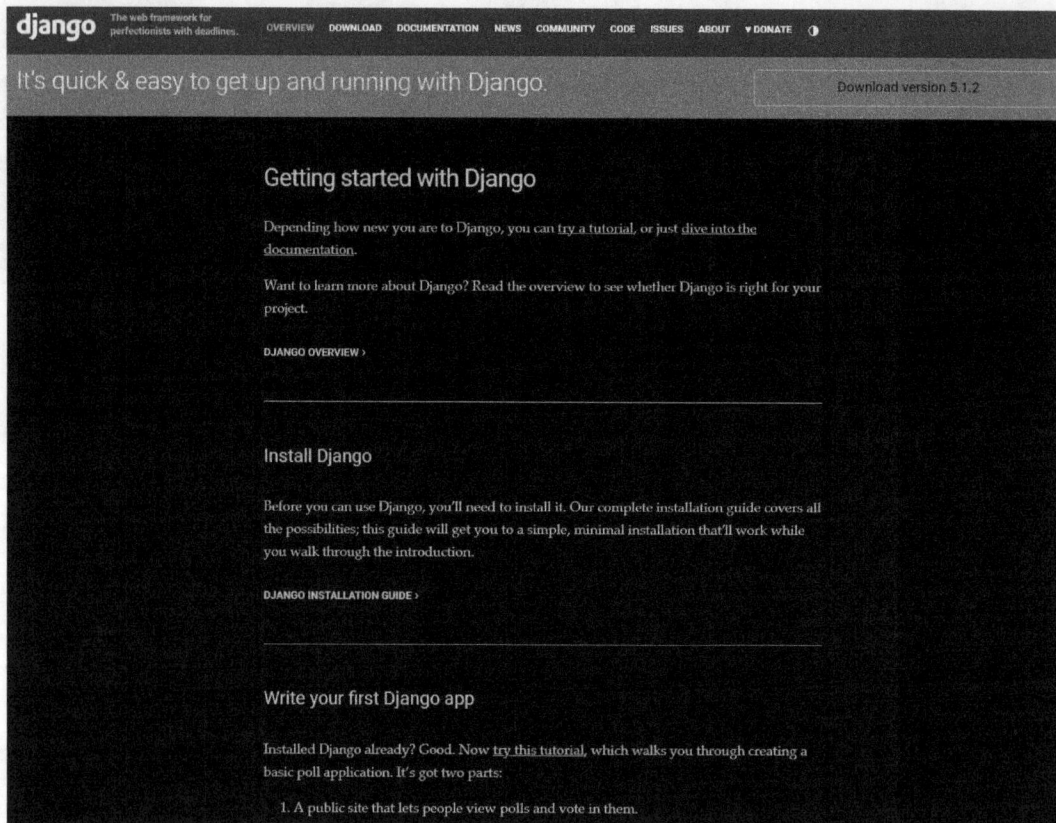

Figure 14.4: The Developer Poral for the Django Framework

AI as the tool for generating code and documentation

A further advanced use of prompt engineering is for the generation of code and automation of documentation. Through the proper cueing, AI models can write boilerplate code, those reusable blocks of code that developers sometimes require. This tooling helps accelerate development by eliminating the repetitive effort so developers can concentrate on more difficult problems. Suppose a developer asked to create an API endpoint and got prompted, **Create a Flask route for registering users.** The AI would generate code as a reference, handling error and authentication logic.

AI can also help in writing technical reports and manuals. The developers or technical writers can easily get overwhelmed by scribbling APIs, software libraries, or deployment flows. AI's first draft on provocation can save time, as well as assure continuity. For instance, a prompt could instruct the model to **Provide API documentation for the user registration endpoint** so that you have a logical breakdown of purpose, parameters, and output. Likewise, reports summarizing system activity or project progress can also be automated using AI. This way, teams can be sure of getting timely, accurate documentation with minimal time-consuming manual work.

Being able to create code and documentation, in general, has wide-ranging implications, especially for agile teams that need to make fast changes. By introducing prompt engineering into the process, development teams can improve productivity and consistency and prevent human mistakes.

AI in decision-making

The decision support applications that make AI available to manage the analysis of massive amounts of data are increasingly applied in the area of decision-making. Prompt engineering design has a goal to gain value out of the prompt, to deliver digestible and useful information to you. Business intelligence work, for instance, AI models will provide summaries of KPIs for executives to use. A command such as **Draft the monthly sales data and select three best performing regions** allows the model to provide a distilled summary.

Data summarization is very handy when it comes to large or multifaceted data sets. So, instead of reading dozens of reports or spreadsheets, decision-makers can use AI-constructed overviews that report on trends, issues, or critical problems. A financial analyst, for example, can get a prompt to analyze quarterly revenue and query the model for observable changes with an explanation. This method is also time-saving and prevents missing important information.

In addition to summary, AI can also be used for predictive analysis and help you know what is happening or will not happen in the future from the past. In a supply chain function, for instance, a company could initiate a projection of inventory levels using historical sales history. Such predictive tools enable businesses to take preventive actions, for example, by monitoring inventory levels before the stock runs out, or by targeting marketing efforts to best take advantage of the future demand.

The power of AI in the real world can be seen in more sophisticated examples of prompt engineering. Custom chatbots and virtual assistants, backed by platforms such as Flask and Django, create personalized experiences and automate customer journeys. AI code, automation of documentation, and faster development time make it easy for developers to work on things they can do better. Further, AI-assisted decision-making gives companies the capability to analyze information, create reports, and make predictions.

Rapid engineering within these more advanced use cases open-up new levels of productivity and innovation for developers and organizations. These real-world examples demonstrate how rapid engineering, combined with AI models, enables building intelligent systems to improve workflows, accelerate development, and give decision-makers new capabilities. Prevent engineering will remain an essential attribute in AI development and will drive the next wave of business applications.

Challenges and future trends in prompt engineering tools

In conjunction with developing platforms and technologies, you must keep up to date on the trends that will impact the future of prompt engineering. This chapter addresses some of the more urgent issues like preventing prompt bias and addressing API restrictions, before looking to the future with key technologies such as multi-modal AI and tools like Gemini and Copilot.

Limitations and bias mitigation

Prompt engineering presents a huge problem with regard to inherent bias in AI-based responses. AI models such as GPT are based on massive sets of data that depict human actions, language, and culture. Unfortunately, it also implies that the models might mirror the biases, stereotypes, and prejudices in the data. The ability to detect these biases is a critical piece of work in use cases where equity and impartiality matter. A financial advice chatbot, for instance, might unintentionally favor certain types of people or offer skewed suggestions if the prompts are not properly designed.

Effectively countering bias in immediate engineering takes a calculated approach. Developers need to be aware of the language, structure, and assumptions of their requests. An option here is to test prompts rigorously in different environments and among user groups to see if you catch intentional biases. Keep in mind that systems that implement prompts need to ensure ethicality. Prompt engineering involves transparency and accountability. Prompters would need to formally write down the design decisions of their prompts and be clear about the limitations of AI models they develop. It is a transparent way of creating credibility among users and letting them know what the model is good for and what it is bad for. Bias mitigation is not an isolated event; it is an ongoing process, one that needs to be continually assessed and optimized as new data and use cases come along.

Handling API limitations and failures

Another barrier in prompt engineering is a technical API limitation. APIs allow programmers to connect to AI models, but they also have limits, like rates and short outages. Rate Limits determine how many requests a developer can execute in a specified amount of time and usually need to be optimized so workflow does not interrupt. This bind must be navigated by contingency plans and coping mechanisms. An all-purpose solution is to use caching, where the most common response or data is cached locally and, therefore, requires fewer API calls. This not only saves the API from additional load but it also makes sure that apps do not break when they experience connection issues.

Along with caching, developers can develop fallback plans by using different APIs. If, for example, an OpenAI API fails, then the system might just use another language model, such as Hugging Face or Anthropic, to continue running. With such contingency measures in place, disruptions are minimized, and the user experience is standardized. As APIs shift and adapt, developers will need to remain up to date with rate caps, pricing, and performance trends in order to ensure they are properly doing their work.

Trends to watch

Prompt engineering is growing in leaps and bounds and there are some exciting developments on the horizon. Perhaps the most consequential one is the emergence of multi-modal AI. In contrast to traditional text-based models, the multi-modal AI is able to work and generate data in text, images, audio, and video. This opens up the potential for prompt engineering, where one prompt could generate a text summary, an infographic or even a video narration. Designers will have to learn how to design prompts for all these modes, making multi-modal experiences natural and immersive.

New services such as Gemini and Copilot are also revolutionizing rapid engineering. Gemini, from Google DeepMind, would challenge large-language models using sophisticated thinking and memory methods. Microsoft's Copilot, meanwhile, is putting AI models in everyday products such as Microsoft Word, Excel, and Visual Studio Code to allow developers and end users to create content right inside existing apps. They create new opportunities for prompt engineering because developers will be able to customize prompts to specific workflows in those tools. As an example, writing a prompt for Copilot can mean instructing the model to generate code lines following an enterprise's in-house coding standard.

The second area of interest is the rising emphasis on responsible AI. As the ethical stakes in AI become more widely acknowledged, rapid engineering will be required to make a greater match to models of responsible AI development. Not just to prevent prejudice but also to be transparent, equitable, and accessible. Also, keep in mind that the compliance and regulatory landscape is rapidly evolving.

Dealing with API constraints will also be a part of coding secure, scalable apps and fallbacks and optimization will be required skills.

Towards the future, things such as multi-modal AI and other startup ecosystems like Gemini and Copilot will impact the developers' practice of prompt engineering. They are exciting new opportunities to build deeper, more compelling user experiences, but they also require novel methodologies and practices. Meanwhile, increasing pressure on responsible AI will also push developers to ensure innovation is ethical, making AI transparent, equitable, and accessible.

Prompt engineering is not a mechanical talent; it is an evolving practice situated between tech, ethics, and creativity. As AI evolves, those who welcome such challenges and stay ahead of the curve will be best placed to harness the full potential of prompt engineering, creating systems that are powerful yet also sensitive and sustainable.

Testing and evaluating prompts

Writing good prompts involves continuous validation to make sure that the AI responds correctly and uniformly. You test simple instructions and sophisticated ones as developers learn more about the model's interpretation of the instructions. A sample prompt could be: **Explain the story of Moby Dick in 50 words.** If the answer is not specific enough you can always make a modification to the overarching model to be used. Let us continue with the example of looking at *Moby Dick* where you can update your prompt by adding: **Put the emphasis on the character of Captain Ahab** which could then produce a more useful summary.

The task of evaluating the result is to validate it in terms of consistency, validity, and innovation. Coherence guarantees that the answer logically makes sense, relevance guarantees that it complies with the intent of the prompt, and creativity can be judged by task. For creative writing, fancies and inventiveness in the response is encouraged; for informational summaries, tight topic adherence is required.

Developers often use evaluation tools, such as BLEU and ROUGE, to measure the output quality. BLEU is a tool that calculates the alignment of the text to a collection of references, so it is helpful for things such as translation. ROUGE, however, calculates the overlap between the output and the source text (which is very useful for summarization). With those metrics and subjective analysis, developers can see which prompts are most efficient and which ones require a little more tuning.

Testing also consists of trying parameters like temperature, max tokens, and penalties. A lower temperature is less deterministic, giving you predictable results and a higher temperature brings randomness and creativity. Designers can experiment with how changing these parameters affects output quality until a balance is slowly found for their use case.

Example of creating a content generator

Let us take another potential example of automation, which would be to create an automated blog content creator. Here, this means creating cues telling the model to produce good-looking and consistent articles for a certain topic. For instance, the initial request might read: `Event a blog post about the importance of sustainable energy.` Once the results are in line with standard blog content, the request can be further filtered to determine the form: `Enter a 500-word blog post about the importance of sustainable energy. Add an introduction, three key benefits, and a conclusion.`

For production environments, content creators may be used in tandem with automation scripts for pipelines. For instance, a Python script could query the OpenAI API to write a blog post, then convert it to Markdown or HTML, and finally publish it directly into a CMS such as WordPress. Developers can even integrate error handling into the script to identify API timeouts or inconsequential output, making sure the process runs flawlessly without manual intervention.

Making the prompt better over time is the trick to good quality outcomes. To improve initial outputs, developers can update the prompt with examples or statistics. This can also be provided by editor or reader feedback for further improvement. The content creator can be made more powerful by adding additional prompts to create headlines, summaries, or even **search engine optimization (SEO)** keywords to make the task even faster. Think about a situation where you could have content creators write an initial detailed outline and use the tool to help give a recommended detailed outline that the content creator could use. A GPT-enabled AI agenda could then parse through all the text and automatically identify the SEO summaries that would accompany it as it Is published. You could even build this into your publication pipeline so it is automated end to end.

Conclusion

In this chapter, you learned about tooling and frameworks that can help you automate and write your tool GPT-based toolsets. You learned how to integrate them and were exposed to some advanced use cases with some focus on challenges in developing platforms that use AI.

In the next chapter, we will speak to ethics in AI and machine learning. This is an area of focus in more and more prompt engineering tooling as AI models are used by so very many people today in so many ways.

CHAPTER 15

Ethics in Artificial Intelligence

Introduction

This chapter will focus on an area that is quite a bit in the news today, which is ethics in AI. Today, AI is something on the precipice of potentially monumentally impactful across many aspects of human life. From faking images to creating false beliefs to imposing a specific point of view, a view of ethics is critical for any AI conversation.

Structure

In this chapter, we will talk about the ethical side of AI. Anytime humans create a system, there is a possibility it can be used in a negative manner, either intentionally or accidentally. We will cover the following items:

- AI and ML ethics
- Bias and fairness in AI
- Privacy and security concerns in AI
- Securing AI models
- Societal impact of GPT and advanced AI
- Addressing bias and fairness in AI models
- Best practices to follow for AI ethics

Objectives

In this chapter, you will learn the overview of ethics in AI, talk to bias and fairness. You will also learn to take privacy and security into account while considering the impacts generative AI has had as well as learning about how to avoid bias and learn best practices.

AI and ML ethics

Ethics in AI and ML are guidelines, principles, and standards that govern design, development, deployment, and use of these technologies. Ethics in AI is ultimately about the way in which AI systems are human-compatible, ethically, and socially permissible – not to harm them, but to be fair, accountable, and transparent. AI ethics is not only a matter of obeying laws but of questioning the consequences of the AI systems we build, of making conscious decisions in human interests, and of holding oneself responsible for the consequences of AI behavior. One example where this is very top of mind today is how AI can be used to drive disinformation in elections. *Figure 15.1* highlights a piece about how AI today is being used today to potentially sway individuals with false information:

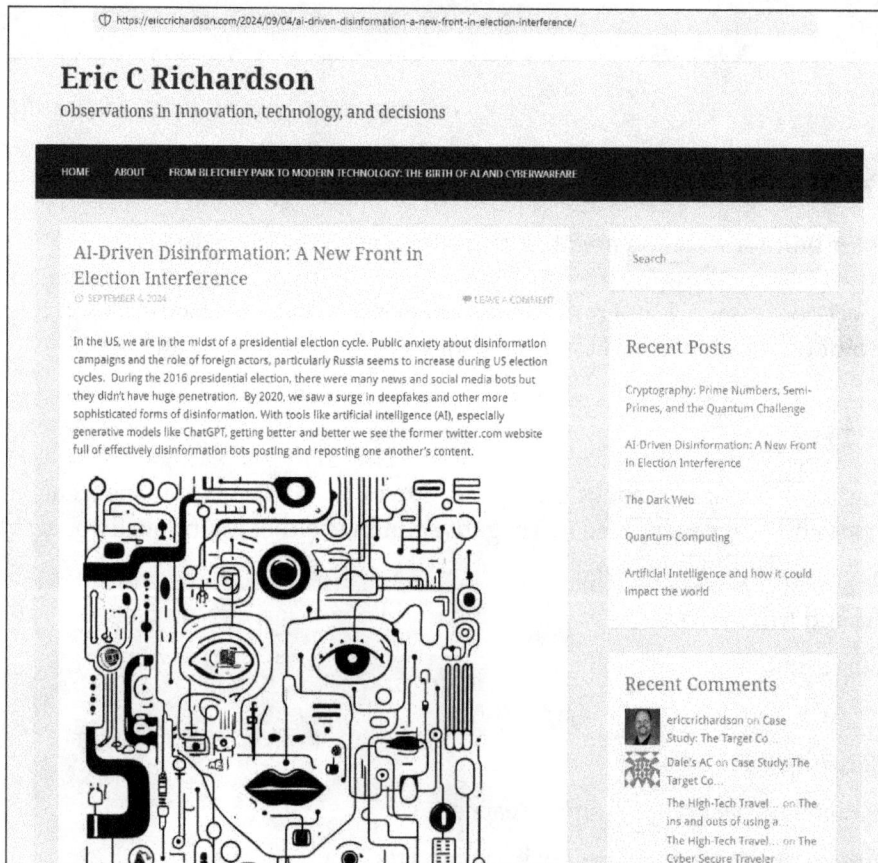

Figure 15.1: Dis-information is a major AI risk

Defining ethics in AI and machine learning

Machine learning (ML) models work by spotting the regularities in large datasets that often replicate real-world complexities, biases, and inequalities. ML ethics demands that such algorithms be designed and developed to mitigate these problems. Models for, say, hiring, criminal justice, or medical care recommendations must be modeled on the principle of equity. In ethical AI design, we incorporate principles of data integrity, diversity, and avoiding algorithms with malicious biases, as well as accepting the risk of unintended consequences in cases where ethical considerations are not present.

Reasons ethics matter in AI development

Morality in AI design is grounded in the ever-growing widespread and social reach of AI-based systems. AI and ML are part of technologies that influence every aspect of life, from healthcare to financial management recruitment to law enforcement. Amounts that matter to individuals and societies are usually algorithms, so evaluating the ethical suitability of these systems is key.

Ethics matters in a key way because biases or errors in AI models can lead to harm. A skewed model might discriminate against applicants, disadvantage underserved groups in criminal justice systems, or create unequal lending approval processes. This weakens trust in AI and pose a legal and reputational threat for companies.

Additionally, ethical AI development needs to lead to transparency and accountability. AI systems operating in "black box" state cannot be easily quantified. This anonymity makes no sense in areas where explanations are important for accountability – like diagnostic information for medicine or autonomous vehicles.

The ethical development of AI matters, as well as public acceptance. To make AI operate as a benefit to society expect it to act accordingly. With that in mind, people will trust this and the benefits of AI are realized by all. We have to ensure that all AI systems support this view and do not stray into any nefarious intention. The notion of "human in the machine" is a concept of having trusted humans review AI systems to ensure they keep best intents in mind.

Overview of ethical challenges

Ethics issues related to AI and ML are varied and complicated and sometimes intermix with matters of bias, openness, accountability, and privacy. These challenges need to be understood by everyone who has a role in the design and use of AI systems — engineers, policymakers, researchers, and executives. The following are some major ethical challenges:

- **Algorithmic bias and fairness:** Among AI's most major ethical issues, algorithmic bias arises when an AI system outputs in a systematically biased manner due to incorrect ML assumptions or biased data. AI biases may take many different shapes: gender bias in recruitment algorithms or racial bias in facial recognition systems. Algorithmic bias must be solved as it has direct implications for fairness, inclusion, and social justice.

- **Transparency and explainability:** Another ethical challenge is insufficient transparency and explainability of AI systems. If companies adopt AI systems that affect people's lives, then we need to make these systems explicable and allow stakeholders to grasp the logic behind automated decisions.

- **Privacy and data security**: AI models depend on huge amounts of data, including personal information. This reliance on data has vital ethical concerns around privacy and data security. Protect user data, use data anonymization tools, and adhere to data privacy laws (e.g., the **General Data Protection Regulation (GDPR)**) all need to be protected when undertaking moral AI studies. If privacy and data security are not properly taken care of, we risk data breaches, reputational harm, and fines.

- **Autonomy and responsibility**: With the emergence of AI systems, there are questions about accountability and responsibility. Autonomous AI systems make errors or harms, and it is difficult to attribute responsibility. It is a particularly pressing concern for areas including self-driving cars, **artificial intelligence (AI)** for military purposes, and health diagnosis. Responsible AI development need mechanisms to apportion blame and responsibility in the case of mishaps or misapprehension.

- **Social effects and economic devastation**: AI could be used to significantly impact employment opportunities and the economy in the world, with moral implications for the loss of jobs and economic inequality.

- **Fake news and deepfakes**: With the advent of generative AI, for example, **Generative Pre-trained Transformers (GPT)** and deep learning video synthesis, fake news and deepfakes spread. Deepfakes can also be used in bad ways to perpetrate deception, influence opinion, and target individuals. Dealing with the ethical impact of these technologies will require active surveillance, regulation, and appropriate use of AI-generated content.

Ethics in AI and ML are foundational to the responsible development and deployment of AI systems. Defining ethics in the context of AI involves a commitment to fairness, transparency, accountability, and the prioritization of human values. As AI becomes more pervasive, the importance of ethical considerations will only increase, given the potential consequences for individuals, organizations, and society. Addressing these challenges requires a multidisciplinary approach, incorporating insights from technologists, ethicists, sociologists, and policymakers to create AI systems that are not only intelligent but also just and trustworthy.

The focus on ethics in AI serves as a guiding principle for subsequent discussions on more specialized topics such as bias, fairness, privacy, and security. By laying a strong ethical foundation, we can better navigate the complex landscape of AI and ensure its alignment with human well-being and societal progress.

Bias and fairness in AI

AI model bias is an important issue that relates to many aspects of the modelling process from the data collection, algorithm design, and model training phases.

Types of bias in AI models

Knowing what kind of biases exist in AI systems can help us minimize their detrimental effects. Let us look at some biases:

- **Data bias**: One of the most widely prevalent sources of bias in AI models is data bias. It happens when the training data from which an AI model is generated are ill-matched with target individuals or reflect inequalities in society. A facial recognition system, for instance, which was originally trained on light-skinned faces, might do extremely badly when examining people with darker skin. Data bias also can be further divided into other kinds of biases, including sampling bias (in which some groups are underrepresented) and label bias (data have wrong or biased labels applied to them).

- **Algorithmic bias**: Algorithmic bias is when the AI algorithm that has been designed or used generates, by its nature, unjust effects. This could be the consequence of applying some mathematical formulas, cost-functions, or optimization models that attach higher priority to one factor than another. For example, an AI job seeker algorithm that prioritizes traits like college experience may disadvantage similarly skilled people who did not attend college through socioeconomic discrimination.

- **Measurement bias**: Measurement bias is introduced when the variable or features supplied to the model are poor proxies for the model being modeled. A credit scoring algorithm based on, say, a homebuyer's zip code may be potentially socioeconomically biased owing to its relationship to income or race.

- **Interaction bias:** An interaction bias is based on users' engagement with the AI system. Chatbots or recommendation engines that use users to entrain their models, for example, risk reinforcing old biases if people always choose certain kinds of content. These networks can ultimately lead to stereotypes and biased behaviors being reinforced in perpetuity.

- **Historical bias:** Historical bias is when an AI model reproduces historical biases. Predictive policing algorithms that model crimes in the past, for instance, can unfairly target particular groups of people – evidence of institutionalized biases in the way police work. This kind of historical bias is especially difficult to eliminate since it tends to be so embedded in social patterns and historical injustices.

Detecting and addressing bias in data

It is a three-phased process of data, model output, and performance measurement monitoring of AI systems to detect and remove biases. Technology and moral strategies aimed at overcoming bias are employed in the fight against bias to ensure that AI simulations provide just and inclusive outcomes.

Let us look at some of the major key strategies to overcome bias:

- **Statistics to find the inaccuracy of data**: Status allows you to see what is going on in terms of quality. performance, accuracy, etc. in your AI model where you can ensure it is providing the right data at the right time. Demographic parity, for example, means that everyone in a protected group (whether white or black) gets the same treatment.

- **Procedures to measure and inspect fairness**: AI developers can calculate fairness to inspect the models and verify if they are biased. These metrics include equalized odds (AI model produces the same accuracy for both sets of users) and predictive parity (prediction value remains the same for both sets). This choice of the fairness parameter is important and also varies depending on the context and objective of the AI model.

- **Bias reduction algorithms**: AI models can reduce bias using a variety of algorithms. These in-processing techniques involve training the learning algorithm to obey fairness constraints during model training. For instance, the fairness constraints on the cost function will force the model to produce better outcomes. When models can predict after training (for instance, to balance the decision limit between classes), post-processing is implemented.

- **Human-in-the-loop methods**: Bringing humans into the modeling process is one promising approach to detect and fix bias. By involving subject matter experts and affected groups, developers can learn where bias lies and how to engineer countermeasures to alleviate actual issues. Human input can help make sure that AI models are not simply technological but morally and socially acceptable.

Case studies on algorithmic bias

Application case studies help to understand algorithmic bias in AI applications and how it can be overcome. Following are some examples of algorithmic bias in the real world and the need for prevention:

- **Biased criminal justice algorithms**: The most familiar algorithmic bias is found in criminal courts — the **Correctional Offender Management Profiling for Alternative Sanctions (COMPAS)** risk-based system for recidivism. It turned out that, despite all the other conditions, the COMPAS algorithm rated African American defendants as more dangerous than white defendants. This kind of example shows how biased decisions can make the highest-level decision and how openness and accountability must exist.

- **Gender bias in AI hiring algorithms**: AI hiring algorithms are gender-based. Many of the companies faced allegations of gender-based AI hiring algorithms. One tech company designed an AI candidate-selection mechanism to exile men simply because they filled in applications in female-speaker jargon (such as *women's chess club captain*). The model was based on the company's long track record of hiring (it is pretty similar to the company's gender stereotypes).

- **Healthcare algorithms and racism**: In medicine, one healthcare allocation algorithm was racist because it overestimated the healthcare needs of black patients. That was because the algorithm took care of cost data to be a proxy of medical need and hence landed on distorted results. This example shows the importance of using the right features and taking into account social factors overall when constructing AI models in highly vulnerable domains.

- **Systemic inequality in facial recognition:** Face recognition software was racially discriminatory across different groups. They also found that face-recognition algorithms are not very good at recognizing dark-skinned or trans individuals. Such bias has always been a result of inaccurate training data, and it proves how crucial it is to obtain data from a population that is diverse and inclusive.

Achieving equity and inclusivity through fairness

In fairness, the aim of AI models is not merely to remove bias but to actively seek equity and inclusion in designing, manufacturing, and implementing AI systems. Justness is a matter of context – and it is a matter of what each society wants and needs:

- **Fairness and equity:** AI's fairness is contextual, and it may or may not be dependent on an application that might demand a different fairness standard. Egalitarianism in algorithmic recruitment, for example, could consist of avoiding gender or race discrimination, or egalitarianism in algorithmic medical care would consist of treating different socioeconomic groups fairly.

- **Fair data collection**: The fairness of data collection is a critical measure of the AI model fairness. Consider building diverse perspectives and marginalized groups into learning datasets to help remove data access bottlenecks and the exclusionary and marginalizing effect of data collection on particular constituencies.

- **Community building and participatory AI**: It is vital that we involve communities of harm in the creation of inclusiveness and responsibility around AI design. Through including the citizens in decision-making and soliciting public views on equitable actions, creators can design AI platforms more closely responsive to the interests and issues of the citizens whom it is collaborating with. Active AI involves sharing control and the development of AI technologies.

- **Transparency and explainability**: Explainability and transparency, when it comes to AI models, are very important elements of fairness. If AI models can be explained and outcomes can be identified from the reasons for creation, stakeholders can know how and why outcomes are produced.

- **Ethics and legality:** It is critical to act both ethically and legally. Organizations need to be able to design their AI development strategies around equity, accountability, and openness.

Privacy and security concerns in AI

The more AI tools enter into the norm of life, the greater the privacy and security issues that need to be tackled with urgency and care. Such systems usually use a large set of personal data to train and function, which might open them up to hacking or theft. Further, sometimes, the opaque algorithms of AI algorithms can conceal the way that the data is used, and it is not possible to make sure that anyone is held responsible and that they are following privacy laws.

Privacy risks in AI-powered applications

In fairness, the aim of AI models is not merely to remove bias but to actively seek equity and inclusion in designing, manufacturing, and implementing AI systems. Being just is a matter of context – and it is a matter of what each society wants and needs.

The following are several approaches to help ensure privacy goals are achieved:

- **Fairness and equity**: AI's fairness is contextual, and it may or may not be dependent on an application that would demand a different fairness standard. Equality in algorithmic recruitment, for example, could consist of avoiding gender or race discrimination, or egalitarianism in algorithmic medical care would consist of treating different socioeconomic groups fairly.

- **Fair data collection**: The fairness of data collection is a critical measure of the AI model fairness. Developers will need to seriously consider building diverse perspectives and marginalized groups into their datasets. Those include the elimination of the data access bottleneck and the exclusionary and marginalizing effect of data collection on particular constituencies.

- **Community building and participatory** AI: It is vital that we involve communities of harm in the creation of inclusiveness and responsibility around AI design. By including the citizens in decision-making and soliciting public views on equitable actions, creators can design AI platforms more closely responsive to the interests and issues of the citizens whom it is collaborating with. Active AI involves sharing control and the development of AI technologies.

- **Transparency and explainability**: Explainability and transparency when it comes to AI models are very important elements of fairness. If AI models can be explained and outcomes can be identified from the reasons for creation, stakeholders can know how and why outcomes are produced. This increases trust in AI infrastructures and makes it easy to monitor and report.

- **Ethics and legality**: For AI to be just, we must act ethically and legally. Organizations need to design their AI development strategies around equity, accountability, openness.

Data anonymization and privacy-preserving techniques

Making data anonymous for privacy measures is critical to ensure any user of an AI system's data stays private. Anonymization removes any information that could be considered personally identifiable, that is, **personally identifiable information** or **PII**. PII means you can tie data to a specific person, and that is something to be avoided. You need to stay ahead of methods trying to tie people to data to keep it anonymous and safe.

These issues are met by some new, powerful privacy-protection methods that are increasingly popular, like the following:

- **Differential privacy:** Differential privacy is a set of mathematical principles that attempts to ensure a strong privacy assurance by introducing random noise into the datasets. By this it avoids making AI model outputs reveal individual data-point specifics. Big companies such as Apple and Google are beginning to deploy differential privacy in their analytics to increase user privacy.

- **Federated learning**: This allows AI models to be trained over a decentralized network or server without sharing data. Rather, only model changes are distributed, preserving the information local to users' devices. The method is now common for data privacy-sensitive applications like mobile health apps or targeted advertising.

- **Homomorphic encryption**: Homomorphic encryption is a modern cryptographic technique that enables calculation over encrypted data that has not been decrypted. This is an especially helpful method in a privacy-sensitive field like financial or medicine, where calculations need to be made with private information. By using homomorphic encryption, AI algorithms can offer actionable insights without harming the privacy of the data.

Securing AI models

As the usage of AI systems becomes increasingly commonplace, they become targets of different cyber-attacks. If you are going to trust these technologies, you need to be able to trust AI models. However, encryption of AI models is tricky in a new way because algorithms and data are so complicated. Following are some of the biggest risks to AI models:

- **Model inversion attacks:** In model inversion attacks, attackers obtain an AI model's outputs and use them to deduce important information regarding the training data. For example, an attacker could exploit facial recognition models to re-build a user's face by asking the model repeatedly with crafted responses.

- **Data poisoning attacks**: A data poisoning attack is when an attacker puts a piece of bad or false information in the AI model training set. This can create models that are incorrect or ethically biased. Attacks such as this are especially problematic in critical applications, such as self-driving cars or medicine, where the wrong model outputs can cause catastrophic outcomes.

- **Adversarial attacks**: Adversarial attacks aim to take advantage of the weaknesses of the AI models by making small, often imperceptible changes to the input information, leading to false or misleading predictions. Particularly, adversarial examples can fool image recognition systems with a small change in the values of pixels that makes the system mistaken for objects.

- **Model theft and reverse engineering**: AI models (especially if highly specialized or proprietary) are intellectual property that many companies hold. This is the model theft and reverse engineering attacks, which aim to take out the information on the model's architecture or data and thus steal an organization's competitive advantage.

Ethical considerations for data usage

Ethical data use forms the foundation of responsible AI research. As more and more AI algorithms rely on personal and sensitive information, developers need to follow good moral practices when harvesting, analyzing, and using that information. There are a few factors that need to be taken into account:

- **Informed consent and transparency**: The user needs to know exactly what data is being acquired and used and what can happen if that does not go well. This requires transparency and user-friendly consent. Transparency will be a keyway of winning and keeping trust with the users by making them understand what data is being used for in AI systems and how it could impact them.

- **Purpose limitation and data de-cache**: AI designers need to limit data to legitimate, limited needs and minimize data collection. This premise tends to be amplified by privacy laws like the GDPR, which requires that data processing is for the stated purpose and the minimum amount of data needed is obtained.

- **Collection bias**: Responsible AI requires attentiveness in data collection and the selection of training data. Biases in data collection can reach far reaches and result in discriminatory AI. Developers should try to take the lead to remove bias from datasets and bring people's voices in order to make it just and inclusive.

- **Sharing and responsibility:** At a time when we have so much data sharing between platforms and organizations, who is responsible and owns it is of great importance. Ethical issues must focus on the right of users to own and manage their personal information, even when it is used to train AI models.

Societal impact of GPT and advanced AI

The onset of GPTs and other advanced AI has revolutionized employment and caused immense opportunities as well as challenges. Automation of repetitive work and the capability of AI models to conduct high-level mental computations are changing the way workers operate in industries in the following ways:

- **Automation and the future of work:** Effective AI algorithms such as OpenAI's GPT have already been automating physical tasks and cognitive functions such as decision-making, natural language processing, and problem-solving. GPT can create a report or even program codes or even provide customer support through chatbots, for instance. This saves some human labor but also means catastrophic job cuts. The most rote jobs (such as entering data, basic analysis, and reporting) are especially vulnerable to automation.

- **Skills retraining and the new market for labor:** Not all industries are expelled by AI. Rotational work might be shrinking, but the opportunities for AI-development, monitoring, and maintenance jobs are growing. The trend highlights how to train the workforce to work in an AI economy. Governments, schools, and private entities need to work in partnership to offer reskilling programs that help displaced employees find alternative jobs (as AI ethics advisers, data analysts, and human-AI interaction designers).

- **Economic inequality and access to AI opportunities:** An obvious concern with AI's job-creation effect is economic inequality. While AI may also save money and improve efficiency, the effects might not be reflected equally. Big companies that are financially able to spend money on AI technology could stand a chance; little companies could be left behind. Not only that, but workers on low incomes are also prone to displacement, doubling inequality.

- **AI-enhanced functions and efficiency:** In the best of all possible worlds, AI is not just a job killer but also an enhancement to human capabilities. We are implementing a lot of jobs in AI tools to make employees more efficient and creative. For instance, in the legal profession, AI can help to analyze contracts allowing lawyers to concentrate on more important areas such as strategy and client-facing. The AI-human coupling is disrupting what it means to be productive in the 21st-century workplace.

Role of AI in misinformation and deepfakes

With the development of GPT and other types of AI, a variety of changes have been enacted to the job market, which has come with great promise and with challenges. Automation of manual processes and the capacity of AI models to perform specialized cognition are forever changing the workplace in various sectors.

Deepfakes made by AI are another big problem in the world of misinformation, as these advanced forgeries can manipulate audio and video to systematically fabricate believable false images of people or events. Deepfakes use powerful ML and AI algorithms to recreate the images and voices of real people in order to produce false news, fake public figures, and fabricate evidence that can be used to damage media credibility, influence the public's views, and derail democratic systems. The more accessible the technologies are and the harder it is to separate them from reality, the more misuse they are likely to unleash, and the more urgent and concerted governments, technology companies and civil society must respond with tools, laws and public education programmes designed to protect us from AI-generated misinformation.

Implications for trust and public perception

When AI technologies of the highest order are adopted at scale, it could spell great peril for the public's confidence and social order. At stake in AI systems is whether we trust them enough to adopt them and integrate them into society. However, a number of things undermine this trust:

- **Transparency and explainability**: You do not want your users to doubt the accuracy of your information. That inaccessibility creates an opportunity for distrust and potentially fear – particularly when the stakes are high in fields as vital as health care, criminal justice, and money. Even efforts to devise explainable AI approaches are making attempts to ease those concerns.

- **Concerns about bias and injustice**: AI is strongly associated with AI's negative public opinion because of AI model bias and injustice. When AI systems act with bias, then you lose your confidence that they will provide equal services to the public. These can be remedied by proactive efforts of regular audits, inclusive data collection, and fairness principles.

- **Secure, reliable, user-friendly AI**: AI must be designed to be safe, reliable, and user-friendly if trust is to be gained. From a development standpoint, ethics, standards-keeping and stakeholder engagement should be on developers' agenda. It is the motto of **trustworthy AI** that calls for rigor, accountability and openness when building and using AI models.

- **Sensitivity and inculcation:** The users should be taught about the AI technologies so they can believe them. Having tools for programming to decode AI, how AI models work and what their limits are can facilitate engineers' adoption into the user base. Awareness initiatives and open discussion of AI risks and opportunities also help to create well-formed trust.

Regulation and governance of advanced AI

Technology around AI will continue to move forward very rapidly, and governments have taken notice of AI in a substantial way. We can assume more and more regulation is on the horizon. This is where the legal systems of various countries meet ethics and social concerns.

There are several areas where new laws and AI ethics converge, here are ones to keep in mind:

- **The rise of AI laws**: With the rise of AI models like GPT, they will have wider applications in areas such as financial decision-making, law enforcement, and health care. However, despite the lack of strict regulations, this totally unregulated space where anything can happen has created a scenario where developers and organizations can accept very little responsibility for their AI systems' missteps. In order to fill this in, national and international governments are looking at broad AI policies geared toward safety, privacy, justice and openness.

- **International movements and policies:** While the National Institute for Standards is US-based, there are many other nationals involved. In the EU, you will see that there is already a proposed AI intelligence act that aims to focus on assigning categories of risk, with strict regulations on high-risk systems.

- **Ethical AI governance standards**: Non-governmental entities such as the **Institute of Electrical and Electronic Engineers** (**IEEE**) have published its Global Initiative on Ethics of Autonomous and Intelligent Systems to try to create AI standards that focus on ethics regardless of the industry in which they are used.

- **Overlapping entities governance**: AI governance must be rolled out to multiple stakeholders, that is, government, technologists, businesses, and civil society. It will take public participation in AI policymaking to understand what matters to those audiences. Multi stakeholder governance mechanisms can ensure universal, scalable, and human values-based AI policy.

Addressing bias and fairness in AI models

Training data is the backbone of any AI model. It contains the datasets to train ML machines to identify patterns, predict, and create decisions. Yet there are biases in training data that may also appear unwittingly in the outputs of AI models and cause unjust outcomes. Understanding and countering such biases is the key to creating ethical and ethical AI systems.

Identifying and mitigating biases in training data

There are various types of bias in training data, such as bias due to past experience, sampling error, and bias due to human labeling. History bias is where training information points back to inequalities or biases. Let us look the following areas you can look at to reduce AI bias:

- **Sources of training data bias:** existing in society. A hiring algorithm, for instance, that is fed with previous job application data might inadvertently choose more candidates from underprivileged backgrounds if past hiring processes were discriminatory. Sampling error - When there are any groups that are under or over-represented in the dataset, then the data will be biased. Human labeling biases arise when the data licensor (conscious or unconscious) adds his/her personal point of view to the dataset.

- **Training data bias detection statistical and algorithmic methods:** There are many statistical and algorithmic methods to identify bias of the training data. Statistical tests like estimating group differences in outcome or feature distributions can indicate if any of these demographic categories are getting undercut by the model. Further advanced approaches include fairness audits – which assess whether an AI model's results differ significantly from each other across demographic samples in ways that are not explained by pertinent differences.

- **Data preprocessing and cleaning:** This involves adjusting and cleaning the learning data. Such as reweighting or resampling data points to have a better distribution of data and decrease group differences. There are also domain specialists who can assist in ensuring data labeling standards are neutral and universal to eliminate bias.

Techniques and strategies for an inclusive AI design

Ensuring that AI keeps inclusion central to have an output that is equitable and takes the diverse needs of those consuming the AI into account. There are many approaches to use for the AI development lifecycle, like:

- **Differentiated and representative datasets:** Diversity and representational datasets is perhaps one of the most important strategies for inclusive AI. Creators should always strive to build in data representing all of the relevant groups, including those who might be disproportionately underrepresented. That could be in the form of selective data collection, synthetic data used to enrich datasets, or partnerships with local institutions to collect representative samples.

- **Model design:** Fairness constraints can be built into model training to give AI algorithms fair results.

- **User-centered and participatory AI design**: With a wide range of stakeholders at the forefront of decision-making, developers can better understand how AI models could be perceived by various communities and devise interventions to meet those concerns. Participatory AI design allows co-design and cooperation in such a way that AI platforms appeal to the needs and interests of target groups.

Auditing and monitoring AI for fairness

Despite the very best design, AI models are subject to bias upon execution. Hence, continuous auditing and tracking of AI systems is necessary to spot and eliminate bias that arises in practical use.

With the following steps, you can take to put specific auditing steps into place to help identify bias:

1. **Establishing fairness metrics and benchmarks:** In order to review AI models, it is essential to define fairness metrics and benchmarks in order to measure model performance for different demographic groups. Demographic parity, equalized odds, predictive parity, and others can be considered fairness indicators depending on the context and objectives of fairness. Benchmarks are to help build benchmarks of model quality, and to determine areas for comparison that require analysis.

2. **Bias audits and periodic review:** We have to regularly audit for bias to be sure that AI models get even with time. Bias audits analyze AI model for bias on some measures to detect groups' differences. These audits can be done once a year or other times, for example, in the event of a change in the reporting or regulatory demands.

3. **Feedback and real-time analytics**: AI models need to have feedback loops to record user suggestions, bugs or unintended consequences. Live monitoring helps the developers monitor the model over time and detect any biases or errors in real time. Online companies, for instance, could rely on feedback to report inaccurate recommendations of content and correct them.

4. **Transparency and the ability to explain:** Trust is built on transparency. This is very relevant in arenas of fairness. Having transparent models for AI with proper metrics supporting them are the mechanism of accountability for reporting and bias-mitigation.

Real-world examples of fair AI implementations

Some examples from the real world illustrate how organizations and developers are doing a great job of addressing bias and advocating for AI models that are fair. The following cases offer valuable lessons and examples of how to make AI fair and inclusive:

- **Equity in healthcare algorithms**: Healthcare data is based on the long-time definition of what a standard patient is. Too often, over history, that is male-heavy, thus making medical AI somewhat limited in female patient information. This also applies to socioeconomic areas where more well-to-do individuals historically make up the definition of a standard patient. These blind spots could be causing dramatic unintended consequences.

- **Egalitarianism of educational AI systems**: AI systems in education have started to be used to track students' performance and give individualized learning tips. Yet such processes must be able to minimize stereotypes and disadvantage some students. For example, an AI grading system that takes only standardized test results into account might unintentionally privilege the wealthy. Developers have, therefore, built fairness checks that take multiple aspects of student achievement into consideration and allow human supervision.

- **Bias control in facial recognition software**: Facial recognition software has been criticized for its bias control across several demographic groups, including people of color and women. Some vendors have also implemented more inclusive training datasets and fairness controls in order to achieve higher accuracy and lower inequities.

- **AI in hiring algorithms**: Similar to medical data, hiring data for HR has too often been defined by a narrow racial and societal economic sets. So, in this case recruiters in companies should ensure they do regular fairness audits so that their hiring algorithms are on target for the company's diversity and inclusion policies.

Best practices to follow for AI ethics

The best practices in AI ethics (such as privacy by design, data governance, quality data, etc.) are all critical for trust and accountability, elimination of bias and individuals' rights in the use and creation of AI.

Privacy by design using privacy-centric AI

Defining AI systems with privacy in mind is a central moral imperative. Privacy by design emphasizes including privacy in the design and development of AI technologies early, not late. This involves in advance, foreseeing potential privacy vulnerabilities and establishing protective measures to safeguard user data over the entire AI development process. Privacy by design follows guiding principles such as proactive, user-friendly, and default privacy settings. Developers need to ensure they take privacy into account, as well as the way the data is gathered, processed, and stored. These may include data minimization (storing only the information needed) and purpose limitation (only using data for the purpose it was collected for).

Do not miss the importance of transparency and consent mechanisms for user safety. The consent process must be transparent and accessible so that individuals know exactly what they are agreeing to. Software developers can build real-time notifications or dashboards for the user to access their data preferences, unsubscribe from data collection or request to have their data removed.

Data governance and ownership in AI systems

Data governance is the process of governing the integrity, availability, usability, and security of data in AI systems. Good data governance practices guarantee that AI models are built from a high-quality and ethically produced dataset.

Ensuring robustness and resilience in AI models

Robustness refers to the model's ability to perform consistently under a variety of conditions, while resilience emphasizes its capacity to withstand and recover from adversarial attacks or failures:

- **Robustness and edge case testing**: Robust AI models are repeatedly run on diverse, hard cases to validate their credibility. You need to provide strong adversarial examples (where the goal is to deceive the model) to test how those attempts succeed or are caught.

- **Gaining strength against adversarial attacks**: AI models also get attacked by adversaries, where someone can make slight adjustments to the data flow to control the output. To provide more resilience, you can also add defenses such as adversarial training (coordinating adversarial training information) and anomaly detection that warns about unwanted inputs during training.

- **Monitoring and analytics during the life of the platform**: AI platforms should be monitored continuously to detect and fix any errors that appear in the installation process. Monitoring can track the performance data, faults and error logs to let developers learn and update the model. It is important to regularly update and patch to stay resilient against threats and data breaches.

Securing the AI development lifecycle

Security at all stages of AI development lifecycle: this is key to deter malicious attacks and data loss and to ensure the security of AI applications. It is about implementing security best practices from data collection to deployment and monitoring.

Things that can be done are, for example, safe data acquisition and preservation, which is the first step towards data security throughout the AI lifecycle and securing the data that AI models depend on. Using end-to-end encryption for your data, whether it is at rest or moving, as well as tightly controlling access. Security is first and foremost.

You can also ensure you are doing security during deployment and tracking, which comes after the AI model is implemented; businesses should implement live monitoring to find anomalies or possible attacks. From patching to watching the network to ensure nothing untoward is occurring.

Conclusion

In this chapter, we learned about the importance of ethics in AI and ML. We learned about how to recognize bias issues and how to mitigate them, we learned about privacy concerns and the broader impacts AI has on society. Lastly, we learned how to address bias issues and best practices.

In the next chapter, we begin our last leg of our journey together and will begin to talk to the aspect of cost, pricing etc. for running AI models.

Join our book's Discord space

Join the book's Discord Workspace for Latest updates, Offers, Tech happenings around the world, New Release and Sessions with the Authors:

https://discord.bpbonline.com

CHAPTER 16

Finances of Prompts and Cost Management

Introduction

This chapter will get super practical and focus on the dollars and cents of prompt engineering and running an AI service yourself. AI is not free, whether you are consuming it or running your own service. So, knowing about cost management and financial considerations is critical. We will also learn about optimizing your spending for both consuming and running an AI service with some analysis points and tips.

Structure

In this chapter, we will cover the following topics:

- Cost management in AI
- Financial considerations in prompt engineering
- Efficiency in writing prompts
- Cost management in running own AI service
- Financial optimization techniques for AI services

Objectives

When you complete this chapter, you will be well-versed in the economics behind prompt engineering and AI services. You will be able to consume AI services efficiently but also acquire skills to if you so choose, consider building out your own AI service. Many individuals and companies today are making substantial money in the AI space, so whether you are involved in running your own service or using them, you will get the most for spend.

Cost management in AI

Artificial intelligence (**AI**) is an important part of any business approach today, mainly for innovation and automation. In AI, prompt engineering – designing specific inputs to steer machine learning algorithms such as **Generative Pretrained Transformer** (**GPT**) to the outputs they are supposed to have — has been given considerable weight. However, one important thing that we do not often talk about is how much it costs to run and scale prompt engineering. In this intro, we cover the cost-efficiency factors in great detail, which are the two dominant AI platforms — Microsoft and Google — and other AI platforms that will enable you to run your own GPT services.

Cost management importance in prompt engineering

From the perspective of a company or individual trying to run an AI service, the prompt engineering work is based on creating efficient queries that lead **large language models (LLMs)** such as ChatGPT or GPT-4. However, running the model in the first place quickly becomes costly, especially for large datasets. When companies try to apply AI in a multitude of areas, cost control is of paramount importance. However, when the cost is not managed properly, then the benefits of AI cannot be realized when not scaled or optimized.

Prompt engineering costs most in the overhead of the cloud: the computing resources for data processing, storage and training/inference. Instead of ordinary programs, AI models take up a lot of compute resources (especially in case of extremely large data or real-time workloads).

The computational cost of AI models, such as memory space and hardware, such as graphics, as controlling the number and complexity of prompts, directly impacts the bottom line. Advanced prompts, which may be multi-step instructions or higher-order reasoning, generally take up more space than simpler prompts. It takes a calculated approach to maintain the accuracy of prompts while also not consuming as many resources. Cost management is one area that, if not managed properly, companies may end up investing more in AI than originally planned, which would negatively impact other business functions.

These issues should be addressed through the planning and implementation of effective cost-management activities by organizations. Such practices must consider reducing overhead, maximizing AI utilization, and making financial investments in AI bear fruit. Decisions are to be made on AI platforms to use scalable and efficient resource management, like optimizing models to eliminate computational cost outages.

Microsoft and Google AI platforms

Two powerhouses of the AI cloud are *Microsoft* and *Google*. Both companies provide powerful engines and environments to execute LLMs, including services explicitly built for cost management in rapid engineering. So, let us see how each platform deals with cost optimization.

Microsoft Azure's AI services offer a full suite of AI development tools, from services that are optimized to the use of language models such as GPT. Azure provides comprehensive monitoring and cost-analysis capabilities to assist developers with evaluating how the compute resources are being consumed.

This is the best part of Microsoft Azure's pay-as-you-go model, where you only pay for what you use. This is a very useful model to accommodate costs, in case of changes in demand. Azure *reserved instances* are a second approach to managing cost by committing to discounted prices over time.

Azure's services also provide a dashboard called Azure Cost Management + Billing to developers, where they can view AI-related costs on a granular level and configure notifications to use up past predefined limits. You will see your all up Azure view there but you can drill down to see your AI services.

Azure also has some advantages when it comes to prompt engineering. Users can adapt to their own rapid engineering on the API level. Further, Azure is multi-tier for the compute resources, which allows enterprises to grow or contract depending on the project requirement, so you do not have to overprovision and spend a bunch of cash.

Another AI development and fast engineering solution is Google Cloud AI. Among them, the most prominent one is Google's attention to machine learning cost reduction in their *Vertex AI* platform for end-to-end development, deployment, and scaling of ML models, such as GPT for LLMs.

For cost management, Vertex AI has several resources available, like budget planning, resource allocation tools, and pipelines, which have already been set up in advance and so, need less manual work. Google Cloud also offers *sustained use discounts* for those who stay long-term to plan the cost and forecasting.

In order to speed engineer, Google Cloud's AI service comes with many useful resources that make it easier to keep the query complexity and number to models such as GPT in check. Their **AI Explainability** tool also tells you how models arrive at their predictions and it can be used by the user to adjust the prompts and the accuracy of the responses, eliminating repeated querying, a huge cost savings.

Another factor is Google Cloud's AI-focused hardware, specifically their **tensor processing units (TPUs)**, a special category dedicated to machine learning tasks that cost less than traditional **graphics processing units (GPUs)**. TPUs accelerate ML workloads with a lower total cost of ownership than other hardware options. This is especially true for enterprises that want to scale their AI without massively raising operating costs.

Lastly, Google Cloud provides a *Cost Insights* dashboard, just like Microsoft Azure cost management system, to developers to view usage and budgets. With Google's billing notifications and cost-forecasting tools, companies know what costs to expect based on historical usage trends and thus keep the costs under control.

Other AI GPT service platforms

While Microsoft and Google do seem to have it all, there are also some other options for running your own GPTs. These are usually flexible, open-source solutions or cheaper than the giants when the needs of an organization warrant it.

Through OpenAI's API, organizations can add high-level language models to their applications without the cost of their own hardware. However, prices go up quite fast if you are running in a lot of use cases since you pay according to how many tokens you are mining (both in and out).

There are a couple of cost reductions with OpenAI, like tiered pricing arrangements that give volume discounts to bigger companies. Optimization of prompts — shorter, more relevant queries can lead to lower costs through OpenAI's API.

Hugging Face is an open-source AI system that offers various models of which GPT based models. Hugging Face's Transformers library enables you to customize and run your own models, which is an analogous and potentially cheaper way to get a fully managed service, such as Microsoft Azure or Google Cloud.

The great advantage of Hugging Face is that models can be run on users' own systems and there is no need to pay for cloud hosting. This does mean more technical knowledge and hardware upfront, but can save companies a ton of money if you scale models.

Hugging Face also provides hosted solutions for companies that do not want to host their own infrastructure but still need powerful AI models. They are usually less expensive than fully managed services from large cloud providers and are a great solution for startups to small and medium sized businesses who want to use GPT without going broke.

Amazon Web Services (AWS) has a multitude of AI and machine learning tools like SageMaker which lets you create, train, and scale ML models. Cost management tools, including model tuning and monitoring automation, are available in SageMaker which ensure that resources are well spent. Amazon Bedrock is their service that allows developers to create and build out generative AI applications with choices of many foundational models.

AWS even offers pre-configured ML instances, both cost-effective and performance-friendly, for the deployment of LLMs such as GPT. Additionally, AWS is deeply integrated with other enterprise solutions, so organizations that are already in Amazon's ecosystem will have a seamless experience.

Financial considerations in prompt engineering

When businesses include prompt engineering in their business, knowing the cost implications is an essential part of the project. AI (particularly massive language models such as GPT) can introduce complex costs. Money decides whether AI projects will be viable or sustainable, from the creation of first prompts to full-scale deployments. Here, we explore the economics of prompt engineering – service pricing models, fixed and variable cost, usage-based pricing, etc.

Economics of AI

At the basic level, AI model development and execution price depend on the computing power, storage, and difficulty of the tasks that need to be run. Prompt engineering is when each request or task is asked by a model, and it is an expense of computational power to receive the prompt and output a response. As you can imagine, the rough perspective is the more compute, storage, and network you consume, the more the cost.

When running a few small prompts at first, it seems cheap. However, the bigger companies go, the more prompts we see, and the more expensive these models are to operate. High-level prompts — complex or asking us to reason, predict, or do a multistep task — take more computation power and time, and they are more expensive. Hardware costs (especially if the business owns its data center) are a major part of prompt engineering economics as well. Also, learning AI models from scratch or tuning already existing models to match specific business requirements takes lots of data and a lot of computation, so it is even more expensive.

AI model deployments are not without their financial issues. Once prompts have been created and optimized, companies have to take care of the infrastructure that can provide AI. This usually includes cloud computing platforms, data storage, and AI infrastructure to run and scale apps. Monitoring and sustaining such systems can get quite expensive, particularly in real-time or high-availability applications where downtime is unacceptable.

In short, the prompt engineering economic chain starts at the relatively cheap price of design and refinement of prompts and can grow.

Pricing models of AI services

When it comes to managing prompt engineering, it is important to consider the cost the right AI service provider and know the different price structures these platforms have.

Microsoft Azure also utilizes the OpenAI models to offer enterprises advanced language models, such as GPT-4, for different tasks. For these AI services, Azure bills by usage — that is, companies only pay for what they consume. To be precise, Azure charges for tokens passed in prompts, where tokens are what the model is reading out and importing. For example, a word such as *AI* can be made up of 1 or 2 tokens depending on the model language, higher levels words/sentences will contain more tokens. The more tokens a prompt contains, the more expensive. Azure, too, comes with tiered pricing, where you may get a discount for volume users, making it affordable for big enterprises with large-scale AI programs. Depending on the provider and model, the new one with many features could potentially be less expensive due to how it is optimized, so take care to investigate that.

Microsoft has a licensing model for larger customers based on volume sales, which could really get confusing, but just know that in some situations when organizations who require dedicated or reserved instances would be able to acquire them as needed. These plans allow organizations to buy blocks of compute power at a discounted price for projects that last a long time and are cost-controlled because they have fixed usage for a period of time.

Google Cloud is also an AI solution with similar, powerful AI capabilities, but pricing is also based on use. Google Cloud *Vertex AI* platform offers turnkey solutions for creating, training, and deploying ML models, such as LLMs (GPT). Google Cloud's prices are based on token usage. The thing special about Google Cloud's pricing strategy is that they provide discounts for extended usage that automatically occur for those customers who are using the services for a longer time. Such discounts decouple longer-term AI projects and encourage businesses to continue to make use of Google's network. Then, there are the volume discounts provided by Google Cloud, which makes it even cheaper for big enterprises who receive a lot of prompts.

Google provides ready-made AI environments to reduce resource consumption, so companies do not have to pay for complex AI simulations. These infrastructures simplify AI workload management and free businesses up capital for fine-tuning and executing language models such as GPT.

Knowing fixed versus variable costs

Businesses can face fixed and variable cost in AI services which comes with their own budgetary and financial implications. Costs are best managed by separating these two costs.

Fixed costs are costs that are set in stone, no matter how much the AI system is used. They are often infrastructure expenses like buying specific hardware (GPUs, CPUs, TPUs) or long-term software licenses. Fixed costs also include maintenance and operational costs for running these systems if an organization owns its AI models locally or in a private data center.

Fixed-costs are normally fixed and hence can be budgeted for over the long term by businesses. However, they are also costly upfront, especially if you are an enterprise and you have to deploy AI solutions at scale. Fixed costs are not scalable: once you have the infrastructure up and running, companies have to pledge to keep it running no matter how much users use it.

Variable costs, meanwhile, are dependent on how much the AI system is employed. The biggest variable cost in an AI cloud system is often compute resources, for example, the number of prompts that need to be processed, the number of datasets that need to be processed, and the amount of storage that needs to be accessed in the cloud. Variable costs directly correlate to how many prompts are processed and how complex they are, and if they are not managed well, can skyrocket.

Variable expenses are the more elastic, but also volatile, component of AI budgeting for companies that utilize a pay-as-you-go model on a cloud such as Microsoft Azure or Google Cloud. If immediate usage spikes due to greater demand or higher complexity of query, then prices can go way up. Therefore, companies must monitor usage and take measures, such as maximizing prompts to control variable costs.

Usage-based pricing

A popular price model in prompt engineering is the usage-based pricing model, in which companies are billed by the extent of use they get out of the AI services. It is a flexible and scalable model but one that comes with some issues in budgeting and cost predictability.

Use case-based pricing: price will depend on the amount of prompts passed to the AI model. In enterprises undertaking prompt engineering work, this could be quite a budgetary mess since it is not always known how much resources will be needed at a given time.

You need tooling and measures to track usage and consumption metrics which often are supplied by the various cloud service providers which will alert you when you cross certain monthly thresholds. These are tools you need for anticipating costs and staying on track with AI projects.

Companies can develop plans for making efficient use of prompts and saving money. For instance, by building more efficient prompts – queries that require less computing or produce better outputs – companies can reduce their variable costs without losing the quality of the AI results. You can tweak the models you use by looking at each task to also try to reduce the number of overall prompts handled.

It is for sure harder to predict the budget with usage based pricing models as the AI workloads are naturally unpredictable. To mitigate this, companies need to be proactive in budget management based on historical data to predict costs in the future and to invest in contingency funds to cover overruns. Firmly understanding the financial requirements of Prompt engineering can be successfully managed by businesses continually tuning their cost-management plans.

Efficiency in writing prompts

You can imagine that a strong relationship exists between length and complexity of a prompt and how expensive it could be for the model to give an answer. If you are trying to do this efficiently then there are tips you can take into account from the prompt engineering perspective.

Understanding token consumption pricing

The biggest driver of costs in prompt engineering is token use. Recall we spent an entire chapter (*Chapter 9, Understanding Tokens*) delving deep into tokens. Many AI vendors, such as Microsoft Azure and Google Cloud, charge based on the number of tokens they have sent and received. So, longer or more detailed prompts and responses will use more tokens and, therefore, be more expensive.

Some AI platforms even offer functions that can forecast how many tokens will be used per prompt in order to schedule and coordinate interactions with the AI model; users can budget their prompts more cost-effectively if they are informed on the spending of tokens.

Optimizing prompt length for cost control

The most cost-efficient solution for prompt engineering is to make the prompts as long as possible. It might seem obvious to offer the AI model detailed, complicated instructions, but this quickly becomes costly as you have to consume more tokens. The goal of optimizing prompt length is to be as detailed as possible while still keeping out too much verbosity.

The strategies you can apply for maximizing prompt length are the following:

- **Be concise**: Do not make your explanation lengthy, and do not use extra information. We have discussed this many times, but not flooding the model with extraneous information is a best practice to always follow.

- **Do not over-describe**: Initially, when in doubt-keep it short. While it is always good to give context to complexities, explaining too much leads to consuming too many tokens.

- **Learn from your prior interactions**: There are AI systems that support session-based interactions, in which the model can remember previous prompts and answers. So be sure that you are not repetitive and do not provide the same information in subsequent prompts, thus saving tokens.

- **Use system messages effectively:** A trick is to set up a persona that the AI will respond in (that is, *be a fixed rate mortgage calculator*, etc.). This prevents us from rewriting individual instructions for every prompt during the session and makes the use of tokens even better.

Using these methods, the length of the prompt can be trimmed by users, saving tokens and costs without sacrificing high quality and accurate output from the AI model.

Strategies to minimize prompt iterations

In prompt engineering, for example, the single source of inefficiency and overhead is repeated prompts. Every iteration – in which the user inputs a new or reworked prompt in response to an imperfect output – is also expensive because the AI model needs to learn something new each time.

Users can take the following measures to get iterations as low as possible at lower costs:

- **Get the problem down in the very first place:** A clear problem / question structure, in the beginning, saves lots of time when working on prompts. Provide enough information in the prompt for the AI model to get a sense of the context and goal of the task. Uncommitted or vague calls are also more likely to give the wrong or useless answers and will require reruns.

- **Apply examples where needed**: When the problem becomes more advanced, specifying examples of output you are after will guide the model in the right direction. By indicating what is expected, the user does not have to phrase or refactor the prompt many times.

- **Use prompt templates:** Find out something that works and turn it into a template. This gives you consistency and speed in the future for similar prompt needs.

Using low-resource models for simple tasks

Not all AI is done with the most complex, resource-hungry models. If your use case is merely data extraction, text classification, or standard content generation, then a low-resource architecture can make savings at no loss of performance.

Low-resource models are usually smaller, cheaper to compute versions of larger models such as GPT-4o. Though they are not as advanced for sophisticated jobs, they can also handle simple ones at a lower price point. Almost every AI platform exposes the different types of models, from the high-end models to the low-resource models.

These are some things that users need to take into account when selecting a model:

- **Complexity of the task**: If the goal is numeric analysis or something like that a model with a lower resolution will be fine versus *reasoning* or more complicated language.

- **Response time**: In low-resource models, the responses come in quicker than the more complex ones, which will save you both money and time. If you are running an application where speed of response is important, then a lighter model could be a time and cost-saving solution.

- **Price/price tradeoffs**: If you need general direction versus very specific accuracy for something, once again a lower resolution model might be a more effective and less expensive way to go.

Using less expensive AI models for non-critical operational analysis allows users to lower AI costs and store advanced, resource-heavy models for when they really do need them.

Batch processing prompts

The other way to increase cost-effectiveness when it comes to prompt engineering is to batch process prompts. Batch processing means clustering similar or related prompts and sending them as one request to the AI model instead of each prompt being processed separately. This could result in major cost savings in terms of fewer interactions with the model and more token utilization.

Batch processing offers several advantages, like the following:

- **Lower overhead**: Each interaction with an AI model is impacted by some overhead, from the initial computation of the prompt and any context-switching. When you execute several prompts in one longer string your per prompt cost is less- so batch them up when logical.

- **More efficient resource usage:** If multiple prompts in a batch are handled by the AI model, then the task is done more efficiently, for instance, if the task is similar. This saves the model's computational time and lowers the overall expense of timely execution.

- **Workflows streamlined**: Batch processing enables the user to streamline workflows by bundling similar tasks into fewer interactions with the AI model. This not only saves money but also makes it easy to monitor and report AI interactions.

- **More cost transparency:** Since prompts are sent in batches, it is easier for users to calculate how many tokens will be spent and budget accordingly. This helps with cost estimation and management, particularly in environments where rapid demand varies.

  However, keep in mind that batch processing only works when the prompts are linked or have a common structure. The attempt to batch process a lot of different prompts could be inefficient as the AI model may have trouble keeping context between tasks.

Batch processing can be a very effective cost-optimization tool for Prompt engineering. When you bundle related triggers together and reduce the number of times you interact with the AI model, you can save resources and reduce costs.

Cost management in running your AI service

Many of you might want to create your own AI service for internal use, as many companies are or as a service to sell as its own GPT model. These include resource optimization, scaling, limiting the number of API calls, and knowing the cost of fine-tuning models for certain functions. As businesses continue to use AI for business purposes, it is important to have visibility into these costs and best practices to stay in the black. Here, we will dive into all the things that determine AI service running costs and how you can best manage them.

Price is always a factor when you are running your own AI service, either on a self-hosted or cloud platform. Running a GPT model is very expensive and is dependent on the usage of compute power, memory, storage, and network. Making the right choices about how to use the resources and which model to use can have a big impact on the total cost of running the AI.

Allocating resources

Clearly, GPT models consume a great deal of network, computer, and more of services. They have to as there is a huge amount of data moving through those models. This is an integral part of cost control, to grasp the impact of these resources on price:

- **Compute power**: Compute power means how much processing power we need to process the AI models. This usually calls for more powerful CPUs (or GPUs, or TPUs, for efficiency). GPUs and TPUs are dedicated hardware that runs the parallel computations that are needed for machine learning and AI computations, in large-scale systems such as GPT.

  Computing power will be expensive based on the number of processors, hardware acceleration, and whether you need the power immediately or wait for it. Services like Microsoft Azure, Google Cloud, and AWS all have tiers with customers paying for what they need when they need it or receiving discount by pre-booking in the long term. If you are running your own GPT model, you will want to select the appropriate ratio between on-demand and reserved compute based on your anticipated usage.

- **Memory**: Lack of memory results in performance degradations, inefficiencies, and even downtime, both of which are pricey.

  The amount of memory should be scaled to the model. If you over-provision, you can be charged for unused memory space. In case you under-provision, you risk waiting times that make your running costs more expensive and reduce the system performance. Monitoring and scaling memory capacity is one cost-saving strategy.

- **Network bandwidth**: Network bandwidth also is a major expense when using models across regions in the cloud or on a distributed model. Every time a GPT model is asked for a request (prompt), the data needs to be sent across the network. High request per second AI operations at scale can rack up huge bandwidth overheads. Optimizing the location of your AI infrastructure (i.e., near users or data points) and minimizing unnecessary network traffic can manage these expenses.

Model selection optimization on use case basis

It is a huge amount of cost in determining the AI model for your business use case. GPT models are available in various sizes, and the larger models (like GPT-4) use a lot more resources than smaller ones (such as GPT-3.5 or GPT-2). Sometimes you might need a high-powered model.

An older and less complicated model, like GPT-3, will probably work fine for some tasks like simple text-generation or simple questions-answering. Choose your model carefully based on the task, and you will be able to save a lot of money.

Also, some use cases can be solved using custom-trained models instead of the big pre-trained models that are being sold on the market. Adapting a small model for your particular field could deliver output comparable to a general-purpose GPT model for a very reasonable price.

Scalability and cost scaling

Scalability is one of the major selling points of implementing AI on a cloud, but scalability comes with immediate costs. Scalability: Adding more capacity (compute, memory, storage) when demand rises helps the system to cope up with increased demands. If not controlled well, scaling up your AI services can result in cost multipliers.

The majority of providers provide horizontal (the increase of instances of a service) and vertical scaling (more instances). It is best to have auto-scaling technologies that automatically scale resources in response to customer demand to control costs. This avoids overprovisioning (paying for unused capacity) or under-provisioning (causing system slowdowns which increase costs).

Moreover, AI models must be containerized and managed using orchestration such as Kubernetes to distribute load on different servers. Containerization is useful for resource balancing as several workloads can be executed on the same machine without resource conflict. It can save money by not having to buy extra hardware and make your system run better.

Managing API calls and minimizing latency

API calls can be a huge expense for any company with AI services. There are application programming interfaces that enable the systems to interact, and calls to an AI model in the cloud are usually expensive. The more API calls there are the more it is costly. Hence, preventing unnecessary API calls is one of the best ways to cut costs.

Organizations can also batch process requests to reduce the number of API calls as well as make multiple prompts into a single API call. This removes the overhead of multiple data sending and receiving and lowers the associated fees. Moreover, AI services can be configured to parse data at a later stage, avoiding API calls at runtime.

The other crucial thing is latency — how long it takes to get the response when calling an API. The longer the latency, the more compute is needed, especially for AI services that are deployed in real-time.

Cost implications of fine-tuning models

To fine-tune a GPT model, you will need to train it on another specific dataset to make it better for some tasks. Fine-tuning can result in better outputs for specialty applications, but it also costs more because it needs more compute resources to train. Fine-tuning is normally done by retraining the model on new data, which can take days or weeks, depending on the size of the model and the dataset. During this period, the AI service will take a lot of compute power, which might push prices sky-high. However, fine-tuning can be cheaper over the long run if it leads to a model that is more efficient for certain tasks. A better-fit model, for instance, might take fewer tokens to generate correct output and thus lower operating costs over time. For businesses, fine-tuning must be viewed as a cost-benefit calculation between the training costs and any long-term savings in improved performance.

If they are using custom models, organizations need to weigh up the upfront training expenditures with the benefits of a model that is built for them. A custom model provides higher accuracy, faster inference time, and possibly a lower total cost of ownership. Training custom models, however, is a cost-prohibitive task, especially for large datasets, and should be executed with a clear picture of the ROI in mind.

Cloud providers usually offer managed fine-tuning services — where the platform does the training and optimization for organizations that do not have the staff to fine-tune models internally. These are a costly service, but they are also appealing to organizations that lack the technical know-how or infrastructure to perform fine-tuning on their own. The cost of running your own AI service is very important, especially for high-resource models like GPT. Businesses need to be mindful of resource allocation, model selection, infrastructure scaling, and API calls (at the lowest costs). There are also cost savings from fine-tuning and custom models (assuming that the short-term training costs are taken into account). Companies can take these steps to make their AI services more efficient and cost-effective.

Financial optimization techniques for AI services

As AI becomes a part of the daily business workflow, the cost of operating AI services becomes an issue that cannot be overlooked. AI deployment (both on-premises and through the cloud) offers great business value but new financial issues. In-house AI models, or cloud-based services, to cost-cutting measures — businesses should be strategic in how they spend on AI. This article details key financial optimization practices such as cost-benefit analyses, discounting and reserved instances, multi-cloud approach, monitoring and alerts to keep the costs under control.

In-house models versus cloud-based costing

Embedding in-house AI models means hosting and maintaining the AI environment in house. This usually means buying custom hardware (such as GPUs or TPUs) for big datasets and machine learning tasks. They also require powerful data centers to host and support them, which means upfront capital investment and recurring operating expenses.

A major benefit of in-house models is predictability — once the initial capital expenditure has been covered, costs of operations can be more stable and perhaps even lower in the long term than on the cloud. For large organizations with heavy AI workloads, the return on investment can be higher than the upfront price, particularly if they can leverage their hardware resources to save money without incurring charges from cloud.

However, having in-house models comes with some drawbacks as well. It costs too much upfront to even start up small businesses, and the infrastructure has to be maintained by an in-house team that can deal with hardware, software, and data flow issues.

One popular offering are AI services which allow a company to outsource the day to day running of their infrastructure. These vendors offer 24/7 access to high-performance AI models and compute power that can be accelerated for various demands. The biggest benefit of the cloud is scalability and adaptability; businesses can start low, only pay for what they need, and scale as they grow.

The other benefit is that cloud providers take the responsibility for hardware maintenance and upgrades and deliver you the newest AI without having to do this in-house. However, the cost-reduction trade-off is that costs of operations can rapidly pile up in the cloud if workloads are not kept under close watch and optimized. If your business does use AI frequently or at scale, the cloud is likely going to become more expensive over time than running your own model.

Ultimately, there should be a cost-benefit analysis for both the in-house and cloud AI models based on usage patterns, technical know-how, capital, and scalability. Hybrid solutions (where the high-priority AI workloads are performed on-premise and the lower-priority tasks outsourced to the cloud) can be the best solution for an organization in terms of cost-efficiency and efficiency.

Leveraging discounts and reserved instances

Discounts and reserve instances are the best financial optimization tools for cloud AI solutions. Cloud providers provide several pricing models that are geared towards long-term consumption and allow companies to reduce their total expenses:

- **Discounts for long-term commitments**: Large cloud vendors such as AWS, Microsoft Azure, and Google Cloud provide sustained use and committed use discounts to customers who commit to long-term use. These discounts reward enterprises who can forecast their AI workload correctly and agree to deploy a certain amount of compute resources for a long time (typically, one to three years).

  For instance, AWS offers savings plans and reserved instances that enable companies to buy cloud space cheaper than on-demand. The same thing goes for Microsoft Azure — they offer reserved **virtual machines** (**VMs**) which enable users to commit lower costs on VMs for a one- or three-year period. These rates often offer significant savings — up to 50 percent or more — when compared to pay-as-you-go.

  The problem, though, is that businesses have to be clear about their future AI needs. If a reserved instance is overused by the organization or its workload is reduced, or a transition to a new technology makes the reserved instances obsolete, resources are wasted. Forecasting and workload analysis must be handled carefully so that reserved instances are suitable for the organization's AI strategy.

- **Spot instances and preemptible VMs**: Spot instances (AWS) and preemptible VMs (Google Cloud) are great for businesses that have a flexible workload. These instances allow organizations to sell idle cloud capacity at a lower price. Spot and preemptible instances are up to 90% cheaper than conventional on-demand instances and a compelling choice for interrupted workloads like non-critical batch processing or model training.

The disadvantage of these cases is that they can be paused at any point when the cloud service provider wants the space back. They are, therefore, ideal for non-time-sensitive tasks and easily reusable if interrupted.

Financial optimization techniques for AI services

Financial aspects are central to prompt engineering in both the design and deployment of AI systems. In the cost of developing good prompts, we pay for skilled labor: engineers and developers with a specialization in AI and linguistics are needed to write prompts that work best with AI models. There is also the fact that training, testing, and execution time of these AI models can be expensive, especially in larger systems where processing power and storage space is required. Businesses also have to plan for recurring cost to upgrade and sustain AI systems to respond to changing data and changing user demands. However, perhaps costs associated with ethical adherence and reduction of biases in AI output, which would require ongoing monitoring and development. It is very important that Prompt engineering finances are managed strategically for a high ROI, quality, reliable, and ethical AI services to be provided.

Multi-cloud strategies for cost management

Another excellent financial optimization tool is multi-cloud. This means you use multiple cloud providers in order to reduce cost, improve performance, and reduce risk. Rather than concentrating on one vendor, enterprises can leverage multiple vendors for different strengths and cost-per-seat.

Pricing of compute power, storage and network are different across cloud providers. When using multi-cloud, companies can cherry-pick the most economical services from each service provider. One organization could, for instance, use Google Cloud's TPUs for machine learning and AWS's **Elastic Compute Cloud** (**EC2**) instances for more general computing. This scalability enables enterprises to reduce AI workload cost from one platform to another.

Moreover, with multi-cloud architecture, you will be able to avoid vendor lock-in, which occurs when all of the services are available with one cloud service provider. In case a cloud provider increases their prices or loses their service, multi-cloud companies can easily move workloads to a new provider to avoid downtime and save money.

However, multi-cloud plans are not free of obstacles either. Integration, data transfer, and security is added complexity when you have more than one cloud. Companies must have strong cloud management solutions and processes for a seamless transition between the different environments. Also, the cost-savings from multi-cloud should be closely watched by organizations in all of these different platforms to ensure the added overhead of management is not incurred.

When a multi-cloud solution is successfully run, companies must take advantage of cloud cost optimization tools that provide a granular view of spending across multiple platforms. Such resources enable companies to find out how to price match, save money, and better allocate resources.

Monitoring usage and setting budgets

Perhaps the most important aspect of financial optimization in AI is a constant rebalancing of consumption and the creation of budgets and warnings so that costs do not spiral out of control. Cloud platforms also provide some tools and functions to monitor how organizations spend and use resources better in real time.

Providers like AWS, Microsoft Azure and Google Cloud have pre-built resource consumption monitors built-in. They are the tooling that gives an up-to-date view of the compute power, memory, and network bandwidth usage to allow organizations to see where inefficiencies are occurring and how they can optimize their workloads.

AWS has Cost Explorer, for instance, where you can view the trends, usage, and costs in detail. The same goes for Google Cloud Cost Management tools which allow enterprises to track their usage across services and identify ways to save. These applications can also save organizations money by uncovering unused resources (e.g., under-used VMs) or suggesting the right infrastructure size for a given workload.

 For unforeseen overruns, companies can budget for cloud services and setup alerts that notify when spending crosses predefined levels. The majority of cloud providers let you set monthly or quarterly spending caps on your AI services and trigger alarms that email you or integrate with apps such as Slack.

Microsoft Azure has cost management notifications that inform users when the budget is slipping or the use of resources changes significantly. In a similar way, Google Cloud Budget and Alerts lets companies set their own custom thresholds for services and get alerts when spend exceeds the budget.

Easily configure real-time alerts so that businesses can act on excessive spending and trim the usage before it becomes unbearable. This proactive mode helps keep AI service expenses on track and within limits.

Cost management for AI services calls for an entire set of financial optimization techniques. Businesses have to consider the pros and cons of in-house versus cloud, access discounts and dedicated instances, think multi-cloud and employ sophisticated monitoring and budgeting functionality to monitor spend. With such approaches, organizations can cut costs on AI in half and keep their AI systems consistently producing optimum outcomes.

Conclusion

In this chapter, we learned all about the finances behind using and running an AI service. We learned about cost management moving into broader financial considerations, then learned about cost efficiency in writing prompts before moving into learning about the financial side of running your own AI GPT service. At this point our foundation is solid, next chapter we will begin to head towards closure of the book and investigate and discuss the future of prompts, AI and AI models.

Join our book's Discord space

Join the book's Discord Workspace for Latest updates, Offers, Tech happenings around the world, New Release and Sessions with the Authors:

https://discord.bpbonline.com

CHAPTER 17

Future Directions and Challenges of AI and ML

Introduction

This chapter will look forward to what the future may hold for both **artificial intelligence (AI)** and **machine learning (ML)**, and we will look at them from a prompt engineering perspective where possible. We will also cover the new advancements and discuss the direction the future holds for AI and ML.

Structure

In this chapter, we will spend time focusing on:

- Advancements in artificial intelligence and machine learning
- Improving prompt engineering using cutting-edge AI
- Future prospects for prompt engineering at scale
- Potential future applications
- Artificial intelligence for social good
- Future of AI-driven prompt engineering

Objectives

AI is very much the current cutting edge of technology; it permeates all businesses and is becoming nearly ubiquitous whether you realize it or not. The big cloud players like *Microsoft*, *Google*, and *Amazon* are racing to create their own AI stack in competition or collaboration with the innovative smaller companies such as *OpenAI* and *Anthropic*. This chapter will help get you up to speed on what is coming in the future, looking at the rapidly advancing technology in AI. Prompt engineering is going to evolve very fast, and we will try to talk about what is happening in that rapid evolution. At the end of the chapter, you should have a strong understanding of the changes the near and medium-term future holds.

Advancements in artificial intelligence and machine learning

AI and ML are changing fast, and advancements in model architecture, training, and interindustry usage will define the ways in which these technologies will influence industries and societies over the next few years. AI and ML are not standalone technologies but are layered upon other technologies. AI can do things that other computer systems just cannot do— from IoT to blockchain and quantum computing, opening new doors and introducing new obstacles. For AI and ML, looking toward the future requires understanding recent developments, current trends, and how they will likely evolve in the near and long term.

Next-generation artificial intelligence models

The AI models of the future are being engineered to solve individual problems but to generalize in multiple fields. The present scene is characterized by developments in language model architectures, training algorithms, and the increasing emphasis on the scalability and performance of models:

- **Developments of language model architectures**: **Large language models (LLMs)** are now at the core of most AI applications. Examples such as OpenAI's **Generative Pre-trained Transformer (GPT)** and Google's **Bidirectional Encoder Representations from Transformers (BERT)** show how far language model architecture has advanced in recent years. Future work here could be more modular – that is, with models that change as context and need change. These could soon produce models that can interpret and produce content even more fully, with even more subtlety, cultural context, and user intent. In the long run, such models could become more autonomous agents, armed with situational awareness and capable of undertaking projects on their own. This shift could change everything from customer service to content production and even code creation (which automating the code is already taking root).

- **Innovative training techniques**: The next-generation's model success depends on this kind of training technique innovation. They are designed to combat computational overhead and a massive amount of data that comes with training large models. Part of this process would involve using specialized data sets to fine tune the results. The use of techniques such as **Reinforcement Learning from Human Feedback (RLHF)** and curriculum learning (in which models are trained in a systematic way with increasing difficulty tasks) is making models smarter and more efficient. Over the next few years, adaptive training is going to become the thing. Selected data sampling techniques, for example, can be used to train models on high-value or difficult data points, which can help make training more effective and less performant. The future could see AI that is self-teaching and can optimize its training over time, eliminating all human oversight and removing the technological barriers to AI deployment in tech-poor sectors.

- **Improved model scaling and performance**: The bigger the AI models gets, the more computational and ecological they are going to be. Models are currently being developed for more efficient and scalable models to deal with these problems. Sparse modeling, in which only the most important parts of the model are called up for action, distillation and pruning which reduce models without lowering precision, are showing promise.

These developments will democratize AI, in the short term, for organizations with lower budgets and will increase the capability of advanced AI in areas like education and medicine. In the long term, perhaps there will be AI chips and services for this type of purpose-built AI, scalable, green AI solutions, which are less harmful to the environment in the process of large-scale AI deployments.

Alignment of AI with other technologies

The potential of AI comes when it is co-operated with other novel technologies. This fusion opens new applications to which neither technology could alone be applied and opens up new possibilities, like:

- **AI and IoT**: AI and IoT integration are an epochal technology and business development. Using AI, IoT systems can crunch real-time data from a huge number of connected devices and build more intelligent and responsive systems. For instance, in cities with AI, IoT networks might automatically control traffic signals to reduce noise or regulate energy use across a city block. AI-based IoT solutions will be very significant in the future in fields like manufacturing, healthcare, agriculture and other industries where processing of real-time data and taking decisions will enable massive enhancement in productivity and outcomes. In the longer term, AI and IoT will be integrated into truly autonomous machines to take over functions like running cities, customizing healthcare, or reducing energy use in society.

- **AI and blockchain for more secure data**: Since blockchain can offer safe and decentralized records, AI would be a natural fit for it, particularly for applications involving strong data protection. With AI on the blockchain, businesses can have data to train AI models to be secure and transparent, eliminating data manipulation and bias.

  Immediately, AI-blockchain integration would be of great use to financial, supply chain and healthcare industries where secure and transparent data exchange are essential. In the long term, AI's predictive powers, coupled with blockchain's safe data storage, might lead to self-regulating infrastructure that will autonomously monitor and regulate security parameters to deliver safer digital ecosystems for finance, government, and more.

- **AI and quantum computing**: Quantum computing is one of the best avenues for AI. Although still experimental, quantum computing could dramatically speed up AI by performing calculations that would otherwise take a hard-wired computer indefinitely. Quantum AI, for example, might disrupt drug discovery, climate modeling, and cryptography by cracking the most difficult of problems – much faster than modern supercomputers.

In the near future, we will see hybrid systems in which quantum computing utilizes certain areas of AI (complex logistics and supply-chain optimization problems, for example). In the long term, quantum-AI collaborations might be converted into an emerging kind of computational intelligence, allowing AI to solve previously impossible problems.

Improving prompt engineering using cutting-edge AI

Insofar, prompt engineering is the key to a successful implementation of AI and ML models. With carefully thought-out prompts, developers and end-users can make AI outputs as efficient, accurate, and relevant as possible. Prompt engineering is accelerating, with AI advancements enabling prompts to be ever more fluid, contextual, and responsive to users' demands. It is a sign of an era when timely, AI-enabled engineering personalizes and optimizes the user experience on a scale never before imagined.

State-of-the-art prompt design

With prompt engineering, there are methods based on real-time learning, context awareness, and dynamic response. These advancements guarantee not just efficient interactions but a response to the moment's demand from the user, reacting smartly to what is needed:

- **Real-time learning dynamic prompts**: Dynamic prompt engineering is designing prompts that change over time as a response to user input and the context changes. **Real time learning** (RTL) helps AI models learn from real-time input from users, so prompts are more intelligent and more relevant to the user's intent. For example, if a user continuously requests an explanation, a pro-active prompting system might be programmed to get more information in the future.

In the near-term, dynamic prompt systems will probably come into play in customer service, personalized education, and digital marketing, where agility in real time is the key. We might teach customer service bots to anticipate follow-up queries, and education sites might simplify material as a student continues. In the long term, dynamic prompts would be the equivalent of completely self-adapting AI systems that respond but also adapt to user behavior, tastes, and even emotions, rendering human-computer interaction much more natural and anthropomorphic.

- **Context-aware prompt systems**: Context-sensitive prompting is a revolutionary AI-human interaction in that AI models retain and make use of context over the course of more extensive interactions. This ability allows the AI to offer not only the response for the current question, but also for the discussion/session that is currently happening thereby making the conversation more cohesive and meaningful.

The prompt systems might one day take context-awareness to the next level for use in conversational AI, virtual assistants, and learning platforms. Contextual prompts in the short term could allow virtual assistants to store preferences during a session or even between sessions for a more individualized and effective experience. An AI shopping assistant, for example, might *remember* a customer's preferences over multiple visits to make it easier to find the exact thing one is looking for because it knows what customers have already seen or does not suggest any extra items. It can employ *projects* to recall for longer-term development projects. Longer-term, context-aware prompt engineering might also help to create virtual partners as repeatable, memory-rich guides to everything from healthcare to career counseling; in other words, virtual spouses that are able to tune in to the particular life situations of individuals. This feature set helps reduce the amount of data hallucinations and allows for stronger personalization.

Artificial intelligence and customizing user experience

AI prompt engineering is democratizing personalization, enabling AI models to create interaction based on user data, behavior patterns, and interests. This ability plays a growing role in boosting user adoption, happiness, and productivity.

Adaptive AI – one that learns, evolves and interacts with each user's needs, tastes and preferences, as does context and memory which are both attributes which help in this area – is revolutionizing the experience in AI-enabled apps. This model uses personalization data to generate prompts tailored to each person's individual taste and desire, allowing for more relevant and interesting AI interactions.

More quickly, adaptive AI will be able to allow the development of personalized tutoring platforms where prompts adapt to the learner's prior knowledge and teaching approach, making content appropriately challenging and motivating. Likewise, adaptive AI could enhance digital guides by sensing users' preferences for shorter, straightforward responses or longer, more elaborate ones and tailoring requests accordingly.

In the future, prompt personalization could become a foundational feature of areas such as mental health, where AI-enabled tailored support would change prompts in response to mood, emotional state, or therapy outcomes. Such systems might eventually be able to support therapists by offering immediate, tailored insights or extending care beyond the session. Adaptive AI in the office could act as a virtual assistant that can not only identify work tasks and workflows associated with a job title but also adapt its response to suit each employee's preferred mode of operation, providing a productivity boost.

Long-term projections for prompt engineering

As AI progresses, prompt engineering will likely move beyond personalization and toward more general use cases — possibly changing how humans relate to tech. Advances in adaptive, contextual, and dynamic prompts are not done.

It is possible that in the future, the AI can derive potential emotions from the text context and respond accordingly. Always ethical considerations and concerns around privacy need to be considered. They could potentially respond with a degree of empathy if someone seems sad, for example.

Predictive prompt systems would guess user demands using past experience and real-time information. This would allow applications to be able to pre-emptively provide information, suggestions, or actions by anticipating and meeting users' needs before they even express them. Such a capability may prove invaluable in the healthcare field (prompts that can advise preventive actions from a patient's data) or project management systems (prompts that can help prioritize tasks).

Autonomous digital agents with integrated prompt engineering could be more commonplace. In the long run, adaptive, context-aware, and predictive prompts may provide us with completely autonomous digital agents. Such agents would be companions or servants for the long term, able to learn from, remember, and change along with the user. A personal productivity aide, for example, could handle all of the user's schedule, tasks and messages, always on top of shifting priorities and individual preferences.

The age of prompt engineering with deep AI is set to transform the way people work with computers. With advanced methods in dynamic, context-aware, adaptive prompting, AI can provide richly personalized, contextual, and natural experiences. In the short term, they will be game changers in certain areas, including customer service, education, and digital health. In the long term, they will transform the way we engage digitally in daily life – both by offering convenience and efficiency and an authentic connection and sense of knowing between humans and machines. Prompt engineering could go from command-based systems to more elaborate, self-learning architectures that get AI as close as possible to truly human-like interaction. This transition will bring new possibilities of engagement, accessibility, and customization that will allow AI to become a part of life, work, and personal growth.

Future prospects for prompt engineering at scale

As AI and ML continue to transform industry and society, it is facing major hurdles that could hinder its growth. These challenges have two broad pillars: technical and ethical and regulatory. It is important to address these challenges to make AI and ML systems responsible, equitable, and sustainable for their creation and application. Through our detailed exploration of these challenges, we will know exactly what to expect and be ready for current and upcoming challenges.

Technical hurdles

AI and ML's technical challenges are more of a problem of limited technology, computational complexity, and environmental costs. Basically, the same issues of any cloud computing service; it is made up of compute, storage, and networking:

- **Computer costs and environmental impact**: Models will continue to increase in size and sophistication as the amount of high-performance hardware — including GPUs and AI chips — becomes exponentially higher.

  Something we will soon see is that we could overcome the computational overhead and environmental problems that AI development creates by using training methods to efficiently make more efficient use of resources. Model pruning (optimizing models by discarding unused portions) and distillation (smoothing a large model into a small model) will minimize training energy without sacrificing performance. We see billions being invested today to build out more and more data centers, AI is very expensive and energy-intensive.

  Long-term remedies could include the design of more resilient hardware, including more energy-efficient CPUs for AI applications. Furthermore, scientists are developing distributed training, which would train models in multiple, geographically distributed data centers, thus minimizing the environmental impact of each site. These improvements might make AI more accessible and less polluting but still involve a steady commitment to research and development.

- **Issues with current model theory**: Though improved recently, AI and ML models remain deeply limited in both comprehension and reasoning. The majority of models are built using correlations of statistics between data rather than a genuine understanding of what is being presented and can be misleading, particularly when dealing with complicated or subtle scenarios. Language models, for example, can create responses that seem to be right, but lack context-sensitive insight and produce errors that a human will flag as incoherent.

Modeling improvements can include the emergence of methods for increasing contextual awareness and customizing responses within different domains or applications. Researchers try to interpret models more easily, enabling users to understand how models get particular results. This is the area of mechanistic interpretability which is a huge area of research leading to emergent behaviors in AI. This openness is vital in industries like healthcare and finance, where mistakes have far-reaching implications.

The future of model-based reasoning could involve more sophisticated methods for **Artificial General Intelligence (AGI)**, or AI, that can be taught and act upon information from multiple areas just like a human. AGI could overcome many limitations of model-based knowledge, but it is still a lofty target that requires new innovations in computational neuroscience, cognitive modelling and interdisciplinary research.

Future state ethical and regulatory challenges

Two chapters ago, we focused on ethics in AI and ML, but what does the future hold? As we know ethical and regulatory issues for AI and ML are multidimensional. Fairness, bias, privacy, and accountability are all issues that have become more important with the emergence of AI systems to make decisions across the board. These are the problems that need to be solved if we are to earn public trust and keep AI deployment within society's norms. Let us look at the challenges in detail:

- **Being fair and reducing bias**: Amid ethical issues of AI, one of the biggest is fairness and diminishing bias of model results. AI models are based on data, and if the data to which AI models are trained is biased or unrepresentative, then the model reproduces or even magnifies those biases.

  Techniques like adversarial testing – stress-testing models against hard or special cases – can detect and correct biases before a system is deployed. Additionally, organizations are already using different datasets for different types of populations to make model training more equitable and inclusive.

  From an objective fairness perspective, we may see models evolve and change from their architecture to how they are trained to what data sets are used in training, etc. Data scientists and computer scientists are actively working on making AI models as aware of their fairness as possible. In some cases, they actually are implementing narrow focused AI systems to monitor the input and output of other AI systems to try to mitigate any kind of bias.

- **Privacy issues and data security**: AI tools usually need big data to improve accuracy and speed, but this data dependence is a privacy and security issue. Often it is private data – identifying details, bank or health information – that is fed into the model. Inadequate data processing could cause privacy breaches, data breaches, and user trust deficits.

   The short-term solution to privacy issues could be to use privacy-preserving methods like federated learning and differential privacy. Federated learning lets models be trained on distributed data sources without having to send raw data to a central server, which decreases data exposure. Differential privacy, however, *noises* data so that privacy is preserved, and patterns and trends can be monitored.

   Long-term goals of data governance can include the development of ethical guidelines and regulations for data management in AI. Such systems might mandate the truth in data collection, relegate data use to narrow ends, and keep data subjects in control. This helps with lifecycle management sovereignty as well as bias reduction. There is also cryptography — homomorphic encryption — that would allow AI to run on encrypted information and in so doing, give privacy and usability.

- **AI deployment regulations regulatory environment**: The rapid proliferation of AI has been faster than the growth of regulation so most AI systems are not properly controlled by any obvious legal or ethical framework. Without a regulatory framework, no one holds AI providers and users accountable, and AI can be misused, misappropriated and misunderstood by the public.

   We are seeing a movement of policymakers and the private sector trying to come up with initial rules of thumb for AI creation and use. Policies like the European Union's **General Data Protection Regulation (GDPR)** and the US' National Artificial Intelligence Initiative Act are aimed at establishing regulations for the processing of data, transparency, and accountability in AI systems. These rules lay the groundwork for AI use with conscience, and they build trust.

Future AI regulatory approaches will have to wrestle with thornier questions like what counts as AGI morality and what the impact of autonomous AI systems can be on society. The regulatory solutions might be creation of AI oversight organizations, international treaties on AI ethics, and reformable policies to meet changing technologies. Developing a unified regulatory system is a worldwide process, which will take the cooperation of governments, tech firms, and civil society.

Potential future applications

With AI, ML and prompt engineering evolving at a rapid pace, endless opportunities and uses open up. Such potential uses do not only span improvement in current technologies but include domains where society could benefit from them. If we look at hybrid models and AI's many social use cases, we can start to see what a game-changing role AI will have in everything from healthcare to education.

Hybrid models and integration of AI tools

AI hybrid models represent a new frontier where generative learning, or producing new content, is mixed with other AI methodologies (predictive modeling, reinforcement learning, symbolic reasoning, etc.). They are hybrid models that can achieve higher efficiency in highly complex tasks with better predictions, more flexibility, and enriched outputs by combining different strengths.

Examples of hybrid implementations that have been well done (Case studies):

- Effective hybrid AI implementations show that it is possible to use several types of models together to achieve outcomes that single models cannot. A scenario would be a hybrid system with a fine tuned model that has a built-in fallback to something like perplexity. Using **generative adversarial networks (GANs)** with predictive models has, for example, worked well in the medical imaging context, where GAN-generated synthetic images are used to enrich data and diagnosis accuracy for unrepresented patients.

- **Financial sector**: Hybrid AI models using a generative algorithm with NLP to forecast stock price movements, artificial data, and synthetic data. Such models produce future market scenarios based on historical evidence and compute the probability of different scenarios. In manufacturing, hybrid AI is streamlining supply chains by blending reinforcement learning (learning from the environment) with predictive algorithms for stock optimization, demand forecast and waste elimination.

  In the upcoming years, hybrid models will still be used in other very difficult domains like urban planning, where predictive and generative skills get used together to model traffic flows, simulate infrastructure development and aid city planning. Longer-term uses could be in robotics, with hybrid AI systems in which generative algorithms to simulate and calibrate robots for their task, together with predictive and adaptive algorithms to increase safety and effectiveness.

- **Predictive modelling with hybrid AI**: Predictive prediction has always been an essential part of AI and hybrid models are building on top of that with generative and contextual features. Hybrid AI models for maintenance forecasting equipment failures, for instance, are now used to build artificial operational data on top of real-time performance data to make predictions more confident and reduce downtime.

  For public health applications, hybrid AI models combine predictive analytics with generative models to simulate the spread of diseases, healthcare resource requirements, and intervention effects. As a result of modelling the possible futures for multiple possible scenarios, they provide information to support policy choices and investments. In the future, such systems might even form part of state planning – providing predictive tools for disaster management, infrastructure construction and the management of resources.

- **Longer-term, hybrid AI predictive models as the foundation of personalized medicine**: Predicting health course is augmented with generative simulations of treatment effects. Such integration would make it possible to tailor treatment and proactive care management to avoid disease development in the first place.

Artificial intelligence for social good

The possibilities for the good of society through AI are huge, from the field of medicine to the environment and education to the one directly impacting people's lives. We can take advantage of AI for social benefit to solve the world's greatest challenges and create infrastructure for a more equitable and sustainable future.

AI in health care, from screening to therapy

AI has already done incredible work in healthcare, but there is more radical promise in the future. Biologically informed diagnostics are yielding better early diagnosis: for example, those systems scan radiology images, genetic data, and electronic health records to determine cancer, heart disease, and neurological diseases with near-perfect accuracy. We are seeing today AI being used to do *virtual biopsies* via real time tissue analysis with very specific medically trained models.

AI use cases in medicine will stay diagnostic-centric and therapeutic-based in the short term. Patterns missed by human clinicians can be picked up by models trained on a range of datasets, making diagnosis faster and more accurate. The models of AI in radiology, for instance, can scan thousands of medical images in less time than a human, so doctors can attend to high-risk patients.

Longer-term AI might even be used for treatment, especially with personalized medicine. Adapting to a patient's individual genetic and molecular makeup, AI might suggest personalized treatments which would be more effective and less invasive. Also, AI-powered drug discovery promises to boost the pace of new treatments and shorten the duration and cost of life-saving medications.

AI in environmental protection

AI is of course essential for environmental protection, whether that be environmental monitoring or combating climate change. Satellite data can be crunched by ML algorithms to track deforestation, wildlife populations, and illegal fishing – all in real-time – so conservationists can respond as needed.

In the short term, AI is being deployed to cut energy bills, emissions and waste. AI-powered smart grids, for example, can coordinate supply and demand, incorporate renewable energy, and mitigate energy waste. Precision agriculture is also aided by AI systems, based on information about soils, weather, and crop production, in order to reduce consumption and secure food supply.

In the long term, AI might be central to climate change mitigation. Forecasting could give governments real-world feedback on policy effects, and self-regulating surveillance systems could enforce environmental laws in the middle of nowhere. AI could also support carbon capture and storage by optimization to capture the CO_2 out of the atmosphere. These developments might turn out to be powerful weapons in the climate wars to save the world for the next few generations.

AI in schools for intelligent education

AI is going to completely change the way people learn by creating personalized learning environments based on individual students' strengths, weaknesses, and learning styles. Algorithms that learn from student performance data can use it to tailor lessons so that students are challenged and supported as required.

AI-powered education platforms are giving students targeted feedback, adaptive exercises, and bespoke content. Students who find it hard to learn certain topics can get extra practice materials or individual tutoring sessions with AI-powered teaching assistants, for example. Such systems can also monitor students' progress and enable teachers to spot patterns of difficulty and intervene as appropriate.

Looking a bit more long-term, you can expect AI in schools might even become fully personalized, autonomous learning spaces. Combining AI with **virtual reality** (**VR**) and **augmented reality** (**AR**), students might learn more interactively at their own speed and interest. A history student, for instance, might spend time in interactive, AI-created past environments to learn more experientially. When these technologies get sophisticated, they might close the gap between education and providing students everywhere with quality, individualized education, regardless of socioeconomic status.

Future of AI-driven prompt engineering

With the progress of AI and ML, AI-powered prompt engineering will grow, allowing for a natural, more autonomous, and more impactful user-machine interaction. The process of prompt engineering, or designing inputs to maximize AI responses, is emerging as a fundamental part of AI system usability and performance. Looking ahead and focusing on the current trends will enable us to see how prompt engineering will evolve to address growing demands for enhanced, contextual, and user-centric communications.

- **Trends for AI-based prompt design**: The realm of prompt engineering is evolving rapidly as new technologies and approaches come to the fore to enable AI to provide useful, accurate, and contextual responses.

- **Evolution of prompt autonomy**: Traditional prompt engineering requires manual prompt design with expert supervision to optimize inputs and achieve AI answers. However, advances in ML are enabling self-learning prompt systems that can generate, train, and modify prompts in real-time without context and learning.

The short term will likely be an evolution toward AI systems that detect user interaction and respond in real-time, reworking prompts to make them more relevant and coherent. For example, autonomous prompt systems might identify situations in which the user requires a greater level of detail and modify their responses without being explicitly asked. These devices could even respond to the tone, difficulty or form of the user's response, giving a unique experience that adapts over time.

In the future, autonomous prompt engineering would make human-AI interaction incredibly tailored and proactive. Artificially intelligent prompts might learn users' preferences and evolve to reflect changes in conversational language or objectives over time. Autonomous prompts could accelerate interactions in sectors such as customer service, education and professional consulting. Fully autonomous prompt systems could also allow us to build digital companions and AI aides that are able to engage in sustained, thoughtful conversations, learn from previous interactions, and be more responsive to users' needs and personalities.

Augmented and virtual reality compatibility

A convergence of AI with VR and AR is occurring. One example we are seeing today is Meta's smart glasses, where the Meta AI is accessible via verbal commands. We are also seeing AR and VR tools being deployed in educational, medical, and entertainment contexts for facilitating immersive experiences, and AI-based prompts will become a fundamental part of these experiences in facilitating them as highly immersive and responsive. Short-term AR and VR apps using AI-driven prompt systems could guide people through the virtual world, deliver contextual data, or provide real-time support in simulated environments. For example, in an online training environment, an AI-powered prompt system could track the user's behavior and provide personalized comments or advice. Likewise, in educational AR, AI could modify prompts to meet a student's level of completion, giving them tips, feedback or support as required.

Eventually, the combination of AI-inspired prompts with AR and VR could lead to fully immersive, intelligent virtual environments that adapt naturally to user actions and interests. Now, think of a VR office where a virtual assistant offers prompts in real-time to help manage projects, facilitate brainstorming, or make suggestions in creative processes. In these immersive spaces, AI prompt engineering could bridge the gap between human and digital intention for improved efficiency, creativity, and learning. Such seamless interplay between AI and immersive technology could change the way we work, learn, and connect and enable environments that feel receptive and individualized.

Conclusion

In this chapter, you learned about what the future could hold for AI and ML. We explored potential future applications of AI, and highlighted hybrid models that combine generative AI techniques with other AI methodologies to enhance capabilities and efficiency. We also discussed the concept of AI for social good, focusing on how AI can drive positive societal impacts and address significant global challenges. This section offers a hopeful perspective on how AI can contribute constructively to various aspects of human life and environmental sustainability. In the next chapter, we will focus on the legal framework that exists for AI. There are legal conversations almost every day about what AI, ML services are doing or can do.

Join our book's Discord space

Join the book's Discord Workspace for Latest updates, Offers, Tech happenings around the world, New Release and Sessions with the Authors:

https://discord.bpbonline.com

CHAPTER 18
Legal Framework for Artificial Intelligence

Introduction

This chapter will look in depth at the ever-changing legal framework around **artificial intelligence (AI)**. While AI has opened up many new avenues of human learning and knowledge acquisition, there are very clear legal and compliance impacts. From artists being concerned about AI-generated art effectively to the government implementing standards for AI use. Of all the material in the book that is likely to change quickly, this is at the top of the list. We will dig into these issues and talk about where we are now, the issues out here, and how governments are getting involved.

Structure

In this chapter, we will focus on:

- Existing legal frameworks
- Intellectual property and artificial intelligence
- Data privacy and security
- Ethical considerations in prompt engineering
- Compliance and enforcement mechanisms

Objectives

At the completion of this chapter, you will have learned about country-based legal frameworks; you will also learn about how intellectual property is being impacted today by AI and the issues occurring due to AI-generated content. You will learn about the major privacy laws which are impacted here. You will also learn about security challenges that exist in AI development and learn about various compliance areas, such as standards and best practices for prompt engineering.

Existing legal frameworks

The development of artificial intelligence has created new regulatory issues between different countries, all trying to weigh innovation against moral application and control. Laws are in the development stage, but a number of countries and territories have set or are proposing rules for the responsible use of AI.

Current national and international AI laws

It is important to understand these rules for prompt engineering because the decisions made during prompt formulation can be the difference between compliance and non-compliance. They are as follows:

- **U.S. regulatory landscape:** It is becoming more important to regulate AI and the goal for governmental regulators is to design a framework that considers ethics, makes AI applications transparent and accountable, and protects consumers' and data privacy, while at the same time adapting to technological developments and the special issues facing AI in every industry. An example is Colorado Senate Bill 24-205, which, as of the 1st of February 2026, will require organizations in Colorado companies who use AI in hiring to disclose it publicly.

- There is no federal AI law in the US, but generally, AI has privacy, security, and consumer protection laws. The **Federal Trade Commission (FTC)** and the **Department of Justice (DOJ)** monitor data protection and antitrust issues, which impact AI deployment by proxy. The **National Institute of Standards and Technology (NIST)** also created the *NIST AI Risk Management Framework* for voluntary guidance in the design of trustworthiness in AI systems. These are the rules that will prompt engineers to hold AI-generated results accountable and just.

  In recent times, some U.S. states have made or will make AI regulations about algorithmic transparency and bias prevention. Illinois, for instance, enacted the Artificial Intelligence Video Interview Act to make it more openly transparent how AI is employed in the process of an interview. This is particularly true if prompts connect with consumer-facing systems or process personal data, which makes it more important for prompts to know about these standards in order to understand them as they become an increasing part of AI workflows.

- **European Union and General Data Protection Regulation (GDPR)**: The **European Union (EU)** is at the forefront of AI regulations, with its GDPR regulating the processing of personal data with stringent requirements and ramifications on AI systems. This future EU Artificial Intelligence Act will lay out specific rules for AI applications on the basis of risk; high-risk applications will be held to high standards of transparency, data integrity, and privacy.

Any AI-based system (and prompts) that processes personal data needs to ensure lawful processing, data minimization, and the right to an explanation for individual-based decisions according to GDPR. Prompt engineers within the EU or on AI applications processing EU citizen data should design prompts to remove redundant data collection and outputs that respect the rights of the data subject. That means developing triggers that do not inadvertently ask for or process personal information (respectively, staying within GDPR guidelines).

Other key jurisdictions

Other important places, such as China, Japan, and Canada, have already or are considering AI-specific rules:

- **China**: Chinese regulation of AI centers around data sovereignty and algorithmic transparency, and tightened regulation of AI technology (especially for personal information and social control). Their Algorithm Regulation Policy calls for algorithms used by internet companies to be transparent and focused on privacy and data localization.

- **Japan**: The Japanese philosophy on AI is human-centered AI research, morality and openness. While not as draconian as the EU, Japan's regulation pushes companies to abide by its government's AI R&D guidelines related to privacy and data security.

- **Canada**: The Canadian government has proposed the **Artificial Intelligence and Data Act (AIDA)**, a bill to legislate high-impact AI systems. AIDA would likely include a section on transparency and accountability, where prompt engineers in Canada are encouraged to factor data privacy into prompt designs.

Local regulatory variations are a must for on-time engineers. Complying with China's data laws, for example, might mean avoiding invitations to use personal information that is stored outside China. Each state's differences in how data is handled, how it is open, and what it takes to comply with ethics determine what prompts are allowed under the law.

Important legal principles and guidelines

Outside of specific rules, principles are emerging state-by-state that will determine how AI machines, including prompt-driven models, have to function to stay on track. These values (transparency, explainability, fairness, accountability, and ethics) are the core principles of law compliance and are fundamental to creating and fine-tuning AI prompts:

- **Transparency and explainability**: Transparency is the key requirement in AI systems where people can see how decisions are made. These are also the same principles that apply to prompt engineering because how you design a prompt will make a huge difference in how transparent or opaque an AI's answer looks.

  Transparency means being able to show users the process by which an AI model interprets inputs when they could make outcomes. Explainability refers to an AI's ability to give comprehensible reasons for its output, and this is particularly relevant for prompts that might attract legal or ethical consequences. For example, when designing prompts for AI-based financial advisory systems, prompt engineers need to create prompts that are going to generate actions in line with transparency requirements (for example, prompts explaining why certain recommendations have been made).

  In order to satisfy these demands, prompt engineers need queries that ask models not just to take away information but also to describe their decision-making path or mention sources of information used to make responses. For difficult domains, such as healthcare, prompt engineers could make use of prompts to provide contextualized and clear answers based on the transparency norms. An example is the Utah state bill using *clear and conspicuous* disclosure of use of generative AI, or California's SB-942 which will provide AI detection tools to the public to ID AI generated content.

- **Equity, accountability, and morality of AI**: Honesty, responsibility, and ethics are the other big legal prescriptions in AI development, with regard to bias, accountability, and social impacts. Fairness asks that AI systems yield unbiased results, which are not discriminatory. Controlling what the developer and the operator can do means that they can be held accountable for AI results, something that is harder to do with automated, immediate tasks.

  The trick for prompt engineers is to write prompts so they will not get biased results. For example, equity demands that designers act promptly to take into account language and dialect variations so as not to create biased biases that are unintentionally harmful. Even better, fair and unbiased answers can be obtained through counter-prompts — questions that examine for bias.

  Privacy, consent, and non-discrimination are moral concerns in prompt engineering. Prompts that are stricter or more limited in terms of their inclusion or deletion of sensitive personal data are fundamental to ethical compliance. What is more, in areas with a high value, such as legal advice, prompt designers have to create prompts with certain guardrails that prevent them from providing legal advice in the first place, and still provide relevant, ethical information.

  The most important legal rules — transparency, fairness, and accountability — together form the compliance regime of prompt engineers. These ideals point to prompts for explainable, objective, and moral AI action, despite shifting legal landscapes.

In taking care of these issues in prompt engineering, AI engineers and prompt designers can proceed while adhering to current laws and ethical principles and preparing for new AI governance rules. This is not only for legal compliance but for user trust and ethics in AI-powered services.

Intellectual property and artificial intelligence

AI **intellectual property rights** (**IPR**) are now a very entangled subject, with implications for the design, implementation, and sale of AI. To early engineers and companies using AI-based services, this framework should be familiarized to comply with and reduce risk when employing and creating AI content. These are patents and copyrights for AI systems, specific licensing problems, and ownership problems in AI-based content (like liability and responsibility).

Patents and copyrights in AI systems

As AI engines take hold in the content production process, the use of a standard IP regime like patents and copyrights changes. Patents are for inventions and techniques; copyrights are for original works of authorship. In AI, both are applicable to prompt engineering and to the infrastructure of AI-generated content more generally, but with different difficulties.

- **Patentable features of AI-assisted prompt systems**: Patenting AI technologies is especially tricky as machine learning algorithms and AI system design are always changing. Patents for AI-based prompt systems could include aspects of architecture, specific algorithmic designs, and how certain prompts are produced. However, it is difficult to patent algorithms that learn dynamically based on user input because these algorithms often fall into the category of **abstract ideas**, and they are not patentable in the US.

  This is especially important for prompt engineers who want to develop new methods of prompt designing or bespoke prompt architectures that deliver patentable AI outputs. Not the algorithms themselves, but a way to implement prompt frameworks or unique applications of prompts within specific industry use cases might be patentable. For example, if a fast-acting engineering solution consistently boosts the response rate in compliance-intensive applications such as healthcare or financial, it can be protected by a patent.

  Even the newer **US Patent and Trademark Office** (**USPTO**) rules make a tentative attempt to treat AI-related patents as such, but variations still exist across the globe. Methods with human-machine cooperation may also be exempt from the requirements of patent eligibility in countries like the European Union. This difference affects prompt engineers working globally because prompt system protection differs from country to country.

- **Copyright issues in prompt design**: The copyright issues of AI have been whether prompt-generated content (e.g., text, images or summaries of data) can be copyrighted, and if so, by whom. Copyright is still, at least for now, a human authorship requirement, so that the ownership rights over content produced by AI responses to prompts are often hard to establish.

  This legal loophole means for prompt engineers to be wary of designing prompts that might be contentious or inventive. A prompt that leads to a data-driven story or artwork, for example, may not, by traditional definitions, be copyright material due to human originality. In addition, where prompt engineers apply generative AI to produce custom outputs for commercial use, knowledge of copyright constraints can avoid IP claims, particularly when generated content is derived from copyrighted data on AI training datasets.

  New legal definitions are looking even to the prompt engineer as a creative actor. However, prompt engineers will still need to design prompts with the understanding that what results might not have explicit rights of ownership. Organizations that use AI-based content creation prompts might have to adopt content rights policies on an internal level to protect their IP.

- **Licensing issues and open-source architectures**: License issues come when you use open-source AI models and prompt engineering for specific tasks. Open-source architectures allow collaboration but can be restricted by licensing to how AI-generated content is distributed or sold.

  For example, an ask used in an open-source AI environment with a closed license might prohibit the production of the outputs or stipulate some disclosures. Prompt engineers writing custom prompts on open-source frameworks also need to take into account whether their prompts will fit under licensing. Questionnaires developed in open-source AI projects have to stay away from the terms of the open-source licenses like GNU **General Public License** (**GPL**), which require derivatives to stay open-sourced.

Open-source frameworks such as OpenAI's GPT models or TensorFlow have an already vast community which could result in the problem of a derivative product, especially if an organization plans to make use of the frameworks for its own proprietary uses. Managing open-source benefits against licensing limits can be challenging for prompt engineers because they need to be well-acquainted with IP rights so that the built prompts do not unintentionally prevent commercial usage.

Ownership issues in AI-generated content

Who gets to own AI-generated content is still one of the most controversial aspects of AI law. When compared to more traditional content creation (where authorship is obvious), machine generated content raises new problems — particularly responsibility and ownership. Ownership issues matter to prompt engineers and companies, especially in situations where AI-based content is commercialized or subject to law.

This is because machine-generated content – entirely or partly produced by AI – presents a unique legal problem in its fuzziness about authorship. There is no human direct intervention in some AI-generated content, and therefore, these works are questionable as to copyright. If there is no human authorship involved, content that is created on prompts cannot be governed by standard IP protections, leaving organizations open to misuse or misattribution.

For agile engineers, a realization of these limitations is critical. When cues are applied to create human-like content — marketing copy, art, or music — companies must also be mindful that IP rights can be weak or absent. In response to such concerns, prompt engineers might create prompts that have little creative input but instead real or technical outputs free of IP hazards. We have seen in recent years Gfetty Images suing AI image generation services for training on their copyrighted data, for example.

Ownership of content in prompt engineering

The problem of title in quick engineering is equally as redressable to the generated content's owner. The majority of states do not assign AI **authorship** – ownership remains up to the company or person who is running the AI. However, what about when there is more than one player involved in prompt creation, for instance, prompt engineers collaborating on a complicated AI project?

In joint scenarios, companies need to spell out ownership in their rapid engineering policies. Others might specify that the company owns all the output produced by AI on its own invitations. Others could define co-ownership if rapid design and AI results are joint creation.

For agile engineers, this means being aware of company rules and contractual content rights. With clear ownership rules for both types of prompts (for example, prompts that enable creative outputs and prompts that enable functional outputs), disagreements can be avoided and IP management in projects is standardized.

Content moderation and liability responsibilities

Mediating and liability issues are also on the rise with AI content as entities are held liable for inaccurate or destructive outputs. Asks that are designed to produce specific kinds of answers can have unintended consequences of generating outputs that are illegal or regulatory in nature and could create liability issues for those institutions using them.

Prompt engineers must keep in mind that prompts designed for public, or client systems could have legal implications. If, for example, a prompt results in false financial advice, then the company could be held responsible. Setting up guardrails for fast inputs and outputs and including fast audit procedures are key to preventing such threats.

Data privacy and security

Privacy and security around data is the foundation of the regulation of AI, especially for personal data use cases. When we are talking about timely engineering, following these rules and having good security in place are very important to build trust from users and legal compliance. This chapter focuses on privacy laws that affect AI prompts such as the GDPR and **California Consumer Privacy Act** (**CCPA**), anonymization and pseudonymization, etc. It also tackles the special security issues with AI deployment, which include data security policies, prompt engineering security, and prompt application risk management.

Privacy laws on AI prompts

International privacy regulations dictate data management and processing – this makes a big difference for the design of prompts, especially when used in systems that might receive, process or react to personal information. These are rules prompt engineers will want to keep in mind to avoid inadvertent breaches, since prompt models based on or requiring personal data could come into breach:

- **GDPR and its consequences for prompt engineering**: The GDPR is a regulation by the EU, which is among the toughest and most complete data privacy regulations in the world. It limits the collection, processing, and storage of personal information of EU citizens with a focus on data minimization, purpose limitation, and data subject rights including access, correction, and deletion. GDPR-compliant AI apps that could be in use of prompts that include personal data, either directly or indirectly, need to be GDPR compliant.

  GDPR is an area that prompt engineers have to think a lot about, whether in the way prompts are worded or what kind of data they trigger. Requests for personal data (like names, health or financial data) need to guarantee GDPR lawful basis for processing. Prompt designers cannot create prompts that automatically request irrelevant personal information. For example, rather than asking for a personal identifier, asks can be created to solicit anonymous responses or aggregated data at a lower risk to privacy. Also, if prompts create outputs that could impact on the rights of individuals (automated profiling or decision-making, for example), GDPR would want to know about these practices and explain them. Do not, or the penalty could be huge fines and reputational harm.

- **California Consumer Privacy Act and emerging privacy laws**: The CCPA is a comprehensive privacy law in the US, only for residents of California, which empowers consumers to be aware of what data is collected, deleted, and to not sell it. Others in the United States and other countries are also rolling out privacy laws, making for a maze of regulations for rapid engineering.

As part of the CCPA, AI prompts used by companies that solicit or process personal information about Californians must be made so as not to inadvertently violate these consumer rights. For instance, asks that solicit the collection of behavioral or preference information must take into account CCPA's consent and opt-out rules. Not only must prompt engineers adhere to this, but prompts should also be able to accommodate data deletion requests by designating interactions so that they do not record persistent or identifiable data. In addition, as states such as Virginia and Colorado have enacted privacy bills, prompt engineers now find themselves in a more complicated compliance landscape that demands flexibility in privacy-sensitive prompt designs from jurisdiction to jurisdiction.

- **Anonymous and pseudonymizing practices**: Anonymization and pseudonymization are ways of protecting data that is anonymous or otherwise impossible to trace. Anonymization erases information that can never be recovered, while pseudonymization replaces identifiable information with pseudonyms that can be reconstructed under a controllable regime. Both of these are necessary for privacy protection in AI systems because they avoid privacy infringements and allow data use in prompt-based applications. Getting it right means to irreversible removing any personal identifiers allowing any follow-on effort to re-identify an individual.

Anonymization/Pseudonymization is important for sensitive data handling for prompt engineers in prompt design. Asks can be formatted to capture anonymized data – we do not ask for information on specific things – and are less likely to endanger privacy. In apps that support pseudonymization, they might prompt for pseudonyms or IDs rather than explicit personal information, so data can be tracked or analyzed with a degree of privacy. For example, in a medical environment, triggers that collect patient data can ask for generic symptoms rather than unique personal details to prevent privacy disclosure. These methods inside prompts are especially helpful when you are doing analyses that do not violate data privacy, which is in accordance with GDPR and CCPA.

Security challenges in AI deployment

Besides privacy concerns, there are specific security issues for AI deployment in terms of data integrity, access control and model security. Cyber-attacks — be it hacking, data breaches, or malicious attacks — can weaken AI outputs and punish the company through regulation. Rapid engineering also requires secure practices to keep users trusting and confidential data safe:

- **Data security principles and encryption**: Data security guidelines like the ones of the **International Organization for Standardization (ISO)** and the **National Institute for Standards and Technology (NIST)** cover data security in AI. Data encryption is a very important security feature for in transit and at rest to make sure that data cannot be read by anyone without permission even if it gets intercepted.

To a augment this work, things like access controls and authentication measures with audits and vulnerability assessments are critical.

When considering data security, prompt engineers have to make sure to include data security considerations into prompts, especially when the data is sensitive or personal. Encryption can be implemented within prompt-based systems for securing inputs and outputs from the users, especially in financial or healthcare applications. For instance, prompts in banking apps should be encrypted for data exchange and should not be intercepted by others. In addition, security norms like ISO 27001 information security management or NIST cybersecurity framework can prompt engineers to create strong security standards, so prompt based interactions stay compliant and safe.

- **Quick engineering for safe model connections**: Secure model interactions — means that the AI model cannot be accessed by an eavesdropper or prompts are not used to gather confidential data. Secure prompts are a must because, when prompts are not designed well, it open the door to leakage of data or to attacks.

Prompt engineers can ensure security by building prompts that do not have too much generic or opaque language that may generate unintended results. For instance, a customer support prompt cannot be accidentally shared personal data or sensitive information. Prompt engineers can also add access controls to control who can access which prompts according to roles or permissions. This is especially true in business applications where requests might come in contact with sensitive business information. **Multi-factor authentication (MFA)** and **role-based access control (RBAC)** for prompt-based systems can be used to further secure model interactions by limiting who can open sensitive prompt-based applications.

- **Prompt-Based Application Risk Management (PbBA):** Risk management is key in AI systems, especially when it comes to prompt-driven apps that work with the user and deal with sensitive data. The proper risk management for prompt engineering is to see if something is vulnerable, assess the risk of security attacks, and have measures in place to control them.

Risk management could include regular audits of prompt inputs and outputs to stay in line with privacy and security policies for prompt engineers. Monitoring the prompts for suspicious/atypical activity will reveal security issues before they become major. Engineers can also add prompt *guardrails* to constrain inputs in high-risk areas like financial advice or medical diagnosis, where false prompts would produce destructive or non-compliant outputs. Making prompts elicit safe interaction without compromise on functionality takes a fine balance between high-risk mitigation and regular refresh of prompt architectures.

Ethical considerations in prompt engineering

AI is becoming more and more embedded in modern life with so many AI applications that people how have access to. Moral prompt engineering is crucial to make AI systems just, open and responsible. Here we discuss two fundamental moral concerns about prompt engineering: bias and fairness of prompt output, and responsibility in automated systems. To quick engineers, these ethical dimensions directly affect law-compliance and user-trust.

Bias and fairness in prompt outcomes

AI systems may exhibit bias if the models give outputs favoring some groups or views (for example, because data biases or prompt structure inadvertently feed into prior biases). In contrast, fairness in AI means systems should be fair to everyone, without discrimination against individuals due to their race, gender, income level, or other empathetic qualities. For prompt engineering, the structure, wording and context of prompts all influence whether AI responses are reduced or increased in bias.

We will now look at several methods to keep bias from occurring in your results via how you structure your prompt:

- **Reducing bias through prompt structuring**: Among the best means we have for inducing bias is thoughtful, prompt construction. This means creating prompts that use as little language or assumption as possible that might create biased outputs. For example, prompts that make AI generalize based on demographic properties reinforce stereotypes. This can be fought by prompt engineers, who can organize prompts in general, open language that does not make any assumption about a group.

  By using counterfactual prompting (a test of the prompts in a variety of different possible worlds), for example, engineers can see how the AI system respond in different environments and design prompts to minimize issues. Moreover, the non-discriminatory or gender-neutral terminology can prevent prejudice or intolerance. With prompt phrasing tightened away from loaded terms, prompt engineers can do their bit to develop more just AI systems. Using specific prompts up front to instruct the AI to consider diverse perspectives and avoid stereotypes will also prove to be very useful.

  If you are designing for a hiring, financial, or healthcare application where unfavorable results can impact reality, prompt design matters more than ever. In an AI-powered hiring assistant, for example, asks must be arranged in a way to score candidates on relevant skills, not demographic factors. These are steps to ensure prompt engineers do not run the risk of being charged for discrimination so that prompt output meets regulatory fairness requirements.

- **Testing and auditing for equality**: Testing and auditing are the gold standard for uncovering and correcting bias in prompt engineering. Several audits per year will show bias that you might not notice in early testing and help engineer correcting quickly. Tests are the evaluation of AI response from prompts with multiple use cases, to make sure the system works well for all user groups.

  In practice, prompt engineers can use fairness testing algorithms to measure the effect of prompts on AI outputs based on protected groups (e.g., age, gender, ethnicity). The A/B testing (different prompt versions are run against each other to see different outputs) allows prompt engineers to pick out the least biased prompts. Bias mitigation mechanisms (by introducing controlled variables or de-biasing prompts) can also be used to further improve prompt structure.

Compliance with ethical principles is increasingly required by regulatory bodies and industry best practices through fairness audits. For regulated sectors, like banking or insurance, early engineers might have to carry out regular audits and file fairness reports. This also ensures that prompt-based systems are not unfairly disadvantaged to any user group and aligns the AI system with both the ethics and the law for non-discrimination.

Accountability in automated prompting systems

Accountability in AI is a fundamental ethical issue, especially when it comes to systems that work independently and influence lives. Accountability makes sure that there are no intractable sources of blame for AI choices and outcomes – especially if they are not wanted or adverse. In prompt engineering, responsibility means creating prompts that produce safe, repeatable behaviors and in which any unexpected consequences can be traced back to specific decisions or designs.

As early engineers are responsible for making AI systems ethically compliant, prompt engineering has a direct bearing on the scope and direction of AI outputs. Building prompts is embedded in ethical engineering that do not abuse user agency, do not contain toxic material, and do not offer false or misleading information. It is the job of predicting how prompts might be misappropriated and implementing controls that minimize risk of misconduct.

For applications where rapid results can have real implications – whether for legal, financial or medical decision-making – prompt engineers must introduce ethical checks and balances on rapid design. For instance, in medical AI, a request would be to instruct the AI to respond in a positive, informative way without any a priori medical diagnosis or diagnosis, which could lead to a false-positive. It is a method that keeps ethical lines up since offering non-supervised clinical treatment could be deemed illegal.

In promoting transparency, prompt engineers also encourage morality. Clean and specific prompts to understand what is and is not supported by AI output enable end-users to evaluate the accuracy of AI results. This transparency engenders trust and gives organizations a means of showing that they care about AI ethical practices.

When AI systems do anything nefarious or undesirable, the user has few options of recourse – especially when liability is not part of the early design process. Legal recourse: What can users or other affected individuals do if the AI system generates a bad or harmful output? Accountability systems for prompt engineering can mitigate these risks by guaranteeing that systems deliver their outputs in an acceptable way and creating avenues for recourse when they do wrong.

Predictable engineers might include risk mitigations like disclaimers, response filters, or escalation mechanisms to deal with high-risk scenarios. In a financial advice chatbot, for instance, calls can be made to remind the user to reach out to human advisors before making investments. These types of disclaimers save both the user and the organization from unintended financial damage and minimize the possibility of a claim.

Accountability mechanisms like prompt logging and version control allow organizations to trace the origin of individual AI responses as well. This can be vital in a user complaints case because it is transparent about how and why an AI system came up with a certain result. If organizations store copies of prompts and outputs, then they can analyze adverse effects and see if something needs to be changed to achieve better ethical compliance in future prompts.

In the case of high-impact use cases, there are legal processes that now mandate accountability. The EU's Artificial Intelligence Act, for example, puts a premium on responsibility in high-risk AI use cases: traceability and human monitoring are required. These are things prompt engineers should take into account when designing prompts and interactions in a way that complies with law to protect users and hold them accountable.

Compliance and enforcement mechanisms

As more and more industries have embraced AI, compliance tools and regulation are needed more than ever. As AI algorithms are used more for decisions, monitoring, and analytics, legal and ethical compliance becomes a must to safeguard users and maintain public trust. This part will describe how AI compliance enforcement is happening at the present time, where regulatory agencies at national and international levels exist, as well as standards and best practices that are relevant to AI prompt design. The insights from these compliance processes are for prompt engineers who want to build AI prompts within legal and industry standards.

Standards and best practices impacting AI prompts

National and international agencies that enforce the law on AI enforcement enforce compliance and punish in the worst case. These regulatory authorities set regulations, audit, and provide advice to stop AI systems from being used improperly or unscrupulously. An enforcement layer that is national and international in scope, since AI technology is transnational, can have an impact on consumers across borders:

- **National-level regulatory bodies**: National authorities are the ones that enforce AI legislation in national jurisdictions and, when appropriate, define sectoral policies for specific requirements and risks. For instance, in the US, the FTC enforces data privacy and consumer protection laws for AI systems. AI apps, including prompts, are prevented from defrauding or compromising user privacy by the FTC.

- **Trade commission for rapid engineers in U.S. companies**: The regulation of AI compliance in the EU is enforced by various bodies and the GDPR is enacted by national data protection authorities across the EU. GDPR dictates data use and privacy in AI applications and will affect prompt design for data minimization and consent by the user. The data protection authority of each member state can check for violations, fines and corrective measures for AI systems that are in violation.

  Other nations, such as China and Canada, have also established regulators in this area. China's cyberspace administration regulates AI technologies to keep it in sync with data sovereignty and security ambitions. Canada's Office of the Privacy Commissioner keeps an eye on AI privacy and recently issued a policy for AI systems processing personal information. In international scenarios, for prompt engineers with national regulatory expectations, prompts will follow jurisdictional regulations without risk of compliance.

- **International cooperation on AI compliance**: Since AI is a technology that is ubiquitous, global cooperation is necessary to come up with united standards for AI enforcement and compliance. Collectives like the **Organization for Economic Co-operation and Development (OECD)** and the **International Telecommunication Union (ITU)** seek to align AI laws to resolve transnational problems and foster responsible AI use.

  The OECD's AI principles, endorsed by more than 40 countries, provide an overarching guide for fairness, accountability, and transparency in AI deployment. These values govern prompt engineering by favoring design based on international best practices, for example, no discriminatory output and prompts that incentivize ethical conduct. At the same time, the ITU, a UN special authority, advocates for AI principles states could use to protect users' rights and preserve public confidence.

International treaties like the upcoming AI Act of the EU aim to create uniform standards of application across member states. The act proposes risk categories for AI applications and stronger regulation for high-risk use cases, including biometrics and healthcare diagnostics. These cross-national collaborations for prompt engineers also mean applying a common set of ethics to design prompts in the context of cross-national applications. Putting prompt engineering in synch with these international standards enables companies to behave ethically in a range of regulatory contexts.

Standards and guidelines for AI prompts

Outside of the regulatory apparatus, there are standards organizations that have set best practices for the safe and ethical development of AI technologies, such as timely engineering. Standardization is an assurance that AI processes are trusted, safe, and just, fostering both user and industry trust. It is essential to the workflow of prompt engineers to be aware of the following guidelines if they want to design prompts in line with law and industry standards:

- **ISO and NIST guidelines for AI systems:** The ISO and NIST are the leading standards-setting agencies in AI that determine prompt engineering. A governmental international standards body called ISO has issued AI standards like ISO/IEC 22989 for AI concepts and ISO/IEC 24029 for bias detection. These guidelines will aid AI developers in identifying and avoiding bias, improving transparency, and maintaining data integrity — all in service of prompt engineering. ISO/IEC 24029 can, for instance, be applied to prompt design: it enables prompt engineers to design bias-free prompts that produce fair and accurate outputs.

  A U.S. government agency, NIST, has similarly created AI risk management standards, such as the NIST AI Risk Management Framework. It defines best practices for handling AI system risks (transparency, fairness, security etc.). When it comes to prompt engineering, NIST guidelines support prompt designs where the chances of bias or misinformation are as small as possible. Prompt engineers should enlist the support of NIST to bring prompts used in such high-risk domains as healthcare and finance up to par for equity and accountability.

- **Implementing prompt engineering standards (Standards):** Implementing a standard for prompt engineering means applying known rules to AI prompts. It is about structuring triggers in such a way that they adhere to data privacy, security, and ethics guidelines while still producing high-quality, impartial output. Standard-following prompt engineers can develop prompts that are consistent with corporate policies and regulations.

  The practical application of standards could be to design prompt templates that are data-minimizing and consent-driven, with prompts that only gather relevant data and are user-privacy friendly. For instance, requests for personal information need to be constructed with clear consent mechanisms (e.g., a message telling users why they are being asked for the data and the ability to decline). Besides that, applying standards means designing reminders to avoid data abuse, particularly when dealing with private information such as medical data or financial information. As part of ISO and NIST best practices, quick engineers could have regular audits and testing so that the best practices are met promptly.

  Another way to implement standards is to design responsive prompts that can adjust themselves for context, and so prevent bad-behavior when playing high-stakes games. For example, prompts for medical or legal advice could be set to provide unspecific content that directs users to professionals for particular instructions. This way prompt based systems are useful and aligned with best risk management practices.

- **Compliance-driven prompt templates**: Compliance-driven prompt templates are frameworks used to guarantee prompts always adhere to regulatory and ethical requirements. These templates act as guides for prompt engineers to create prompts that conform in real-time with the law and minimize the chance of a breach. These templates can come in handy in high-security industries, like healthcare, finance, and legal, where accuracy and privacy compliance are of paramount importance.

Compliance-driven templates will direct prompt engineers to develop prompts that do not gather too much personal information or elicit bias. For example, a customer support chatbot template might restrict requests to common questions that do not intrusion into private data. Compliant templates can also have common disclaimers so that users know what AI-driven responses cannot do. For instance, in a finance application, a prompt template could have a disclaimer for users to seek financial advice for investment decision-making so that users do not have to resort to AI-generated responses for complex financial decisions.

When building these templates, you will want to know everything you can about the law and all the dangers with each prompt type. Templates can be customized for specific industry standards, like health insurance privacy regulations like the **Health Insurance Portability and Accountability Act (HIPAA)** in healthcare or GDPR in Europe. When prompt engineers factor in the aspects of compliance within prompt templates, creating legally compliant prompts that are consistent with organizational and regulatory requirements is easier.

Conclusion

In this chapter, you learned about the very complicated legal framework that exists today around artificial intelligence. It is fast-moving and rapidly evolving. You should have an understanding of some of the major legal frameworks that exist today for AI, but also legal issues that have arisen from AI, such as intellectual property, etc. You also learned about several of the current standards and laws that need to be followed when considering using AI and learned about how privacy is critical in AI prompt generation to ensure people using the systems who wish not to be tracked. This will conclude the main body of the book, with the next chapter being practical examples of using AI with a chapter of examples to get you started.

CHAPTER 19

Practical Examples of Chatbots and AI Systems

Introduction

This chapter will cover in detail some of the latest advanced chatbots and AI systems that are dominating conversational AI at present. The chapter starts with examples that will work with some well-known systems like ChatGPT and ChatGPT Plus, how they work and what the technology is. It also goes over Google Gemini and Gemini and what they are suitable for, especially with more advanced queries.

Using several examples from real-world use, this chapter illustrates not only the breadth and scope of current AI technology but also their implementation in industries and sectors. It can also be an important read for those who want to understand how and what these technologies mean in practice.

Structure

In this chapter, we will focus on:

- Simple and helpful prompts
- Complex examples
- Chatbot planning
- Simple chatbot example

Objectives

This chapter is a bit of a different format from other chapters in this book as it focuses on real-world examples you can copy and use right now in most cases. Those examples will run from moderately basic examples to more complex ones. You will also focus on what to consider maximizing an AI service by effectively using well-planned prompts to turn an AI service like ChatGPT, Claude, or Gemini into a chatbot to help you. We will also create a helpful and real in-session chatbot for you to use and modify in the future.

Simple and helpful prompts

Let us start with lists of some very simple prompts. You, as the writer, would just need to put in the variable information in the brackets [] and prompt away:

- **Creative writing prompts**:
  - `Create a fiction story about a [character/scene].`
  - `Produce a poem in the same style as [poet].`
  - `Write me a [genre] novel plot.`
  - `Give a background to a character from the fantasy universe named [name].`
  - `Pick other endings for a popular story such as [story].`
  - `Say something like: [character 1] and [character 2] talking about [sequence].`
  - `Make a list of writing prompts for [genre] stories.`
  - `Cool opening paragraph for an article on [thing].`
  - `Tell me about this paragraph in a [voice/styling] different voice: [text].`
  - `Scribe me a short film about [idea] screenplay.`

- **Informational problem-solving and analysis prompts**:
  - `Description [difficult idea] in plain language.`
  - `Compare and contrast [two concepts].`
  - `What is the upside and downside to [option]? Help me analyze.`
  - `Extract main points from this article: [copy/paste].`
  - `How can [problem] be solved?`
  - `What's the risk/benefit of [choice].`
  - `Do some research on [thing] and put it in words.`
  - `Describe what it takes to solve [sequence of problem].`
  - `What should be of the essence when I perform [action]?`
  - `Suggest a SWOT analysis model for [project/idea].`

- **Entertainment and leisure prompts:**
    - Recommend books similar to [title].
    - What are the best movies of [genre] genre?)
    - Help me throw [name of theme] party.
    - Tell me about video games for [game/genre].
    - Create trivia questions about [topic].
    - Build a list of weekend things you can do near [location].
    - Compose a joke about [ex: topic].
    - Suggest a playlist for [mood/activity].
    - Share a peaceful meditation practice I can use.-Tell me.
    - So, what are some cool hobbies that I can kick off with [key thing]?

- **Personal development prompts:**
    - Tell me how to set SMART targets for [target].
    - Can you tell me how to speak better?.
    - How do you think [skill] should be built?
    - Build an energy- and attention-boosting morning routine.
    - How do I develop more discipline for [task/habit]?.
    - How do I develop emotional intelligence?

Complex examples

Now that we have established simple prompts let us take it one step further and get more complicated using what we have learned in previous chapters. Notice how these set up a scenario and let the AI know the persona to take on. Although the examples we just looked at are much more detailed and will elicit a better first-time answer so you can modify from there:

- **Creative writing:**
    - Suppose you're a long-time science fiction and fantasy literary agent. Tell me what a good opening line would be for a book about time travel, a supposedly morally questionable protagonist and a world headed for ruin.

    - You're a famous poet acting in the persona of [poet]. Write a modern sonnet about technology and human feeling.

    - I'm a world-builder who knows mythology, so help me build the political, economic and cultural infrastructure of a fantasy kingdom at war.

o   You're a Hollywood blockbuster screenwriter consultant. Write this dialogue again, for extra impact and drama: [copy-paste dialogue].

o   Suppose you are a Pulitzer Prize-winning author. Read this paragraph of my work and make corrections to tone, pace and imagery: [insert text].

- **Productivity and organization prompts:**

   o   You are a Project Management Professional (PMP). I need you to create a Gantt chart breakdown of 3-month project to create new e-commerce website.

   o   Suppose you are a popular productivity coach. Tell me how to structure my day so that work, exercise, and family time go smoothly, when I have 10 hours of work week, and two infant children. (I work 10 hours and have 2 small children.)

   o   You are an entrepreneur when it comes to remote team time management. Tell me how I can build a process to define tasks, deadlines, and dependencies for a team of 5 working from different time zones.

   o   You are Marie Kondo the organizer. Show me how to clean my virtual desk, cleaning email inboxes, cleaning cloud storage, cleaning task lists.

   o   Imagine you are an executive coach who is focused on OKR (Objectives and Key Results) alignment. Create 3 real-world OKRs for my team to churn out 25% more customers in Q1.

- **Informational problem-solving and analysis prompts:**

   o   Be a senior data scientist. Evaluate what could happen if we add a new machine learning component to our product in terms of user adoption, cost and scalability.

   o   You are an investigative journalist. Help me figure out questions and perspectives to use when I am doing some research on the ethical use of AI in hiring.

   o   Suppose you're an historian of ancient cultures. Show how the social hierarchy of Ancient Rome affected economic policy — for the same as contemporary cultures.

   o   You're an intellectual property lawyer. Examine potential risks and possible violations in using generative AI for the creation of branded marketing materials.

   o   Trust an advisor who is knowledgeable in cryptocurrency. Let me check the upsides and downsides of blockchain startup investment.

- Entertainment and leisure prompts:

  o Suppose you are a travel blogger who has been to more than 100 countries. Recommend 10 days itinerary for both adventure and rest in Japan, hints and tips.

  o You are a sommelier and foodie. "Plan a five-course meal with wine pairings for a dinner party that I have coming up, it must be fall.

  o Suppose you are a trivia pro. Prepare a series of more difficult questions related to Marvel Cinematic Universe in beginner, intermediate, and expert mode.

  o You are a film critic for a big magazine. Tell a person who likes character drama films 3 film and why they are impactful?

  o Imagine you're a real party planner. Create a murder mystery party with character roles, rules and a breakdown of event timeline.

- Personal development prompts:

  o You're a clinical psychologist who is doing cognitive behavioral therapy. Teach me to recognize and reset the negative thinking habits that stop me from going after a new job opportunity.

  o Suppose you're an Olympic fitness trainer. Build an upper body and core strength program using limited equipment for four weeks.

  o You're a meditation master, and a neuroscientist. Give me a meditation to be focused on, to not get stressed out in stressful situations.

  o So, suppose you are a life coach to superstars. Help me conquer procrastination on big uncertain projects.

  o You are the public speaker; you are a storytelling genius. Give me a 10-minute keynote on how AI is changing personal productivity to write and practice.

- Cross-category advanced prompts:

  o You're a philosopher, technologist, sociology buff. Explore how generative AI will impact human creativity in the next 10 years, and how society could be affected.

  o Become a team-building coach for technology companies. Create an offsite event to support collaboration and creativity with shared communication issues.

  o Assume you are an accessibility UX/UI designer. Test out this app design: [describe app], suggest changes to make it accessible to blind users.

- You're an environmental scientist and a city planner. Ideas for green methods to reduce traffic jams and enhance air quality in a medium-sized city.)

- Now suppose you are an AI moralist. Be specific in why and how you think AI can be used for personalized education with fairness, equity, and privacy issues.

Examples of prompts and responses

This section will look at different approaches to make a query and an answer, or a prompt and a response. We will examine each prompt type in a brief way and then show examples of user input and possible AI reactions. Following is a rough idea of what this might be like:

- **Informational prompts**: You want to pull the correct and formatted data from the AI:
  - **Task challenge**: Tell me what deep learning is and what is machine learning.
    - **Prediction**: You will get a list of names and definitions for applications and algorithms of ML/DL" (or machine learning/deep learning).
  - **Task example**: Sell me 5 cyber trends and impacting in 2019.
  - **Desired response:** Current cybersecurity standards, zero-trust model, AI powered threat analysis, etc., briefly explained.

- **Creative prompts**: The idea is to create something unique or original, i.e., fiction, poetry, or non-fiction:
  - **Question**: Coach, make me a short horror of a seaside town.
  - **Expected views**: An action-packed horror thriller with character-driven gore and a suspenseful twist set in a beach town.
  - **Challenge**: If you're a sci-fi writer, compose a dialogue between a 2300 time-traveler and a medieval blacksmith.
  - **Predicted response**: A crude, fantasy dialogue between time-traveler and blacksmith about technology, culture, and normal life in each other's era.

- **Instructional/Process prompts**: They are intended to be taught to perform instructed behavior or actions:
  - **Response objective**: Tell me how to enable two-factor authentication on my Gmail account.
  - **Prediction**: Step-by-step instructions on how to enable two-factor authentication on Gmail.

- o **Problem/Exam**: `Define the overall approach to building a machine learning model using Python.`

- o **Goal**: A list of actions (e.g., collecting data, choosing a model, training, testing, etc.) with brief explanations for each.

- **Analytical prompts**: To represent or compare hard content, such as that found in technical domains:

  - o **Test question**: `Tell me how blockchain makes payments fast?`

  - o **Expected response**: Comprehensive description of the strengths (security, transparency) and weaknesses (scalability, energy) of blockchain for the capital markets.

  - o **Exercise question**: `Discard supervised and unsupervised learning.`

  - o **Expected response:** An introduction to each learning approach, what it is best at, what are its drawbacks, use cases, and how it is applicable.

- **Summarization prompts**: The idea is to provide digests of very long works or of some very large topic:

  - o **Explanation question**: `Listen to GDPR regulations basics.`

  - o **Expected impact**: A brief primer of the GDPR's principles, its data privacy centricity, and which organizations will be held to account.

  - o **Challenge**: `Do the experiment of summarizing this AI ethics article in 100 words.`

  - o **Potential response**: A broader review of the paper's conclusions and more emphasis on ethics, such as bias, responsibility, and transparency.

- **Personalized/Advisory prompts**:

  - o The goal would be to get a customized recommendation.

  - o **Quiz**: `I'm a cybersecurity professional and I need to understand machine learning. So, what do I do now to progress?`

    - ▪ **Upon completion**: You will get a list of machine learning materials, classes, as well as career paths to blend cybersecurity and machine learning.

  - o **Practice**: `Pair one to one I enjoy reading – fantasy, conflict.`

    - ▪ **Expected response**: A clear answer for a sci-fi book that will satisfy the characters and plot richness, like Dune or Hyperion.

- **Task automation prompts**:

  - o The goal is to automate repetitive actions, such as create templates.

- o **Test case: Make an email template for alerting customers about price increase due to market conditions.**
  - ▪ **Expected solution**: A professional-looking email template that explains why we are requesting the price hike and focuses on quality and service.
- o **Task description: Form a generic status report on a project, which will contain updates, risks and action items.**
  - ▪ **Expected response**: You would have a template of the project status report that contains structured sections and placeholders for project status, risks, timelines, and actions.

- **Technical/Code generation prompts:**
  - o The goal is to create some sort of technical solution.
  - o **Example: Write a python function that calculates the factorial of a number.**
    - ▪ **Expected response**: A practical Python formula for factorizing factorials with a negative error checking.
  - o **Q&A: Execute a SQL query to retrieve all purchase for the past 30 days.**
    - ▪ **What to expect**: An SQL query with valid date range and customer id filter to retrieve recent purchases.

- **Exploratory/Research prompts:**
  - o It is about learning something new.
  - o **Type of question: Now we have quantum computing.**
    - ▪ **Predicted answer**: Basics of quantum theory: qubits, superposition, entanglement.
  - o **Assignment: What are the main differences between reinforcement and supervised learning?**
    - ▪ **Expected answer**: Reward Learning vs. Supervised Learning.

- **Conversational prompts:**
  - o It is designed to promote speech or thought.
  - o **Assignment: Let's brainstorm a cognitive wellbeing mobile app using AI.**
    - ▪ **Everyday answer**: A mood-checker, meditation app or daily affirmation chatbot – a little introduction to each.

- o Deeper question: `What does AI look like for the future of medicine?`
    - ▪ **Expected of answer**: An in-person call to get a 360 degree view of AI healthcare solutions, like diagnostics, tracking, and analytics.

- **Legal and compliance prompts**:
    - o It is to familiarize with laws and regulations or run regulatory-responsive processes.
    - o **Assignment**: `State the top 3 small business GDPR (The General Data Protection Regulation)-related tasks.`
    - o **Searching for the answer**: Learn key GDPR compliance issues for small businesses — Processing, Consent and Protection of Data.
    - o **Experiment**: `What are the laws on AI in healthcare?`
    - o **The future**: Data privacy, patient safety, AI care in the right hands.

- **Planning and organizational prompts**:
    - o Project management, process, plan oversight, etc.
    - o **Task example**: `Determine a date to release a new piece of software.`
    - o **Prediction**: An adaptable roadmap with milestones per phase (research, development, testing, release) and timeline in general.
    - o **Assignment**: `Essay me how I would build an action plan to make a mid-market company more data secure.`
    - o **Specific response**: The plan is kind of a broad security roadmap (including policy risk mitigation, technical solutions like encryption, network monitoring, etc.).

Chatbot planning

Creating a chatbot within ChatGPT using only prompts can be achieved through structured prompt engineering without any need for coding. Here is a guide on how to set it up:

- **Purpose and voice of the chatbot**: You want to create a chatbot to help figure out financial planning items
    - o Choose the role, character, and purpose of the chatbot. For example:
        - ▪ **Goal**: To answer customer support, provide product data or walk users through a step.
        - ▪ **Speech style**: Friendly, formal or informal, based on the target.

Create a context prompt

Create a context prompt of your entire chatbot to establish its behavior. The following is its starting point for its solutions:

- **Sample callout:** `You are a helpful customer support representative known as ChatBot. You are to answer a user's questions about [name of subject] in a simple, engaging, and concise manner. Be non-complex and if you don't have the answer, then tell the user and encourage them to get in touch with our support.`

- **Design system-level:**
  - System-wide commands to assign generic commands. Here is an approach:
    - **Knowledge scope prompt:** `Just ask questions about [topic] and don't talk about unrelated things.`
    - **Tone and style rule:** `Be polite and friendly but keep answers professional and concise.`

- **Create multiple-selection prompts for different cases:** Look for typical queries or activities that the bot might need to answer and create responses to them. Examples:
  - **Fill FAQs:** `If a user has a question about [specific FAQ], reply with a very brief and clear response.`
  - **Edit user's input:** `If the user input is unclear, ask them to correct it politely.`
  - **Step up to human support:** `If the user has an advanced question, say: 'I'm available to assist, but you can get a deeper answer from our support team [contact info].`

- **Design follow-up and continuation prompts:**
  - Make conversations flow to allow the chatbot to be a social agent:
    - **Call to Action:** `If the user is unsure or requests further details, ask a little more and check if that helps.`
    - **Reject user request:** `Never reject the user's request. For example, 'Oh yeah!' or 'I'm good with that!' before you say something.`

- **Handle edge cases and limitations:**
  - Prevent the situation where the bot lacks information or when action needs to have limits.

- o **Unknown questions:** `If a user queries something outside the bounds of the specified field, gently respond with, 'I'm not qualified to answer that, but you can know more by [other source].`

- o **Negative requests:** `If the user requests something inappropriate, say, "Hey, I'm available for [question].`

- o Add personalization and memory (Simulated).

- o As ChatGPT does not store memory in every session if you do not adapt it via API, simulate it inside the session:

- o **Personalized greetings:** `Ask the username at the top and insert in responses where appropriate.`

- o **Session-scoped memory:** Use prompts to "remember" in conversation. For instance, `If the user has shared a specific interest, include that into future responses this session.`

- **Prompt chain for a simple customer support Chatbot example:**

  - o **Welcome prompt:** `Hello! I'm ChatBot, your support assistant. How can I help you today?`

  - o **Topic response:** If someone is saying, `When can I visit you?` you could respond, `We are open Monday – Friday 9 a.m. – 5 p.m.` ET. `What exactly do you need someone to help with during those periods?`

  - o **Follow-up question:** After the user replies, `Yes, can you do the billing?` you say `Yes, I can do the billing. So, you're asking for payment methods, billing period, etc.?`

  - o Chaining prompts will give the chatbot a hierarchy, answering many of the requirements with no additional code.

Simple Chatbot example

Let us put what we learned together here and use prompt engineering skills to create a very simple chatbot within ChatGPT itself.

Setting up the prompt

We will use an example of a calculation that is a bit complicated where you might want to run it several times with different parameter values. So, that means we will need to ensure it retains the information it needs from one prompt to the next prompt, so you will not need to restate anything:

- **The foundation:** Be a chatbot.

- **The persona to use:** Act as a financial planner.

- **The inputs**: You are to start with **how much are you starting with** (let us ignore units for now) and then ask, **how much is being invested** and **how many years of you plan to invest**.

- **The Math**: Assume that 10% return is likely, which of course is optimistic, but we will do that for science anyway.

Note: There is no mention of future value of money calculation given here. The assumption is that ChatGPT would have already been trained on that- but that would be something to verify with the first prompt.

Running the prompt

Now, let us run with the text from the following prompt. Note that *Figure 19.1* shows the set up in ChatGPT:

Let us create a financial helper chatbot. Act as a financial planner for someone. You will assume they are investing and ask, **how much are you starting with**, then you will ask **how much are you investing each year** followed by **how many years do you plan to invest**? You will assume that they will be investing in stocks and recall that the average return over the last 30 years is 10% and assume that is the number to work with. At the end of the questions, you will calculate their total investment at the conclusion of the investment years:

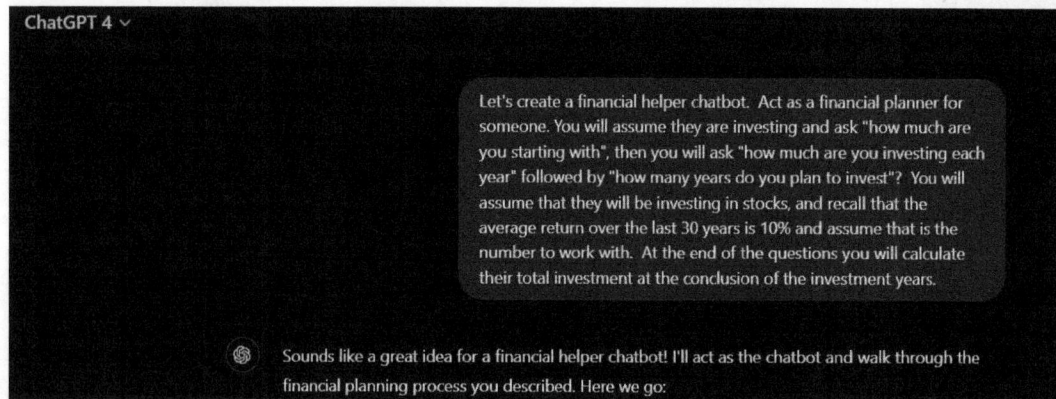

ChatGPT 4 ⌄

Let's create a financial helper chatbot. Act as a financial planner for someone. You will assume they are investing and ask "how much are you starting with", then you will ask "how much are you investing each year" followed by "how many years do you plan to invest"? You will assume that they will be investing in stocks, and recall that the average return over the last 30 years is 10% and assume that is the number to work with. At the end of the questions you will calculate their total investment at the conclusion of the investment years.

Sounds like a great idea for a financial helper chatbot! I'll act as the chatbot and walk through the financial planning process you described. Here we go:

Figure 19.1: The prompt starting off the chatbot

The interaction would look like this:

ChatGPT:

Hello! I'm here to help you plan your investments effectively. To start, could you please tell me how much money you are starting with for your investment?

Your first answer would be "**2500**", your second "**12000**" and your third "**25**". *Figure 19.2* shows those questions being answered:

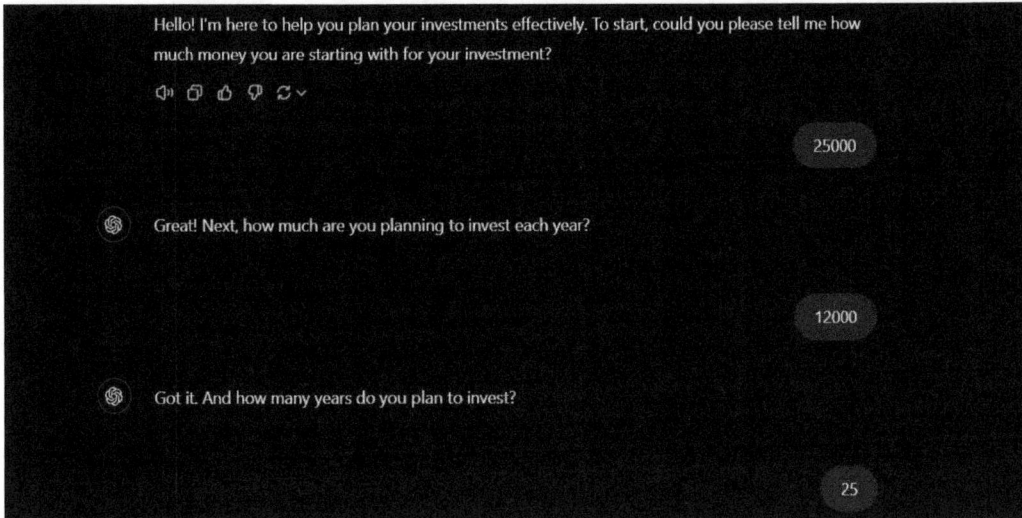

Figure 19.2: The in-window simple chatbot asking and
being answered according to the parameters given in the prompt

Then the response from ChatGPT is as follow:

Thanks for providing all the details. Let's calculate your total investment value at the end of 25 years, assuming an average annual return of 10%.

To calculate the future value of your investment, we'll use the formula for the future value of a series of cash flows (annual investments), combined with your initial investment growing at the same rate.

The formula to calculate the future value FV of an investment undergoing regular annual investments is given by:

$FV = P \times (1+r)^n + PMT \times (((1+r)^n - 1)/r \quad)$

where:

P is the initial amount invested ($25,000),

r is the annual return rate (10%, or 0.10),

n is the number of years the money is invested (25 years),

PMT is the amount invested annually ($12,000).

I'll calculate this for you now.

At the end of 25 years, with your initial investment of $25,000 and annual investments of $12,000, at an average annual return of 10%, your total investment would grow to approximately $1,451,032.36. If you have any more questions or need further assistance, feel free to ask! [>-]

Two things to note: It was not given the **future value** (**FV**) of money calculations but was previously trained on it, and it assumes Dollars as the currency, but the name of the units is not important, and you could always call them out. You can see the ChatGPT interaction in *Figure 19.3*. The second thing to note is to look for the **[>-]**; that is a link to the analysis:

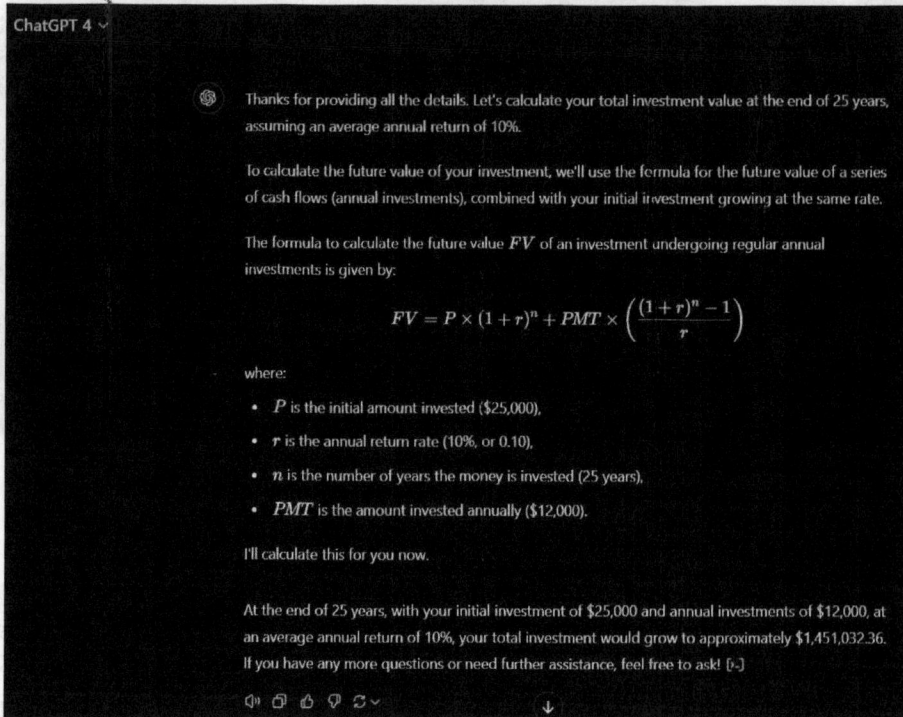

Figure 19.3: The answer and detailed explanation given by ChatGPT for this example

The analysis, in this case, will give you details in the calculation with a code snippet given in Python that you can copy and paste to run yourself. Figure 19.4 shows the analysis pop-up you get by clicking on **[>-]**:

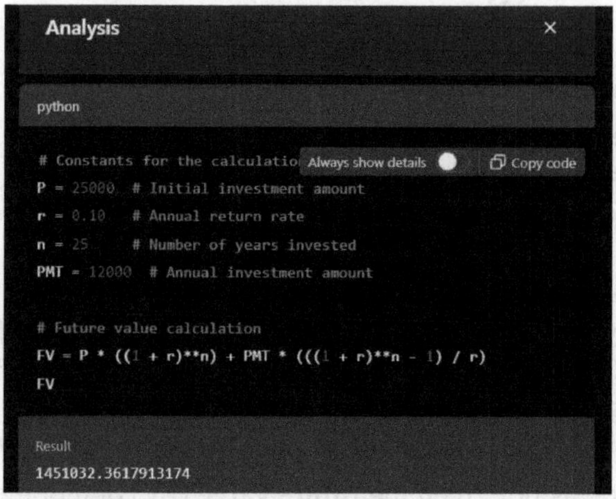

Figure 19.4: Analysis of the calculation with code snippet in Python with variables

Lastly, this relies on it to have a memory of the current session so you can change your question without having to re-ask everything. For example, if you want to change the initial investment from 12000 down to 2000, it would recall it. *Figure 19.5* shows that very interaction:

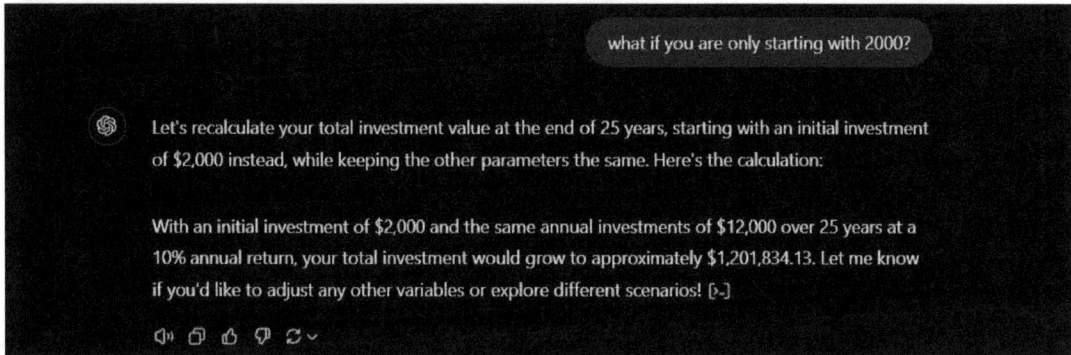

what if you are only starting with 2000?

Let's recalculate your total investment value at the end of 25 years, starting with an initial investment of $2,000 instead, while keeping the other parameters the same. Here's the calculation:

With an initial investment of $2,000 and the same annual investments of $12,000 over 25 years at a 10% annual return, your total investment would grow to approximately $1,201,834.13. Let me know if you'd like to adjust any other variables or explore different scenarios!

Figure 19.5: Recalculating the question while the session retains the initial prompt parameters

Conclusion

In this chapter, you were exposed to many ready-to-use prompts you can use right now in your favorite AI service. You also got more detailed and complicated prompts, ending with a real-world example of using a detailed prompt to effectively program your session to act as a rudimentary chatbot with no coding but just using prompts. In this book, you have learned a great deal about prompt engineering, from history to architecture to legal and ethical frameworks. You should have a strong grounding now to move forward with this knowledge to enhance your prompt engineering skills.

Join our book's Discord space

Join the book's Discord Workspace for Latest updates, Offers, Tech happenings around the world, New Release and Sessions with the Authors:

https://discord.bpbonline.com

Index

A

Aackpropagation Algorithm 28

Aackpropagation Algorithm,
    history 28

Adaptive Prompts
  about 140
  architecture 140
  challenges 142
  characteristics 140, 141
  use cases 141

Adaptive Prompts,
    practices 142, 143

AI, architecture 8

AI, challenges
  Environmental
    Protection 295, 296
  Health Care 295
  Intelligent Education 296

AI Communication 147, 148

AI Developer, steps
  OpenAI Playgroud 237
  Prompt Effort,
    setting up 236, 237
  Prompts Testing 238
  Results Interpreting 238, 239

AI Developer, tools
  Emerging Platforms 235, 236
  Hugging Face
    Transformers 233, 234
  OpenAI API 235
  OpenAI Playground 232, 233

AI Developer, use cases
  Custom Assistants,
    building 241, 242
  Decision-Making 243
  Documentation, generating 242, 243

AI-Driven Prompt Engineering 296
AI-Driven Prompt Engineering,
    demands 296, 297
AI Ethics, practices
  AI Development, securing 265
  Data Governance 265
  Privacy-Centric AI 264
  Robustness, ensuring 265
AI, factors
  Accelerated Development/
    Innovation 32
  Big Data 30
  Computational Power 30, 31
  Large Datasets/Databases 31
  Model Robustness 32
  Performance, enhancing 31
  Scalability/Infrastructure 32
AI/GPT, evolutions 15-17
AI, milestones
  Code Breakers 2-4
  Dartmouth Conference 4, 5
  Turing Test 4
AI Models, risks
  Adversarial Attacks 258
  Data Poisoning 258
  Inversion Attacks 258
  Reverse Engineering 258
AI, players
  Claude 201
  Google Gemini 200, 202
  Meta LLaMA 199
  Microsoft Copilot 203, 204
  Midjourney 204, 205
  OpenAI ChatGPT 198
AI-Powered Applications 256

AI-Powered Applications,
    approaches
  Community, building 256
  Fair Data Collection 256
  Fairness/Equity 256
  Legality 257
  Transparency/Explainability 257
AI, technologies
  Cognitive Computing 9
  Deep Learning 8
  Expert Systems 9
  General AI 8
  Narrow AI 8
  NLP 8
  Robotics 9
Algorithmic Bias,
    case studies 254
Artificial Intelligence (AI) 7

B
BERT 66
BERT, areas
  MLM 66
  NSP 66
BERT, industries
  AlphaFold 68
  Efficiency, improving 68
  Ethical/Societal Impact 68
  Multimodal Transformers 68
Bias 253
Bias, strategies
  Bias Reduction 254
  Human-in-the-loop 254
  Inspect Fairness 254
  Statistics Data, inaccuracy 254

Bias, types
  Algorithmic 253
  Data 253
  Historical 253
  Interaction 253
  Measurement 253
Boltzmann Machine 48
Boltzmann Machine, concepts
  Energy Function 48
  Neurons 48
  Stochasticity 48
  Weights 48
Boltzmann Machine, steps
  Energy Calculation 48
  Initialization 48
  Learning 48
  State Updating 48

C

Chatbot Planning 323
Closed-Ended Prompts
  about 128
  architecture 128
  Challenges 129
  Use Cases 129
Computational Costs 164, 165
Computational Costs,
    points
  Model Performance,
    enhancing 166, 167
  Operational Expenses,
    lowering 165
  Resource Optimization 165
  User Experience/Response Time,
    improving 165

Contextual Prompts
  about 135
  architecture 135
  challenges 136, 137
  use cases 135, 136
Cost Management 268
Cost Management,
    impact
  API Calls, managing 279
  Cost Implications 279
  Model Selection,
    optimizing 278
  Resource Allocating 277, 278
  Scalability/Cost Scaling 278
Cost Management, terms
  AI GPT Service
    Platforms 270, 271
  Microsoft/Google AI
    Platforms 269, 270
  Prompt Engineering 268, 269

D

Data Anonymization 257
Data Anonymization,
    methods
  Differential Privacy 257
  Federated Learning 257
  Homomorphic Encryption 257
Data-Driven Models 23
Data-Driven Models,
    challenges
  Bias/Data Quality 25
  Generalization 25
  Interpretability 25
  Privacy/Security 25

Data-Driven Models, scope
  Computer Vision 25
  Healthcare 25
  Natural Language
      Processing 25
  Recommendation
      Systems 25
Data-Driven Models, terms
  Algorithmic Innovations 24
  Computational Advances 24
  Data Availability 24
  Neural Networks/
      Deep Learning 23
  Statistical Foundations 23
  Statistical Learning 24
Data Privacy 306
Data Privacy, terms
  AI Deployment 307, 308
  AI Prompts 306, 307
Data Training 10
Deep Learning 34, 35
Discriminative Model 41
Discriminative Model,
      benefits 43, 44

E

Efficient Prompts 168
Efficient Prompts, ability
  Accessibility/Inclusivity,
      enhancing 170
  AI System,
      efficiency 169, 170
  Cognitive Overload,
      reducing 168, 169
Efficient Prompts,
      architecture 170, 171

Efficient Prompts, evolutions
  Automation/Efficiency 174, 175
  Gen AI 174
  Performance, adapting 175, 176
Efficient Prompts,
      optimizing 171-173
Efficient Prompts, points
  Clarity/Specificity 216
  Context/Relevance 217, 218
  Tone/Style Considerations 219-221
Ethical Data, factors 258
Exploratory Prompts
  about 130
  architecture 130
  Challenges 131
  Effectiveness, enhancing 131, 132
  use cases 130, 131

F

Fairness 255
Fairness, terms
  Community Building/
      Participatory 255
  Equity 255
  Ethics/Legality 256
  Fair Data Collection 255
  Transparency/Explainability 256
Financial Optimization, techniques
  AI Services 281
  Budgets, monitoring 282, 283
  Discounts/Reserved Instances,
      leveraging 281
  In-House Models/Cloud-Based
      Costing 280
  Multi-Cloud Strategies 282
Fine-Tuning 79, 80

G

GANs, configuring 51, 52
Gaussian Mixture Models
    (GMM) 44, 45
Generative Adversarial
    Networks (GANs) 51
Generative/Discriminative Model,
    differences
  Application 42
  Complexity 42
  Purpose 41
Generative Model 38, 40
Generative Model,
    architecture 38, 39
Generative Model, areas
  Creative Applications 39
  Data Augmentation 39
  Data, identifying 39
  Simulation/Prediction 39
  Unsupervised Learning 39
Generative Model, benefits 42, 43
Generative Model,
    configuring 40
Generative Model, types
  Boltzmann Machine 47
  Gaussian Mixture Models
    (GMM) 44, 45
  Hiddent Markov Model
    (HMM) 46
  Markov Chains 46
  Naive Baynes 45
  Probabilistic Graphical
    Model (PGM) 46
  Variational Autoencoders
    (VAEs) 49

GPT 66
GPT/Advanced AI 259
GPT/Advanced AI, areas 261
GPT/Advanced AI,
    implications 260
GPT/Advanced AI, role 260
GPT/Advanced AI, ways 259
GPT Models 96
GPT Models, architecture 97
GPT Models, components
  Feed-Forward Networks 98
  Layer Normalization 98
  Multi-Head Self-Attention 98
  Positional Encoding 98
GPT Models, evolutions
  GPT-1 98
  GPT-2 99
  GPT-3 99
  GPT-4 99
GPT Models, impacts
  Chatbots/Virtual Assistants,
    enhancing 102
  Creative Applications 103
  Education Content
    Creation 104
  Language Translation/
    Summarization 102
  Marketing Opportunities 103
  Sentiment Analysis/
    Text Classification 103
  Turning Test 104
GPT Models, training 99, 100
GPT, process
  Supervised Fine-Tuning 67
  Unsupervised Pre-Training 67

GPUs, terms
  Speed/Efficiency 33
  Tensor Processing Units
    (TPUs) 33, 34
  Wide Adoption 33

H
Hiddent Markov Model
    (HMM) 46
HMM, concepts
  Emission Probabilities 47
  Initial Probabilities 47
  Observations 46
  States 46
  Transition Probabilities 46

I
Intellectual Property Rights
    (IPR) 303
IPR, terms
  AI-Generated Content 304, 305
  Patents/Copyrights 303, 304

L
Legal Frameworks 300
Legal Frameworks, rules
  International AI Laws 300, 301
  Key Jurisdictions 301
  Legal Principles/
    Guidelines 301-303

M
Meta Prompting 181
ML/AI, concepts
  Algorithms/Models 7
  Statistical Analysis 6
ML/AI Ethics 250
ML Ethics 251

ML Ethics, challenges
  Algorithmic Bias/Fairness 251
  Data Security 252
  Deepfakes 252
  Economic Devastation 252
  Responsibility/Autonomy 252
  Transparency/
    Explainability 252
ML Ethics, reasons 251
ML, evolutions 65
ML, types
  Supervised Learning 10
  Unsupervised Learning 11
Multi-Modal Prompts
  about 132
  architecture 132, 133
  challenges 133, 134
  Directions, synthesizing 133
  use cases 133

N
Neural Networks 26
Neural Networks, architecture 27
Neural Networks, layers 27
Neural Networks, terminology
  Adaptation/Learning 26
  Layered Structure 26
  Neurons/Nodes 26
  Weights/Connections 26

O
OpenAI 90
OpenAI, architecture 91
OpenAI, concepts 90, 91
OpenAI Contextual, reference 91

OpenAI, resources
  GPT-2 92
  GPT-3 93
  GPT-4 94
Open-Ended Prompts
  about 126
  architecture 126, 127
  Challenges 127
  Use Cases 127

P
Procedural Prompts
  about 137, 138
  architecture 138
  challenges 139
  practices 139
  use cases 138, 139
Prompt 111
Prompt, anatomy 112
Prompt, architecture 111
Prompt Ecosystem 108
Prompt Ecosystem, importance
  AI Significance 110
  Text Generation 110, 111
Prompt Ecosystem, strategies
  Analogies/Constraints 120
  Effective Prompts,
      crafting 113
  Interation/Refinement 114
  Specificity/Precision 118
  Style/Edge Cases 122, 123
Prompt Ecosystem, terms
  AI-Driven Models 109
  AI Subsystems 109
  Shaping Model 109, 110
Prompt Efficiency 162

Prompt Efficiency, architecture 163
Prompt Efficiency,
      outcomes 163, 164
Prompt Efficiency, role 163
Prompt Efficiency, scope 162
Prompt, elements
  Clear Objectives 115, 116
  Context Providing 116, 117
  Contextualization 116
  Prior Knowledge,
      managing 117, 118
Prompt Engineering 72, 73
Prompt Engineering,
      architecture 73
Prompt Engineering,
      challenges
  API Limitations, handling 244
  Consequential Emergence 245
  Content Generator 246, 247
  Limitations/
      Bias Mitigation 244
  Testing/Evaluating 246
Prompt Engineering, concerns
  Accountability 310, 311
  Bias/Fairness,
      occurring 309, 310
Prompt Engineering,
      configuring 73, 74
Prompt Engineering,
      functionality
  Ambiguity 222
  Bias 223
  Complexity 223, 224
Prompt Engineering, implications
  Accuracy Tradeoff 191

AI Task Execution 191, 192
Iteration Results 192
Prompt Engineering, insights
AI Prompts,
    impacting 311, 312
Standards/Guidelines 313, 314
Prompt Engineering,
    methodologies
Effective Prompts,
    crafting 81, 82
Parallelism 83
Prompt Efficacy,
    measuring 82, 83
Prompt Engineering, methods
Failures, resolving 229
Iterative Refinement 224
Metric/Quality Assessment 227
Prompt Chaining 225
Templates/Automation 226
Prompt Engineering, outcomes
Incorrect Responses 229
Model Limitations 229
Performance, evaluating 230
Prompt Engineering, parts
Economics AI 271
Pricing Models 272
Usage-Based Pricing 273, 274
Variable Costs 272, 273
Prompt Engineering, points
Long-Term
    Projections 290, 291
State-of-the-art 288, 289
User Experience 289
Prompt Engineering, practices
Audience 206

Essential Lesson 209
Feedback/Metrics,
    leveraging 207, 208
Real-World Applications 208
Refinement/Iterative
    Testing 207
Prompt Engineering,
    prospects
State Ethical/
    Regulatory 292, 293
Technical Hurdles 291, 292
Prompt Engineering, purpose
Conversational AI 84, 85
Generative Tasks 84
Language Translation/
    Summarization 85-87
Sentiment Analysis/
    Test Classification 87, 88
Prompt Engineering,
    techniques
Few-Shot/Zero-Shot
    Learning 209, 210
Multi-Turn Conversations,
    handling 212, 213
Prompt Tuning 210-212
Prompt Engineering, terms
Fine-Tuning 79
Transfer Leaning 80
Prompt Engineering, tips
Batch Processing Prompts 276
Low-Resource Models 275
Prompt Iterations 275
Token Consumption 274
Prompt Engineering, trends
AI Development 193, 194

Human AI-Collaboration 194, 195
Human Syntax, adapting 193
Prompt Engineering, workflow
  Continuous Scaling 240, 241
  Version Control/
        Collaboration 240
  Workflow Automation 239
Prompt, running 326-329
Prompt, setting up 325, 326
Prompt, types 112, 113

R
Rule-Based Systems 23
Rule-Based Systems, limitations
  Acquisition Bottleneck 23
  Adaptability 23
  Scalability 23
  Uncertainty, handling 23

S
Sentiment Analysis 78, 79
Supervised Learning 11
Supervised Learning, techniques
  Few-Shot Learning 12
  Zero-Shot Learning 12
Support Vectors 28, 29
Support Vectors, architecture 29
Symbolic AI 20
Symbolic AI, configuring 20, 21
Symbolic AI, factors
  Adaptability/Scalability 22
  Computational Power 22
  Data Availability 21
  Mathematical Foundations 22
Syntactical Precision 183

Syntactical Precision, practices
  AI Responses Influence 185-187
  Prompts Clarity,
        structuring 184
  Syntactical Pitfalls 185
  Unambiguous Languagae 183, 184
Syntactical Precision,
        techniques
  AI Responses,
        employing 188, 189
  Keywords/Phrases 188
  Simplicity/Complexity,
        balancing 190
  Sophisticated Outputs,
        leveraging 189
Syntax 180
Syntax Ambiguity,
        analyzing 182, 183
Syntax, architecture 180, 181
Syntax Variations, optimizing 181

T
Tensor Processing Units
        (TPUs) 33, 34
Tokenization 149
Tokenization, approach
  BPE 150
  WordPiece 150
Tokenization, architecture 154, 155
Tokenization, challenges 151
Tokenization, configuring 151, 152
Tokenization, languages
  Chinese 151
  Japanese 151
Tokenization, preventing 155-157

Tokenization, process
Input Normalization 150
Spaces, splitting 150
Subwords/Characters,
splitting 150
Tokenization, roles 155
Tokenization, scenario 158, 159
Tokenization, trends 157, 158
Tokens 146
Tokens, architecture 146, 147
Tokens, importance 148, 149
Tokens, limitations
Effective Prompts,
designing 153
Memory/Processing Power 152
Tokens, methods
Context Windows 154
Memory-Based Model 154
Training Data 261
Training Data, points
Biases, mitigating 262
Fair AI,
implementing 263, 264
Fairness Audit/
Monitoring 263
Inclusive AI Design 262
Transfer Leaning 80, 81
Transformer-Based Models 56
Transformer-Based Models,
ability
Contextual, improving 75
Long-Range Dependencies,
handling 75, 76
Parallelization/Scalability 76, 77

Transformer-Based Models,
components
Layered Architecture 58
Positional Encoding 58
Self-Attention Mechanism 58
Transformer-Based Models,
history 57, 58
Transformer-Based Models,
importances 56, 57
Transformer-Based Models,
mechanisms
Connected Network 62
Encoder/Decoder Layers 62
Feed-Forward Neural
Networks 59
Input Tokenization 60
Multi-Head Attention 63
Optimization/Training 63
Positional Encoding 62
Scalability/Efficiency 63
Self-Attention
Mechanisms 59, 60
Vectors Tokenization 61, 62
Transformer Models 90

V
VAEs, steps
Decoding 49
Encoding 49
Loss Function 50
Sampling 49
Variational Autoencoders
(VAEs) 49
Virtual Reality (VR) 297
Vocabulary 150